T0247598

The Last Ships from Hamburg

ALSO BY STEVEN UJIFUSA

Barons of the Sea
A Man and His Ship

The Last Ships
from Hamburg

Business, Rivalry,
and the Race to
Save Russia's Jews
on the Eve of World War I

Steven Ujifusa

HARPER

An Imprint of HarperCollins*Publishers*

HarperCollins books may be purchased for educational, business, or sales promotional use. For information, please email the Special Markets Department at SPsales@harpercollins.com.

FIRST EDITION

Designed by Leah Carlson-Stanisic

Library of Congress Cataloging-in-Publication Data has been applied for.

ISBN 978-0-06-297187-6

23 24 25 26 27 LBC 5 4 3 2 1

To my maternal great-grandparents, Isaac and Anna Shlefstein,
Maurice and Lily Brooks, and all those who come to America to seek
better lives for themselves and their descendants

Contents

The Last Ships from Hamburg

Introduction

_____

_____

_____

Between 1881 and 1914, over ten million people crossed the Atlantic from Europe to America, the largest mass migration of people from one continent to another in human history. Over 2.5 million of them were Jews from Central and Eastern Europe. Most of them were from the Russian Empire. While many European nations relaxed their ancient restrictions on Jews, Russia did the opposite. Jews were faced with a difficult decision: survive in menacing circumstances, convert to Christianity, or leave everything behind for a chance at a better life in a distant place.

Many chose to travel to America. During this thirty-three-year period, the industrializing United States had a largely unrestricted immigration policy. American business enterprises wanted cheap labor, and new arrivals provided it in abundance. The Russian Empire, however, did not easily permit its subjects to leave its confines. For most Jewish immigrants, their escape meant at least one illegal border crossing in order to get to the great seaports of Hamburg, Bremen, Liverpool, Antwerp, and Le Havre, where ships took them to America.

It was a journey fraught with anxiety and peril, but for the steamship lines and the international investment banks backing them, the mass immigration across the Atlantic was a financial bonanza.

Three titans made this mass exodus of humanity logistically possible. Albert Ballin, managing director of the Hamburg-America Line (also known as HAPAG), created a transportation network that allowed Jews to travel seamlessly from Russia to America by train and steamship. Jacob Schiff, managing partner of the investment bank Kuhn, Loeb & Co., used his immense wealth to encourage and to help Jews to leave Russia for a fresh start in America. J. P. Morgan, mastermind of the International Mercantile Marine (IMM) trust, tried to take over the lucrative transatlantic steamship business that Albert Ballin had created, aiming to run it in the same ruthless way he ran his banks and railroads.

In her 1882 ode to the Statue of Liberty, the poet Emma Lazarus called New York Harbor the "golden door" to America. But the immigration gateway slammed shut in 1914, when Europe became a battleground and all movement between nations, with the exception of armies, ground to a halt. Russia's remaining Jews were trapped in a maelstrom of violence, war, and revolution. The German transatlantic steamship companies collapsed, and with them the intricate transportation networks that allowed Jews to escape to America.

By 1923, the American public had become first uneasy and then frightened by unrestricted immigration, and Congress passed a series of discriminatory laws that barred almost all new arrivals from Southern and Eastern Europe. It was a victory for a small group of socially elite racists in Boston and New York who felt that Jews and Italians were polluting the genetic makeup of the United States with supposedly inferior stock. Their racial theories, presumed to be scientific, mirrored the Nazi Party's racial policies toward Jews that would culminate in Hitler's Final Solution a few years later.

Those who made it across the North Atlantic faced privation and poverty upon their arrival in America. Some did not last a generation, victims of industrial accidents, disease, or despair. Those who survived created new lives for themselves and their children, and breathed new energy into the American economy and culture. Among the Jewish immigrants were Supreme Court justice Felix Frankfurter, songwriter Irving Berlin, artist Mark Rothko, journalist Abraham Cahan, and labor organizer Emma Goldman. Children of immigrants included composers Leonard Bernstein and Aaron Copland, Hollywood mogul Louis B. Mayer, and actress Lauren Bacall. Tens of thousands became doctors, lawyers, bankers, professors, teachers, and owners of businesses large and small. Most of them achieved success, material and otherwise, that their grandparents in the shtetls of Russia could have never imagined.

These three powerful personalities—Albert Ballin and Jacob Schiff,

Jews themselves, and J. P. Morgan—were all driven by very different motives, but the convergence of their ambitions helped make the Second Exodus a reality for millions of people. They did not survive to see the world they helped create, but their impact resonates to this day.

This is their story.

Part I

CHAPTER 1

The Jew Boy of Morris & Co.

———————————————————————

———————————————————————

One needed to have seen the wonderous eyes of
this person in order to feel the degree to
which goodness and pleasantness were united
in him. This strange little man had the charm
of a woman, and what seemed even stranger,
the sensibility of a woman.

—CARL FÜRSTENBERG ON ALBERT BALLIN

In the early 1900s, the Lower Elbe Regatta was the social event of the year for all in Germany who loved sailing. Here, sleek racing yachts spread their canvas and sliced through the choppy waters of the North Sea under the June sun. The yachts were only part of the celebration. The gathering was also a stage for royals, diplomats, and industrialists from all over Europe to socialize—and to push their various private agendas. Battleships from Germany, Great Britain, and other nations were anchored in formation, bedecked with flags, brightwork polished to a gleam, and crews standing at attention.

At the center of the Lower Elbe Regatta was Kaiser Wilhelm II, who made annual appearances at the event beginning in 1889, the year he was crowned emperor of Germany. Typically sporting a blue admiral's uniform gleaming with gold braid and medals, the Kaiser did his best to hide his shriveled left arm, which was injured during his birth. Even with that disability, or because of it, he was impulsive and bombastic.

Aristocrats, merchants, and the just plain rich of imperial Germany all vied for an invitation aboard the Kaiser's royal yacht *Hohenzollern*, a sleek, white-hulled swan that always anchored in the prime viewing spot for the sailing races. Wilhelm, the eldest grandson of Britain's Queen Victoria, had a strong admiration for all things British: ocean liners, naval uniforms, and fast sailing yachts. In addition to the *Hohenzollern*, Wilhelm owned a succession of sailing yachts, the biggest of which was the sailing schooner *Meteor III*, built in New York City in 1902 and christened by President Theodore Roosevelt's daughter Alice.

But the real master of ceremonies of the Lower Elbe Regatta was Albert Ballin, managing director of the Hamburg-America Line, the largest shipping company in the world. He stood just over five feet tall; his head was balding. A set of gold-rimmed pince-nez sat on his prominent nose. According to Theodor Wolff, a journalist with the *Berliner Tageblatt* and a friend, this man "could not hide the fact—he did not for one moment want to hide it—that he was a Jew, and it was impossible for anyone else to fail to observe it. His facial type, and striking details like the strong lips under his moustache, sufficiently revealed it." Yet it was his "truly 'speaking' eyes" that grabbed the attention of those who knew him, of friend and foe, of royalty, employees, and his own family. Those eyes, Wolff noted, "from moment to moment expressed everything, grave thought and humor, dominant will and kind-heartedness, anxiety and contentment."

Ballin did his best to fit into the so-called kaiserly constellation, and by all appearances did so quite nicely. Although no sailor himself, he loved dressing the part, donning summer whites and yachting cap. But he felt most at home aboard one of his HAPAG ships, entertaining the elite of German society and international power brokers at the end of a strenuous day on the water. He felt comfortable as long as he was stage-managing whatever was happening, as he was that day at the Lower Elbe Regatta.

The Kaiser soon took a liking to the brilliant but enigmatic little man, even if his wife the empress couldn't bear the sight of him and everything Jewish he represented. Ballin's relationship to the Kaiser was "based on the honorable wish to awaken an awareness of economic topics in the appropriate places," according to his friend, the banker Max Warburg. "Here, too, he was never afraid to share his opinion, though he encountered resistance that he was not able to overcome."

Yet for all his accomplishments, Ballin was only a hired man, a manager of a shipping line's passenger division, not the owner of a big business operation or a landed aristocrat. Some called him worse: "the Jew Boy of Morris & Co.," Wolff wrote, referring to his father's failed business. Snobbish wags in Hamburg even had a new nickname for him: "the king of steerage."

Fellow Jews criticized him, too, as an exploiter of his own people.

But Albert Ballin did what he felt was best for his company, his country, his people, and his family. For it, he learned what it meant to be mocked and despised. He kept those feelings close to his heart, though perhaps those who knew him well saw it in his eyes.

*   *   *

Albert Ballin was an unlikely mastermind of the Second Exodus of the Jewish people—his people. He was born in 1857 in a narrow house near the Hamburg waterfront. His father was Samuel Joel Ballin, a portly Danish Jew who ran a small emigration agency. His mother, Amalia, was the daughter of a prosperous Hamburg Jewish merchant. Samuel already had nine children with his first wife before her death. Amalia bore him four more, of whom Albert was the last. Albert hated talking about his childhood. In a letter to a friend, he hinted at the pain he suffered as a boy. "I think you and I were never young. This involves freedom from cares— and in this respect we are both badly burdened." Even when dressed for yachting parties like the Lower Elbe Regatta, partaking of "the care-free enjoyment of the pleasures of society," Ballin was never carefree.

BALLIN'S FATHER had emigrated from Denmark to the Free Hanseatic City of Hamburg as a young man. There, he petitioned the city authorities to register in his own name a piece of rural land upon which he intended to construct a wool dye works. His plan was to employ "21 to 30 people of the working class," maintaining that "their number will grow steadily corresponding to the company's flourishing. I want to add that I will follow the principle of hiring primarily Christians and not Israelites as my factory workers." To bolster his case, he claimed that his dye works would produce the same quality of woolen goods being imported from Great Britain, but at a fraction of the cost.

Yet his request was denied.

Stung, an enraged Samuel Ballin wrote an appeal to the city authorities. "Of course, one can't deny the existence of legal regulations according to which Jews shouldn't be able to register properties," he said, "but these regulations date from the time of darkness and intolerance and shouldn't be observed anymore in our time of light and enlightenment."

Ballin argued that Jews, as taxpaying citizens of Hamburg, should have the same property rights as Christians. "Why shall Israelites be inferior to their Christian fellow citizens with regard to the acquisition of property when they meet their obligations to the state just as well as them, or when they even have heavier burdens to carry than them?" he said. "No logical reason for their discrimination can be recognized, what is being said about the growth of their influence is muddled, especially as it's actually by no means prohibited for them to buy property, they're just not allowed to register [the property] in their names. Who might find a real difference here?"

Jews like Samuel Ballin dreamed of complete integration into German society, a hope kindled by the Enlightenment and the humanistic aspirations of the French Revolution. One of the guiding lights of the eighteenth-century "Jewish Enlightenment" (the Haskala) was the philosopher Moses Mendelssohn. Even the intensely anti-Semitic regime of Frederick the Great granted Mendelssohn the status of "protected Jew," which meant that the philosopher could live free of harassment in the Prussian capital of Berlin. His descendants rose so high in German society that they eventually abandoned the Jewish faith altogether, choosing to assimilate by embracing Lutheranism. His son, the Hamburg banker Abraham Mendelssohn, added the Germanic "Bartholdy" to the Mendelssohn surname to signal his distance from his Jewish heritage. But for many among the German social elite, a Christian Mendelssohn was no more possible than a Jewish Confucius. His grandson, the composer Felix Mendelssohn-Bartholdy, despite his family's conversion (and new, hyphenated last name) never denied his Jewish origins. The composer died in 1847. He was world famous, having toured internationally as a pianist, organist, and composer. As for Mendelssohn's extended family, they grew rich as the owners of the Berlin-based bank Mendelssohn & Co.

The Mendelssohns were the exception rather than the rule. Most of Germany's Jews were like Samuel Joel Ballin. Even if they converted, they did not have the wealth or cultural capital to fully assimilate into German society. The poet Heinrich Heine, whose lyrics Mendelssohn and others had set to music, claimed that his conversion was his "ticket to admission to Europe culture." In reality, he did it to apply for a university position, something he never received given the anti-Semitism in German academic circles. Another composer, Salomon Jadassohn, achieved eminence as a professor of music at the Leipzig Conservatory. Still, nationalistic music critics derided the music of Jewish composers as dry and lacking in soul. The most vociferous of the critics was the composer Richard Wagner, famed for his musical transformation of old Norse myths into Germanic grand operas. "Mendelssohn has shown us that a Jew can have the richest abundance of talents and be a man of the broadest culture," Wagner wrote in his essay "Judaism in Music," "but still be incapable of supplying the profound, heart-seizing, soul-searching experience we expect from art."

Even German humanists tended to be wary of Jews. The prominent philosopher Johann Gottfried von Herder, the rector of the University of Berlin, declared that the Jews were an "alien, Asiatic people." The Old Testament Jews were worthy of admiration, he argued, but not those he saw on the streets of Berlin, whether they were rabbis, moneylenders, merchants, or peddlers. No matter how much Jews aspired to become part of Germanic culture, they would still be regarded as imitators, frauds, and deceivers. They could try to buy their way into German society, but they could never become true members of *der Volk*, who drew their identity not from trade but from the land. It wasn't even a matter of religion, or a patent of nobility, but of something intangible: "blood and soil."

Eventually, Samuel Ballin was able to acquire the land and build his dye works. For a while, he prospered. Following the death of his first wife, he met and wed Albert's mother, Amalia Meyer. They had seven children together, including Albert, the youngest, who was born sickly. But following the great Hamburg fire of 1842, Samuel was forced to close his hard-won company and found himself in financial trouble. Desperate to support a growing family, Samuel decided to take advantage of the surge of immigrants leaving Germany for the United States. He opened a small immigration ticketing agency that he, for some reason, gave the English-sounding moniker of Morris & Co. As a Jew without social connections, it was one of the few avenues of business open to him. Hamburg was teeming with shipping firms that did business through all the major ports in Europe, but employment was not available to the likes of anyone in the Ballin family. Even though he had founded his own company, Samuel's future as a player in the city's transatlantic passenger business was far from secure.

The major player in that business was the Hamburg-Amerikanische Packetfahrt-Aktien-Gesellschaft, known in Hamburg by the abbreviation HAPAG and in the United States as the Hamburg-America Line. HAPAG began operations in the late 1840s with a fleet of wooden packet ships that carried passengers and mail between Hamburg and New York City. In the next decades, HAPAG took a major gamble and began to replace its sailing ships with steam-powered paddle-wheel vessels. Within a decade, screw propellers replaced paddle wheels on large transatlantic steamers. They specialized in cargo, and largely catered to first-class passengers. Tens of thousands of people left Germany for the United States in those years. Among them were revolutionaries such as Carl Schurz, who risked his life in the German Revolution of 1848 to bring democracy to the ossified states that made up the German Confederation, and later fought as a Union general in the American Civil War before being elected a U.S. senator from Missouri. Others, such as the teenage barber's apprentice Friedrich Trump of Kallstadt, fled military conscription in the king of Bavaria's army. And then there were thousands of ordinary poor families who were fed up with the poverty and rigid class structure of the society in which they lived. Some were Jews, but most were Catholics and Protestants. All were willing to brave a one-to-two-month voyage in the bottom of a reeking sailing ship to get a new start in America. Many were bound for New York and other cities along the East Coast, but others planned to join the westward movement of settlers into the fertile farm country of America's heartland in Ohio, Illinois, Wisconsin, and Missouri. (This is how beer came to Milwaukee and St. Louis.)

Several ports in North Germany catered to the immigrants bound for the New World. Hamburg was one of them, but its rival, Bremen, had the better navigable location because its port district of Bremerhaven was situated directly on the North Sea, rather than sixty miles up the Elbe River. Bremen's premier transatlantic line, and counterpart to HAPAG, was the Norddeutscher-Lloyd Line, also known as NDL or North German Lloyd. Beyond the geographic advantage, to prospective immigrants from Germany and beyond Bremen had a much better reputation as a layover destination than Hamburg. For all its ancient hauteur, Hamburg was teeming with swindlers who were notorious for taking advantage of people passing through its hostelries, especially if they didn't speak German.

For its part, HAPAG felt that immigrant agents were unscrupulous and preferred not to employ them to procure steerage passengers. Employing agents such as Samuel Ballin, who was a minor player in the hardscrabble, cutthroat business, would tarnish HAPAG's reputation. The city fathers also frowned on the new booking business. Hamburg specialized in the exchange of cargo, particularly with Great Britain. This included wheat, coffee, and finished goods such as textiles. The city was ill equipped to handle a vast influx of immigrants seeking passage to America anyway. The waterfront slums were already congested. The Hamburg Senate imposed onerous restrictions on new arrivals to the city, hoping to mitigate overcrowding in that area and the spread of diseases such as cholera, smallpox, and influenza from those who stayed there. Politically, the Senate spoke to the worries among the citizenry that many of the migrants would choose to settle in Hamburg rather than move on to America. A major influx of outsiders, the city fathers feared, would threaten the old fabric of Hamburg's tight-knit, insular mercantile community.

Despite facing more and more restrictions, Samuel Ballin persisted. Although HAPAG specialized in cargo and first-class passengers, its management grudgingly acknowledged that it needed steerage to survive financially and passed along bundles of tickets to Morris & Co.'s dreary little office. The ticket agency business was simple: Samuel would buy steerage tickets in bulk and then sell them at a markup to migrants looking for passage to the New World. But by the 1860s, Ballin found himself locked out by the shipping companies, which switched course and decided to sell tickets directly to the public, cutting out middlemen.

To finance his beleaguered operation, Samuel Ballin had invested most of his wife Amalia's inheritance from her father's estate. He hoped his new venture would redeem him from his failed dye works in the eyes of the Hamburg Jewish community. He also wanted to leave something behind for his children. But as little Albert grew older, he noticed that his family kept on moving to shabbier quarters, closer to the noise and dirt of the waterfront, and farther and farther away from the stately villas that ringed the Alster Lake. These were the homes of Hamburg's prosperous upper class of shipping families.

SAMUEL AND AMALIA could have moved to America to seek a better life for their children, like so many other German Jews. But they didn't. They felt their roots in Hamburg were too deep.

Albert liked to explore other parts of the city, places like the Rotherbaum neighborhood, where wealthy Jewish families lived. There, at Mittelweg 17, lived Moritz and Charlotte Warburg, heirs to the banking house of M. M. Warburg & Co. The Warburgs used their know-how and relationships to finance Germany's nascent industrial complex and overseas trade. One day, they would prove crucial to Albert Ballin's rise from obscurity to shipping titan.

Albert knew his mother had once mingled with the likes of the Warburgs, and it must have saddened him to realize that his father had diminished his family's standing. As the youngest son in a large family, Albert knew he would have to fend for himself in life. But all the while Albert was growing up, Amalia doted on her sickly, slight son, who according to one friend was "subject to all sorts of maladies and constitutional weaknesses."

As a student at Professor Goldmann's academy, Albert apparently showed no sign of brilliance. In a home that doubled as office space for Morris & Co., the constant comings and goings of prospective migrants seeking passage to America meant not much peace and quiet. Instead of attending to his studies, Albert spent his time helping his father with his struggling business. This meant keeping the books, running errands, and convincing desperate people to buy tickets that his father had purchased on credit.

As young Albert Ballin slaved over his father's books, the Free Hanseatic City of Hamburg was swallowed up by a new nation. This event would affect the young entrepreneur in ways big and small. In 1871, after France's defeat in the Franco-Prussian War, Prussian chancellor Otto von

Bismarck declared the creation of a new, unified German Empire. The new emperor would be Wilhelm I, head of the Prussian House of Hohenzollern, the dynasty that had produced the military genius Frederick the Great—the man who had given, many years before, Moses Mendelssohn the status of "protected Jew." The announcement, which took place at the Hall of Mirrors at Versailles, was the result of a decade's worth of planning on Bismarck's part to unify many independent German-speaking states into a single nation under the rule of Prussia's Hohenzollern family. For centuries, Great Britain, France, and the Austro-Hungarian Empire had benefited from an economically, politically, and culturally fractured Germany. True, the German region might have shared a common language, but its states were governed by competing (if often intermarried) ruling families. Some states, like Prussia and Hanover, were predominately Protestant, while others, such as Bavaria, were predominately Catholic. Stretching from the Austrian Alps of the south to the Hanseatic ports of the north, and from the Rhenish coal regions of the west to the rich farmlands of Prussia of the east, the new German nation felt ready to compete with the older, established nations of Europe.

Bismarck worked with the Jewish banker Gerson Bleichröder to help finance the growth of Prussia as a force on the European stage. This financial muscle would help allow Prussia's Kaiser Wilhelm I to claim supremacy over Austria as the ruler of the unified German states. Bleichröder's most notable social triumph came in the 1860s, when he personally bailed out a 915-mile-long railroad in Romania and saved the fortunes of several prominent German families that had invested in the venture. In 1872, the year after German unification, Gerson Bleichröder received a patent of nobility from Emperor Wilhelm I for his service to the state, making him only the second Prussian Jew allowed to use an honorific "von" between his first and last names, and the first who chose not to convert to Christianity.

For the new empire's five hundred thousand Jews, from the rich like Gerson von Bleichröder to the poor like Albert Ballin, it was an exhilarating time. They were granted full citizenship rights, could vote, could serve in the military, and theoretically could rise into the mercantile bourgeoisie. In the burgeoning cities of Hamburg, Düsseldorf, Munich, and the capital, Berlin, there were new opportunities in banking,

manufacturing, and merchandising that would in time give rise to a prosperous and increasingly integrated Jewish middle and upper class. There
was an exception made: in the newly "liberal" German Empire, the ruling Prussian state still barred Jews from the governing class of officers
and diplomats in Berlin.

Samuel Joseph Ballin did not live long enough to benefit from a new
Germany. In 1874, he died penniless. A panic in the United States devastated the American labor market, stanched the flow of immigrants out of
Hamburg, and tanked the family business. Although young Albert had
to drop out of school at seventeen to help support the family, he alone
of his siblings decided to stick it out at Morris & Co., making a bet that
economic conditions and the demand for labor in the United States would
improve and that Europeans would again want to undertake the transatlantic journey. Soon enough Morris & Co. was back at selling tickets.
By the late 1870s, as the depression in America lifted, Albert chose not
to court HAPAG but instead was already at work on behalf of small
shipping lines, as he plugged his business into Hamburg's long trading
relationship with England and booked migrants on vessels bound for
Liverpool and London. The travelers would then board British liners
to continue their voyage to America. Known as "indirect" migration,
the arrangement was ideal for shipowners less established than HAPAG.
Relatively small coastal ships could travel the relatively short twelve-
hundred-mile sea voyage between Hamburg and England.

Although Ballin found ships interesting, what really intrigued him
was connecting with people. The deep pain he had experienced growing
up produced a capacity for empathy that would help allay the fears of
anxious immigrants. That skill was crucial to his success. He was, it also
turned out, a brilliant manager, able to assess people, ideas, and logistics
better than anyone in the Hamburg business world, and he was able to see
the weak spots in the competition's armor and exploit them.

A member of the Hamburg elite began to take notice of Ballin's business prowess. He was Edward Carr, a scion of Hamburg's Robert M.
Sloman & Co. shipping business. The Slomans knew something about
looking for talented outsiders. The firm's founder, Robert M. Sloman Sr.,
was the son of a British ship captain who had settled in Hamburg at the
end of the eighteenth century. During the mid-nineteenth century, the

Sloman Line competed with HAPAG on the transatlantic steamship run. But when the line's brand-new flagship, the state-of-the-art steamer *Helena Sloman*, sank in a storm on her third voyage, HAPAG drove the weakened Sloman Line out of the North Atlantic shipping lanes, leaving the company dependent on sailing ships that plied the waters of northern Europe. Then Edward Carr, a British-born nephew of the founder's son Robert Jr., started a shipping line with a couple of small steam freighters that chugged back and forth between Hamburg and the British Isles. This was a workaday, steady business, but Ballin had a big idea for Carr's little fleet: he saw synergy between Carr's family operation and his family's struggling immigrant ticketing business.

For the Carr Line to succeed against the likes of HAPAG, Ballin concluded, it would have to steal their business. In 1881, he began to book immigrants on Carr's fleet and other small British ships bound from Hamburg to Liverpool, England. There the emigrants would board larger liners bound for New York. Because of their greater length and longer layovers in intermediate ports, these "indirect" voyages were cheaper than those that sailed from Hamburg to New York. The snag, however, was that Ballin had to split commissions with British immigration agents. Even so, Morris & Co. actually began to make money.

But Ballin hated being a middleman. He decided what he really wanted to do was control the entire immigrant journey from start to finish. He looked at two of Carr's small steam-powered freighters, the SS *America* and the SS *Australia*, and proposed to convert their upper decks into sleeping spaces for about eight hundred immigrants. Ballin promised Carr enough customers to justify the costly renovations. The selling point was that passengers would receive clean, comfortable accommodations at a reasonable price. And unlike other passenger vessels, in which steerage was consigned to the lowest and least desirable space on the ship, immigrants would receive "run of the ship" privileges.

Edward Carr gambled and bought into Ballin's business plan. In 1881, the first year of their partnership, Ballin supplied the Carr Line with four thousand immigrants, followed by eight thousand the next year, and in 1883, over sixteen thousand. For Yiddish-speaking immigrants from Eastern Europe, taking a Carr Line ship presented some risks. The stopover in Liverpool was just as fraught as time in Hamburg. For anywhere from a few days to a few weeks, they would have to deal with more un-scrupulous locals and yet another foreign language.

Ballin managed the ticketing side of the business, wooing prospective immigrants, while Carr ran the shipping line. Business was so good that the two men decided to build a series of new, improved versions of their vessels. During the 1880s, Ballin began to make regular trips to Great Britain, a nation upon which Hamburg's trading fortunes, including his own, depended. Now in his element, and feeling for the first time full confidence in the way his mind worked, Ballin mastered the English language, an invaluable skill in the British-dominated world of international shipping. He also grew to admire everything English, especially haberdashery.

In Great Britain, Ballin also noticed that British Jews were quickly rising to the top of society, even joining the ranks of the nobility. Among them were Lord Rothschild and Prime Minister Benjamin Disraeli, who still had a strong Jewish identity despite having converted as a child to Anglicanism. Here, Ballin thought, was a society that blended traditionalism with meritocracy to an extent even greater than in Hamburg.

Ballin felt at home in England in a way he never truly did in Germany. He was welcomed by a liberated and assimilated group of British Jews, among them Gustav Christian Schwabe, a wealthy Liverpool merchant who had converted to Protestantism, and his nephew Gustav Wilhelm Wolff, who had established the Harland & Wolff shipyard in Belfast, just across the Irish Sea from Liverpool. Harland & Wolff's main business was building ships for the White Star Line, run by the tough-as-nails Liverpool businessman Thomas Ismay. Ismay had purchased the bankrupt White Star Line in 1867 for a mere one thousand pounds.

White Star was carrying passengers and cargo between Great Britain and Australia. Schwabe, however, convinced Ismay that a better use of his new shipping company would be to inaugurate a new steamship service between Liverpool and New York City, transporting rich passengers in first class and immigrants in steerage. Ismay agreed to the proposition. One night, over a game of billiards, Schwabe and Ismay came to a gentleman's agreement: Schwabe would finance the White Star Line under Ismay's ownership and management, while Wolff would build all of White Star's ships.

In the early 1870s, the White Star Line began to unveil a new set of six iron-hulled transatlantic liners that boasted luxurious accommodations for 166 first-class passengers and over 1,000 immigrants in steerage. To save on fuel, White Star used revolutionary new compound engines, which funneled steam in three or four cylinders before it was expelled into the condenser. White Star's main rival in the immigrant trade was the Inman Line, also based in Liverpool, whose large, clipper-bowed liners also carried a small number of passengers in ultra-luxurious first class and many in steerage.

Ballin's Carr Line filled some of these steerage berths with his "indirect" travelers from the Continent, mostly Germans and ethnic Poles from East Prussia. The rest of the berths were filled with immigrants from the British Isles and Scandinavia. Britain's oldest and most prestigious transatlantic steamship company, the Cunard Line, mostly specialized in carrying first-class passengers. It operated under an older business model that dated from the 1850s, in which the well-heeled traveled on steamships and the poor traveled by sailing ship. Steamship companies' operating losses, mostly because of fuel costs, were made whole by healthy mail subsidies from the British government.

Ballin looked at how White Star ran its business and saw the future. He realized that White Star and other British lines had made the steamship business pay by cramming as many immigrants as possible into their hulls. He could not help but notice that the White Star Line and Harland & Wolff had built a successful, symbiotic business relationship. Compared to the conservative and spartan German vessels, Ismay's advanced steamships boasted improved comfort for both first-class and steerage passengers. The upstart White Star proved to be a worthy rival to Cunard.

In due course, Albert Ballin would give the White Star Line a run for its money, both as a carrier of immigrants and a purveyor of luxurious transportation.

Perhaps, Ballin thought, he could put together enough capital to build White Star–style ships that could carry first-class *and* steerage passengers directly from Hamburg to New York, cutting out the British middlemen.

He soon garnered an important supporter in the Hamburg establishment, the businessman Carl Laiesz, whose family owned the famed

"Flying P" line of nitrate-carrying sailing ships that plied the route between Hamburg and Chile. Among his many business interests, Laiesz held a board seat at HAPAG.

There was an opportunity for Ballin—if he could seize it.

Theodor Wolff observed that Hamburg's mercantile society had become expert at maintaining appearances but had lost much of the drive that had made it so wealthy in the first place. "Many scions of the old Hamburg families had nothing left in them of the traditions of the Free City," Wolff wrote. "Their ideal was to belong to one of the feudal students' corps, and such vestiges as they still retained of Hanseatic sturdiness were to be found only in their jealous distaste for parvenu Berlin with all of its new ideas and excessive energy."

Albert Ballin personified that excessive energy. He also realized that in order to get along in Hamburg society, he had to temper his drive with a genteel façade, and to be less talkative and more measured in his approach to those born into higher social circles than his own. He would work all his life to contain emotional outbursts and would reveal grave self-doubts only to a select few of his closest friends.

The biggest threat to his plan was not HAPAG but the long-standing Norddeutscher-Lloyd. Founded by a circle of Bremen merchants, NDL ran a fleet of luxurious and fast steamships not just to New York but to Baltimore, the West Indies, and Australia. It also entered a partnership with the Baltimore & Ohio Railroad in exchange for favorable rates for its passengers and freight for transport into the American interior. Compared to NDL, HAPAG's fleet had become dull, dowdy, and unprofitable. For its part, HAPAG saw the Carr-Ballin collaboration as little more than a pesky little mutt nipping at its heels. Its arrogance would be its undoing.

There were a few things Ballin would need to manage first. By 1882, Albert Ballin, a twenty-five-year-old ticket seller, had put away enough money to purchase civil rights in the city of Hamburg. The following year, on October 26, he married Marianne Rauert, the daughter of a prosperous cloth dealer. Three years older than Ballin, Marianne was blond, stately, and a head taller than her new husband. The marriage ceremony took place in a Lutheran church, but Ballin made a point of not converting to his wife's faith. Whether Ballin's mother, Amalia, objected to the marriage is unknown, but Marianne's brother Paul, a prominent Hamburg lawyer, was strongly in favor of the match. Bucking the bigotry that separated Jew and gentile in Hamburg, Marianne saw a remarkable young man on the rise, and for the rest of her life, would support him in all his endeavors, even if she never really felt comfortable in the heights to which he would one day rise.

Though there were many factors Ballin could influence, there were some over which he had no control. Economic conditions in Germany and the rest of Northern Europe had improved enough in the early 1880s so that fewer people wanted to leave for a new life in the United States. The same was true for Great Britain and Ireland. There was a fear among shipping executives in Hamburg, Bremen, and Liverpool that the immigrant trade would decline again, this time permanently. But tragic events unfolding in Russia would change Albert Ballin's fortunes forever and allow him to take on HAPAG, the shipping company that had refused to do business with his father only a decade earlier.

For liberated German Jews like Albert Ballin, the future seemed bright. For the Jews of Russia, especially the poor ones, conditions grew unbearable enough that thousands considered risking everything to get out and sail to America. This meant passing through Germany to get to one of the great port cities of Northern Europe, there to board ships that would take them to America. Ballin aimed to control those ships.

In Russia, an absolute ruler did everything in his power to control his empire. Czar Alexander III blamed all his country's Jews for killing his father. And he wanted revenge.

CHAPTER 2

Convert, Emigrate, or Disappear

And it came to pass, when Pharaoh had let the
people go, that God led them not through the
way of the land of the Philistines, although
that was near; for God said, Lest peradven-
ture the people repent when they see war, and
they return to Egypt:
But God led the people about, through the
way of the wilderness of the Red Sea: and the
children of Israel went up harnessed out of
the land of Egypt.

—EXODUS 13: 17-18

The Second Jewish Exodus began with a bomb blast on March 13, 1881.

Czar Alexander II had just stepped out of his carriage to inspect the damage. Seconds earlier, a bomb had exploded under it, seriously injuring several of his Cossack guards. The carriage was a bulletproof gift from the deposed Emperor Napoleon III of France. It had worked—Alexander emerged unharmed.

"It's too early to thank God," a young man screamed into the crowd that had gathered on the St. Petersburg street.

Then came the second bomb. It landed at Alexander's feet and exploded. Police Chief Dvorzhitsky pushed his way through the smoke and saw the czar lying on the ground. "Thinking he was merely wounded heavily, I tried to lift him but the czar's legs were shattered," he recalled, "and the blood poured out of them. Twenty people, with wounds of varying degree, lay on the sidewalk and on the street. Some managed to stand, others to crawl, still others tried to get out from beneath bodies that had fallen on them. Through the snow and debris, you could see fragments of clothing, epaulets, sabers, and blood." His legs shattered, his abdomen torn open, Alexander II gasped to his guards that he only wanted to be taken back to the Winter Palace to die.

Compared to his predecessors, Alexander II was a thoughtful moderate who sought to bring reforms to his empire while still retaining the Divine Right concept of monarchy that had defined Russian culture for centuries. He had been known as the "Liberator" for freeing Russia's serfs in 1861, two years before Abraham Lincoln signed the Emancipation Proclamation in America. Alexander II had enacted a series of reforms that loosened restrictions on the press. He was also making small moves to guide Russia toward a constitutional monarchy along British lines. Conservatives in St. Petersburg scoffed at the czar's flirtation with liberalism, feeling that it would only embolden radicals within the realm.

In fact, Alexander II's reforms were met with derision by a small group of radicals known as Narodnaya Volya, or "People's Will." Composed mainly of the sons and daughters of Russia's middle class, Narodnaya Volya felt that gradual legislative reforms were a sham. Terror was the only way to achieve the dream of a socialist society, in which food and other resources were distributed fairly to all, rather than being hoarded by a small, elite group of Russia's aristocrats, who, despite the loss of their serfs as actual property, still lived lavishly off the proceeds of their estates while doing virtually no work themselves.

Alexander II's son, Alexander III, watched his father breathe his last in his study that fateful day. Enraged, the young man turned his back on his father's legacy of reform as soon as he became czar. Instead, he embraced Russian nationalism, one that placed the Russian people above all others within the empire. His motto was one used by his archconservative grandfather Nicholas I: "*Pravoslávie, samoderzhávie, naródnost*" ("Orthodoxy, Autocracy, and Nationality"). Within weeks of his coronation, Alexander III decided it was time to wage a war against enemies of the state, real and imagined.

The young czar needed scapegoats. In the cities, these included professors, students, journalists, and other members of the so-called intelligentsia. In the countryside, they included unassimilated minorities who might have yearnings for independence from the Russian Empire: Georgians, Poles, Mongols, Tartars, Uzbeks, and Kazakhs. And highest on the list were one of Russia's largest minorities, the Jews.

The earliest recorded presence of Jews in the Russian Empire dated to the 700s, when small communities existed in modern-day Ukraine, Belarus, Moldova, and western Russia. Their customs were a mix of the Ashkenazi Jews in the German states and the Sephardim who lived on in the Middle East after the Roman expulsion from Jerusalem. Under the early czars such as Peter the Great, Russian Jews faced similar restrictions as Jews in other European states. Forbidden from owning land, they could only make a living as merchants, tradesmen, and moneylenders. But because their numbers were relatively small, the Jews in the empire were not viewed as a significant threat by the Russian Orthodox establishment.

Not all European rulers felt threatened by the Jews. Poland's King Casimir III welcomed Jews from Spain, France, and German states who were fleeing the violent pogroms sparked by the Black Death in the mid-fourteenth century. Again, Jews became scapegoats. Some of the most devastating massacres took place in the German river cities of Mainz, Cologne, and Frankfurt am Main, where angry townspeople raged through the ghettos, slaughtered Jews, and drove out those who survived. After deaths from the plague subsided, a few Jews returned to their German homes and restarted their lives. Countless other German Jews sought refuge in the kingdom of Poland, where they worked as agents for the Polish landowning nobility or as tradesmen or middlemen.

Poland's lack of natural borders between Prussia and Russia made it virtually defenseless, and its fertile farmlands made it a tempting target for land-hungry aristocrats from the German states and Russia. In 1772, 1773, and finally in 1775, the two great powers forcibly partitioned Poland, and as a result, the Russian Empire acquired large Jewish populations. Under the rule of Catherine the Great, the growing Russian Jewish population was confined to the southwestern section of the empire, an area that became known as the Pale of Settlement. The Pale was not a giant ghetto per se. Jews and Christians lived side by side in places such as Belarus, Bessarabia, and Ukraine. Yet Jews were forbidden to live outside of the Pale and were largely barred from the major Russian cities of St. Petersburg and Moscow. It was Czar Nicholas I, who ruled Russia from 1825 to 1855, who imposed especially harsh restrictions on Jewish life, and specifically targeted Jews for military service and forced assimilation.

Although some Jews settled in big cities within the Pale such as Kiev, the typical Jewish family in nineteenth-century Russia lived in small villages known as shtetls, which were predominately, if not entirely, Jewish communities located within the Pale of Settlement. All were poor places of subsistence living. A few Jews grew prosperous enough to hire servants and live in substantial houses, but there was always the lingering fear that they would be beaten up by gangs, killed by Cossacks, or have their property confiscated or vandalized by jealous neighbors. Yet almost all of Russia's Jews, no matter how poor, made sure to educate their sons in the local Talmud Torah schools, where they would learn Hebrew Scripture and prepare to become bar mitzvah at thirteen. So Russia's Jews had a much higher literacy rate than their gentile neighbors.

A few Jews in imperial Russia were able to break free of the restrictions put upon them by the czarist government. And a tiny few rose to great wealth as industrialists and merchants in big cities such as Warsaw and Kiev. One scholar of Jewish culture and language, Abraham Harkavy, became head of the Oriental Division of the Imperial Public Library, an appointment granted during the relatively liberal reign of Alexander II. But most Russian Jews remained trapped in the Pale of Settlement, barred from the professional classes such as law and medicine, as well as from the ownership of land. To provide for their families and to support their synagogues and Talmud Torahs, they worked as tanners, blacksmiths, furriers, and at assorted other trades like the proverbial dairyman Tevye of Sholem Aleichem's stories on which *Fiddler on the Roof* was based. Those with modest capital tried their hand at playing the Rothschilds' game by loaning out money at interest. Still, most men made time to read and study Torah.

For the Jews, a devotion to learning was a tradition to be guarded. For Alexander III and other believers in absolute monarchy, a literate population was a threat, especially when it was heavily skewed toward a group that placed no spiritual faith in the Orthodox Church. Alexander III had a special epithet for the Jews, meant to incite the populace into violence: Christ killers. In 1881, the full force of the czar's wrath swept through Jewish communities in both cities and shtetls as saber-wielding Cossacks on horseback and peasants bearing torches and clubs descended upon a helpless population.

The Jews of the Russian Empire had withstood centuries of persecution and abuse, and had survived. But the pogroms of the 1880s were so ferocious and terrifying that a growing number of Jews considered a journey previously thought unthinkable, one that would take them halfway around the world to a foreign land. Some Jews thought that the idea of moving to America was madness. Why abandon all that was familiar, as wretched as it was, for a totally alien place so far away from what they knew? Others decided that the best places to move were the burgeoning industrial cities of Poland, such as Warsaw and Lodz. Here, one could get a job in a factory, open up a store with many more customers than in the shtetl, and become a rich man. Or at least raise a family with dignity or even lose one's self within the urban crowd, far away from the prying eyes of the police and the sabers of the Cossacks. Some Jews moved to the relatively tolerant city of Odessa, on the Black Sea, where there was a thriving Ukrainian Jewish community of craftsmen, bankers, physicians, architects, and wholesale businessmen. Between 1873 and 1897, the city's Jewish population grew from 51,000 of a total of 193,000, to 198,000 of 403,000. A few Jewish families, such as the grain merchant Ephrussi clan, achieved tremendous wealth and married into other elite European Jewish families such as the Rothschilds. Yet even in Odessa, they were subject to bigotry and intimidation, usually by Christian business rivals who declared that the city's Jewish population's effort to assimilate was merely a ruse to aid "the exploitation of Christians and masters at the hands of heretics and foreigners."

In addition to the violent pogroms, Alexander III strengthened an initiative that sent shock waves of fear throughout the Pale of Settlement: military conscription. Although Jews were denied full citizenship rights, they were still fully eligible for the draft. Mass conscription into the czar's army was nothing new. Alexander's grandfather Nicholas I had instituted mandatory conscription quotas on Jewish communities as early as 1827.

However, under his grandson's reign, military conscription came with a terrifying new caveat: the drafting of Jewish children into the army. By taking boys as young as eight away from their parents, the czar hoped to deprive them of their religion and culture as part of a program known as Russification. This meant learning Russian instead of Yiddish, and more often than not, a forced conversion to Russian Orthodoxy. Like other non–Russian Orthodox minorities, Jewish soldiers were classified as *inorodtsy* (alien believers) and were treated very harshly by their commanding officers, even for the most minor infractions. To countless mothers in the Russian Empire, forced conscription led to heartbreaking separations from their young sons. The boys who survived the rigors of military service and war often returned to their villages as virtual strangers to their families and their faith.

Obstinate, gruff, and not especially bright, Alexander III refused to back down from his new policy of state-sanctioned anti-Semitism. No matter that the Romanovs were among the richest families on earth and lived in a series of grand palaces, he saw himself as a strongman, whose rough manners and simple tastes mirrored those of his subjects.

Alexander III thought of intellectuals as dangerous, but he did revere one teacher: Konstantin Petrovich Pobedonostsev. A professor at Moscow State University, Pobedonostsev was one of Russia's most prominent legal theorists and had personally tutored Alexander in jurisprudence. He thought so highly of Pobedonostsev that he asked him to do the same for his own son Nicholas. Pobedonostsev received a big boost to his legal arsenal when he accepted a new position: Supreme Prosecutor of the Holy Synod. Now he had the power not only of Russia's legal apparatus behind him but the national church as well.

Following the summer pogroms of 1881, Alexander III tasked several high-ranking aristocrats with investigating the so-called Jewish Question. A year after he ascended the throne, he promulgated the May Laws, whose main purpose was to single out and punish the Jews for the death of his father. It was also a way of distracting his troubled empire from the real problems plaguing the nation—among them, the grinding poverty of the recently freed serfs, labor unrest in the rapidly industrializing cities, and simmering hatred among the educated middle classes for the czarist surveillance state. Despite its vast size and enormous army, Russia was still playing catch-up to the other great powers of Europe—Great Britain, France, and the newly unified Germany.

The May Laws, proposed by one of the czar's appointed aristocrats, Count Ignatiev, and drafted by Pobedonostsev, placed a number of severe restrictions on the business and personal lives of Jews living in the Pale of Settlement, excluding Poland:

1. As a temporary measure, and until a general revision is made of their legal status, it is decreed that the Jews be forbidden to settle anew outside of towns and boroughs, exceptions being admitted only in the case of existing Jewish agricultural colonies.

2. Temporarily forbidden are the issuing of mortgages and other deeds to Jews, as well as the registration of Jews as lessees of real property situated outside of towns and boroughs; and also the issuing to Jews of powers of attorney to manage and dispose of such real property.

3. Jews are forbidden to transact business on Sundays and on the principal Christian holy days; the existing regulations concerning the closing of places of business belonging to Christians on such days to apply to Jews also.

4. The measures laid down in paragraphs 1, 2, and 3 shall apply only to the governments within the Pale of Jewish Settlement [that is, they shall not apply to the ten governments of Poland].

The May Laws also severely limited the ability of Jews to make a living in Russia's emergent industrial economy. "Jews may be admitted as members by a majority vote of the stockholders," the laws said, "but they may not hold appointments as officers of such companies. Only a certain proportion of Jews, moreover, may be admitted, the number being limited to one-tenth of the total number of shareholders."

IN RUSSIA, there was a clear-cut answer of who was Russian and who was not: a Russian was a white Caucasian communicant of the Russian Orthodox Church and a loyal subject of the czar. A Jew could never be a true Russian, even if he or she converted to Christianity. Konstantin Pobedonostsev made a cold prediction of the future of Russia's Jews: "One third will die, one third will leave the country, and the last third will be completely assimilated within the Russian people."

After the promulgation of the May Laws, Konstantin Pobedonostsev granted an interview to the British journalist Arnold White, who himself was an advocate of restricting Jewish emigration to the United Kingdom. "The characteristics of the Jewish race are parasitic; for their sustenance they require the presence of another race as 'host' although they remain aloof and self-contained," he told White. "Take them from the living organism, put them on a rock, and they die. They cannot cultivate the soil." When asked about whether Jews could be a productive middle class of artisans and businessmen, Pobedonostsev doubled down. "The Jewish artisans are not really artisans, only colorably so. And they adopt the calling of artisan in order to become brokers, hucksters, and middlemen." He then cited a Russian government study that supposedly found that out of thirty Russian Jewish watchmakers, only two truly knew their trade, and the other twenty-eight were merely moneylenders and middlemen. White claimed that his interview of Pobedonostsev was done at the behest of Baron Maurice de Hirsch, one of Europe's most generous benefactors of Jewish emigration from Russia, as part of a fact-finding mission.

The pogroms and the May Laws were a loud and clear signal: the Jews were no longer safe in Russia. Beyond Odessa, Great Britain had long been a beacon for Jewish liberty. Several prominent Jewish families had already been elevated to the peerage during the reign of Queen Victoria. Lionel de Rothschild blazed a trail by becoming the first practicing Jewish member of Parliament in 1858. After refusing to take his seat three times because as an MP he had to swear his oath on a Christian Bible, he relented when he was allowed to use a copy of the Old Testament.

Yet for most Eastern European Jews, there was only one true beacon of hope that promised escape from the anti-Semitism that pervaded the Russian Empire. That beacon was the United States of America. There was one problem: Getting out of where they lived as safely and inexpensively as possible.

Albert Ballin and the German lines would solve that problem.

Across the Atlantic Ocean, another Jew, named Jacob Schiff, used his great wealth to help. He was an immigrant success story, but as devout as he was, he also felt somehow different from his Russian coreligionists. Superior, in fact.

CHAPTER 3

Schiff, the Immigrant Success Story

The surplus wealth we have gained, to some
extent, at least, belongs to our fellow beings. We are only temporary custodians of our
fortunes.

—JACOB HENRY SCHIFF

In the 1890s, shopkeepers on Fifth Avenue could set their watches to Jacob Henry Schiff's daily walk. Every morning, in good weather, a short man with a pointed beard, blue eyes, and a top hat would march briskly down the street, a flower in his buttonhole and a mirror shine on his shoes. Before leaving his townhouse at 965 Fifth Avenue, he would kiss his two children on their heads before they were whisked off to school, Frieda to Brearley on the Upper East Side and Mortimer to the Sachs Collegiate Institute on the Upper West Side. Of Dr. Sachs's Institute, Morti's uncle James Loeb wrote: "Herr Doktor Sachs was a stern Old World schoolmaster whose uniformed boys, in smart black suits and starched, stand-up collars, were seldom spared the rod. He emphasized the classics, languages (including German), and Teutonic discipline." It was a far cry from the strictly religious education that Jacob had received in the airless rooms of the Frankfurt Talmud Torah.

Schiff was the personification of this blend of Jewish piety and Germanic discipline. He would walk sixty blocks to Union Square, where he would then take a carriage the rest of the way to the office of Kuhn, Loeb & Co. at 52 William Street. Here Schiff met with railroad titans like

Edward H. Harriman of the Union Pacific and James J. Hill of the Great Northern Railroad. Though just over five feet tall, Schiff could command a room. He was confident. His speech was clipped and authoritative, with a strong German accent. He was resourceful. Through his network of European investors, Schiff was a master at raising capital for American corporations. He was also smart. He kept an eye on what was happening across the Atlantic, especially in his native Germany and in Russia. When he had time, he corresponded with influential friends outside of finance, including President Charles W. Eliot of Harvard University.

At the end of the day, Schiff would walk back to 965 Fifth Avenue. At sundown on Friday nights, he gathered with his wife, Therese, his children, and other members of his large extended family in the top-floor music room to celebrate the Jewish Sabbath.

Devoted to his family, Schiff had no rich man's interests or hobbies. His townhouse on Fifth Avenue was elegantly furnished, with objects from both Britain and Germany, but its walls boasted only a few Old Master paintings, nothing like the world-class collection Henry Clay Frick was steadily amassing not far away in the townhouse he was renting from the Vanderbilt family. "My father collected paintings, chiefly of the 19th century French school," his daughter, Frieda, recalled, "Oriental jades and crystals, and he gave commissions to several artists, including Harrington Mann and Eduard Veith." Pride of place was the bas-relief of Frieda and Mortimer executed by the sculptor Augustus Saint-Gaudens. It was a gift from his friend Sir Ernest Cassel, one of Britain's most prominent bankers. "We never forgave Sir Ernest for having done it just that time," Frieda said of it, "because we had to spend our entire Christmas holiday posing for it."

Collections aside, Jacob Schiff owned no yachts, shunned polo and golf, and belonged to no clubs, not even the fashionable Harmonie Club, a must for every upwardly mobile German Jew. Schiff cast a fisheye at those who lived lives of willful leisure and luxury. "I drastically became aware of its great temptations," he said of the city, "and at the same time I found how limited were the opportunities for those, possessed of greater aspirations than to satisfy alone bodily wants and desires."

As one of America's premier railroad bankers, Schiff loved making money and roaming the halls of power, but Judaism was his true passion.

"I have, for a long time, made it a rule not to go into anything of which I understand little or nothing," he said. "In my younger years I was not as conservative, but I wish I had been." If there was one thing he believed he understood more than banking, it was Judaism. He was proud of his religion. He was also convinced that America was the new Promised Land for the Jews. Schiff never forgot that he was once an immigrant, and always felt something of the outsider. He also had no problem pouncing on any whiff of anti-Semitism that he sensed from America's ruling establishment.

Jacob Schiff had no qualms taking on Henry Codman Potter, the Episcopal bishop of New York and religious pillar of the city's social elite. On January 11, 1898, Potter relayed in a letter to Jacob Schiff the sentiment that many in the American Protestant elite felt that the Jews might have brought persecution upon themselves. "Of course there are liars, thieves, and swindlers everywhere," the bishop wrote to Schiff, "but the contention made among the people whom I have again and again approached on the subject is that the hostility to the Hebrew is because, in ordinary business and personal transactions, he is tricky and untrustworthy, and unless held by a written agreement is sure to evade it and overreach the person with whom he is dealing." These traits, he suggested, also have been said of American Jews on Wall Street, who, "I am told that it is the only race on Wall Street whose word is not as good as its bond, that is, among business men of recognized rank and character."

Jacob Schiff was indignant at the bishop's accounts of anti-Semitism in elite gentile circles. "Strange to say," he responded a week later, "notwithstanding you have been told that the Hebrew race is the only one in Wall Street whose word is not as good as its bond, quite a number of the firms who, as I have just explained, have risen in standing and in credit, both in the actual and the moral sense of the word, are composed of Hebrews, while on the not small list of firms who have lost in prestige and credit, also both in the actual and the moral sense of the word, hardly one can be included of like composition."

Jacob Schiff made it his mission to show the world that Jews could be good Americans. Yet for all of his assuredness, he must have wondered whether even he could escape the frequently virulent anti-Semitism infecting so-called polite society at the time.

The *New York Times*, the bastion of the city's conservative establishment, did not think highly of Schiff and his ilk. When he purchased the mansion at 965 Fifth Avenue, one of the grandest homes in New York, for $450,000, the paper mockingly wrote: "Mr. Schiff looked at the property, said he thought it would answer his purposes very nicely, and there was no more ado over the rest of the transaction than there would have been had the subject of it been a box of cigars."

Schiff's militant optimism was a survival mechanism. In his long and eventful life, Jacob Schiff always saw the anti-Semitism in German culture, while ignoring, at least publicly, its uglier dimensions. He did the same with America as well. Only in Russia, he believed, was anti-Semitism not only ugly but violent.

* * *

Jakob Heinrich Schiff was born in the Jewish ghetto of Frankfurt in 1847, ten years before Albert Ballin. The Schiffs could trace their origins in Frankfurt to 1370, a time when many Jews were expelled from German cities after being blamed for the bubonic plague. The Protestant Reformation, led by the intensely anti-Semitic Martin Luther, resulted in further expulsion of Jews from the German states. Many of these erstwhile German Jews found temporary welcome in the kingdom of Poland, which would eventually be absorbed into the Russian Empire.

Frankfurt was one German city that did not expel its Jews. Yet this hardly meant tolerance. Until the late eighteenth century, Germany's remaining Jews were confined to specific neighborhoods, known as ghettos, a term first used in Venice centuries earlier. As Germany was a patchwork of small states, principalities, and free cities, treatment of the Jewish population depended on the good graces of the ruling monarch or city senate.

Jacob Schiff's parents, Moses and Clara, instilled in the young man a deep commitment to family and to Judaism. The family had produced generations of rabbis and Talmudic scholars. Schiff's father had an important contemporary connection. He supported his family by working as a broker for the Rothschilds, the most famous family to emerge from the crowded tenements and airless streets of the Frankfurt *Jüdengasse* (the lane where Jews lived). In fact, the two families acquired their German surnames from images painted onto their adjoining houses: a red shield and a sailing ship.

Jacob Schiff attended school until the age of fifteen, receiving a thorough grounding in the Torah, the German language, and mathematics. He then worked as an apprentice broker. A traditional university education was out of the question, as Jews were barred from attending the University of Frankfurt am Main. At the age of nineteen, after his parents encouraged him to seek his future in America, Jacob wrote several merchant houses in America, asking for work. "I spent the years of my apprenticeship in one of the best mercantile concerns in Frankfort [*sic*]," he wrote a friend of his father's in St. Louis, "and then entered the banking business in which I am still connected. I am therefore able to accomplish something in either of these fields. I know that my greatest difficulty will arise in connection with the Sabbath, but perhaps you will be able to procure a position which will leave me free on that day, because I am inclined by principle to devout religious observance."

As the carriage waited outside of the door of the family home, Jacob's father, Moses, would only give his blessing to his son's departure if the young man promised he would do his best to uphold Jewish law in the New World. Jacob carried with him about five hundred dollars in cash, or about ten thousand dollars today. This was more than enough to set him up with food and lodging upon his arrival in America, as well as pay for his fare.

Thanks to his family's relative affluence, Jacob probably booked a private cabin, rather than a communal steerage berth, on a transatlantic packet ship sailing from either Bremen or Hamburg. Along with his other worldly possessions, Jacob also carried with him a package of kosher meat—most likely salted beef or chicken—that he hoped would last six to eight days at sea. Food and bedding were often not included in the fare of most of these ships, especially for immigrants. For Schiff, the package of meat was not just a sign of keeping the faith but would also be a marker to everyone along the way that he was a Jew. While other passengers would dine on ham and salted pork, Jacob would eat alone.

Schiff set sail from Germany sometime in late spring, and he arrived in New York City on August 6, 1865. Due to his family's connections in Frankfurt, as well as his immense energy, he quickly found work at a brokerage firm named Frank & Gans. His timing was perfect. Already flush with cash from the Civil War, New York City was about to become the financial center of America's industrial boom, channeling money into railroads, steel, telegraphy, coal mining, and eventually into innovations such as the telephone and electricity. Older tycoons such as Cornelius "Commodore" Vanderbilt clashed with a new generation of financial card sharks such as Jay Gould, Jim Fiske, and Edward Harriman, who were determined to use fair means or foul to gain control of the lucrative and volatile new sectors of the American economy. Capital, foreign and domestic, was in strong demand, as were sharp financial brains.

Jacob Schiff was one of millions of Germans coming to America looking for a better life. The year after Schiff's birth, a series of revolutions rocked the old monarchies of Europe, especially in the patchwork of kingdoms that made up the yet-to-be-unified German Confederation. Following an outbreak of poorly planned demonstrations and uprisings by students and social liberals, the ruling aristocrats, spurred by the fear of the second coming of the guillotine, cracked down with brutal force. The result was a mass immigration of Germans to America. Some were Jews, but most were Protestants and Catholics. Many of the German Jews who settled in the United States hit the back roads of the country as peddlers. Some used their earnings from selling pots, pans, and assorted tchotchkes to start brokerage houses. Two such German Jewish immigrants were Abraham Kuhn and Solomon Loeb, who started a dry goods firm in Cincinnati, Ohio. In 1867, two years after the Civil War ended, the two men formed the investment house of Kuhn, Loeb & Co. and moved their operations to New York City.

Solomon Loeb bought a townhouse in the Murray Hill section of Manhattan, an area popular with affluent German Jews. His partner, Abraham Kuhn, was looking to expand into the investment banking world, much as the Lehman brothers of Selma, Alabama, had done with their dry goods business a few years earlier. Loeb had heard good things about Jacob Schiff, who had started his own brokerage house after leaving the Frank & Gans firm in 1867. Although Schiff had become a naturalized American citizen, he had by then returned to Germany to take up a position with the Hamburg branch of the London & Hanseatic Bank.

There Jacob Schiff first encountered the Warburg family, very much at the top of the small but steep Jewish social pyramid in Hamburg. Moritz Warburg, the family patriarch, was so impressed with Jacob that he offered him a job at the family banking house, M. M. Warburg & Co. Jacob might have contemplated returning to his native land since Germany had just been unified under the rule of the Prussian monarchy thanks to the scheming of Chancellor Otto von Bismarck. Commercial prospects in the new German Reich now seemed rosy, as the new country was poised to become an industrial powerhouse. But Jacob Schiff, as much as he wanted to be close to his mother in Frankfurt, realized he had to "reemigrate" back to America. As he wrote her when he returned, "The opportunity is enormous here. The coming expansion of the United States, in railroading and all that, is so large that I myself don't feel there will be a foreign branch for some time to come. There is more than enough to keep us here."

During his brief time in Hamburg, Jacob Schiff might have run into Albert Ballin at the local synagogue, seated in a pew with his own mother, Amalia, his ill-looking father, Samuel, and their several other children. If he did, Schiff might have wondered why that family didn't emigrate to America, just as he had. Yet he also understood that the Warburg family gave generously to Hamburg's Talmud Torah, to make sure that all the city's Jewish children, including less fortunate children such as those in the Ballin family, received some sort of religious education. That was probably a factor in keeping the Ballins in Hamburg.

Two years after the unification of Germany, the American stock market and many financial banking firms cratered in the Panic of 1873 from too much speculation in the securities of the nation's railroads. Despite this turn, in the eight short years between the end of the Civil War in 1865 and the onset of the Panic, the industrialization of America had picked up momentum, as the population of the cities of the Northeast exploded and newly emergent enterprises such as railroads, textiles, steel, and mining absorbed tens of thousands of workers. The new concerns, often massive, needed all the cheap labor they could get, as well as vast amounts of capital to keep themselves going. And the source of that capital was Europe, which had long supplied promising American corporations with money to start and expand. The two big players in funneling European capital to the United States were Baring Brothers & Co., based in London, and the Rothschild partnership, with branches in London, Paris, Frankfurt, and Vienna. Both firms, gentile and Jew, had their powerful agents in major American cities, especially New York. These early gentile and Jewish spheres of finance capitalism foreshadowed the eventual structure of Wall Street investment banking firms in the decades to come.

Across the Atlantic, the Panic of 1873 caused a massive drop in immigration to America, and hastened the bankruptcy and death of Albert Ballin's father. Kuhn, Loeb & Co., on the other hand, survived the disaster, and Abraham Kuhn offered Jacob Schiff a job at his investment house. Kuhn knew that Schiff was smart and ambitious. But the young man also came with connections to some of the most powerful financiers in continental Europe.

Jacob Schiff joined Kuhn, Loeb as a junior partner. He met, and fell in love with, Solomon Loeb's daughter Therese. She found the young man's interest more than a bit hasty, but Schiff was persistent in courting her. Schiff had a powerful ally: Therese's mother, Betty Loeb. Smart, ambitious, and demanding, Betty brought up her five children in a whirlwind of lessons: dancing, music, riding, tennis, and languages. After one of her children performed a musical piece, she would either say approvingly: "*Das war Musik!*" Or sneer: "*Hmph! Musik?*"

Therese was used to being fussed over and pampered. Jacob appreciated her intelligence, but also sensed that, because of her strict upbringing, she would not challenge his authority. He wrote his mother, Clara, back in Frankfurt, about the concerns she might have about the match:

> I know you haven't any clear conception of what an American girl is like. You may think she is rather uncultured and even a feminist—but don't imagine that of the girl I've selected. She might have been brought up in the best of German families.

Clara wrote back, urging Jacob to curb his snobbery, if not his ambition. "A word spoken hastily in anger would leave lifelong scars," she warned. The recently widowed Clara Schiff was certainly relieved that her beloved Americanized son was not marrying a gentile. Not like August Belmont (originally August Schönberg), the German-born agent of the Rothschilds in New York, who had married Caroline Slidell Perry two decades earlier and had joined the Episcopal Church.

Jacob Schiff aimed to outdo Belmont in every respect, while still being a religious Jew. He avoided all the temptations of gentile society, outside of the business sphere. After Jacob and Therese married on May 6, 1875, Schiff's father-in-law, Solomon Loeb, elevated him to a senior partnership at Kuhn, Loeb & Co., a position Jacob did not see as a sinecure. Schiff surveyed the investment banking landscape of New York City and decided to make it to the top. This meant taking on not just J. W. Seligman & Co., the other prominent Jewish firm in the city, but also the formidable and thoroughly gentile Drexel, Morgan & Co., led by the established Philadelphian Anthony J. Drexel and the up-and-coming Hartford, Connecticut, transplant John Pierpont Morgan.

Although Jacob Schiff mingled with the plutocrats, he refused to live like one. He ate well, exercised frequently, and tried not to let stress get the better of him. He walked around Manhattan as if God himself protected his every step. The rules of the Schiff household were unfailingly Jewish. The Gilded Age staples of oysters and lobsters were banned from the dinner table, as Schiff insisted on a kosher kitchen. The Sabbath would be kept on Saturday, and he would be the guiding family patriarch. So powerful was his faith that he even cajoled his agnostic in-laws Solomon and Betty Loeb into becoming more observant Jews. As a warning shot to the rest of the extended Loeb-Schiff family, Schiff stipulated in his will that if either of his children married a non-Jew, they would be permanently disinherited.

To those who looked up to Schiff, he was the model Jew, the immigrant success story. He was ethical, assured, and unfazed by bullies, especially of the anti-Semitic variety. But his own family was terrified of him, such was the strength of his will and ambition. Soon after rising to the partnership of Kuhn, Loeb & Co., Schiff decided that his own father-in-law was too weak and timid for the good of the bank. He began a steady and calculated effort to take over the firm. First, he showed up earlier to work than Solomon, then started leaving a barrage of memoranda and questions on the old man's desk. Solomon, who was a workaholic himself, hated any sort of conflict. Bewildered by the memos, he would show up at his son-in-law's desk immediately after getting one of these missives to speak to its contents.

Soon, Solomon Loeb was so overwhelmed by Schiff's energy that in 1888 he went into semi-retirement. Even if he felt shunted aside at his own firm, Loeb knew that his son-in-law's energy was paying off, as were his connections to prominent Jewish banking families such as the Warburgs in Germany. Solomon tried to establish some dynastic continuity by pressuring his son James Loeb into going into the business after his graduation from Harvard. James was brilliant, but was much more interested in music, art, and literature than in railroad finance. Schiff immediately felt threatened by the Harvard-educated golden boy and did what he could to make life miserable for his brother-in-law. Schiff especially objected to James's mysterious, unnamed love interest, a gentile girl he had met while at Harvard. Loeb eventually left the partnership and moved to Munich, Germany, where he lived the life of an eccentric, and very lonely, gentleman philanthropist. He never married.

With his brother-in-law James Loeb out of the picture, Schiff was now the undisputed heir to the banking kingdom. Leveraging his strong connections to European banks, Schiff turned Kuhn, Loeb & Co. into an adviser for blue-chip transportation clients such as the Pennsylvania Railroad and Union Pacific. Over the course of his career, his work for the Pennsylvania alone amounted to close to one billion dollars in public offerings and loans. Scrupulous to detail, Schiff preferred learning from experience and people rather than from books. He did have a head for numbers but took real joy from gathering information firsthand and understanding how small weaknesses could lead to massive problems in the flow of passengers and freight. He couldn't stand the sloppiness he saw everywhere in America in the name of saving money. In his memos, he told his clients of dirty passenger-car windows, tracks overgrown with weeds, and drunken conductors. Service and care mattered, even for the lowest-paying passengers. Spending money on the little things, he believed, paid off in the long run.

Schiff also believed that companies in trouble often represented opportunities. One of them was the Union Pacific, the company responsible for the final spike that completed the transcontinental railroad. Like Ballin's

HAPAG, the railroad had a long history, but had suffered from years of poor management. Most recently, the ruthless Jay Gould had bled it dry, leaving it bankrupt and close to death. Despite its rail connection to California, no one seemed to want it.

Jacob Schiff decided to take on Union Pacific as a Kuhn, Loeb client and then have the firm reorganize the railroad into a profitable company. But Schiff was opposed by Edward H. "Ned" Harriman, who wanted to do the same thing and integrate the Union Pacific into his Illinois Central system. Both men knew what it meant to be outsiders. Harriman, once a poor clergyman's son from Hempstead, New York, had become one of the richest and most hated men on Wall Street. Schiff decided that to get his way, he would have to make a pact with the devil. So he offered Harriman a position on the railroad's executive committee in 1897. Harriman accepted. Next, Schiff used his connections with European banks to funnel capital into rebuilding the railroad from the ground up. The two men would turn the Union Pacific into one of the most profitable railroads in America. It would make them both multimillionaires.

By selling securities for the Union Pacific, Jacob Schiff deepened his relationship with European investors, including Sir Ernest Cassel in London. Cassel had a deep desire to cultivate close ties between his native Germany and his adopted homeland of Great Britain. Born a Jew, he had converted to Catholicism upon his marriage to Annette Maud Maxwell. By the 1890s, Cassel had become one of Great Britain's most successful bankers, with large stakes in mining and heavy industry.* Schiff was quick to criticize Jews like Cassel who he felt had forsaken their faith, especially members of his own family. Even so, Cassel became a close friend of Schiff and a confidant of Edward, Prince of Wales, who very much enjoyed the company of Jewish bankers and businessmen.

Unlike August Belmont, however, Cassel never forgot who he was. He would serve as a major link in the financial chain that aided Jews trying to escape Russia after the first wave of czarist pogroms.

In New York City, prominent and wealthy German Jews such as Jacob Schiff took notice of Russia's increasing persecution of its Jewish pop-

---

* Sir Ernest Cassel's granddaughter Edwina married Lord Mountbatten, a relative of King Edward VII, in 1922.

ulation. More alarmingly, they began to notice strains of anti-Semitism creeping into their own daily lives, no matter how assimilated they thought they had become.

* * *

America had been struggling with issues of assimilation well before the Revolution. Although primarily an English nation, colonial America had pockets of German, Dutch, Spanish, and Sephardim (Jews of Spanish and Portuguese origins). All these groups were considered "white." The two tragic exceptions were African Americans, even in states where slavery had been abolished, and Native Americans, whose tribal lands had been expropriated from them by white settlers.

One prominent American who took a stand against bigotry was the poet Emma Lazarus, who could trace her family lineage to colonial times but recognized that her ancestors, too, arrived as penniless refugees. Born in 1849, Emma was the daughter of a wealthy New York sugar refiner. Both her parents could trace their ancestry to Sephardic Jews who had arrived in the Dutch colony of New Amsterdam in 1651 aboard the *St. Charles*. This group of Jews was seeking refuge from the scourge of the Portuguese Inquisition in Brazil. The Dutch governor of New Amsterdam, Pieter Stuyvesant, tried to turn the group away, writing to the Dutch West India Company that members of "the deceitful race,—such hateful enemies and blasphemers of the name of Christ,—be not allowed further to infect and trouble this new colony." The Dutch West India Company, which had ultimate control over the colony of New Amsterdam, ordered their governor Stuyvesant (a company employee) to accept the Jewish refugees.

The American Jewish community remained minuscule until the Civil War. In 1861, there were only 150,000 Jews in America, with most of them residing in big coastal cities such as New York, Philadelphia, Charleston, and New Orleans. Because of their relatively small numbers and their colonial roots, Jews in America had been left mostly undisturbed by discriminatory practices. When the German Jews arrived en masse, they did face backlash from the Sephardic Jews who had established family fortunes before the Revolution and considered themselves the equal of the Protestant upper crust. By and large, they considered the German Jews brassy, unpolished, and uncouth. A group of German Jews, for example, was prevented from joining the Union Club, New York's most prestigious social organization, one that counted several Sephardic families on the rolls. To retaliate, the new immigrants founded the Harmonie Club, an organization that ostensibly was about German choral singing but in reality was a German Jewish version of the Union Club.

The Lazarus family was at the top of mid-nineteenth-century American Jewish society. The family had wealth, status, and social acceptance. Emma's father had lavished on her the best education money could buy. The Lazaruses had also intermarried with Jewish families of German ancestry who had settled in the United States in the years since the Revolution. Yet despite all her privilege, she felt troubled by the anti-Semitic pogroms in Russia and could not in good conscience ignore that news as a Jew in a gentile world. Emma knew that soon the trickle of Jews coming to America would turn into a flood. And she was "perfectly conscious that . . . contempt and hatred underlies the general tone of the community towards us."

Already clubs such as the Union and the Knickerbocker, as well as hotels and other gathering places, were closing their doors to Jews. Anti-Semitism in the United States, especially in elite society, was on the rise. The seminal event that made flagrant anti-Semitism acceptable in broader American society was the so-called Hilton Affair. On June 13, 1877, Joseph Seligman, a partner in the investment banking firm of J. W. Seligman & Co., arrived at the Grand Union Hotel in Saratoga Springs, as he looked forward to breathing the country air, soaking in the mineral waters, and spending time placing bets on horses at the racetrack. Besides being one of America's premier railroad bankers, he was a founder of the Union League of New York and an ardent supporter of the Northern cause during the Civil War, having almost single-handedly placed $200 million worth of American war bonds. He was also a longtime president of Temple Emanu-El in New York City. Seligman had patronized the Grand Union Hotel for years. But that spring, when he showed up to check in at the front desk along with his wife and retinue of servants, the hotel clerk refused the family admission because they were Jewish.

Seligman was shocked. He had dealt with anti-Semitic slurs when traveling the American countryside as a young peddler and largely shrugged them off. He protested, but the clerk said that the hotel's owner, Judge Henry Hilton, had decreed members of the "Hebrew race" were no longer welcome. Although Henry Hilton was no friend of the Jews, the real reason for the snub was personal: Seligman had not invited Hilton to a dinner he hosted in honor of President Ulysses S. Grant several years earlier.

The Seligman-Hilton Affair outraged many Americans, and there were many editorials condemning Hilton's actions. On June 19, the *New York Times* blared in multideck headlines:

A SENSATION AT SARATOGA

NEW RULES FOR THE GRAND UNION.

NO JEWS TO BE ADMITTED—MR. SELIGMAN,

THE BANKER, AND HIS FAMILY SENT AWAY—

HIS LETTER TO MR. HILTON—

GATHERING OF MR. SELIGMAN'S FRIENDS

AN INDIGNATION MEETING TO BE HELD.

When asked to apologize for what he did, Hilton flatly refused, citing his constitutional right to deny people access to his personal property. "As [yet] the law . . . permits a man to use his property as he pleases," he wrote in a published letter, "and I propose exercising that blessed privilege, notwithstanding Moses and all his descendants object."

Seligman suddenly found his former friends turning against him. His son was denied membership in the Union League of New York, an organization Seligman himself had helped found. Dispirited and ill, Seligman died in 1880, on the eve of the assassination of Czar Alexander II. Those who knew the banker suspected the Seligman-Hilton Affair had hastened his death.

Emma Lazarus, meanwhile, came to realize that, privileged as she was, she didn't feel fully safe in her own country. She concluded that the way to counter hatred against Jews was not by denying her own heritage but by asserting it and insisting upon the broad acceptance of Jews in American life. In a letter to her friend Philip Cowen, she noted that a recent anti-Semitic article in the *New York Sun* was "so coarse and vulgar that it deserves no reply from any self-respecting Jew." For her, the letter was not an exception to the rule. "It represents the habitual light in which we are regarded as a race by the Christians," she said, "but it happens to be couched in somewhat more offensive terms than usual."

As an heiress to a fortune, Emma Lazarus had the time and the leisure to pursue poetry and activism for Jewish causes. As part of a fundraising campaign to build a base for a copper-clad Statue of Liberty, she penned a poem called "The New Colossus" at the urging of former secretary of state William Maxwell Evarts.

Designed by the sculptor Frederic Auguste Bartholdi, the 151-foot-high statue was completed in 1876, just in time for the Centennial Exposition in Philadelphia. The sculpture was the female representation of a principle enshrined in 1776 by Thomas Jefferson in the Declaration of Independence (life, liberty, and the pursuit of happiness) and asserted by the French Revolution in the 1789 Declaration of the Rights of Man ("freedom to do everything which injures no one else; hence the exercise of the natural rights of each man has no limits except those which assure to the other members of the society the enjoyment of the same rights").

For the next ten years, the disembodied head and torch were exhibited around the country. Bartholdi hoped to prompt the American people to find a site for the statue and raise money for the construction of its base. Most people thought of the project as a needless extravagance. Also, the sight of a giant disembodied copper hand holding a glass torch rising above Madison Square Park struck many passersby as more than a little disturbing.

The statue had form and symbolism, but she did not have a voice. After thinking about the meaning of liberty in America, Emma Lazarus wrote her sonnet to give human voice to the allegorical figure. Her thoughts turned to the pogroms in Russia and Czar Alexander III's hatred of the Jewish people, and to how Old World suffering and the New World hope of immigrants arriving in New York for the first time would renew the meaning of liberty in America:

> *Not like the brazen giant of Greek fame,*
> *With conquering limbs astride from land to land;*
> *Here at our sea-washed, sunset gates shall stand*
> *A mighty woman with a torch, whose flame*

Is the imprisoned lightning, and her name
Mother of Exiles. From her beacon-hand
Glows world-wide welcome; her mild eyes command
The air-bridged harbor that twin cities frame.
"Keep, ancient lands, your storied pomp!" cries she
With silent lips. "Give me your tired, your poor,
Your huddled masses yearning to breathe free,
The wretched refuse of your teeming shore.
Send these, the homeless, tempest-tost to me,
I lift my lamp beside the golden door!"

The poem was published in the *New York World*, owned by Joseph Pulitzer, another prominent Jew. Within three years, enough money had been raised for the architect Richard Morris Hunt to start construction of a great stone pedestal on Bedloe's Island, right in the middle of the Upper Bay.

Lazarus never saw the completed statue. She was in Europe the day of the official dedication, on a two-year extended tour where she met many literary and cultural figures, including the Christian socialist William Morris and the poet Robert Browning. By 1887, however, she had been diagnosed with Hodgkin's lymphoma, which was untreatable at the time. She decided to return to America to die. As her steamship sailed past the Statue of Liberty in September of that year, Lazarus was too weak to get up from her berth and see the completed "New Colossus" through her porthole.

She died on November 19, 1887, at age thirty-eight.

Emma Lazarus's outspoken activism spread throughout German Jewish society. As a proud Jew and adopted American, Jacob Schiff believed he had to fulfill the mission so beautifully expressed by Emma Lazarus. Beginning in the 1880s, when he was still relatively young, Jacob Schiff started to donate large sums of money to virtually every Jewish charitable organization in New York City. In accordance with the traditional Jewish principle of *tzedakah*, he donated 10 percent of his income to charitable causes. In the absence of any sort of modern welfare state to take care of the poor, Schiff determined that he would build one from scratch for poor Jewish Americans. It would be a top-down enterprise, dependent on the philanthropy of the now-successful German Jewish merchant class of New York City, who themselves were only one or two generations away from immigrant status.

Jacob Schiff approached the problem in the same way he looked at the railroad business. He surveyed the network of Jewish charities in New York and found them disorganized, underfunded, and ill prepared to handle the needs of thousands of impoverished Russian Jews arriving at the Castle Garden immigration station each month. The principal charitable umbrella organization was the United Hebrew Charities, established in 1874, when the city had a mere sixty thousand Jews, most of them of German and Sephardic ancestry. Fifteen years later, that number was approaching five hundred thousand, and most of them were of Russian, Romanian, Polish, and Austro-Hungarian origin.

Jacob Schiff gave to charities on the condition that he have a firm hand in directing what they did. This meant strict adherence to Jewish principles, and making sure that they encouraged the new arrivals to learn English and maintain clean habits. In turn, the money would flow to the Henry Street Settlement House (run by his friend Lillian Wald), the Educational Alliance, and Montefiore Hospital. Besides giving away large amounts of his fortune to Jewish charities, Schiff started to get involved in Republican politics. Given his wealth and his close ties to the railroads, politicians were more than happy to listen to him. He lobbied mainly to keep the country's mostly open immigration policy in place despite resistance from Republicans like Congressman Henry Cabot Lodge of Massachusetts, who was pushing for literacy tests and other measures that would restrict the flow of Eastern and Southern European immigrants into the country. Nativists like Lodge felt that the new wave of immigrants would destroy the nation the Civil War was fought to preserve, a nation that did not include Jews from Eastern and Southern Europe.

The Seligman Affair aside, Jacob Schiff felt that anti-Semites represented a vocal but minor sideshow. The bigotry of a small group of snobs, he believed, paled in comparison to the state-sponsored violence of Czar Alexander III. Most Americans were people of goodwill, and certainly the U.S. Constitution served as a bulwark against anti-Semitism in his adopted country.

By the 1890s, Jacob Schiff had turned Kuhn, Loeb into a top-tier Wall

Street bank, second only to J. P. Morgan & Co. He was also a millionaire many times over. Jacob and Therese owned not only a townhouse on Fifth Avenue but a summer house in Sea Bright, New Jersey, and another summer house in Bar Harbor, Maine. Despite his strong German identity, he fell under the sway of the British branch of the Rothschilds when it came to the art of living. He consulted his friend Sir Ernest Cassel on matters of paintings, home decoration, and attire.

Jacob and Therese Schiff were uncompromising on the studies and deportment of Frieda and Morti. Above all, Jacob wanted them to be good Jews. Being late for Shabbat services meant a beating from Papa, and it was usually Morti who got spanked. Schiff, however, found himself irresistibly drawn to the Groton School, one of the most gentile institutions in the United States, as he considered Morti's schooling. Founded in 1880 by the Reverend Endicott Peabody, an Episcopal priest, it had been modeled on British boarding schools such as Eton, Marlborough, and Cheltenham. Among its founding trustees were the two Morgans, father, Junius, and son John Pierpont, and the Boston Brahmin clergymen Phillips Brooks and William Lawrence. Schiff wrote Peabody, asking that Morti be admitted to Groton, but be excused from all Christian instruction and chapel services. Peabody demurred. He respected Schiff's religious beliefs but wrote back that religious instruction in the Anglican tradition was compulsory at Groton. Schiff gave up and decided that it would be best for Morti to finish his secondary education among other rich German Jewish boys at Dr. Sachs's Institute in New York.

Along with a fear of apostasy, Schiff was terrified of his children becoming spendthrifts, even going so far as keeping Morti from enrolling at Harvard because he feared that his son would pick up bad habits being around so many rich gentile boys. Morti went to Williams College instead for two years, and then was called back to New York by his father to get a practical training at Kuhn, Loeb & Co. A couple of years in the mountains of western Massachusetts with not a synagogue in sight was too much for Schiff to bear. It didn't help that Morti bought a brand-new bicycle without asking his father's permission, an unpardonable sin in the Schiff household.

Mortimer dutifully joined the Kuhn, Loeb & Co. partnership in 1891. Schiff then oversaw his son's marriage to Adele Neustadt, the daughter

of one of the partners at Hallgarten & Co., another German Jewish banking house, albeit a much less powerful one than Kuhn, Loeb. It was a
poor match. Morti and Adele didn't get along, but Jacob Schiff didn't
care. What mattered was that the two came from rich Jewish families
and would perpetuate the faith of their ancestors. "As to your surprise at
the resentment which Hebrews show to so-called Christian social exclu-
siveness," Schiff wrote in an otherwise caustic letter to Bishop Potter, "I
am entirely at one with you. That Jew and Gentile will socialize but not
thoroughly mix is a natured result of the reluctance on the part of both
to intermarriage, the uniting of the sexes in wedlock being, after all, the
main stimulus to all social intercourse."

Schiff had already begun to fret about his progeny's control of the
bank. In 1895, a dashing young man named Otto Hermann Kahn joined
the bank, soon after marrying the socially ambitious Adelaide Wolff, the
daughter of Abraham Wolff, another Kuhn, Loeb partner. A native of
Mannheim, Germany, Kahn had an elite education and also spoke with a
clipped British accent acquired from his time in London. He was initially
trained as a musician but soon gravitated toward finance. Unlike Morti
Schiff, Kahn genuinely loved the financial and logical complexities of railroad banking. He also took up rich men's hobbies such as coaching sports
teams and patronizing the opera, and did his best to join Protestant society.

None of it worked. Despite serving on the board of the Metropolitan Opera, Kahn was still refused his own box because he was Jewish.
But Edward Harriman liked Kahn's skill with the finances of the Union
Pacific as well as his suave demeanor. Jacob Schiff had no choice but to
tolerate the young upstart. Kahn might have been a nonobservant dandy,
but he was also a mathematical genius who had the same knack for reorganizing railroads as his boss.

Even if the smart but troubled Morti was all but assured a partnership
at Kuhn, Loeb, Schiff still felt he needed a good son-in-law to ensure his
progeny's future. He didn't like Kahn, who, besides, was already married.
Dynastic salvation of a sort came in 1894, when the Schiffs were vacation-
ing in Frankfurt. Frieda, then eighteen, was bright and inquisitive, but
thanks to her father's strict control—he guarded her as he would a vestal
virgin—woefully naïve. At a dinner hosted by the Dreyfus banking family in honor of the Schiffs, Frieda met two of the Warburg brothers, Max

and Felix. She fell instantly for Felix, whose easy smile and bon vivant ways contrasted so sharply with the austere ways of her father. To assess what might happen, Felix's parents invited the Schiffs to a dinner at their home in Hamburg. "The charm of the Warburgs was deeply impressed on me," Frieda recalled.

There were few more accomplished Jewish clans in Germany than the Warburgs of Hamburg. The five Warburg brothers—Aby, Max, Paul, Felix, and Fritz—had all received fine instruction in languages, mathematics, history, and Torah. Everyone lived under the watchful eye of the fearsome grandmother-matriarch Sara Warburg. Father Moritz loved fine wines, cigars, and music. Mother Charlotte was a member of the prominent Oppenheim family of Frankfurt. She not only knew her Goethe and played piano brilliantly but kept a perfectly organized account book that tracked every penny of household expenses. Charlotte and Moritz Warburg led Hamburg's sixteen-thousand-strong Jewish community, as they gave generously to the Jewish hospital and other charities—including the synagogue that the Ballin family visited.

As newly emancipated Jews in the German Empire, the Warburgs were symbols of what was possible in an enlightened society open to talent, but only to a point. Despite their wealth, the specter of hate, institutional and on the street, still hovered over their daily lives, making them insular and suspicious of outsiders. Sara Warburg sent her famous Passover buttercakes to Chancellor Bismarck each year, until she got wind of the court preacher's anti-Semitic sermon, and the gift giving stopped.

The court preacher was Adolf Stoecker, one of the most outspoken anti-Semites in Germany, who argued that the German Jews, no matter how hard they tried to assimilate, would never be part of the German *Volk*. In addition to his religious duties in Berlin, Stoecker was also the organizer of the Christian Social Workers' Party, which advocated for conservative social values and the economic protection of the German working classes, or *Mittelstand*. In 1879, Stoecker delivered an address that swept the nation by storm. He said:

> *The Jews are and remain a people within a people, a state within a state, a separate tribe within a foreign race. All immigrants are eventually absorbed by the people among whom they live—all save the Jews. They pit*

their unbroken Semitic character against Teutonic nature, their rigid cult of law or their hatred of Christians against Christianity. We cannot condemn them for this; as long as they are Jews, they are bound to act in this way. But we must, in all candor, state the necessity of protecting ourselves against the dangers of such an intermingling.

The new German nation, Stoecker argued, had to impose strict limits on Jewish participation in all sectors of life. "Either we succeed in this," he concluded, "and Germany will rise again, or the cancer from which we suffer will spread further. In that event our whole future is threatened and the German spirit will become Judaized." In 1881, Stoecker was elected to a seat in the Reichstag, where he continued to spew anti-Semitic hatred.

Reverend Stoecker and his ilk aside, the Warburgs fervently believed that they could be good Germans and good Jews. For the youngest generation of Warburgs, however, the temptations of assimilation into German culture were very strong. Max, the second son of Moritz and Charlotte Warburg, was a charming, easygoing child who dreamed of going into the German military. His parents didn't much mind that Max wasn't an especially good student. His older brother Aby was brilliant, and was first in line to inherit a partnership in the family bank when only one son of each generation could go into the business. But the erratic Aby wanted instead to become a scholar of Renaissance art. Max, meanwhile, dreamed of cavalry horses, uniforms, and joining the ranks of Hamburg high society, not of mastering any part of the Torah. Then there was Felix, a playboy, and Paul, the serious scholar. There was a daughter, Olga, who was engaged to Paul Kohn-Speyer, scion of another German Jewish banking family. Youngest were a set of twins, Fritz and Louise. The Warburg boys (Aby, Max, Felix, Paul, and Fritz) were collectively known as the "Famous Five."

Theirs was a life full of garden parties, yachting, music lessons, private religious studies, art appreciation, and a carefree devotion to one another that German Jews liked to call *familiengefühl* ("family feeling"). As heirs to one of Germany's most important banks, their future seemed serene and assured, despite what people like Adolf Stoecker said.

And yet Jacob Schiff had his doubts about the match. For all Felix Warburg's charisma, or perhaps because of it, the serious-minded Schiff didn't like the young man as a prospective son-in-law. His nickname in Germany was the "Black Prince." He seemed more interested in golf, tennis, and music than in the rigors of finance. He also seemed too handsome and lighthearted for his own good, unlike his more serious brother Paul, a genuine intellectual and financial wizard who was simultaneously courting Therese Schiff's niece Nina Loeb. Neither did Jacob like Felix's lack of seriousness about his Judaism, a rebellion no doubt against his own parents' piety.

Divine intervention was provided by Sir Ernest Cassel, who not only took a paternalistic interest in Frieda but also knew that stronger ties between Kuhn, Loeb and M. M. Warburg & Co. were good for business. At Cassel's urging, Jacob and Therese Schiff met with Moritz and Charlotte Warburg at the Belgian resort of Ostend to see if the two clans could get along as in-laws as well as business associates. When the waiter placed a quartet of steaming hot lobsters on the table, Jacob Schiff blew up. To him, such a flagrant breach of dietary laws was not just an abomination but an insult. Yet Frieda didn't bow to her father's rage. In 1895, Frieda and Felix were married in New York City at the Schiff townhouse. Soon after the wedding, a somewhat reluctant Schiff admitted his son-in-law to the partnership of Kuhn, Loeb & Co. Even then, it took him a while before he could refer to Felix with the familiar "*du*" rather than the formal "*sie*." As it turned out, Felix would one day prove himself a completely worthy member of the Schiff family as a father, a philanthropist, and a Jew.

By the time of this august transatlantic marriage, the fetid conditions of the Frankfurt *Jüdengasse* were a distant memory for Jacob Schiff. What held constant from the ghetto to Fifth Avenue was his own sense of *familiengefühl*. To Schiff, his true religion was his family, and he relished being an Old Testament patriarch.

As for his native land, Schiff held no resentment toward the "Fatherland." He was proud of how Germany had rapidly evolved from a hodgepodge of small principalities into a unified empire with a thriving industrial and commercial economy. Despite the vicious treatment of Jews in German history, he felt that the people of the recently united Germany had made enormous strides in welcoming its Jewish subjects into the national fold. A ferocious optimist and a deep believer in the promise of America, he felt, too, that anti-Semitism could be conquered in the United States, just as it supposedly was in Germany.

For Schiff, it was czarist Russia that was the great enemy of the Jewish people. Reports of the increasingly brutal pogroms and military conscriptions of Jewish boys enraged him. As a banker, he could call out for regime change in Russia, but the power of the Romanovs made that extremely unlikely. He concluded that if Alexander III remained on his throne, the only way for Russia's Jews to improve their lot was to get out and come to America. Here there were constitutionally protected rights (not "Divine Right" autocracy) and relatively lax immigration laws. For the Russian Jews to assimilate into American life, however, they needed to reform their ways and become more like him and the German Jewish elite. If a Jew such as himself could rise as high as he did in American society, then why couldn't every Jew do the same?

So Jacob Schiff, one of the richest men in America, decided it was time to put virtue ahead of profit and give away his time and money to save his people from the tyranny of the czarist government. As he grew richer, he devoted more of his time to Jewish causes and less time to the lucrative goyish railroad business. Jacob Schiff would become the most outspoken and tireless advocate for Jewish life and culture worldwide.

But for all his zeal, not everyone took kindly to his sense of mission or his sense of superiority.

In spite of Jacob Schiff's efforts, the Russian Jews of downtown and the German Jews of uptown lived in completely different spheres. What linked them together were the charitable aid groups that were funded by the German Jews and patronized by the Russian Jews. Most of the aid came from charities overseen by Jacob Schiff. The largest and most well-funded was the Hebrew Emigrant Aid Society (HEAS), which was a mutual-aid enterprise unlike any other in history. By subsidizing the cost of steamship tickets and by giving Jewish immigrants small amounts of money to feed their families, pay rent, and start small businesses in America, Schiff and his colleagues hoped to make these transplants over in their own image, as patriots and devout Jews both.

The Eastern European Jews who settled in America in the 1880s and '90s did not always share Schiff's rosy sentiments about assimilating with the establishment. For them, the worlds of uptown and downtown were irreconcilable, no matter what aid Schiff and HEAS provided them. For most, their first impressions of America were not uplifting but horrifying.

For months and years after passing through Castle Garden and Ellis Island, countless immigrants wondered whether the hardships of America were worth the sacrifice. Most stayed because the alternatives—pogroms and military conscription—were far worse.

And yet, those who survived the ordeal of the tenements did eventually find joy and hope, even if they never did reach the Upper East Side and the rarefied world of Jacob Schiff and the Warburgs.

So family members left behind and neighbors who heard good news kept on coming to America by the hundreds of thousands, and increasingly more so on the ships built and run by Albert Ballin.

CHAPTER 4

Albert Ballin Takes Over HAPAG

Really, when those Hamburg magnates pocketed
their family pride and sent for the young
Jewish fellow, they did a good stroke of business. He bore no resemblance to the portraits
in their long line of forefathers, but he
had not the feeling of so many heirs that he
was entitled to a comfortable existence, and
whatever else might be thought of his blood
it had not been attenuated by caste interbreeding.

—THEODOR WOLFF, *THE JEW BALLIN*

In 1886, when Albert Ballin had turned twenty-nine, his Carr Line had become the undisputed first choice as the carrier of immigrants to the United States via the United Kingdom. Recently married and increasingly successful, Ballin was a man on the make. But he had ambition that reached well beyond the indirect steerage business.

That year, HAPAG decided that the only way to compete with Carr was to buy him out. And so for running its flailing passenger division and for his expertise in the immigrant business, HAPAG agreed to pay Ballin the handsome salary of ten thousand marks a year, plus a commission on ticket sales.

As the new manager of HAPAG's passenger division, the young Albert Ballin had engineered an improbable backdoor takeover of one of Hamburg's most prestigious companies. He took one look at the decrepit, out-of-date HAPAG fleet, decided it needed a major makeover, and quickly borrowed the funds needed to construct four steel-hulled express liners. These ships would bear his distinctive taste for luxury, at least for first class. Although Ballin's background was in the no-frills, hardscrabble immigrant business, he was trying to attract rich passengers who could pay for the finer things in life.

Ballin planned to use the new ships to showcase German engineering prowess. The most revolutionary advance in design was the use of twin propellers instead of one, a first for a transatlantic steamer built outside the British Isles. At 475 feet long and grossing 7,600 tons, they were among the largest ships in the world, and he hoped among the fastest. It would be Germany's first attempt to challenge Great Britain's supremacy on the high seas, in both the luxury and the immigrant markets.

Although some board members were a bit startled by the new head's willingness to experiment, HAPAG's board chair Carl Laiesz was impressed. Laiesz admired Ballin so much that in 1888, he led a successful effort to get Ballin a directorship on the company's Board of Control. It was a crucial stepping stone for Ballin into the city's business elite. Yet when Ballin pestered Laiesz to pay the shareholders larger dividends, the old man snapped back, "Young man, according to paragraph 1 of our bylaws, the purpose of this company is the operation of ships, not the distribution of dividends!" The gruff-mannered Laiesz, who loved sporting a sailor's cap even when not at sea, felt no need to pull punches with anyone, especially with someone as young as Ballin. In time, the intelligent but green Ballin would adopt his own self-assured, autocratic manner. And his own sailor's cap.

The timing for a renewal of HAPAG's dowdy image was perfect. There was great hope in Germany when Friedrich III became the second emperor of the newly unified state on March 9, 1888. Breaking with the conservative militarism that defined the ruling house of Prussia, Friedrich was a liberal thinker who was sympathetic to the idea of moving Germany toward a British-style constitutional monarchy. He was almost certainly influenced by his wife, Victoria, who was Queen Victoria's eldest daughter. But Friedrich, mortally ill with cancer of the larynx upon his ascension to the throne, died at Potsdam after a ninety-nine-day reign.

His eldest son, Wilhelm, was crowned third emperor of Germany on June 15, 1888, at the tender age of twenty-nine. Kaiser Wilhelm II was by no means stupid, but he was sensitive to slights and easily swayed by flattery. He loved pageantry, medals, fancy uniforms, and big military processions. Chancellor Otto von Bismarck feared he had all the makings of a megalomaniac.

The official portrait of the new emperor by Max Koner captured his grandiosity: he takes a theatrical stance, staring off into the distance, his right hand holding a scepter, his left hand (shown without injury) grasping a sword. He wears the collar and mantle of the Prussian Order of the Black Eagle, and the Protector's diamond-encrusted cross of the Order of St. John around his neck. His crown is off to one side, sitting on a table. This portrait set the tone for the so-called Wilhelmine style of art and architecture: neo-baroque, traditionalist, pompous, and deferential to the monarch and the military.

Whatever the new monarch's flaws, he was good for Albert Ballin and HAPAG. All of a sudden, the newly crowned Kaiser had ships on the mind. He obsessed over them, in fact. The first year of his reign, the Kaiser told a group of Hamburg merchants, "You are the ones who connect our fatherland with invisible ties to distant parts of the globe, trade with our products, and more than that; you are the ones who transmit our ideas and values to the wider world." Assessing the new government from his desk at HAPAG, Albert Ballin concluded that for his shipping company to grow, he had to play to the Kaiser's German nationalism. This wasn't going to be hard for Ballin. As a Jew, he was himself intensely eager to assert his own German identity, even while he was keenly aware that the Hohenzollerns had historically been less than tolerant toward the Jews in Prussia. The same was true for Chancellor Otto von Bismarck.

On December 1, 1888, at the A. G. Vulcan yard at Stettin, the first of HAPAG's new ships was christened SS *Augusta Victoria*. Three others would soon follow: *Fürst Bismarck*, named in honor of the chancellor responsible for unifying Germany (built by A. G. Vulcan in Stettin, Germany), *Normannia* (built at the Fairfield yard in Govan, Scotland), and *Columbia* (built at the Laird Brothers yard in Birkenhead, England). All four were built according to the same plans, but Ballin wanted to compare the techniques of British and German yards, to see who did the best job.

Acutely sensitive to status, Ballin had his own desire to use his ships to elevate his own place, and his company's, in German society. Investing some of the money he made in the immigrant business in the *Augusta Victoria,* he created a magnificent vessel that would capture royal eyes. She was a yacht-like beauty, boasting three buff funnels, three masts, and a black hull picked out with gilded filigree. Inside, she was wired for electricity throughout and heated by the ship's massive steam plant.

For the elite passengers, Ballin wanted nothing short of a floating grand hotel. To outfit her first-class spaces, he hired an architect from Bremen named Johannes Pöppe. Pöppe was a known quantity in the German shipping world—he had designed the interiors of ships of HAPAG's archrival North German Lloyd, as well as many public buildings and villas for the North German elite. His style was an unabashed German baroque revival: classical murals, stained-glass skylights, dark wood paneling, and gilded cherubs holding electric lights. Some found these spaces magnificent. Others felt them oppressive. Ballin realized that for ships to be built in the future, he would have to take the spaces down more than a notch. It was Wagner's music set in wood, glass, gilt, plaster, and crystal, and framed in steel.

Down below in her cramped steerage quarters, *Augusta Victoria* looked like earlier HAPAG vessels. She was able to carry up to 580 immigrants in open dormitories, with bunks stacked two or three high. Ballin's new ships were the first to have Edison's revolutionary incandescent lighting in the formerly dark steerage areas.

Ballin might have been praised for his vision, but with the first ship he committed an unpardonable error. The empress's actual name was *Auguste* Victoria, not *Augusta.* The royal misspelling was there, in gold letters on the ship's steel hull, for the world to see. Despite his wife's anger at the mishap, and whatever he said about Jews in private, Kaiser Wilhelm II ignored the faux pas. For the Kaiser, Ballin represented what could make Germany a power not just in Europe but on the world stage. The name was corrected, but the young emperor wanted more from his shipping companies.

Auguste Victoria set out on her maiden voyage from Hamburg to New York on May 10, 1889, after which Ballin realized there were serious problems with both the *Auguste Victoria* and her twin sister, *Columbia.* As big and luxurious as they were, they burned too much coal to be profitable. He had also overplayed his hand by giving too much space for the 400 first-class and 120 second-class passengers. Ballin concluded that in order to capitalize on the immigrant boom, future HAPAG ships needed to carry hundreds more steerage passengers. Speed, he realized, did not pay, and luxury only to a point.

Kaiser Wilhelm attended the British Naval Review at Spithead that year. It was a family reunion of sorts, as it was presided over by his grandmother Queen Victoria. Trained as an army officer, Wilhelm was smitten not just by the great British battleships and their big guns but also by the uniforms, rituals, and spit-and-polish pageantry that defined life in the Royal Navy. But what really caught Wilhelm's attention was a passenger liner, the newly commissioned White Star flagship RMS *Teutonic*, representing Britain's merchant marine. At 9,900 tons, 582 feet long, and 57 feet wide, she was one of the largest ships in the world. With *Teutonic* and her sister ship, *Majestic*, White Star's chairman, Thomas Ismay, had created the first true modern ocean liner. She could carry 300 in first class, 150 in second, and 1,000 in steerage, and could cruise at over 20 knots, faster than any battleship.

No ocean liner in either the North German Lloyd or Hamburg-America Line fleets could come close to competing with the two British liners. Since the American Civil War, Britain's commercial fleet had been supreme on the North Atlantic. White Star and its rival Cunard had enjoyed fat subsidies from the British government to carry Royal Mail to the United States and around the world. British naval engineers were at the forefront of marine design, having pioneered the compound steam engine, the screw propeller, and iron-and-steel construction. HAPAG and the German shipyards spent much of the nineteenth century playing catch-up. Wilhelm sailed back to Germany with two things in hand: an honorary admiralship in the Royal Navy (and a uniform to match) and a demand that his country build bigger and faster ships, and soon.

In 1890, Kaiser Wilhelm II declared his independence by jettisoning Otto von Bismarck from his government. He felt that a brilliant personality like Bismarck overshadowed the glory and power of the monarchy. Bismarck, for his part, looked askance at the Kaiser's dream of creating a German navy and an overseas empire to rival those of Great Britain.

The future of Germany, he felt, lay in being a self-contained, largely landlocked nation that depended on agriculture, industry, and natural resources. Between the coal of the Rhineland, the industry of the Ruhr, the ports of the Hanseatic League, the banking of Frankfurt, and the agriculture of Prussia, why did Germany need to engage in overseas expansion for the sake of glory?

Privately, Bismarck felt that the young emperor was incapable of steering the German ship of state, and that he would surround himself with sycophants rather than wise and prudent advisers. Bismarck had used wars with France and Austria-Hungary to consolidate the German Empire, but within carefully calculated limits. His worry was that Wilhelm would stumble into a military conflict that would destroy the hard work of creating the new Germany. He was particularly concerned about political instability in southeastern Europe. "If there is ever another war in Europe," Bismarck said soon after Wilhelm assumed the throne, "it will come out of some damned silly thing in the Balkans."

But to many up-and-coming men like Albert Ballin, the allure of the Kaiser's demand was impossible to resist. Wilhelm's interest in overseas expansion and the growth of Germany's maritime industry aligned neatly with HAPAG's own ambitious business goals. Soon enough, the "Jew Boy of Morris & Co." would get his royal introduction even though HAPAG's dance with the House of Hohenzollern would have consequences, both short and long term, for Albert Ballin.

* * *

When Bismarck left office in 1890, HAPAG didn't yet have the capital to build ships to match the Kaiser's ambitions. Neither did its competitor North German Lloyd. In the interim, Albert Ballin decided to try something novel with the renamed SS *Auguste Victoria*. Rather than having her sit idle or lose money sailing half empty on the North Atlantic, HAPAG announced that the big liner would sail from Hamburg to the Mediterranean on a three-month pleasure cruise. To reassure potential passengers that this was more than a publicity gimmick, the company announced that Albert and Marianne Ballin would be among the passengers. It would be a first-class affair only; the second-class and steerage spaces would be sealed off during the voyage.

Auguste Victoria departed Hamburg on January 22, 1891. Among the all-first-class passengers was Christian Wilhelm Allers, a talented pencil sketch artist whom Ballin had personally hired to document the voyage. Just before the ship sailed, the Kaiser and Kaiserin—who were staying in Cuxhaven, a port city at the mouth of the Elbe—paid a surprise visit. It was then that Albert Ballin met the German emperor for the first time. As one reporter put it, the Kaiser braved the ice-choked Elbe in a launch, drew up alongside the new vessel, and appeared like a "meteor on the bridge." After inspecting the vessel, the Kaiser declared, "See, gentlemen, we can build ships in Germany!" After bestowing the Order of St. Michael on Albert Ballin and the other HAPAG executives, he said, "Take our countrymen out to sea. It will bear great fruits for our nation and for your company!"

Although excited by the prospect of a royal visit, Ballin didn't think much of the first encounter. The Kaiser was known to shower medals and decorations on anyone he found interesting, much to the alarm of established nobles. "He received the honour of a decoration and a few gracious words from His Majesty," Ballin's friend Bernhard Huldermann recalled, but ultimately "did not think that this meeting had established any special contact between himself and his sovereign."

During the next fifty-seven days, Allers sketched his impressions of shore excursions, dinners, and people lounging on deck as the ship wandered from port to port. He also captured Albert Ballin at a celebration of the Kaiser's birthday, dressed in evening clothes, gingerly holding a champagne glass, and wearing a detached expression fit more for a Junker than a shipping executive. He looks in command, suave, even a bit haughty. His mustache is spiked, just like the Kaiser's. A man who only two decades earlier was a poor Jewish boy scrambling to run his father's bankrupt immigration agency now looked the part of the elegant Hamburg gentleman.

At the dinner in the glittering main saloon, Albert Ballin raised his glass and proposed a toast:

Let us, here at the boundary of two parts of the earth, pledge our allegiance once more to the third German Emperor of the House of Hohenzollern. And let us—even if we are far removed from the fatherland—grant him

our most heartfelt and submissive blessings from a piece of German soil, from
a ship that he graced with his most high visitation just a few days ago. Let us
today exclaim "God bless the Kaiser!" May the words echo wherever God's
sun shines, wherever the ocean brings forth her waves, wherever Germans
may be found!

The *Auguste Victoria* pleasure cruise was a tremendous public relations success. By building increasingly larger and elegant ships, Ballin could live out his long attainable fantasy of selling the good life. He inspected his new dream ships rigorously, making notations about defects in the service, the food, and the décor. But Ballin's real gift was his ability to listen carefully to others and then identify what his business offered the public based on human needs and desires, not just numbers and balance sheets.

Kaiser Wilhelm II took great interest in Albert Ballin's trajectory at HAPAG. He also appeared to like individual Jews, as long as they were rich and loyal to the crown. Beginning in the 1890s, Wilhelm took it upon himself to host roundtable discussions with prominent German Jews to discuss issues that were important to the empire's growth and to its increasingly prosperous Jewish population. Albert Ballin and other Jewish businessmen close to Wilhelm were called "the Kaiser's Jews," or *Kaiserjuden*. Chaim Weizmann, the Russian-born Zionist leader, felt that neither Germany nor the United States would ever offer a true safe haven for the Jews. The whole German-Jewish symbiosis, he argued, was all an illusion.

To many in the Kaiser's inner circle, the idea of cooperating with Jews was not only annoying but downright disgusting. This included the Kaiser's wife, the empress. The thirty-year-old Auguste Victoria, or "Dona" as her family called her, represented the landed old guard of the German aristocracy, where anti-Semitism ran deep. Tall and elegant, her main priority was her family, and she looked warily on people she saw as uncouth upstarts. Ships, technology, and finance held little interest for her. But Auguste had her own insecurities. Married off at the age of twenty-three, she had received only a rudimentary education. And although Wilhelm's second cousin, she was not a royal but the daughter of a duke. As such, she was sensitive to hierarchy. For her, men of commerce deeply threatened the ruling legitimacy of the Hohenzollern clan. No matter how much bankers such as the Rothschilds helped finance the nuts and bolts of German economic expansion, they were still mere moneymen, pretentious fake nobles. The empress might have tolerated the Rothschilds—they were impossible to ignore. But the shipping man Albert Ballin was no better to her than a Berlin bootblack. To her, he was ugly, common, obsequious, and a Jew.

The Kaiserin represented the reactionary German old guard. The Prussian landed nobility, who made up the core of her coterie, was full of militarists and anti-Semites. Although the young Ballin was burning with ambition, he realized that no matter how hard he tried, there was no way he could ever ingratiate himself with the Prussian aristocracy. Not socially, at least. Most of the old Prussian elites didn't like him, and the sight of a Jew rising through the ranks of German society made them very uncomfortable. And they did not want Jewish refugees to settle within their borders.

Germany wasn't the only country worried about Russian Jews flooding into its cities and towns. The Austro-Hungarian Empire, which also boasted a relatively liberated and prosperous Jewish community, guaranteed Jews equal rights—but did not welcome Jewish refugees from Russia. Emperor Franz Joseph I, greatly beloved by the Viennese Jewish community, declared that "the civil rights and the country's policy is not contingent in the people's religion." As the Roman Catholic monarch of a multiethnic empire, Franz Joseph decided that the best path to stability was to give Austro-Hungarian Jews as much opportunity as possible. However, anti-Semitic currents in greater Austrian society were strong, even in provinces like Galicia, which had a significant Jewish population. Like Germany, Austria-Hungary was not interested in opening its doors to a flood of Jewish refugees from Russia.

Then in 1891, the Kaiser's cousin Alexander III intensified his already draconian anti-Semitic state policies. He and his uncle, Grand Duke Sergei Alexandrovich, ordered the expulsion of all Jews living in Moscow and several other large cities in the Pale of Settlement. Suddenly, thousands of Jews were now homeless, forced to leave their possessions and businesses behind as they looked for new places to live. Some moved to smaller villages, others to cities not affected by the edicts. Tens of thousands more, however, made the decision to try to get out of Russia altogether, resulting in an immigrant surge.

In reality, Kaiser Wilhelm II's relationship with the Jews was ambivalent at best. He played both sides, happily associating with both Jewish financiers while still exchanging anti-Semitic barbs with the old Prussian Junker class. Unlike Emperor Franz Joseph I of Austria-Hungary, who publicly condemned anti-Semitism and fostered a brilliant flowering of Jewish life in his capital of Vienna, Wilhelm tolerated the Jews but wasn't especially interested in making them feel welcome.

In conservative German society, a gentile social climber was bad enough. No matter how much money one made from industry, manufacturing, or merchandizing, a newly minted tycoon was a nobody unless he knew how to carefully court the favor of the Prussian landed nobility. For a Jew, this path was downright dangerous. The best way to walk it was not only to remain quiet and unobtrusive but also to discreetly allow the old rich to keep their status, their style of life, and their bank accounts. Although Bismarck relied on Bleichröder for all his personal and political financial needs, he never mentioned the banker once in his memoirs. To men like Bismarck and Kaiser Wilhelm II, the Jewish businessman was a tool to achieve their grand visions, but not in any way an equal. For the new Germany, blood and iron were on public display, while gold was kept locked in a vault.

In the years to come, Albert Ballin treasured the many decorations he received from the Kaiser. But rather than displaying them in his office or on his chest, he kept them locked away in a safe. For the next two decades, Ballin would find himself in a delicate dance with the Kaiser and the powers in Berlin. Although the Bremen-based North German Lloyd was a worthy rival, HAPAG, and by extension, the city of Hamburg, would eventually gain the title of the "official" shipping line of imperial Germany, an impression Ballin was determined to protect. He had to cater to both the whims of the rich and the needs of the migrants.

Thanks to Ballin's marketing and the elegant style of his new fleet of ships, HAPAG quickly became the transatlantic line of choice for America's increasingly affluent German Jewish elite. Centered in New York City, but with outposts in Cincinnati, Philadelphia, and Chicago, this group of religiously Jewish but culturally German people had made their fortunes in dry goods, department stores, and merchant banking. They made frequent trips back to the Fatherland to visit family, take the waters at Baden-Baden, or find suitable matches for their sons and daughters.

As much as he liked catering to the rich, Ballin never forgot that it was those in steerage, not first class, who truly paid for the rebuilding of his fleet. He also saw that the tide of immigrants was shifting. For three decades, HAPAG had catered to a mostly German-speaking clientele. Since the failed revolutions of 1848, Hamburg had become a destination for tens of thousands of German refugees seeking a new start in America. By the early 1890s, however, Ballin and the other steamship operators saw impoverished and frightened Russian Jews flooding into the Hamburg railway station, carrying boxes, trunks, and anything else they could manage, and then taking up residence in squalid boardinghouses hard against the noisy and polluted Elbe River.

* * *

The petty machinations of the Berlin court meant little to Russia's millions of Jews, most of whom barely eked out a living and dreamed of a better life across the sea. Germany's growing rail and sea infrastructure provided the crucial link between the shtetl and the sea. For prospective migrants, the hardest part was the difficult decision to leave family and friends behind, probably forever. Farewell meals consisted of schnapps and schav soup, not champagne and oysters. Toasts to best wishes for a new life in America were made not in triumphant German but in expressive Yiddish. Few if any wished the czar good health.

In countless villages, families got into horse-drawn wagons that would carry them and their precious belongings to the nearest train stations. "You know what I see now," one migrant recalled in her old age, "was the peasant with the wagon and hay, to take me, take me away. The whole town was around my wagon. Everybody came to say goodbye, but I didn't know how to say goodbye." A crack of the whip, and the wagon would roll away from the town square, as loved ones waved and cried. All that was familiar, whether it was the tower of the synagogue or the Cossacks on horseback, faded into the distance.

For Russian Jews looking to get to America, the route to the port cities of Western Europe was as long as it was dangerous. Following the first state-sponsored pogroms of the early 1880s, Jewish charitable organizations in Germany, France, the United Kingdom, and the United States started to raise money in anticipation of a massive exodus out of Russia. The United Hebrew Charities started a Russian Relief Committee to help new arrivals get across the border and find jobs in the United States. Its infrastructure was rickety at first. Russian border patrol agents refused to let Jews through, as almost none of them had passports or legal permission to leave the country. Those who did evade the Russian authorities congregated in the border town of Brody, a city in the Austrian province of Galicia, which had a large Jewish community eager to assist their fellow Jews. From Brody, representatives from the Russian Relief Committee would classify and select prospective immigrants for transport by train, three hundred people at a time, to Hamburg. Some traveled to America by HAPAG ships, but others continued on to Liverpool, where they would book passage aboard a Cunard or other British vessel.

The German government decided to take action to make sure the migrants were not transmitting disease during their time in the country. In 1891, the year that *Auguste Victoria* made headlines with her Mediterranean cruise, a new railroad station opened at Ruhleben, several miles outside of Berlin. On the outside, it was a nondescript, half-timbered structure. Inside was a fully operational health station. Here, sealed trains carrying Russian immigrants bound for Hamburg would stop and unload their exhausted and often frightened passengers. After hours of travel through endless Prussian farmland and drab industrial towns, they had briefly glimpsed the lights and spires of the German capital. But like so many things beautiful and wondrous in the world, no coffee or pastries under the glass-and-steel train shed of the Berlin *Hauptbahnhof* were for them. Still, many of the travelers knew that Berlin had a rich and thriving Jewish population that gave generously to the aid societies that had allowed them to escape from Russia.

Upon arrival in Ruhleben, the doors to the carriages were flung open and stern German voices ordered the emigrants to get out. A line of white-uniformed officials then separated the men from the women and children and ordered them to give up their luggage. For many travelers, who had sold almost everything they owned to pay for the trip, parting with their possessions was painful. The bags and trunks were thrown into a huge pile and carted away for fumigation. The immigrants were then ordered to strip and abandon their clothing in another big pile. After showering with disinfectant soap, the bewildered crowd exited the showers to reclaim their now fumigated clothing and their baggage, then reboarded the waiting train for Hamburg or Bremen, where a ship waited to take them to Great Britain or the United States.

The construction of Ruhleben coincided with the building of another facility station, this time on the other side of the Atlantic. By the early 1890s, the crowds of new arrivals by steamship had outgrown the New York immigration inspection station at Castle Garden. Located at the foot of Manhattan Island, the sandstone structure had originally served as a fortress guarding the harbor from British attack. In 1855, it was converted into the Emigrant Landing Depot and jointly managed by the city and state of New York. In 1890, the federal government took control of all immigrant processing, and by consolidating the operations in an island in the Upper Bay, potentially sick arrivals could be quarantined away from the mainland until deemed acceptable for entry into the United States.

The new facility opened on Ellis Island on January 1, 1892, and the first person processed there was seventeen-year-old Annie Moore from Ireland. Seven hundred others followed her that day, with 1.5 million to come during the next five years. The construction of such a large processing facility, in the shadow of the Statue of Liberty, where a plaque of Emma Lazarus's poem could be found for those who knew where to look, raised eyebrows among those who felt that America was perhaps becoming a bit too welcoming.

Also in January 1892, Albert Ballin made a shrewd hire for the American side of his business. He was Emil Leopold Boas. Born in Prussia in 1854, Boas was, like Ballin, an assimilated Jew. Although the Boas family ran an immigration agency in Hamburg, they were much wealthier than the Ballins because they also had interests in banking and the grain business. Boas had received a first-rate education at the Sophien-Gymnasium in Berlin and as a young man worked in America in a rich uncle's business. But Boas preferred the family's immigrant agency, C. B. Richard & Boas Company, and took over the American side of the business in the 1880s. He also joined the board of the Hebrew Emigrant Aid Society, as well as at the Jacob Schiff–funded State Bank on the Lower East Side. By that time, HAPAG had contracted with the Boas firm to be their exclusive ticket agency, selling steamship and railroad packages for families to send home to waiting relatives in Europe. Ballin liked Emil Boas's work so much that he brought his entire operation in-house at HAPAG.

As general manager of HAPAG's American operations, Emil Boas and his wife, Harriet, soon became popular figures among New York's social elite, both Jewish and Christian. Boas consolidated his company's control over its ticketing operations in New York, clamping down on the black market of saloonkeepers, landlords, and other middlemen who sold HAPAG tickets for Lower East Side residents to send back to family in the Old Country. His goal was to bring all ticket sales within the HAPAG network, and he succeeded. As he gained more power at HAPAG, he distanced himself from his Jewish origins. Somewhere along the way, Boas and his wife left Judaism for Unitarianism, which allowed them to dodge anti-Semitism while not fully denying their Jewish ancestry. Boas joined numerous upper-class Protestant clubs, including the New York Yacht Club and St. Andrew's Golf Club, while also being active in German singing societies and cultural organizations.

As for North German Lloyd, its principal representative in America was the equally popular and well-connected Hermann Oelrichs. Oelrichs, the son of a German American merchant from Baltimore, descended from the Boston aristocrat Harrison Gray Otis and was thoroughly gentile. After graduating from Yale, Oelrichs founded the firm of Oelrichs & Co., which served as NDL's agent in the United States. He married heiress and socialite Theresa Alice "Tessie" Fair in 1889. With Tessie's Comstock Lode millions, the Oelrichses proceeded to conquer New York and Newport society. They also had the resources to wine and dine congressmen and senators who might consider voting for a literacy test or any other measure that would restrict immigration to the United States.

As the number of refugees grew from a trickle to a flood, Albert Ballin realized that for HAPAG to maximize its profits from Russian Jewish immigration, he had to curb the influence of the Jewish aid organizations at the border who were steering travelers toward lower-cost British competitors. His goal, ultimately, was for HAPAG to take over the processing of potential immigrants by providing counsel, aid, and, if possible, funds for impoverished immigrants to buy tickets on HAPAG vessels. "Without steerage passengers," Albert Ballin declared, "I would be bankrupt within a few weeks."

He also realized it would only take one epidemic to cause both America and Germany to shut down HAPAG. When it did come, both countries would blame it on the Jews. They always did, whether it was the bubonic plague or, as Ballin would soon learn, cholera.

CHAPTER 5

Immigrants and "Asia's Fearful Scourge"

With the cholera killing people on the wholesale in the ports whence these creatures as-
semble to take passage to the United States,
there is good ground for the present demand
for absolute prohibition.

—*NEW YORK TIMES*, AUGUST 29, 1892

By the early 1890s, Hamburg was the busiest port in the world, just ahead of New York City. Vessels of all kinds—ocean liners, freighters, sailing vessels, tugboats, and ferries—glided up and down the Elbe River. Its wharves and hulking brick warehouses stored coffee, tea, and other valuable imports in demand by the growing German population. Railroads brought all sorts of cargo for export to the farthest corners of the world: steel, wheat, and finished goods.

The city's population approached one million residents. The fortunate middle and upper classes lived in the posh districts of Harvesthüde, Rotherbaum, and Blankenese. Most of Hamburg's residents, however, lived in crowded tenements near the bustling waterfront. Like their counterparts in New York City, the poor people of Hamburg made do without indoor plumbing or running water. Household waste usually ended up dumped in the streets.

And then there were the thousands of migrants arriving each year by wagon, train, or foot from Russia, Poland, Romania, and elsewhere, waiting to board their HAPAG ship to America. For them, the big city was a bewildering environment, so unlike the small villages they knew. Some relied on word of mouth to find their way to a boarding-house or some other form of lodging, almost always in the worst parts of town. Sometimes, forty people slept in a 12 x 15-foot room, on a floor covered with straw, cheek-by-jowl with drunken, foulmouthed sailors. Families with young children would do their best to ignore the sounds coming from the cheap bordellos that also lined the waterfront.

Hamburg was a public health disaster waiting to happen.

In 1892, a year after all Jews were expelled from Moscow, a cholera epidemic spread through Hamburg. For a city that depended on free trade and the comings and goings of merchants and passengers, the epidemic spelled economic disaster. Although the disease spread into other European cities, Hamburg was by far the hardest hit. Some 8,600 residents perished that year. Cholera, carried by waterborne bacteria, is a swift and savage killer. Patients first experience a general malaise, followed within hours by violent diarrhea and vomiting. In the 1890s, the mortality rate for cholera patients ranged between 30 and 80 percent, depending on the bacterial strain.

The American reaction to the cholera epidemic in Hamburg was swift. Public health officials and the press blamed immigrants, especially Eastern European Jews, for spreading the disease and called for restricting their entry into the already crowded tenement districts of New York and other large cities. In the summer of 1892, the *New York Times* published a scathing article that warned that the Jews were bringing the epidemic with them, and that the horrific scenes playing out in Hamburg would soon be happening in New York City:

> *With the danger of cholera in question, it is plain to see that the United States would be better off if ignorant Russian Jews and Hungarians were denied refuge here. . . . These people are offensive enough at best; under the present circumstances, they are a positive menace to the health of the country. Even should they pass the Quarantine officials, their mode of life, when they settle down makes them always a source of danger. Cholera, it must be remembered, originates in the homes of this human riff-raff.*

Albert Ballin did not let the cholera epidemic interrupt the service of his big liners. In late August, HAPAG's two-year-old express steamship, the SS *Normannia*, set sail from Hamburg on a routine summer transatlantic trip to New York. She was about the same size as her sister ship *Auguste Victoria*, and like her was equipped with twin screws and over a thousand Edison-Swan incandescent bulbs. The *Normannia* also had expanded steerage capacity for 700 passengers, along with 428 in opulent first class and 170 in comfortable second.

On the ship's westbound voyage, steerage was only at about 60 percent capacity, with 482 berths filled. Most of them were Eastern European Jews who endured many of the usual indignities. Among them were the Hornishes from Odessa and their three young children. Wending their way down twisting staircases and along narrow companionways, the family found their home for the next ten days: a large compartment, with berths stacked three or four high, that they would be sharing with dozens of other passengers. A few portholes provided glimmers of sunlight. The waves of the Elbe River smacked up against the hull and portholes, and the ship rolled ominously at her pier. They felt a jerk, then another, and the ship's engines rumbled to life. *Normannia*'s whistle gave a blast, and the Hornishes watched the spires and warehouses of Hamburg fade into the distance.

Within a few days of the ship's departure, as *Normannia* tore through the Atlantic, a fifty-seven-year-old second-class passenger named Carl Hegert began to complain of stomach problems, then suffered horrific diarrhea. On August 29, Hegert died and was buried at sea. Because he was a second-class passenger, the officers decided not to label him a cholera victim. Cholera, after all, was considered a disease of the poor. Then, a few decks below in steerage, the Hornishes' daughter Ottlie died the following day. According to a later report:

> *Little Ottlie Hornish died the day after Hegert, and the distracted parents, after watching her tiny body sink into the waves, had to hurry back to their other two children, Willie and Selma, three and five respectively. Both were looking very white and were beginning to complain.*

Over the next few days, as *Normannia* plowed through the rough North Atlantic, six other passengers succumbed to the disease. The ship's doctor insisted that not only the bodies be thrown overboard, but all their luggage and possessions as well. Tragically, the Hornishes' son Willie also succumbed to the disease, and once again, his parents had to watch in absolute anguish as their child's body was thrown over the side and swallowed by the sea. First- and second-class passengers were no longer allowed to visit steerage, "as was customary," according to one newspaper. A small group of stewards was assigned to tend to the sick in an isolated part of the vessel.

When *Normannia* arrived at the mouth of New York Harbor, the health inspectors ordered it to remain outside the harbor for two weeks, the generally accepted time for a disease to run its course. She dropped anchor off the Quarantine station at Staten Island. The passengers on board milled about the decks, some silent, some infuriated, but all powerless. There was a killer in their midst, and there was nothing they could do to escape it. In the meantime, Ottlie's twin brother, Rudolph, and five-year-old sister, Selma, remained sick in the dank, airless confines of steerage, while their parents did everything they could to keep their diarrheal children comfortable.

Normannia wasn't the only HAPAG "plague ship" anchored off Swinburne Island. Two other vessels, *Rugia* and *Moravia*, had multiple cases of the disease on board. Over the next few days, ships continued to show up and were detained outside the city's gates. Back on land, city residents read in the *New York Times* that "Asia's fearful scourge is now fairly trying to force its way into the harbor," and that the city's health authorities "are straining every nerve to block every channel through which it might enter."

Passengers aboard *Normannia* began to grow anxious about their circumstances. Among the first-class passengers were journalist Edwin Lawrence Godkin, the English musical hall singer Lottie Collins, and Senator John McPherson of New Jersey, the sort of rich passengers Albert Ballin was hoping to attract with his new emphasis on luxury in first class. Food and supplies continued to be ferried to the ship as it bobbed off Quarantine, but after days of confinement and uncertainty, the first-class passengers grew increasingly irritable and rude. Godkin complained that the table service and food in the first-class dining room had gone from stellar to wretched, and that this was hardly the sort of voyage he had paid for.

The only communication to the outside world came from Dr. William T. Jenkins, health officer for the Port of New York and chief of the Quarantine facilities at Swinburne and Hoffman islands. A native of Mississippi, Jenkins owed his position more to Tammany Hall patronage than medical qualification. He had been on the job less than a year but he took charge as best he could with the meager resources at his disposal. "It is a very hard thing to get news from the quarantined ships," the *New York Times* reported. "Not even a tug can approach them, unless it flies the yellow quarantine flag to show that it is on an official errand. All news which can be secured has to be got in fragments from Dr. Jenkins when he stops for a short time at the Quarantine station after trips down the bay."

Anxious to get word ashore to their family and friends, first-class passengers tossed messages and silver coins onto the deck of a passing tugboat. Steerage passengers, confined below, couldn't do that. Jenkins assured the world that the passengers on *Normannia* were remaining calm, that the "cabin passengers seemed to feel the gravity of the situation," and that "they and the steerage passengers were exhibiting a desire to cooperate in every way with the physicians in ridding the ships of the disease."

Unmentioned was the panic that one can only imagine was brewing in steerage. Parents in particular worried that their children would be next to die, and that their "contaminated" dead bodies would be thrown overboard just outside the gates to America. And then there were other waves of fear. Would they be sent back to Russia? Would their families be separated?

At the HAPAG offices in Lower Manhattan, the usually unflappable general manager Emil Boas sat morose at his desk. A visiting reporter from the *New York Times* tried to get Boas to make a statement on the cholera ships. Boas refused. The company, he noted, seemed doomed:

> *To have three cholera-scourged ships arrive in port one after the other is a succession of disasters from which no line can readily recover. Emil Boas, the General Manager, was consequently in no mood to talk to reporters yesterday, although he received them with his usual courtesy. He wearily admitted that he was inexpressibly distressed by the misfortune which had befallen*

the patrons of his line, the particulars of which, he said, had been cabled to the home office.

After twenty days in limbo, the Health Department ferried *Normannia*'s first- and second-class passengers to the Surf Hotel on Fire Island, while the steerage passengers were moved to the Health Department's facilities on Hoffman Island. There, the remaining victims of the cholera epidemic were buried. More ships arrived, and more immigrants were detained on Hoffman Island. Even the well-heeled travelers were met by a mob of gun-wielding residents who wanted to stop anyone from the "pest ships" from setting foot at the Surf Hotel.

Abraham Cahan, the immigrant journalist and editor of the Yiddish socialist daily *Arbeiter Zeitung*, sneered at how the press devoted so much coverage to the travails of the rich travelers on the HAPAG steamer but so little to the immigrants:

> *The wealthy gentlemen, poor things . . . raised such a cry about the "unpleasantness" which they had to undergo, that the entire wealthy class took to weeping and wailing over their plight. . . . For the rich first-class passengers they bought a fine hotel, and for the paupers, they put up military tents on a field in which they set up beds.*

IN RESPONSE to the public health crisis, President Benjamin Harrison ordered a twenty-day quarantine for all ships arriving in New York Harbor, which caused a giant backlog of vessels large and small outside of the Narrows. The conditions in the facilities at Hoffman Island and aboard the marooned ships only exacerbated the spread of the disease to healthy people. Aboard *Bohemia*, a group of physicians noted in a report that "there are two water closets near the stern of the boat, accessible from the cabin; one on each side, each with three seats and pans. Adults and children used them promiscuously, the sick and the comparatively well, those with and without diarrhea. The closets, seats, covers, and floors were offensive from soiling with filth and feces."

On Hoffman Island, families shivered in tents and washed laundry on the excrement-fouled beach. On nearby Swinburne Island, they could see the stack of the crematory belching thick black smoke into the sky. The

Statue of Liberty, which they had hoped to see upon their entry to New York Harbor, lay hidden behind the knolls of Staten Island.

Meanwhile, the epidemic continued to rage in Hamburg. Despite its German origins, populist German newspapers quickly began to associate the disease with the Russian Jewish transmigrants arriving by train almost every day, where they lived in boardinghouses and mingled with the general population while awaiting their steamers to America. German scientists such as the Jewish-born Robert Koch worked hard to discern the actual cause of the disease, which many believed was spread by exposure to noxious fumes. Koch ultimately proved that it was spread by exposure to bacteria in human feces that had leached into drinking water. His "germ theory" would revolutionize the field of infectious disease, but the public was still quicker to assign blame to visible causes—foreigners— rather than invisible bacteria.

By 1893, with the death toll mounting and Hamburg's economy in ruins, riots broke out in Germany's working-class districts, where, as the *New York Times* observed, the "poor and ignorant" residents "seem to have a horror of being compelled to observe cleanliness and the ordinary sanitary regulations." The quarantine had also ground Hamburg's mighty maritime industry to a halt. After weeks of unemployment, hunger, and death in the streets, many of the city's residents had had enough. An angry mob cornered one sanitation officer, knocked him to the ground, and kicked and stamped him to death. A policeman intervened, but he, too, was attacked and killed. The soldiers fixed bayonets and steel blades and advanced as members of the mob scattered away into the streets and alleyways of Hamburg.

Mark Twain, who was visiting Hamburg at the time, was aghast. He had gained a reputation as an anti-imperialist and opponent of the racism he saw as endemic in American society. Twain surely knew of Hamburg's reputation as a port of departure for Jewish emigrants and probably saw many of them leaving the shabby boardinghouses or waiting at the HAPAG piers for their ships to depart. After his return to America, Twain would pen an essay called "Concerning the Jews," in which he expressed deep admiration for the hopeful immigrants.

"He has made a marvelous fight in this world, in all the ages," Twain wrote in *Harper's Magazine*, "and has done it with his hands tied behind him. He could be vain of himself, and be excused for it. The Egyptian, the Babylonian, and the Persian rose, filled the planet with sound and splendor, then faded to dream-stuff and passed away; the Greek and the Roman followed, and made a vast noise, and they are gone; other peoples have sprung up and held their torch high for a time, but it burned out, and they sit in twilight now, or have vanished. The Jew saw them all, beat them all, and is now what he always was, exhibiting no decadence, no infirmities of age, no weakening of his parts, no slowing of his energies, no dulling of his alert and aggressive mind. All things are mortal but the Jew; all other forces pass, but he remains. What is the secret of his immortality?"

* * *

With immigration to the United States temporarily barred due to the cholera epidemic, Ballin concluded that he had to make peace with his bitter rival. He boldly reached out to his counterpart at North German Lloyd about forming a German shipping cartel. The company's chief executive, Johann Heinrich Christoph Wiegand, was a lawyer by training—cool tempered, logical, and thoroughly analytical. Ballin, who loved the art of negotiation, was emotional and intuitive. "Occasional explosions of temper," as he called them, "were inevitable." Yet both were outsiders and meritocrats, born to modest parents in snobbish Hanseatic cities, who had risen through the ranks to be managers of modern corporations, not through the closed family operations that had defined the shipping spheres of Bremen and Hamburg. Despite their business rivalry, Ballin and Wiegand respected each other immensely, and felt that the flow of emigrants out of Eastern Europe was big enough for their respective companies to share amicably. While waiting for the disease to run its course and for public opinion to turn, they discussed possible ways to divvy up future immigrant traffic.

By February 1893 a satisfied President Harrison lifted the harsh quarantine restriction on all ships arriving from Hamburg. In all, seventy-six people, mostly steerage-class passengers, had died aboard ships arriving in New York, and another forty-four died while ashore. The cause of all the misery, death, and fear, it appeared, was not the unhealthy habits of the Russian Jewish immigrants. Rather, it was the contaminated Elbe

River. Some immigrants, like the Hornishes, may have contracted the disease while staying in a Hamburg boardinghouse. Others, like those aboard *Bohemia*, may have contracted it from the ship's contaminated drinking water, drawn directly from the Elbe. All of this fell in line with Robert Koch's germ theory.

HAPAG breathed a sigh of relief, as did the other major steamship lines. After a five-month hiatus, Russian Jewish immigrants were allowed back into the United States, and the steamship lines made big plans for the future. Ballin would make HAPAG's immigrant business a model of cleanliness, efficiency, and safety. It would require significant investment in capital—new facilities, new ships, new advertising campaigns—but as Ballin argued to his fellow directors, it would all pay off in the long run.

But the people of Hamburg weren't so sure about letting Russian Jews and other migrants back into the city. Goaded by populist elements, the Hamburg city fathers looked for someone to blame. The best plausible explanation for the plague, they reasoned, was the influx of thousands of impoverished immigrants. In their eyes, Russia was the source of an unclean flood of disease, and the alien Jews were the worst of the offenders. The city's increasingly prosperous Jewish population were perfectly willing to help the Russian Jews on their way to the United States but were not keen on having them settle down with them in Hamburg. Even as the cholera epidemic subsided and the port stirred to life, the Hamburg Senate continued to bar all Russian transmigrants from the city.

Albert Ballin knew that without the immigrant trade, HAPAG could never compete against North German Lloyd, whose port of departure in Bremen was unscathed by cholera and remained open for business to immigrants. Between 1890 and 1900, 776,000 people departed Bremen, almost all for the United States, a figure that would double in the following decade. Unlike Hamburg, where immigrants stayed in boardinghouses, Bremen housed all its port facilities and passenger staging areas in Bremerhaven, located just down the river Weser from the main city.

Summoning up all his courage, Ballin delivered an ultimatum to the Hamburg Senate sometime in 1893. At company expense, HAPAG would build new barracks for incoming emigrants that would be far away from the city center. All arrivals would be inspected for contagious disease upon their arrival at the new facility. After processing, the immigrants would then be ferried by special train or boat to their awaiting ships at a new shipping terminal at Cuxhaven, a port at the mouth of the Elbe River.

If the Hamburg Senate turned down his proposal, Ballin threatened, he would move HAPAG's operations to Bremen and join forces with its archrival, North German Lloyd.

Ballin played his hand well. The city fathers realized that the loss of Hamburg's premier shipping line would devastate the regional economy. If HAPAG could continue the emigrant business while keeping Russian Jews out of sight and out of mind, all would be relieved and happy.

Ballin got his way. Now he had to find a way to deliver on his very expensive promise. The construction of the facilities required a vast outlay of capital, and he had to convince his fellow directors to make this investment as well as construct a whole new class of ships that could carry more immigrants than could the four new express liners. But Ballin still faced stumbling blocks in Berlin. The German government remained wary of the transmigrants from Russia and was at a loss at how to police the porous border between Prussia and the Russian Empire. Small cities such as Brody, Austria, and Tilsit, Poland, simply could not cope with the thousands of people camped out in boardinghouses and hovels.

Ballin then approached Heinrich Wiegand about a novel solution to the border problem: privatization. Wiegand liked the idea. The two men laid out their plan to Kaiser Wilhelm's government. North German Lloyd and HAPAG would assume control of the Russia-Prussia border control stations at their own cost. There, they would inspect all would-be emigrants for contagious diseases and fumigate all men, women, children, and their luggage. Those holding tickets for America would be permitted to pass through easily. Those seeking to stay in Germany would either be turned back or forced to buy steerage tickets to America from one of the steamship companies.

The government in Berlin accepted the proposal.

Wiegand and Ballin knew that a large percentage of these Russian refugees would have neither a passport nor a ticket, but would have some cash on hand. Some had sold almost all they owned. Others had received grants from Jewish aid organizations such as the Alliance Israélite Universelle in Paris, as well as pogrom relief funds organized by wealthy

American Jews in New York, Philadelphia, Boston, and other large cities. The two German steamship lines made plans to divide the unticketed migrants into tranches, working as a cartel—what Ballin had proposed earlier that year.

By the summer of 1893, the German shipping companies were back in business, and the ferries were now regularly carrying hundreds of would-be Americans from the HAPAG piers in Hoboken to the new immigration station at Ellis Island. People thought to have a contagious disease, as well as any physical or mental deformity, were pulled aside by the immigration officials for additional examination and questioning.

BUT EVEN as Albert Ballin tackled these problems, another emerged. Forces in the United States to restrict immigration were now coalescing and growing into a broad-based political movement. Some of the nation's leading medical and public health officials, including U.S. surgeon general Walter Wyman and New York's chief sanitary inspector Cyrus Edson, called for immigration from Eastern Europe to be severely curtailed as a matter of public health.

And politicians like Massachusetts senator Henry Cabot Lodge began to argue that all the new arrivals would fundamentally change the cultural fabric of the United States for much the worse.

CHAPTER 6

The Aristocrats Mobilize

The danger has begun. It is small as yet, comparatively speaking, but it is large enough to warn us to act while there is yet time and while it can be done easily and efficiently. There lies the peril at the portals of our land; there is pressing the tide of unrestricted immigration. The time has certainly come, if not to stop, at least to check, to sift, and to restrict those immigrants. In careless strength, with generous hand, we have kept our gates wide open to all the world. If we do not close them, we should at least place sentinels beside them to challenge those who would pass through. The gates which admit men to the United States and to citizenship in the great republic should no longer be left unguarded.

—SENATOR HENRY CABOT LODGE, ADDRESS TO THE U.S. SENATE, MARCH 16, 1896

Henry Cabot Lodge did everything according to "correct" form. He was rail thin, with a narrow face, blue eyes, and a Vandyke beard. He dressed like an English lord and spoke with a strangely shrill and British-style diction. His education, from undergraduate to a law degree to a doctorate, was all Harvard. He was a pure product of Boston's tight-knit and homogenous upper class. Henry's parents, John and Anna,

were members of a small cluster of Beacon Hill families who had profited enormously from rum and slave trafficking, the opium trade, railroad
building in the hinterlands, and manufacturing of all sorts from cotton to
steel mills.

Unlike Albert Ballin and Jacob Schiff, who never stopped working,
Henry Cabot Lodge had plenty of time to do what he wanted, with
money to spare.

In 1875, as countless Americans lost their jobs and went hungry, the
twenty-five-year-old Lodge went on an extended grand tour of Europe.
The young Bostonian felt great affinity for England, but he was particularly struck by the economic dynamism of the newly unified German
Empire. His PhD dissertation was about the Germanic origins of Anglo-
Saxon law, a favorite subject of his mentor, the famed historian Henry
Adams. Adams and his protégés fervently believed that Great Britain and
Germany shared ancient "democratic" systems of governance, and that
the two countries' recent ascendancy on the world economic stage was no
accident. If America followed their example, the historians reasoned, it
could become part of a powerful cultural and economic triumvirate.

Lodge knew that German Jews, for all of their insular haughtiness,
feared the likes of men like him. Lodge shared much in common with the
Prussian ruling elite who disdained Albert Ballin and all Jews. Nothing
frightened Lodge more than an outsider who aspired to be an insider.
"You can take a Hindoo and give him the highest education the world can
afford," he mused. "He has keen intelligence. He will absorb the learn-
ings of Oxford, he will acquire the manners and habits of the English, he
will sit in the British Parliament, but you cannot make him an English-
man." Lodge felt that the Anglo-Saxon race's superiority didn't rest on
mere intellect. Rather, it rested on "our history, our victories, our future," which could only be weakened by interbreeding with an "inferior
race." The intermixing with "lower races of less social efficiency and less
moral force" would lead to a racially inferior genetic product. Lodge,
of course, saw people like himself as the apogee of Anglo-Germanic
glory.

For Lodge, a man like Albert Ballin, no matter how successful, worldly,
or polished, would forever be a Jew. No matter, as Theodor Wolff wrote,
that Ballin wore his yachting attire "with the careless elegance that only

comes with habit." Men like Ballin were to be tolerated but excluded from society and the halls of power.

In 1886, Lodge won a seat in Congress from Massachusetts. Once in Washington, his fancy degrees and impeccable pedigree failed to convince everyone that he possessed a towering intellect. Though fellow congressman and Speaker of the House Thomas B. Reed of Maine mocked Lodge as a "spoiled child," a pampered creature having arisen from "thin soil, highly cultivated," insults from the son of a Maine fisherman did not bother Lodge. He dismissed criticism from those he considered beneath him and looked for support among his social peers.

Among those Lodge sought to enlist in his cause was his college friend Theodore Roosevelt, heir to a substantial New York City mercantile fortune. Young Roosevelt was making a name for himself in the 1880s as a reformist New York State assemblyman and appeared, even in his twenties, to have potential as a presidential candidate. By the 1890s, he had become the New York City police commissioner. The brilliant, bookish dandy-turned-cowboy loved roaming the slums of Manhattan, catching officers sleeping on duty or taking bribes from saloonkeepers and brothel owners. Roosevelt was not anti-immigrant, but he did believe that new arrivals had a duty to assimilate into traditional American mores and values, and those arrivals included Jews. If Roosevelt were to become president someday, Lodge thought, immigration restriction had a chance.

In 1893, the same year that President Harrison lifted the cholera immigration restrictions, the forty-three-year-old Republican Lodge was elected senator from his home state of Massachusetts. The so-called spoiled child would remain in office for the next thirty-one years and prove to be a hardworking politician and a formidable opponent.

For the good of his country—at least as he saw it—Lodge would make it his personal mission to cut off the mostly unrestricted stream of "huddled masses" from arriving on America's shores, and he had powerful allies and deep pockets to assist him.

In 1895, two years after the cholera epidemic had ground immigration to a halt for those five months, three Bostonians—Henry DeCourcy Ward, Prescott Farnsworth Hall, and Charles Warren—founded a new organization called the Immigration Restriction League. It was part club, part think tank, and part political action committee. The three men met in elegant parlors on Beacon Hill and in the Back Bay, far removed from the crowded immigrant districts of South Boston and Dorchester. Soon they attracted the support of Senator Henry Cabot Lodge, who promised to turn their agenda into law. The core of the IRL membership was drawn from the faculty of prominent universities, exclusive social clubs, and other institutions that formed the backbone of the nation's Protestant East Coast establishment.

The IRL chose Prescott Farnsworth Hall as their secretary. Eighteen years younger than Lodge, Hall was also trained as a lawyer, but thanks to his parents' wealth, never had to work. A pale, balding man, Hall was neurotic and constantly suffering from one ailment or another. But when it came to lobbying for restrictions on immigration, he was tireless. For him, it came down to "educating" those in power as to the gravity of the problem.

"The older men in congress, and of course, most congressmen in middle life," Hall wrote, "tend to think of immigration as it was before 1880, when the very desirable German and Scandinavian colonists settled the middle and northwestern states. Very few congressmen visit the recent immigration in its principal residence,—the slum districts of large eastern cities,—nor do they take the trouble to inspect incognito the landing of these immigrants at our ports."

The IRL's goal was for Congress to block the vast majority of Southern and Eastern European immigrants from settling in America, especially Jews and Italians, by whatever political means possible. Their sworn enemies were Jacob Schiff, Albert Ballin, and the steamship companies.

Most Americans were in favor of open immigration. So was most of big business. Never before had an elite group of Americans banded together to oppose it. Before the Civil War, calls for immigration restriction largely came from the native-born working class, who feared that cheap labor would depress their wages, especially in large cities. The Know-Nothing Party of the 1850s, for example, resisted the wave of Catholic newcomers from Ireland and Germany for both cultural and economic reasons. The party died out without enacting any real restrictions, and by the 1890s many in positions of power concluded that new arrivals from all northern European nations could become integrated into American society.

This time, the fear was different. This elite group of Americans feared that if the nation's genetic makeup changed too much, the nation would face grave peril. Oliver Wendell Holmes Sr., dean of Harvard Medical School, founder of the *Atlantic Monthly* and the man who coined the term "Boston Brahmin," wrote, "If genius and talent are inherited, why should not deep-rooted moral defects . . . show themselves . . . in the descendants of moral monsters?"

In 1895, Senator Henry Cabot Lodge introduced a literacy test bill onto the Senate floor, a measure largely written by his friend Prescott Farnsworth Hall. "German steamship companies making great effort against bill," Lodge cabled Hall breathlessly. "Anything you can do should be done at once." The following year, the House and the Senate both passed the bill, with votes of 195–26 and 52–10, respectively. President Grover Cleveland vetoed the bill, decrying it as a "radical departure from our national policy related to immigration."

Prescott Hall was infuriated. "To hell with Jews, Jesuits, and steamships!" he wrote. Although he did not name HAPAG and Albert Ballin, he believed that the German steamship lines were involved in a vast conspiracy to profit from sending Europe's unwanted to America's shores.

From the New York City police department, Commissioner Theodore Roosevelt wrote Prescott Hall declaring his support for the bill, but declined to offer specifics in writing:

> I do heartily sympathize with this bill; as I understand it is the one introduced by Senator Lodge; but my dear sir, I cannot write to Mr. Reed at present. I will explain this to you personally the reasons when I get the chance. I have written him again and again recently for various measures which I deem of importance, and I feel I have gone to the very limit to which I am willing to go in writing. Moreover, if Senator Lodge can't influence him in favor of the bill, I certainly cannot.

The Immigration Restriction League's first legislative fight was a resounding defeat. Despite friends in Congress, much of the American moneyed class lined up against the IRL. These included big businessmen such as Andrew Carnegie, who welcomed cheap immigrant labor to work in his steel mills, leaders of the Roman Catholic Church, and of course, leaders of the German Jewish elite such as Jacob Schiff. For all of his bigotry and bile, Hall was partially right that Albert Ballin of HAPAG and Heinrich Wiegand at North German Lloyd cultivated relationships in the highest circles of American society to promote and protect their business interests.

A surprising ally of the immigrant cause was Jacob Schiff's friend, Harvard president Charles William Eliot, a man whose elite pedigree easily matched Senator Lodge's. Despite his close ties to the Boston aristocracy, Eliot had no wish to alienate prominent German Jewish donors, who by the 1890s were sending their children to Harvard. He also realized that Harvard was an urban school, and that in order to stay at the forefront of American education, it had to draw immigrant students from urban public schools as well as those from traditional preparatory schools. Eliot joined the board of the National Liberal Immigration League. Eliot believed, too, that Jews should be allowed to come into this country, and attributed their survival, like that of his Puritan forebears, to "their religious faith and the singular purity, tenderness, and devotion of their family relations." He felt that the new wave of Russian Jews fleeing the czar's pogroms were no different from any other oppressed people who had come to America in the past.

Mark Twain, another supporter of the National Liberal Immigration League, wrote that it was the self-declared 100 percent Americans like Lodge and Hall, not the immigrants, who were the true germs infecting American society. Neither did he share much of their obsession with Germanic culture. "I had become instantly naturalized," he wrote in his satire "3,000 Years Among the Microbes," "that is to say, I was to become a real cholera germ, not an imitation one; I was become [*sic*] intensely, passionately cholera-germanic; indeed, I outnatived the natives themselves . . . my patriotism was hotter than their own, more aggressive, more uncompromising; I was the germiest of the germy."

* * *

Despite losing the test fight, the IRL remained undaunted. Sure of himself as always, and never one to back down, Henry Cabot Lodge assured Hall that the fight would continue. In the years after Cleveland's veto, the Immigration Restriction League added a number of prominent aristocrats into their ranks. To get "scientific" credibility, they also won the support of many in the academic community. In 1896, Francis Amasa Walker, the president of the Massachusetts Institute of Technology and a former commissioner of Indian Affairs, wrote a scathing piece in the *Atlantic Monthly* about how the construction of Ellis Island signaled a federal complicity in permitting the entry of the great unwashed hordes. Echoing Lodge's Germanophilia, he wrote: "They have none of the ideas and aptitudes which fit men to take up readily and easily the problem of self-care and self-government, such as belong to those who are descended from the tribes that met under the oak-trees of old Germany to make laws and choose chieftains."

Walker must have rejoiced when, in 1897, Ellis Island burned to the ground. But within a couple of years, a bigger, grander, fireproof structure of brick and concrete arose on top of the ashes of the old one. Barges carted over tons of landfill that allowed for the construction of expanded facilities that included a hospital, dormitories, a powerhouse, a psychiatric observation ward, even a morgue. On opening day, December 17, 1900, over twenty-five hundred new arrivals were processed. To cope with the growing numbers, immigration and public health had gone from improvised to industrialized.

The specter of disease, however, continued to haunt the immigration business on both sides of the Atlantic. The year that Ellis Island reopened its doors, a typhoid outbreak, caused by sewage running through the streets, hit the tenement blocks of the Lower East Side. One disease in particular became associated with immigrant Jews: tuberculosis. Caused by airborne bacteria, the illness spread rapidly in tight living quarters, especially in small, airless apartments and packed garment factories in that part of New York City.

*   *   *

As the cholera epidemic crested in Hamburg, Ballin continued to labor under pressure, some of it self-imposed. Unlike executives at the traditional Hamburg shipping firms, Ballin had no ownership position in HAPAG. He was only one of its directors, with no family connections to ensure his position at the company. His only source of clout was consistently turning a profit for HAPAG's passenger division, and his only path up was someday to become its general director. But if he lost his job, Ballin felt, his work would revert to what it once was, a job as a mere immigrant ticketing agent. The specter of his father's failure haunted him.

But most of the pressure was due to circumstance. The spread of disease had slowed business. Albert Ballin and the Hamburg Senate had agreed to a deal in 1893 that would prevent the spread of disease in the city and save HAPAG from bankruptcy. In exchange for an unlimited flow of migrants into Hamburg, HAPAG would construct a hermetically sealed emigrants' facility, an "Emigrant Village" (*Auswandererhallen*), far from the center of the city. Unlike Berlin's Ruhleben station, which merely inspected and sorted emigrants, this facility would house and feed them as well. This setup would benefit both the city and the steamship company, and not just for hygienic reasons. The facility would also curb the criminal element who preyed on the bewildered Yiddish-speaking arrivals.

Aware of how the migrants communicated by letter and word of mouth, Ballin also wanted to take away much of the shock that hit his passengers upon their arrival in Hamburg and to minimize their wait time in the city. He also understood, of course, that miserable and unhappy immigrants did not make for good HAPAG customers. And sick immigrants cost the company money. Not only did he have to get them away from the swindlers, but also from the city's sometimes contaminated water supply.

The first attempt at an Emigrant Village was a camp located at the Amerika Quay, right where the ships docked on the waterfront. But the makeshift barracks met few immigrant needs, and the city fathers urged HAPAG to build a permanent facility, out of sight and mind from the residents of Hamburg.

Ballin and his fellow HAPAG directors decided to build something unprecedented: a complete, self-contained *Auswandererhallen* on the island of Veddel. The facility would include dormitories for up to five thousand migrants at a time, as well as a church, a synagogue, kosher kitchens, a medical clinic, and fumigation facilities to make sure passengers and their belongings were free of disease. The village would also assuage the fears of the Hamburg population by quarantining the migrants from the rest of the city. The cost for an overnight stay would be a mere two marks.

By consolidating control over the new arrivals, Ballin also delivered a knockout punch to the ecosystem of boardinghouses and swindlers. Although historian Arnold Kludas maintained that Ballin "had some kind of a heart for the emigrants," his move also made simple and great business sense.

The planned Emigrant Village was only part of a larger scheme. Ballin decided that to retain the profits from steerage berths and to get a handle on disease, HAPAG would have to get control of the emigrants' journey from the German border to Ellis Island. This meant the construction of not just a receiving facility in Hamburg but of an entire network of agents and border stations, as per his joint proposal with Wiegand. He also proposed getting HAPAG out of the "indirect" immigration business, meaning that the company's ships would no longer sail from Hamburg to Great Britain, but would sail directly to New York. They would need to build a series of larger ships with vastly increased steerage capacity.

The Emigrant Village was a brilliant response to a crisis for his company. With a masterstroke, Ballin had taken a messy, corrupt, and often terrifying business and turned it into an efficient machine. It also gave concrete proof to the American authorities, especially opponents of unrestricted immigration, that his shipping company was taking the threat of disease seriously.

Thanks in part to Ballin's reforms, Jewish immigration bounced back after the cholera epidemic subsided. In 1895, according to the German newspaper *Freistatt*, HAPAG ships carried 55,097 westbound emigrants in steerage, including 19,461 from Russia. By 1899, that number had grown to 64,214, with 30,941 from Russia.

To fill the steerage compartments of his new liners, Albert Ballin decided to hire a large number of agents who would operate inside the Russian Empire, as well as in Romania and Austria-Hungary. Their job would be to sell HAPAG tickets to Jewish families who were thinking about going to America, with the promise that they would help smuggle them across the Prussian border and facilitate their train journey through Germany to the port of Hamburg. Some agents were Jews, some were gentiles, but all were on HAPAG's payroll.

Ballin's aggressive growth strategy pleased the Kaiser and earned handsome returns for HAPAG stockholders. But the Foreign Office in

Berlin looked on the surge of Russian Jews gathering at the border with increasing alarm. To the steamship lines, the migrants represented a lucrative market, but to the German upper-class bureaucrats, they were a threat to German culture, especially to Prussian domination. What most worried the bureaucrats, many of them subscribers to the nationalist sentiments of philosophers like von Herder, was that Russian Jews would choose to settle in the booming industrial cities of Germany rather than move on to the United States.

Germany, still struggling with the growing pains of unification under Bismarck, was in a poor political position to integrate potentially hundreds of thousands of new arrivals from the Russian Empire. So the government in Berlin passed a series of edicts to keep that from happening. The Prussian government expelled thirty thousand migrant Polish and Jewish seasonal laborers, and also required migrants traveling through the province to carry at least four hundred marks in cash per adult (plus one hundred marks for each child), to pay for an eventual return journey to Russia. For most impoverished Jews, this was an unattainable sum.

Albert Ballin felt that further edicts would crush his business. He also feared that Jews would find ways to bypass Germany at the expense of Hamburg and HAPAG. From Odessa, Jews could travel to Mediterranean ports such as Trieste, and then on to the United States. Through intense lobbying efforts in Berlin, Ballin was able to strike a deal with the Prussian government—a first step in a much grander plan to create an integrated transportation system between the Pale of Settlement and the United States. His next move was to control the business of the Germany-Russia border crossings, and in effect privatize the management of a growing humanitarian crisis.

Count Leo von Caprivi, who succeeded Bismarck as chancellor, decided that Ballin's offer was too good to pass up. In return for eliminating the burdensome cash requirements for transmigrants, von Caprivi's government would allow agents of the steamship companies—working in cooperation with Prussian authorities—to screen all Russians trying to gain entry into Germany. The agents would only allow safe passage to those who held HAPAG or NDL tickets. All others seeking asylum would be turned away unless they could at that point be convinced to buy a steamship ticket to America. Ballin sweetened the deal with one more promise: his officials would turn a blind eye to Jewish immigrants who had steamship tickets but lacked passports or other travel documents.

What outraged critics of the system was that HAPAG was profiting from a humanitarian crisis in the Russian Empire. Noted Berlin Jewish leader Georg Halpern and other left-wing German Jewish critics of HAPAG wanted immigration to be managed by the government, not by a private company, which they felt was inherently exploitative. "Ballin's agents have been holding power at the border and the bourgeois is protected from Russian-Jewish germs by various showers and baths and disinfectant apparatuses," Halpern scoffed. "Only those who have been deemed disease-free by the control stations are allowed to move on; the examination, however, is carried out by odd methods otherwise unknown in medicine." Halpern had no problems calling what Ballin did in the name of profit: *Vergewaltigung*. Rape.

Nonetheless, Russian Jews did hear from those who had gone before that the conditions aboard HAPAG ships were markedly better than those on cheaper lines, and they were willing to pay more if it meant less trouble at the border too. Colorful posters showing the powerful, three-funneled profiles of the *Auguste Victoria* and her fleetmates drew countless migrants into HAPAG's offices.

There were only two things that could end the flow of Jews out of the Russian Empire. One was a change in regime in Russia, something that looked increasingly unlikely given that Alexander III's conservatism hardened as he aged, and his eldest surviving son, Nicholas, did not exhibit liberal inclinations of any sort.

The other was a large-scale European conflict involving Germany and Russia.

*   *   *

And then Alexander III fell ill. On the first day of November 1894, he died of kidney disease at the imperial palace of Livadia on the Black Sea. He was only forty-nine years old. His son, now Czar Nicholas II, was determined to continue the many policies championed by his father, the most prominent of which was the perpetuation of the state creed of Orthodoxy, Autocracy, and Nationality. He also inherited his father's intense loathing of the Jews, whom he saw not just as Christ killers but also as members of a disloyal group of political dissenters—writers, artists, academics, and other freethinkers who championed republicanism, socialism, communism, and even anarchy. Nicholas II frequently derided intellectuals with a term coined by the Russian writer Pyotr Boborykin in the 1860s: *intelligentsiya*. To the new czar, they were political descendants of the People's Will, the anarchist group that had planned the assassination of his grandfather. And like his cousin Kaiser Wilhelm II of Germany, Nicholas regarded the rising commercial class of bankers and industrialists, Jew and gentile alike, with intense suspicion, because they threatened the traditional supremacy of the landed aristocracy.

For his part, Kaiser Wilhelm II was eager to improve relations with Russia, which had suffered during the reign of Nicholas's father. The Kaiser tried to present himself as an ally who upheld the traditional prerogatives of European monarchs, prerogatives that seemed to be in free fall in Great Britain, where the aging Queen Victoria was little more than a figurehead in a constitutional government.

In 1895, as preparations for the coronation of Nicholas II were proceeding apace in Moscow's Kremlin, Albert Ballin was summoned to Berlin for his first formal meeting with Kaiser Wilhelm II. The purpose was to discuss festivities celebrating the opening of the Kiel Canal, a 61-mile waterway that linked the North Sea on the west to the Baltic on the east. The Kaiser wanted a magnificent spectacle to commemorate a German engineering achievement, and the Hamburg Senate was more than happy to send Ballin as its representative.

The Kaiser laid out his vision for the event, a procession down the canal, which would start in the Elbe River basin. The imperial yacht *Hohenzollern* would be the first to sail down the canal, followed by a liner each from HAPAG and North German Lloyd.

Ballin asked for permission to speak. Because the celebration was starting in Hamburg's waters, he reasoned, why shouldn't the HAPAG liner be lined up immediately behind the imperial yacht, with the NDL steamer third?

There was an awkward silence. The Kaiser, somewhat irritated, said that he had already promised NDL second place behind the imperial yacht. Ballin kept his cool. "If the Kaiser had pledged his word, the matter, of course, was settled," he said, and that he would withdraw his suggestion, although he considered himself justified in making it.

A shocked Count von Waldersee pulled Ballin aside after the meeting. "As you are now sure to be hanged from the Brandenburger Tor," the count told the businessman, "let us go to Hiller's before it comes off to have some lunch together." Ballin, although quickly learning the ways of Hamburg society, still had some way to go if he was to bridge the gap between the needs of the business world and royal protocols. He proved to be a quick study in court politics. In 1899, Ballin was finally appointed HAPAG's general director, putting him in the top tier of the German business community and among the most prominent members of the nation's Jewish *haute bourgeoisie*.

Echoing Kaiser Wilhelm II's ambitions and his global expansionist policy of *Weltpolitik*, Albert Ballin gave HAPAG a new corporate slogan: "*Mein Feld ist die Welt*" ("My Field Is the World").

Albert Ballin did not love Berlin, but he cultivated a group of admirers and lobbyists in the capital, including the new prince Bernhard von Bülow, whom the Kaiser appointed to the position of chancellor in the fall of 1900. Bülow came from one of North Germany's oldest noble families yet did not feel threatened by meritocrats like Ballin. Rather, he deeply admired Ballin for what he had accomplished at HAPAG. He also felt that Ballin's friendship with Lord Pirrie, head of Britain's Harland & Wolff shipyard, would prove useful in the diplomacy of the future, especially in avoiding a war with Great Britain. As for Russia, Bülow was well aware that the Prussian government had effectively subcontracted its border control operations to HAPAG and its rival North German Lloyd.

The news of Albert Ballin's new favor at court sounded alarm bells for the Kaiserin Auguste Victoria and her archconservative Prussian coterie in Berlin. Not only was a Jew about to be welcomed into the halls of the Neue Palast but he was also an internationalist who favored cooperation with Great Britain for the sake of commerce, at the expense of the German Army. As the journalist Theodor Wolff recalled, "The Empress did not begrudge her husband his business with Ballin, but she surveilled their friendship with a troubled eye and when the imperial spouse was tied up in international thinking and the creation of his lordly Fleet was touched, then she rose up—warning and defensive—to her duty."

The Foreign Office tolerated Ballin only because Kaiser Wilhelm II admired him. The ministry saw his shipping line as useful, but only if the growing HAPAG fleet could be used for military purposes should war break out between Germany and Great Britain. That was certainly a possibility. But Ballin knew that war would bring an end to HAPAG, and to the immigration business that made it so profitable.

It was politics abroad that proved more unpredictable. What really worried him was something over which he had no control: the unfettered laissez-faire capitalism across the ocean that produced boom-and-bust business cycles. The small federal government in Washington had virtually no tools to mitigate the effects of an economic downturn. There was no central bank to control the money supply and interest rates, and no laws or regulatory agencies to hold corporations and trusts accountable for reckless behavior.

Each time the stock market crashed, millions of people were thrown out of work. Lower East Side garment workers found that orders from department stores plummeted. To stay in business, sweatshop owners cut prices drastically, reduced wages, and forced their employees to work even longer hours. The hardest hit were the family sewing shops run out of tenement apartments. To alleviate the suffering, Jewish aid organizations stepped in to provide food and coal, as did political bosses looking for support in the next election.

The periodic downturns, then called "panics," led organized labor to lobby against unrestricted immigration. More workers would, they believed, exacerbate these conditions. The effort began in the 1890s. Samuel Gompers, a British-born Jew who headed the Cigar Makers Union and the American Federation of Labor, was a committed socialist who shared many of the views of working-class Jews. But he kept his distance from Russian Jews and Yiddish culture, declaring, "I was taught Hebrew, not the mongrel language spoken and written by many Jews of the present age."

Although the immigrant trade provided the bulk of the company's business, it was not all of it. And as these possibilities swirled, Ballin looked to other ports. As a patriotic German, Albert Ballin saw HAPAG as a tool for Germany's entrée onto the world stage as a colonial power. He hoped to expand the shipping line's routes to the Far East and to Africa.

Chancellor Bismarck, an avowed anticolonialist, was asserting that acquisitions abroad were distractions from Germany's destiny as an industrial and agricultural superpower on the European continent. But by the end of his service as chancellor, Bismarck relented and allowed the German military to acquire colonies that made up part or all of the modern-day nations of Namibia, Burundi, Chad, Nigeria, Congo, and the Central African Republic. Of more significance for the city of Hamburg, Germany also acquired spheres of influence in Shanghai and Tsingtao in China. Ballin, for his part, opened HAPAG routes to China and Japan, but the routes remained a small part of his business.

What excited the Kaiser was competing with England in this way. The Royal Navy may have ruled the waves with its big guns, but it was Great Britain's vast, privately owned merchant fleet that made the British Empire a working economic and business proposition. White Star operated combination cargo and passenger ships on the Australian route. Peninsular and Orient Lines connected England with India. Union Castle ruled the London-to–South Africa trade. In their passenger quarters, they carried diplomats, settlers, and military officials. In their cargo holds, they carried wool, grain, cattle, and sundry exotic goods. Most importantly, they carried the mail, and thus earned government subsidies. The privately owned German merchant fleet was beginning to provide the same services to the new German colonies in Africa and the Pacific. With service to Shanghai and Yokohama, as well as a joint service with the Africa-focused Woermann Line, HAPAG had become Germany's premier global shipping company.

Global ambitions aside, the North Atlantic still remained HAPAG's profit center. Disaster struck in 1897 when Ballin's entire fleet was made obsolete by the arrival of a new ship from North German Lloyd, a turn that could have jeopardized HAPAG's stake in the immigrant business too. She was the SS *Kaiser Wilhelm der Grosse*, at 14,000 gross tons the largest ship in the world and an homage to the Kaiser's grandfather, the first emperor of a unified Germany. She was also equipped with the world's most powerful engines, able to drive her at an astonishing 22.29 knots. Her best westbound crossing was five days and twenty minutes from the Needles to New York, making her the first German liner to ever hold the Blue Riband (ribbon) for the fastest crossing of the Atlantic.

The *Kaiser Wilhelm der Grosse* (*KWDG*) was also the first transatlantic liner equipped with four smokestacks. And she had space for over eight hundred steerage-class passengers. The *KWDG*'s silhouette would quickly become synonymous in the traveling public's mind with size and safety. Soon, images of the great ship were finding their way to small villages in Russia and Austria-Hungary, and potential emigrants, already terrified of the prospect of a sea voyage, rushed to book with North German Lloyd, assuming they would sail on that particular ship. To satisfy the craze, North German Lloyd would eventually place orders for three additional four-stackers during the next decade.

HAPAG's biggest new ships of the 1890s were a quartet of slow 13,000-ton liners—*Pennsylvania*, *Pretoria*, *Patricia*, and *Graf Waldersee*. Known as the P-class ships, they were able to carry up to twenty-eight hundred in steerage and only about one hundred in first and second class. They sailed along at a plodding 14 knots, and took almost two weeks to make the crossing. According to Ballin's friend Bernhard Huldermann, these ships represented "an important step forward, which greatly strengthened the earning capacities of the Company's resources." The big immigrant carriers were "extremely seaworthy, and were capable of accommodating a great many passengers, especially steeragers, as well as of carrying large quantities of cargo." These four ships might have made money in the immigrant trade, but there was little glamour about them. As pragmatic as he was as a businessman, Ballin had a weakness for the finer things in life and could not help but envy the new four-funnel liner. *Kronprinz Wilhelm* followed in 1901, *Kaiser Wilhelm II* in 1902, and *Kronprinzessin Cecilie* in 1906. The so-called Four Flyers combined sleek looks, luxurious interiors, and large steerage capacities.

Just after assuming full control of the line, Ballin realized that HAPAG needed a four-stacker. He undertook construction of a new passenger liner, big and luxurious enough to rival the grandest ships from North German Lloyd. She would be named *Deutschland*. Ballin made a strong statement supporting German nationalism by building the liner in Stettin, at the AG Vulcan shipyard, rather than in a British yard. The plans called for a ship 679 feet long, 67 feet wide, and grossing 16,000 tons, making her larger than her competitor. To account for the enormous fuel consumption required to drive the big ship through the Atlantic at over

23 knots, *Deutschland* would be able to carry almost a thousand emigrants in open-berth steerage dormitories.

The new ship made her maiden voyage on July 6, 1900, arriving in New York City just over five days later. Although she didn't beat the *Kaiser Wilhelm der Grosse*'s record, she proved to be an extraordinarily fast vessel, able to steam well above 22 knots. The following summer, after several repeated attempts, SS *Deutschland*'s captain pushed the ship beyond her limits and achieved an average crossing speed of 22.42 knots, sailing from Eddystone, England, to New York in five days, fifteen hours, and forty-five minutes. The record was reclaimed a year later by the *KWDG*'s newer sister ship, *Kronprinz Wilhelm*, but finally in the fall of 1903, Ballin ordered that the *Deutschland* retake the prize, which she did, making the journey from Bishop's Rock Light off Ireland to New York's Ambrose Light in five days, eleven hours, and fifty-four minutes at an average speed of 23.15 knots, a record she would hold for the next several years.

The *Deutschland*, however, had a major design flaw, one that substantially reduced bookings in first, second, and steerage classes. Her engines were so powerful that when the ship was at full speed, they sent shock waves throughout the vessel. The vibrations were especially bad in the steerage dormitories, but shook even the crystal tableware in the first-class dining room. American travelers nicknamed her "The Cocktail Shaker." This did not produce favorable press notice for HAPAG or Albert Ballin.

Even so, because of her extreme speed and novelty, *Deutschland* made HAPAG a tremendous amount of money in her first few years of service. In 1901, *Deutschland* earned a total of 1.9 million marks (about $7.9 million) on her fifteen voyages. By contrast, the twelve-year-old *Auguste Victoria*, about half *Deutschland*'s size and much slower, earned only 327,000 marks (about $1.4 million) the same year. However, the real moneymakers were not the sleek express liners but the four big P-class immigrant carriers. On one summer voyage, the *Pennsylvania* earned 283,761.25 marks ($1.2 million), with a total annual earning of over 1.1 million marks ($4.6 million). This was significantly less than the *Deutschland*, but the caveat was that she and her three sisters burned far less coal and required fewer crew to take care of the passengers, especially since first-class capacity on the P-class ships was minuscule. They might have been big and homely, but as moneymakers, the P-class ships were phenomenal vessels.

Maintaining such a massive fleet was no small feat. A typical big liner in the HAPAG fleet would employ about six hundred crew members. About half of them worked in the hotel department as stewards, stewardesses, chefs, and elevator operators. In first class, Ballin made sure the passengers were waited on with the same polish and courtesy that he would have expected in his own home. Steerage, of course, had a low crew-to-passenger ratio. Nevertheless, for steerage-class passengers, HAPAG provided uniformed servers in the dining saloons—a novelty for people who had never been waited on in their lives. Most of the rest of the crew worked in the boiler rooms, shoveling coal into the furnaces day and night for a week or two at a time.

As the *Deutschland* was being constructed, Ballin made plans to expand the Emigrant Village at Veddel Island to accommodate the growing numbers of passengers for his larger ships. In addition to the barracks, he ordered the construction of a new hostelry, to be called the Hotel Nord et Sud. Geared toward more affluent HAPAG migrants, the facility would offer separate bedrooms for families and full-service restaurants. Even so, the facility would lie within the bounds of the Emigrant Village, walled off from the rest of Hamburg. As it was, the *Auswandererhallen* was basically a ghetto, albeit a transient and efficient one.

For each and every problem that arose in this period—anti-Semitism at home and abroad, regime change, competing ships—Ballin devised a solution. But the effort took its toll.

Part II

CHAPTER 7

A Banker's Charity

Forget your past, your customs, your ideals.
Select a goal and pursue it with all your
might. No matter what happens to you, hold
on. You will experience a bad time but sooner
or later you will achieve your goal. . . . A
bit of advice for you: Do not take a moment's
rest. Run, do, work and keep your own good in
mind. A final virtue is needed in America-
called cheek. . . . Do not say, "I cannot; I
do not know."

—G. M. PRICE, *AN IMMIGRANT'S ADVICE
MANUAL TO NEW YORK*, 1891

Every Friday night, Jacob Schiff gathered his extended family and friends around the table at 965 Fifth Avenue for his weekly Shabbat dinner. Before the meal began, he said grace, not in German or Hebrew, but in English:

> *Our God and Father*
> *Thou givest food to every living being,*
> *Thou hast not only given us life,*
> *Thou also givest our daily bread to sustain it.*
> *Continue to bless us with Thy mercy*
> *So that we may be able to share our own plenty*

With those less fortunate than ourselves.
Blessed be Thy name forevermore.
Amen.

While Jacob Schiff and his family dined in splendor on the Sabbath, hundreds of thousands of Jews gathered around rickety tables in two-room railroad flats on the Lower East Side. They lit the candles, blessed the bread, and did the best they could to keep their ancestral faith alive in difficult surroundings.

This slum—the most densely occupied in the world—was only five miles away from Jacob Schiff's Upper East Side townhouse, but it might as well have been on a different continent. But Schiff was a constant visitor. He spent time at the Henry Street Settlement House, conferring for hours with its director, Lillian Wald, who had forsaken a life of privilege to live among the immigrants as a nurse and educator. Although always immaculately dressed, Schiff refused to drive through the Lower East Side in a carriage. He preferred to walk through the muck of the streets, to be among his fellow Jews and to experience at least some of the life they lived. A leader, Schiff felt, showed no condescension toward those he wanted to help.

Some welcomed his presence and looked up to him. Others didn't, feeling the gulf between their world and his, and between his capitalist prosperity and their socialist dream, was too wide to reconcile.

*   *   *

The Lower East Side had been an immigrant neighborhood for almost a century. Since the early nineteenth century, the so-called Five Points section of Manhattan had served as the first home for newly arrived emigrants. The area was built atop the former site of the Collect Pond, which was for years the city's main source of drinking water. But Five Points gradually became befouled by tanneries, breweries, and other noxious commercial enterprises. And because the landfill over the polluted pond had been badly put down, buildings constantly shifted as the air reeked. Accordingly, the Five Points was the least desirable part of the growing city and the cheapest in which to live.

Five Points was only a stone's throw away from the immigrant processing center at Castle Garden and from the busy East River docks that gave the shipping-based economy of New York City life and sustenance. In the 1850s, it was home mostly to Irish immigrants who had fled the Great Famine and who worked as laborers and domestic servants. It was also a breeding ground for all sorts of vice: gangs, prostitution, saloons, gambling, and pickpocketing. One infamous structure supposedly recorded one murder a day. Soon German immigrants took up residence in the blocks just to the east of the Five Points intersection, moving into townhouses that had been carved up into warrens of small apartments. This neighborhood became known as "Kleine Deutschland." By the 1880s, the Germans and Irish were joined by Italians and Eastern European Jews. As the city grew northward after the Civil War, the Five Points low-income melting pot expanded to a slum that was bounded on the west by the Bowery, on the east by the East River, on the south by Canal Street, and on the north by Houston Street. This came to be known as the Lower East Side.

In the 1890s, the Lower East Side of New York had a population density of 335,000 people per square mile, the highest of any urban area in the world. Converted townhouses had been replaced by four- and five-story brick apartment buildings called tenements. The exteriors of the tenements might have featured a bit of decoration, but inside they were grim and utilitarian, designed to maximize the rental income by cramming as many people per floor as possible. Until 1879, there were no laws regulating the construction of tenement housing. Most had no indoor plumbing. Instead, there were old-fashioned communal privies in the back. Water came from a communal pump, which was often contaminated from the privies and other sources of disease, including seepage from the old Collect Pond.

The typical tenement apartment consisted of three rooms: a front parlor, a dining room that also doubled as the kitchen, and a back bedroom. In the "Old Law" tenements, only the front parlor, which overlooked the street, received any natural light or air. Often, another bed was squeezed next to the coal stove. In tenements built after a new set of 1879 regulations came into effect, all rooms had to have windows that could let in fresh air. These mandated airshafts backfired, as residents dumped trash and chamber pots out their windows onto the ground below, creating ever-growing piles of fetid waste.

For most middle- and upper-class New Yorkers, the slums of Lower Manhattan were a shadowy netherworld. In 1888, a police reporter named Jacob Riis decided to change that. He brought light to the slum in the form of the newly invented flash photography. For nights on end, Jacob Riis and his team went from tenement to tenement, from boardinghouse to boardinghouse, and from saloon to saloon. They opened doors, quickly set up camera equipment, captured an image, then retreated. Most of the subjects had no idea what had just happened.

The following year, Riis gave a series of presentations of his images. Then, in 1890, he released his illustrated book *How the Other Half Lives*. It was a publishing sensation. With its vivid prose and photographs, it pulled back the curtain on the desperate conditions in which more than half of New York City's residents had to live.

Despite his call for tenement reform, Riis did not have kind things to say about the people who lived there. A devout evangelical Christian, he was especially contemptuous of the Jewish residents of the Lower East Side. Rather than admiring their work ethic, Riis repeated standard anti-Semitic tropes about Jews and money. "Money is their God," he said. "Life itself is of little value compared with even the leanest bank account. In no other spot does life wear so intensely bald and materialistic an aspect as in Ludlow Street. Over and over again I have met with instances of these Polish or Russian Jews deliberately starving themselves to the point of physical exhaustion, while working night and day at a tremendous pressure to save a little money."

For their part, most Russian Jews worked hard and saved because they dreamed of making a better life for their children. They made a living as cobblers, butchers, bakers, printers, distillers, and other trades they had practiced in the Old Country. Some even found their way into organized crime. But the most common line of work for Jews in New York was the garment industry. The Yiddish term for this line of work was the *schmata* (rag) trade. The little engine that powered the trade was the Singer sewing machine, a miraculous labor-saving device that an American, Isaac Singer, patented in the 1850s. Powered by a foot pedal, it could rapidly stitch raw cloth into a garment, and made mass production of clothing possible. Russian Jews were familiar with Singer sewing machines because the company had established a thriving branch in St. Petersburg.

The Russian Jews brought their expertise with them. As the nation's biggest manufacturer of women's and men's clothing, New York needed as many bodies in front of sewing machines as possible. In 1897, 60 percent of the Jewish workforce labored in the garment industry, and 75 percent of all garment workers were Jewish. They first worked in garment shops owned by uptown German Jews, and then branched off to form their own operations. In a typical Russian Jewish *schmata* business, the immigrant husband would purchase a Singer sewing machine, usually on an installment plan, and a set of mannequins to be put up in the front parlor. Then the whole family would set to work assembling dresses from raw cloth, using commercial patterns. The roughly assembled garment would be sent on to another shop where finer needlework was done, and it was then put up for sale in a department store like Macy's or Bloomingdale's, owned by elite German Jewish families. If the owner of the *schmata* business was successful, he would hire friends and relatives as they arrived in America. If the owner was especially successful, he would move his operation out of his apartment and into an industrial building farther uptown, usually on Seventh Avenue.

The decentralized production model, known as "section work," provided plenty of employment for Jewish immigrants. Despite New York's relatively high labor costs compared with other cities, the sheer amount of labor available, as well as access to quality materials such as silk from Paterson, New Jersey, and cotton fabrics from mills in Lawrence, Massachusetts, outweighed the high cost of doing business.

Yet not every garment worker dreamed of starting a shop of his or her own. By the 1890s, a growing number of Russian Jews abandoned that path—and their religion—and embraced the mantle of socialism and organized labor. A small but vocal minority became anarchists. For them, traditional Orthodoxy provided little comfort as they confronted the daily hardship of life in America. The rabbis might preach that the Messiah would one day come and right the wrongs of the world, but that prospect did not feed hungry children or provide better working conditions in the here and now.

Left-wing political organizations offered a solution. They took their cue from the German philosopher and political theorist Karl Marx, from Social Democrats, to socialists, to Communists, to anarchists. All were united in a single mission: for the proletariat to wrest control of the means of production from the capitalists. Some thought the best way for this to be achieved was the formation of stronger trade unions, which would negotiate better working conditions and wages. On the Lower East Side, arguably the most colorful advocate of that approach was Joseph Barondess, founder of the Cloakmakers' Union and a sought-after speaker at celebrations, gatherings of all sorts, and even funerals.

Proof of this came on June 3, 1900, when a large group of organizers and garment workers crammed into the main hall of the Labor Lyceum at 64–70 East Fourth Street in Greenwich Village. They came not just from New York's Lower East Side but also from Baltimore, Boston, and Philadelphia. The garment workers, most of them Eastern European Jews, cheered at the announcement of the formation of a new labor union: the International Ladies' Garment Workers Union (ILGWU). It was an organization in which women's rights were linked to workers' rights, the first of its kind in the United States. The organization, which at its launch had two thousand members, had roots in the Jewish Labor Bund movement back in Russia, which was closely allied with the Social Democratic movement in Germany.

JEWISH IMMIGRANTS Emma Goldman and Alexander Berkman, sometime lovers and leaders of the anarchist movement, attended speeches by radical activists throughout the city and penned articles in publications such as *Der Anarchist* and *Die Autonomie* that called for the violent overthrow of the capitalist system. To Goldman, Berkman, and their followers, there was no room for negotiation or equivocation with the plutocrats, the bourgeoisie, and the federal government. In order to achieve a workers' paradise, the whole system had to be taken down and rebuilt from the bottom up.

In 1892, Berkman put his beliefs into action. The steelworkers at Carnegie Steel's Homestead plant went on strike, demanding higher wages and shorter hours. They then surrounded the plant and refused to let managers and scabs enter. Andrew Carnegie decamped to Scotland for a fishing trip, putting his associate Henry Clay Frick in charge of breaking the strike. Frick, who despised unions, sent in a private army of Pinkerton guards to regain control of the plant and brutally beat up the strikers. Berkman traveled to Pittsburgh, gained entry to Henry Clay Frick's office, and shot him in the neck. Frick survived the assassination attempt. Berkman was sent to prison for attempted murder for fourteen years, yet continued to read and correspond with Emma Goldman, who was not charged in the crime.

*　*　*

This, of course, did not seem like a reasonable solution to Jacob Schiff.

In contrast to most of the Russian Jewish immigrant population, Jacob Schiff was a staunch Republican who firmly believed business and culture would uplift his fellow Jews. He truly felt that he could integrate Gilded Age capitalism with the Jewish principle of *tzedakah* as a moral obligation. As a railroad banker, he was suspicious of trade unions. Schiff hoped that, rather than joining a union, Jews would avail themselves of organizations like the Henry Street Settlement, which he lavishly funded. Here, he believed, Eastern European Jews would learn to become proper, sober Americans who practiced thrift, industry, and cleanliness.

Schiff may have been the autocrat of Jewish philanthropy, but he had several powerful lieutenants who put his ideas into action. Louis Marshall was one of America's most prominent constitutional lawyers, a partner in the German Jewish firm of Guggenheimer and Untermeyer. Schiff pushed Marshall to lead two of his pet philanthropic projects: the Jewish Theological Seminary in New York, to which Marshall was appointed chairman of the board in 1905, and the American Jewish Committee (AJC), which the two men cofounded. Among the other well-connected German Jews whom Schiff selected to lead the AJC were the biblical scholar Cyrus Adler, Judge Mayer Sulzberger, and the attorney-diplomat Oscar Straus.

On one hand, his wealth and connections made him an ideal advocate for Jewish immigrants among the rich and powerful. On the other, his autocratic manner and conservative politics made him an object of suspicion among many of the very people he so generously assisted. An 1894 article in the *Yiddische Gazette* summed up how Russian Jews felt when ushered into the domain of the German Jewish philanthropists:

*In the philanthropic institutions of our aristocratic German Jews you see
beautiful offices, desks, all decorated, but strict and angry faces. Every poor
man is questioned like a criminal, is looked down upon; every unfortunate
suffers self-degradation and shivers like a leaf, just as if he were standing
before a Russian official. When the same Russian Jew is in an institution of
Russian Jews, no matter how poor or small the building, it will seem to him
big and comfortable. He feels at home among his own brethren who speak
his tongue, understand his thoughts and feel his heart.*

Russian Jewish immigrants began to start their own mutual aid societies, known as *landsmanshaftn*. These evolved into ersatz fraternities,
separate from the synagogues to which many of them belonged. When
a new arrival from Kiev, Bialystok, Minsk, Lodz, or one of the innumer-
able tiny shtetls set foot on the Lower East Side, often the first order of
business for the father of the family was to set up a meeting with his
hometown *landsmanshaft*. Here, those who had come before would help
his family find a place to live, learn English, and find a job. Women were
almost never permitted to be members. Not only were the *landsmanshaftn*
enclaves of male fellowship but they provided benefits for the entire
household. Should he become unemployed, disabled, or die, his fellow
landsmen would help support his family. Life insurance policies, like those
provided by the Equitable Life Assurance Society of the United States, on
whose board Jacob Schiff sat, were beyond the reach of Lower East Side
immigrant families.

Condescension, both real and imagined, widened the gulf between
the German uptown Jews and the Russian Jews downtown. To bridge it,
Schiff and his close friend Louis Marshall came up with a new approach.
The Henry Street Settlement House and Montefiore Hospital provided
crucial social services for destitute Lower East Side Jews, and HEAS provided loans to would-be small-business owners. But Schiff and Marshall's
new project was different. They planned to start a newspaper, hoping to
ease assimilation with the written word.

There was a radical socialist element in the Yiddish press that Schiff
hoped to counter. To many of the uptown German Jews, the political
ferment on the Lower East Side was not something to celebrate, but to
mitigate. Many of them had made their fortunes in banking, dry goods,

manufacturing, and mining, industries that depended on unrestricted immigration, minimal regulations, and cheap labor. Jacob Schiff's own fortune depended on the lack of regulation on railroads such as the Pennsylvania and the Union Pacific. Radical political ideas threatened Schiff's own financial well-being. All the more reason, he felt, these Russian Jews needed to be assimilated as much as aided. Otherwise, they might find themselves locked out of the country.

He thought that this radical socialist element and the action they inspired—like Berkman's crime—would be detrimental to his long-standing effort to keep the immigration door open for Russian Jews.

In 1902, Schiff helped launch a new Yiddish daily. It was called *Di yidishe velt* (*The Jewish World*), and its masthead boasted that Zvi Hirsch Masliansky was its owner and publisher. A renowned Jewish orator and *maggid*, Masliansky had emigrated from Russia to America in 1895 and gave a popular series of Friday-night sermons at the Educational Alliance, another large settlement house on the Lower East Side. The head of the Educational Alliance was Isidor Straus, one of Jacob Schiff's allies, whose heart, according to New York Supreme Court judge Samuel Greenbaum, "beat in responsive sympathy with his oppressed brethren."

The paper failed within a few years.

Schiff's uplift efforts weren't doing much to change the minds of Russian Jewish immigrants. They weren't doing much to change the broader public opinion either. Gentiles, especially elite ones, increasingly associated Jews with anarchism, communism, and other left-wing causes. For America's Protestant upper class, it appeared that anarchy was in the air. One of them, Theodore Roosevelt, owed his own office to the death of President William McKinley, who had been shot by the young anarchist Leon Czolgosz (a non-Jew) at the Pan-American Exposition in Buffalo on August 31, 1901. Although a lone wolf, Czolgosz had been inspired by the speeches of Emma Goldman to overthrow the ruling class. Other prominent victims of anarchist assassinations, in addition to Czar Alexander II of Russia, were Empress Elisabeth of Austria-Hungary in 1898 and King Umberto I of Italy two years later.

Ultimately, it was fear of politically radical immigrants that led President Theodore Roosevelt to quietly impose more restrictions. Senator Henry Cabot Lodge finally got some of what he wanted. In 1902,

Roosevelt selected a new commissioner of immigration at Ellis Island, whose job was to supervise all activities at the facility. William Williams was very much a man in Roosevelt's mold. A native of New Haven, he was a graduate of Yale College and Harvard Law School and had served as a soldier in the Spanish-American War. A man of independent means, Williams then worked as a Wall Street lawyer after his return from the war.

Like Roosevelt, Williams felt that corruption had to be ferreted out of public agencies. To that end, he sent a number of undercover agents disguised as steerage arrivals through the Ellis Island process, then promptly fired agents who gave "defective" immigrants permission to pass through in exchange for bribes. Although this was productive, he also believed that too many people were being allowed into the country, and that enforcement of standards barring sick and mentally deficient new arrivals was too lax.

Prescott Hall, thrilled to hear about higher rejection rates, wrote Williams asking for updates on his reforms. "It may interest you to know," Williams wrote Hall in 1902, "that during the first twenty-three days of this month this office rejected and ordered deported 810 aliens, or over 3% of the arrivals. Every day the machinery here is being gotten into better shape to execute the laws. In view of the hardship resulting from deportation, I earnestly hope that the steamship companies will have the wisdom to leave ineligibles in Europe, but if they do not, the deportations next Spring will be very heavy."

In public, Theodore Roosevelt expressed no overt anti-Semitism, which was unusual given his upbringing and social class. Like Harvard president Eliot, Roosevelt felt that Jews could be integrated into American society, so long as they accepted "traditional" mores and political norms. Roosevelt's appointment of Oscar Straus as secretary of commerce and labor was not merely an act of philo-Semitism. The cabinet position also gave Straus oversight over the entire Bureau of Immigration, which enforced a new immigration act signed into law by Theodore Roosevelt in 1903. Known as the Anarchist Exclusion Act, the law barred four classes of immigrants from entering the United States: anarchists, epileptics, beggars, and importers of prostitutes. Although not explicitly stated in the law, the radical Russian Jew became the bogeyman of the movement in Congress and eventually among the public.

Schiff had been wrong about what the Russian Jewish immigrants wanted, and needed, but he had been right about Jewish radicals being singled out by anti-Semites as representative of *all* Jews.

That was one obstacle to Schiff's ideal of Jewish assimilation. Another soon emerged, in the shape of a man.

This man, J. P. Morgan, intended to take over the entire North Atlantic passenger business. Even the confident Schiff would admit that he was nervous about doing anything that looked "as if we attempted to play in Morgan's backyard." Here was an implacable rival, a member of the American establishment he could not reason with or charm.

CHAPTER 8

Morganizing the Atlantic

Millionaires operating with the unnumbered
millions of vast railroad corporations have
no financial conscience. . . . The combination may be sufficient to drive the British
and Continental competition off the Atlantic.

—BENJAMIN TAYLOR, "BRITISH AND
AMERICAN SHIPPING," 1902

John Pierpont Morgan was bulky, gruff, and had a flaming red nose. He also had piercing blue eyes that one observer compared to the headlights of an onrushing train. He liked to lock people into confined spaces, then ask them to come up with answers to business problems he posed, after which they could return to their lives on the outside. He would employ the practice at his mansion in New York and on his yacht *Corsair*. In both places, Morgan could also hide from photographers who might otherwise take candid shots of that nose.

While hiding from the press, Morgan could simply pick up the telephone (an invention he helped to finance) and get the president of the United States on the line. And the thought might have crossed his mind many times in 1893, when the United States entered a sharp economic depression, the worst in the nation's history. American railroads were going bankrupt, tax revenues were tanking, and European investors grew worried that the United States government would default on its bonds. During the worst of the crisis, foreign investors had unloaded $300 million worth of U.S. Treasury bonds.

By early 1895, advisers to President Grover Cleveland warned him that the United States would default in two weeks. To meet the demand for dollars to be redeemed into pounds sterling and other foreign currencies, the federal government was forced to send gold bullion across the Atlantic in the hulls of ships. The nation's gold reserves were plummeting, and without the backing of gold, the dollar would become worthless, wiping out the wealth of men like J. P. Morgan.

The near collapse of the American economy sent shock waves through the immigration trade. HAPAG and the other major steamship lines saw demand for steerage berths plummet. The cholera epidemic a few years earlier had already threatened the immigrant trade, as the ports of Hamburg and Bremen slowed the arrival of trainloads of potentially infected migrants. Even as HAPAG and NDL rushed to staff their new, privatized border control stations, news reached villages in Russia that there would be no jobs or work in America, whose economy had cratered.

On February 4, 1895, after setting up a meeting with President Cleveland, J. P. Morgan took the train down to Washington, D.C. He then arranged for a syndicate of bankers under his firm's management to put up funds to guarantee the solvency of the United States government. After some hesitancy, Cleveland agreed to accept the syndicate's offer. Confidence in the American economy returned, and gold started flowing back into the United States Treasury's vaults. The terms of the deal called for the government to buy 3.5 million ounces of gold coin from Morgan's syndicate at $17.80 per ounce, in exchange for $62.3 million in 4 percent bonds to be held by the syndicate. With the price of gold pegged at $18.60 an ounce, the Morgan syndicate made a profit of $3 million. Morgan's group also promised to supply the U.S. government with 300,000 ounces a month within six months.

J. P. Morgan had saved his country from economic collapse and paved the way for a new economic boom. The nation's money supply, he felt, should remain in control of an unofficial Protestant upper class that maintained strong economic and social ties with Great Britain. Morgan, unlike some Boston Brahmins such as Henry Cabot Lodge, saw America's financial future aligned with Great Britain and France, not with Germany. And Morgan didn't like upstarts like Jacob Schiff, nor did he like any deal he considered "too Jewish."

Kuhn, Loeb & Co., as represented by Jacob Schiff, was a direct threat to J. P. Morgan & Co.'s dominance as a funnel for European capital. Both men believed in order over chaos and saw business consolidation as the way to make the American economy work more efficiently. They were pro-trust conservatives, not trust-busting reformers. But they also believed there should be only one person at the top of America's banking pyramid.

Schiff proved to be the one man who refused to bend to Morgan's will, and this impertinence, from a Jewish immigrant no less, was unconscionable to the most powerful WASP in the country. After all, if Morgan could make the president of the United States do what he wanted, why not Jacob Schiff? But what Morgan may have not understood is that while he answered only to himself, Jacob Schiff was firmly convinced he answered to the God of Abraham.

*   *   *

John Pierpont Morgan grew up in a home that was thoroughly American, but with a heavy British influence. His father, Junius Spencer Morgan, a financier, cultivated ties with British banks and looked to forge strong connections between Great Britain's ruling aristocracy and America's emerging and mostly Protestant commercial elite.

Junius Morgan spent much of his business career in London, first as a partner of the Boston banker George Peabody, whose family had made a fortune in the pepper import business. By the 1860s, Junius Morgan had become the London banker for anyone who wanted to invest capital in American government bonds, American corporations, and American business ventures. But Junius needed a partner on the other side of the Atlantic. That person turned out to be not a fellow Yankee but the son of an Austrian immigrant who had come to America to paint portraits but found that his real talent was selling securities. His name was Anthony Drexel, a principal in the Philadelphia firm of Drexel & Co.

Tony Drexel, as he was known among family, believed fervently in the future greatness of America, and used his considerable talents to find ways for European capital to underwrite the nation's expansion. Earlier, he helped underwrite a giant bond offering to support the Union effort during the Civil War. But despite this effort, and his wealth, Drexel felt shunned by Philadelphia society. And so he lived apart from the city's fashionable hub of Rittenhouse Square in a gloomy mansion in the prosperous but not especially fashionable streetcar suburb of West Philadelphia. Here, away from society, this extremely private man could devote himself to raising his family. Born a Roman Catholic, Tony became an Episcopalian and raised his children in that faith.

In 1833, Junius married Julia Pierpont, the daughter of a New England Unitarian minister. Their son John Pierpont was born in 1837 in Hartford, Connecticut. A sickly child, Morgan was educated at the Episcopal Academy just outside of Hartford, and also at the Bellerive School in Switzerland. He then spent two years at the University of Göttingen in Germany, where his father hoped he would master the German language and pick up some useful European contacts for the family bank. Morgan graduated with a degree in art history, and collecting art and rare books remained a deep passion for the rest of his life.

Junius Morgan felt that Tony would be the ideal mentor for his irascible son, who had drifted from job to job after finishing his education at Göttingen. John Pierpont was clearly very smart, but he lacked discipline and tact. Tony took Pierpont into the Drexel bank and created a New York branch for him called Drexel, Morgan & Co. Pierpont had a head for numbers and logic, and proved to be a very hard worker, but despite all of Tony's tutoring, young Morgan never gained facility with words or public speaking. He was a numbers man, someone who loved order and beauty.

By the 1870s, Pierpont had proved himself to be a master of reorganizing business sectors that had run into trouble during the Panic of 1873. Drexel, Morgan & Co. advised railroads and banks on how to buy out the competition. The firm also used its networks in London—usually Barings and the house of J. S. Morgan & Co.—to supply capital to carefully selected corporations in the United States.

As a banker, Morgan came to the conclusion that the American railroad system needed some kind of centralized mode of control. Although railroads were hardly a new technology—the first steam-driven trains had appeared in the 1830s—they were still in the 1870s unwieldy, unregulated, and viciously competitive with one another. A few railroad magnates, most notably the former China merchant John Murray Forbes, applied careful logic and prudence to the running and operation of their lines and produced steady returns for their investors. But most railroad presidents were interested in short-term profit, and their weapon of choice against rivals was the rate war.

As Morgan's confidence and stature grew, he came to realize he could remake New York's financial landscape along the lines of the one he so admired in London. It was also starting to dawn on him that Drexel, Morgan & Co. had to coexist somehow with Jewish competitors, even if he loathed them. What the Jewish House of Rothschild was to the gentile House of Baring Brothers in England, Kuhn, Loeb & Co. was to Drexel, Morgan & Co. in America. The two houses cooperated and even did deals together, but their partners never socialized after business hours in clubs or country houses. One observer called it the "nine-to-five relationship," in which Jewish bankers like Schiff "had close contact with gentile bankers and upper-class clients during the working hours, but none afterward."

Morgan and Schiff shared a profession, but what made them great at it was very different. While Schiff loved learning on the job, traveling across the country to personally inspect rolling stock and rail stations, Morgan preferred to do his analysis at his desk, surrounded by his collection of art. What interested Morgan was risk mitigation. This involved quantifying the risks posed by an array of businesses with varying levels of profit potential and then organizing them into groups of easy-to-manage, publicly traded corporations. In short, Morgan bought companies and created huge trusts.

They differed in their social lives too. Despite his busy work schedule, Morgan found plenty of time for leisure. But much of this leisure was about conducting unspoken business with fellow gentiles long after business hours, in settings where Jews were increasingly not welcome. Exclusive social clubs were as much about forging trusting business relationships as they were about backgammon and billiards. He joined several, all of which by the 1890s began to enact unspoken yet strict bans against prospective Jewish members. He belonged to the Union Club, the New York Yacht Club (of which he became commodore), the Union League, and the Knickerbocker. When one of his associates, the president of the Erie Railroad, was turned down for membership in the Union

Club, the oldest and most exclusive men's club in New York, Morgan stormed off in a huff and founded the Metropolitan Club, upon which he and his fellow millionaires spared no expense.

His busy professional and social life contrasted with a dysfunctional family life. Morgan and his second wife, Fanny Tracy, drifted apart. Both suffered from bouts of depression, but while Tracy coped by drawing closer to her children, Morgan retreated further into the world of his creation. He also took up with a series of mistresses. And because he hated exercise, he was by the 1890s fat and florid faced, his nose turned red by a condition called rhinophyma.

His only son, John Pierpont Morgan Jr., known in the family as Jack, felt enormous pressure to measure up to his father. Jack was the heir apparent, after all. His sisters Juliet and Louisa married proper New York husbands, the former, banker William Pierson Hamilton (a descendant of Alexander Hamilton), and the latter, the lawyer Herbert Livingston Satterlee. His third sister, Anne, remained unmarried and became his father's closest and most loyal companion.

Morgan's fame continued to grow as the master who reorganized competing businesses into profitable corporate trusts that effectively controlled entire sectors of the economy: sugar, oil, rubber, steel, tobacco, and many others. Some applauded Morgan for reining in needless and inefficient competition and creating corporate order that benefited the American economy. Others saw him as a predator who created monopolies that gouged American consumers for the benefit of corporate shareholders. Still, Morgan's influence grew. In 1895, following Anthony Drexel's death, Morgan and his partners renamed the New York branch of the firm J. P. Morgan & Co. The London branch would be renamed Morgan, Grenfell & Co. The Philadelphia branch retained the name Drexel & Co. as Morgan, despite a huge ego, nevertheless chose to honor the legacy of his mentor.

It was through a Philadelphia connection that J. P. Morgan heard about another possible business opportunity, something a bit out of his comfort zone but still interesting. Clement Acton Griscom, a client of Drexel & Co., was an American who appeared to run his international steamship company with the same success as other men of his class ran their railroads. That is, with logistical precision coupled with a healthy amount of government "assistance." Since the Civil War, American international shipping had fallen into steep decline as entrepreneurs (Morgan and Schiff included) turned their attention to railroads. American shipyards with much higher labor costs than their British counterparts contributed to the decline of the sector. Griscom got around these costs by using subsidies from foreign countries and using foreign shipyards to build his empire of ships.

Clement Griscom had all the proper social credentials J. P. Morgan liked in a client. Born in 1841, Clement Griscom was a birthright Quaker, the son of a prominent Philadelphia physician. Like the Jews of Europe, the Society of Friends had experienced vicious persecution in the Old World because they refused to acknowledge the hierarchy of throne and altar. They were also pacifists. Griscom's ancestors had emigrated to the British colony of Pennsylvania in the late seventeenth century to practice their egalitarian faith. Thanks to their asceticism and thrift, the Quakers proved adept at making money, especially in manufacturing, banking, and engineering.

Griscom's family had abstained from all "worldly" pleasures, meaning there was neither a piano nor alcohol in the Griscom household. Much like the Warburgs of Hamburg, the Griscoms of Philadelphia found themselves torn between observing the strict tenets of their faith and the luxuries their financial discipline allowed them to purchase. By the mid-nineteenth century, the trappings of aristocracy—especially the example set by the British upper crust—proved too hard for many Philadelphia Quakers to resist.

Clement Griscom attended Philadelphia's elite Central High School, but dropped out at age sixteen to clerk at a local shipping firm called Peter Wright & Sons. The young man proved to be a natural businessman, so much so that he attracted the attention of an officer of the Pennsylvania Railroad, the biggest corporation in America and Kuhn, Loeb & Co.'s most famous client. Griscom soon became a stakeholder in Pennsylvania Railroad. With the railroad's backing, in 1872 Griscom formed a transatlantic shipping firm that he named the International Navigation Company. The railroad hoped that Griscom's ships would be part of a seamless supply chain that carried Pennsylvania petroleum to markets in Great Britain and beyond. This proved to be hopeless folly. Well-heeled travelers understandably balked at the idea of traveling on ships carrying full holds of reeking, flammable petroleum.

In danger of going bankrupt, Griscom pivoted and decided that the best use for his fleet of ships was the immigrant trade. With backing from Pennsylvania Railroad, he formed an alliance with the Belgian government to carry passengers and mail to the United States. According to Griscom's son Lloyd, he chose Antwerp as his new line's principal European port by rolling out the biggest map of Western Europe he could find, dotting in red ink all the major manufacturing centers, and choosing the port at the middle of the hub. Griscom then sailed for Belgium and pestered the American minister to get him an audience with Queen Victoria's cousin King Leopold II, who had a knack for making money in overseas ventures. One such undertaking led to the vicious subjugation of the people of the Congo and the ruthless exploitation of its natural resources for his personal benefit.

King Leopold, eager to increase Belgium's international standing as a trading power, listened attentively to the young American businessman's proposal of turning the city of Antwerp into a hub of American shipping.

"Your plan seems sound, Mr. Griscom," he said. "However, since it's so late, I'd like you to dine with the Queen and me. Afterward, we can discuss it further."

Like Albert Ballin, Griscom was too naïve to know that one never contradicted a king's wishes, at least not publicly. "Well, Sir, my wife and young baby are back at the hotel in Antwerp. Before I left this morning she made me promise to return for dinner."

Despite Griscom's faux pas, King Leopold responded, "You could not have a better reason. Another time you must bring Mrs. Griscom. And don't worry about a charter or postal subsidy. I'll see that Parliament grants you everything you need."

The venture became known as the Société Anonyme de Navigation Belge-Americaine in 1871, and it established steamship service between Antwerp and Philadelphia. To help pay for the new line, Griscom got a $100,000-a-year subsidy from the Belgian government, the kind of financial support that the United States government was unwilling to provide.

As the only American shipping magnate with a toehold in a European port, Griscom shrewdly realized that Antwerp could be a worthy competitor to the twin German port cities of Bremen and Hamburg in the immigrant business. Over the course of the next twenty years, with the steady backing of the Pennsylvania Railroad, Griscom built up a large fleet of steam-powered passenger liners and freighters flying the Red Star pennant and registered in Belgium. He also purchased the bankrupt Inman Line of Great Britain, which specialized in the immigrant trade, and transferred their two premier liners, *Paris* and *New York*, to the American registry under the new "American Line" moniker.

American law stated that only U.S.-built ships could be registered under the American flag, so a major exception had to be made. In exchange, Griscom agreed to build two big liners at Philadelphia's Cramp shipyard, *St. Louis* and *St. Paul*, which would work with the two "City" ships in a weekly service between New York and Liverpool. The American government hoped that Griscom's company would create jobs for American workers. Yet the two "Saints," which were slightly larger than Ballin's quartet of new HAPAG liners, cost 30 percent more to build than a comparable vessel in a British yard. Griscom found that his American Line was a fairly consistent money loser. He had counted on receiving a $750,000 annual subsidy from Washington in exchange for making his four vessels available to the U.S. Navy in times of war, but Congress only made good on the money for one year before voting down this provision.

Griscom avoided personal financial trouble because of his very diverse holdings in shipping and other industrial enterprises. Thanks to his directorship in the Pennsylvania Railroad, he was a very rich man, living in a big estate on Philadelphia's Main Line and enjoying the best the city's club life had to offer. Unlike his German counterpart Albert Ballin, Griscom did not have to face social ostracism for practicing his faith. Griscom knew that high living ran against Quaker principles, but he did it anyway.

By 1898, Griscom needed a rescue plan for his shipping concern, at least the American portion. All four of his American Line ships—*St. Louis*, *St. Paul*, *Paris*, and *New York*—were commandeered by the navy for service in the Spanish-American War, and although their service was brief, they were much the worse for wear upon their return to Griscom's company. Worse still, these ships were already woefully out of date compared to newer German and British vessels, especially when it came to size, luxury, and passenger capacity. Liverpool was also declining as an immigrant port because of HAPAG and NDL's direct services to New York.

With no help forthcoming from his home country, Griscom decided to invest where the money was. Because of the immigrant business, especially from Eastern Europe, his Belgian subsidiary Red Star was making money. And unlike his American shipping companies, Red Star was not required to build ships in their country of registry. So he planned to use British yards for future builds, which were still significantly cheaper.

By running a profitable international shipping line, Griscom had accomplished what no other major American businessman had since the pre–Civil War heyday of the Yankee clipper ships.

From his desk in Hamburg, Albert Ballin took notice of the success of Griscom's Red Star Line. A small but still significant portion of Jewish immigration was steadily being diverted away from Hamburg and Bremen to Antwerp, from twelve hundred in 1880 to twenty thousand two decades later. That was enough to fill the steerage quarters of several large liners per year. The Red Star Line's most significant competitive edge was that third-class rates on its ships were the cheapest on the North Atlantic. Antwerp, unlike Hamburg, did not fight the steamship companies over the thousands of Jewish migrants who arrived each year at the city's train station. Red Star's competitive disadvantage, however, was that it did not have a formal concession from Berlin for Russian immigrants to pass through Germany on their way to Belgium. Russian Jews managed to get through to Antwerp anyway. Red Star did set up an agency in Warsaw, the capital of the Russian province of Poland, as a way to encourage Jewish migrants to book passage on its steamers. It also printed Yiddish advertisements for distribution in the Russian Empire, competing directly with HAPAG and North German Lloyd. Thanks to the Red Star Line, Philadelphia became a major port of entry for Russian Jews.

In May 1898, Ballin traveled to London to finalize a new agreement that would allocate the immigrant trade among four principal competitors, including Griscom's Red Star Line, but leaving the British lines out of the equation. NDL and HAPAG's control of the Prussian border crossings gave the two German lines enormous leverage. In the agreement, which would expire in five years, North German Lloyd would get 44.14 percent of all westbound steerage traffic, HAPAG 30.71 percent, Red Star Line 15.37 percent, and the Holland-America Line 9.78 percent. The agreement would come to be known as the Nord Atlantische Dampfer Linien Verband, or the NDLV pool.

The formation of this new steamship cartel was how Griscom and Ballin first made contact. How Morgan and Griscom met in 1899 is not recorded, but Drexel & Co. had long served as banker to the International Navigation Company. Perhaps that's how they came to know each other. What was recorded was Griscom's pitch. He sold Morgan on the idea of a big express steamer departing on a transatlantic journey once a week without fail:

> In this way, mails would go forward without delay, and a man who wanted to sail for the other side would not have to wait, unless for his favorite ship. Eventually, it would be as simple as going up to the Grand Central Terminal and getting a train to Chicago or San Francisco on any day of the week.

The idea of a shipping trust greatly appealed to Morgan's sense of order and desire for control. And Morgan liked the railroad language Griscom used to explain its value—a transatlantic trip could be as easy as "getting a train." Although he realized that the special relationship with the Belgian government was nice to have, it wasn't enough to control the North Atlantic passenger market. He decided that he had to woo the shipping companies of Great Britain and Germany over to his side. Given his bank's extensive social and financial ties to Great Britain, Morgan felt that buying out or at least partially controlling the British shipping lines would be easy work.

Germany, however, was a puzzle to Morgan and his partners. Morgan had attended university at Göttingen but did not seem to have acquired much love or affinity for German culture. His heart lay with Great Britain, as his father's had. He may have also associated German financial power with Jewish banking houses, most notably the House of Rothschild, which he tolerated in the same way he did Kuhn, Loeb & Co. Morgan could have approached Ballin. He had already heard reports about

Albert Ballin's brilliance, as well as his skill as a negotiator. Yet Morgan was reluctant to work with him, not least because he was Jewish. He may also have heard that Ballin might be too independent to become any kind of subordinate.

From Hamburg, Albert Ballin kept tabs on the conversations going on between Griscom, Morgan, and the heads of various British lines between 1899 and 1901. His most valuable source of information was Viscount William Pirrie, the head of the Harland & Wolff shipyard and a close friend.

Although Ballin knew that the American railroads were crucial to HAPAG's freight business, he also knew the immigrant business was the most valuable asset in his entire portfolio, and that Morgan would not leave HAPAG alone in its drive to consolidate the shipping business worldwide. Ballin had to keep Morgan at a distance, all the while reassuring Kaiser Wilhelm II that he would not sell out his company to a British-American trust. It was only a matter of time before Morgan would make his move.

Within a few years, Griscom's $13 million financing request from the Morgan bank had grown into a full-fledged takeover bid of almost every shipping company on the North Atlantic. The new corporation would be called the International Mercantile Marine, or IMM for short. Morgan's first target was the Leyland Line, which specialized in cargo. But the chairman of the company, John Ellerman, proved shrewder than anticipated. He was able to charge very high freight rates because Britain needed men and matériel to fight the Boer War. And so he raised his asking price from $8.5 million to $11 million based on the projected new revenue stream. Morgan and Griscom agreed to the price and continued their buying binge. Next came the Atlantic Transport Line of Baltimore, then the Dominion Line, which operated passenger and freight service between Liverpool, New England, and Canada.

In 1901, Morgan and Griscom decided to go after the White Star Line, which operated a fleet of crack transatlantic liners that sailed between Liverpool and New York, as well as a fleet of smaller vessels that operated between Great Britain and Australia. Under the management of Thomas Ismay, the White Star Line had prospered for over forty years. Its fleet consisted of first iron- and then steel-hulled steamships that combined groundbreaking technology and extraordinary levels of luxury in first class. Unlike its competitor Cunard, which built solid, fast, but relatively plain ships, White Star sold a service with an aristocratic feel that aspirational Americans, including J. P. Morgan, really loved. The advances in White Star marine technology were in no small part due to the drive of the Harland & Wolff shipyard, run by Ismay's business partners and Ballin's friend William Pirrie, and the Hamburg natives Gustav Christian Schwabe and his nephew Gustav Wilhelm Wolff. White Star also made some profits from the immigrant trade, as their ships stopped in Cherbourg and Cobh, Ireland, to pick up steerage passengers.

Cunard may have been the recipient of a Royal Mail subsidy, but by the mid-1890s its ships were growing increasingly out of date and dowdy compared to Ismay's glamorous and sleek White Star liners. No matter how big or small, Ismay's ships tended to have a yacht-like elegance to them, a style also honed in the drafting rooms of Harland & Wolff. It was a look that appealed to J. P. Morgan, a frequent passenger, and to Albert Ballin, another passenger. White Star was also a real moneymaker, taking in much more money than Cunard. It earned 50 percent more per ship tonnage than comparable American lines, including Griscom's American Line.

Ismay's successful turnaround and expansion of the White Star Line made him one of England's richest men. A demanding parent, he groomed his eldest son, Joseph Bruce Ismay, to assume control of the company. Ismay died in 1899, and Bruce, as he was known, assumed the chairmanship of the White Star Line at thirty-seven. That was the same year that the self-made Albert Ballin assumed the leadership position at HAPAG.

Griscom knew that he needed a British partner and access to White Star's relationship with Harland & Wolff. Ballin knew that even though the Red Star Line was only a nuisance to HAPAG, it could become a real threat if it gained that partner. And if Morgan could raise enough capital to buy out or control HAPAG or its competitor North German Lloyd, Ballin's career as the "King of Steerage" would be finished.

But there were other players in this game. Harland & Wolff knew that to survive as shipbuilders, they couldn't rely on contracts from White Star alone. Partners Schwabe and Wolff, although nominally Protestant, retained contact with their Jewish extended family in Hamburg, one of whom was Albert Ballin. To expand business, Wolff reached out to Ballin with an unusual offer: he would be willing to offer HAPAG the same "cost-plus" arrangement that his shipyard had previously only had with White Star.

Ballin accepted the offer, and asked Harland & Wolff to build a series of new ships for HAPAG. Although loyal to German yards, he still wanted to find the best deal for his company. Harland & Wolff's first ship for HAPAG had been the SS *Pennsylvania* of 1896, the first of the lucrative four P-class immigrant carriers. The Anglo-Irish yard proved to be a good choice for Ballin, especially because the German shipyards were backed up with orders from North German Lloyd.

Because Albert Ballin had ships big enough to carry immigrants directly from Hamburg to New York, he had no need to rely on the British lines. And Ballin had no need to rely on Morgan's bankroll either. Thanks to all the money coming in from steerage tickets, his good relationship with German banks, and his relationship with Harland & Wolff, HAPAG was easily able to raise capital to invest in new ships and passenger routes, and to do it in style.

Still, Ballin watched Morgan cautiously. Above all else, he wanted to keep Morgan away from HAPAG's hugely profitable immigrant business. Then there was the matter of national honor. For all of his internationalist idealism, Albert Ballin was a patriotic German. Once impoverished, he had created a shipping firm with the same name recognition as other well-known German firms such as Daimler-Motoren-Gesellschaft, the Stuttgart-based producer of the new Mercedes automobile, and Thyssen AG, the Essen-based producer of steel. In first class, Ballin could also showcase the best in German art, design, and cuisine. But he knew very well that the steerage-class passengers, deep in the bowels of the vessel, were the key to his success.

Albert Ballin had one more card to play. HAPAG might have been one of Germany's most visible international companies, but it received no government subsidies, and none seemed forthcoming. Rather, it received an intangible blessing that Ballin considered more important than money: a seal of royal approval. The Kaiser's attendance at company receptions, ship launches, and parties aboard HAPAG steamers at the Kiel Regatta was regarded as the German equivalent of the British "royal warrant of appointment" with which high-quality purveyors were allowed to supply their goods to the royal family.

To survive the Morgan threat, Albert Ballin felt that he needed Kaiser Wilhelm's intervention, and the German monarch was more than happy to oblige. The problem was that tact was not one of Wilhelm's strengths, and Ballin had to carefully manage him without looking like he was doing anything of the kind.

CHAPTER 9

The Kaiser's Jews

Theatrical superficiality, impatience, an
overestimation of his own power in spite of
the best of intentions.

—MAX WARBURG ON KAISER WILHELM II

In the summer of 1901, the new forty-two-year-old general director of HAPAG, Albert Ballin, received an invitation to Potsdam to be received as Kaiser Wilhelm II's personal guest. "Darling, everything a person can become!" Albert wrote to Marianne. "I was picked up by an imperial page and have a splendid room here in the palace and will stay here until around evening. At one I'll join the family at the table. Will I still know how to be around you? With the warmest wishes for all of you and my love to you—Your Albert."

The letterhead bore the crest of the Neue Palast.

In private conversations, Kaiser Wilhelm II fell easily into the casual anti-Semitism that was rampant in Prussian aristocracy. He liked Jews who supported him and the monarchy, but he disliked those he considered socialists, trade union leaders, and advocates of the Zionist cause. They threatened his sense of German nationalism and destiny, and his own very fragile ego.

During his reign, Kaiser Wilhelm II couldn't resist the company of successful Jewish bankers and businessmen, not only because they added luster to his country, but they were helping him in Germany's quest to overtake Great Britain. When the Kaiser caught wind that his country's two shipping lines might be absorbed by a nascent American shipping trust, he knew he had to act. And that meant deploying Albert Ballin to stop the Americans.

As for Ballin, he was nothing if not loyal to the institution of the German monarchy. For all its flaws, Prussian rule of the empire had enabled people like him to rise higher than was ever possible in preunified Germany.

The crucial test for his loyalty to Germany came a few months after his visit to the Neue Palast. On October 16, 1901, Albert Ballin received a special summons from Kaiser Wilhelm II. He and the newly appointed Chancellor Bernhard von Bülow were to travel together to the hunting lodge at Hubertusstock for a two-day session with the monarch. For Ballin, it was a stunning invitation—even more so than the invitation to Potsdam. It also caught him at a very weary time. He had just spent the past few weeks in London with William Pirrie analyzing the new Morgan shipping trust's intentions for HAPAG.

Both men knew that J. P. Morgan was in the middle of negotiating the purchase of one of the biggest prizes in the shipping world: the White Star Line. J. Bruce Ismay, its new chairman, was the majority owner of a privately held entity and stood to profit handsomely should he sell out to Morgan. Ballin could not, of course, sell his company and pocket anything. Although he had amassed a handsome fortune for himself as HAPAG's general director, Ballin was a hired executive, not a company owner. He answered first and foremost to the company directors and shareholders. Unlike Ismay, the son and heir of the founder, Ballin could be unseated at any time for mismanagement. Early in his tenure, he had made enemies among his fellow directors. Ballin couldn't rid himself of the feeling that much of the animus against him did not stem from the business decisions he made but from old-fashioned German anti-Semitism.

Albert Ballin's desire to maintain German control over HAPAG was not out of national pride, although that was part of it. Rather, he felt that HAPAG would be a more profitable concern over the long run if it were not a subsidiary of a larger, American-based company. He also had a gut instinct about Morgan. He didn't think that the great banker really understood the transatlantic shipping business, especially the immigrant trade. If he could stave off being absorbed for just long enough, Ballin figured he could keep Morgan's hands off HAPAG.

Ballin knew exactly how to flatter Morgan. But first he had to flatter the Kaiser yet again. This time, it wouldn't be on Ballin's terms at a sumptuous party on a HAPAG liner at the Kiel Regatta. This time, he had to prove himself on the Kaiser's turf and on the Kaiser's terms.

Chancellor von Bülow and Ballin arrived at the station of Eberswalde on October 17, 1901, where a special horse-drawn carriage met them. They then rode for two hours to Hubertusstock, a squat, rustic, two-story structure of gray stone and dark wood clapboard. This was the Kaiser's special retreat, where he went fishing and deer hunting and engaged in other outdoor pursuits dear to the Prussian aristocracy but utterly foreign to urban Jews like Ballin. If he felt any unease in the setting, Ballin never betrayed it. And if he did, the Kaiser was probably too absorbed in his own thoughts on the agreement to pay Ballin's feelings (or his "speaking eyes") any notice. The Kaiser feared that the Morgan trust was going to take over HAPAG and NDL, just as it had bought out Leyland, Atlantic Transport, Red Star, and White Star, and he wanted Ballin's word that he would act in the best interests of the German Empire, not the HAPAG shareholders. It was only a matter of time before the Morgan trust started to buy shares in the two German lines.

Ballin's job was to reassure the Kaiser that he wasn't about to auction off one of Germany's most valuable and prominent corporate assets.

Albert Ballin enjoyed being admitted into the Kaiser's inner sanctum, away from the prying and often envious eyes of the Berlin court. "I was privileged to spend two unforgettable days in most intimate intercourse with the Kaiser," Ballin recalled of the meeting. "The Chancellor had previously informed me that the Kaiser did not like the terms of the agreement, because Metternich had told him that the Americans would have the right to acquire 20 million marks' worth of our shares. During an after-dinner walk with the Kaiser, on which we were accompanied by the Chancellor and the Kaiser's A.D.C., Captain v. Grumme, I explained the whole proposal in detail. I pointed out to the Kaiser that whereas the British lines engaged in the North Atlantic business were simply absorbed by the trust, the proposed agreement would leave the independence of the German lines intact."

The consummate listener, Ballin knew he had to play along with the Kaiser's harangues and to make it seem like he was in control of the negotiations. His biggest fear was that the Kaiser would step into the actual proceedings by telegramming Morgan, and ruin the whole deal. Albert was doing delicate work.

The other problem facing Ballin was Great Britain's Cunard Line, which was planning to divert steerage passengers from Hamburg and Bremen to ports in the Mediterranean. By the 1880s, when their steamships grew large enough to carry both first-class and steerage passengers, it was Ballin's Carr Line that shipped Continental migrants from Hamburg to the Cunard docks in Liverpool, which then carried them to New York and other American ports.

Yet while Ballin developed warm relationships with other English shipping firms, Cunard's management never seemed interested in any sort of long-term partnership with HAPAG or with him. Cunard preferred to build its ships in Scotland rather than in Belfast, and never once thought about constructing a ship at Pirrie's Harland & Wolff. Because of their mail subsidy, and perhaps because of a streak of British nationalism, Cunard saw itself as a British company, first and foremost. Participating in the NDLV pooling arrangement was an affront to British sovereignty.

A few days after the private meeting, the Kaiser summoned the heads of Germany's two greatest shipping companies, HAPAG and North German Lloyd, to Berlin. Ballin and Heinrich Wiegand had always battled for royal patronage and approval, and to be recognized as *the* national steamship line of Germany. By the time of the meeting, the Kaiser had grown increasingly partial to HAPAG and Ballin. Now, in the face of Morgan's trust, the two men realized that if they did not act as one, both HAPAG and North German Lloyd would lie prostrate before the American giant. Ballin and Wiegand left the meeting under royal orders to come up with a solution: a profit-sharing agreement between Morgan's shipping trust and the two German lines.

The result, as hammered out by the banker Adolph von Hansemann in 1901, was an arrangement in which Morgan's trust paid the two lines a fixed annual sum. In return, the German lines would pay the trust a portion of their future dividends. The two firms could not have received better financial counsel. Hansemann was one of the shrewdest bankers in Germany, and his bank, the Gesellschaft-Disconto, helped finance industries in the Ruhr Valley, as well as imperial enterprises in Samoa, New Guinea, and China. HAPAG was part and parcel of an imperial strategy.

Ballin and Wiegand decided to maintain absolute secrecy. If any aspect of the negotiation was leaked to the press, the public would be outraged and the deal would come apart.

Back in New York, Morgan and his team evaluated the German shipping lines' response. They could make a hostile bid for them or cooperate in a shared community of interest. Morgan decided that with the strength of the White Star Line and an infusion of federal dollars to support American shipbuilding, he could consolidate control of shipping on the North Atlantic without the German lines. But he had another thought about getting the best of HAPAG without having to buy the world's biggest shipping line outright. If he couldn't buy HAPAG, maybe he could buy its brilliant managing director.

Ballin did not know he was part of Morgan's plans. Here's what he did know, in the wake of the deal: He concluded that Morgan's shipping trust was an overcapitalized paper tiger that had paid inflated prices for its British assets. The only way the trust could make money was if IMM swallowed HAPAG and North German Lloyd whole. And it hadn't.

The Kaiser was thrilled that Morgan had agreed to the revised treaty and the new profit-sharing solution. He asked Ballin if he could arrange for a meeting with J. P. Morgan aboard his yacht SMS *Hohenzollern*. Ballin was happy to oblige.

* * *

Meanwhile, as J. P. Morgan focused on shipping in the North Atlantic, another game was afoot—this one in New York. Jacob Schiff decided it was time to show Morgan he was not willing to play second fiddle in the lucrative railroad business. Consorting with Union Pacific president and longtime client Edward Harriman, Schiff directed Kuhn, Loeb to wrest the Northern Pacific Railroad from J. P. Morgan's control. Throughout the spring, Kuhn, Loeb used their ample cash reserves to buy up 420,000 shares of Northern Pacific common stock and 370,000 shares of preferred stock to the tune of $79 million. Jacob Schiff's funding came from a deep-pocketed backer: William Rockefeller Jr., a brother of John D.

Rockefeller and cofounder of Standard Oil. The lesser-known Rockefeller was also a longtime Kuhn, Loeb client.

Jacob Schiff's Kuhn, Loeb & Co. served as the primary investment bank for the mighty Pennsylvania Railroad, the nation's largest and most powerful, and with this move on Edward Harriman's Union Pacific, he threatened Morgan's control over the railroad industry. J. P. Morgan and his bank served as adviser to almost all the other railroads. Morgan himself had direct or indirect financial control of over 55,000 miles of American railroads. He didn't want to lose it.

J. P. Morgan, who was in France at the time, responded by ordering his team to buy up the majority of the remaining stock to retain his control of the railroad. Giddy smaller investors, jumping on the bandwagon, followed suit. Northern Pacific's stock price rose as high as a thousand dollars a share, before crashing spectacularly in May 1901 and nearly bringing the whole New York Stock Exchange down with it.

Jacob Schiff and his Union Pacific backers ultimately failed to gain control of the Northern Pacific, but his personal wealth remained unscathed and his confidence in his own abilities undimmed. He also felt zero remorse about what happened. Schiff had demonstrated to J. P. Morgan that he was a formidable foe. Schiff wrote a sarcastically polite note to Morgan, warning him not to look down on Kuhn, Loeb & Co. Schiff said that his firm was "entirely ready to do anything in reason that you may ask or suggest, so that permanent conditions shall be created which shall be just to all interests and not bear within them the seeds of future strife." He concluded with a pleasantry, that "the rest of your stay abroad be pleasant and not interrupted by any unsatisfactory events."

That Schiff had dared to cross him made Morgan furious. He left France for London, a city mourning the recent death of Queen Victoria. Once there, he made social rounds with members of the British elite, whom the Morgans, father and son, had assiduously courted for half a century. Yet even then, Morgan couldn't quite escape the world of Schiff and Ballin as he toured Windsor Castle with King Edward VII, client and confidant of Sir Ernest Cassel, Schiff's private banker. When Morgan set sail from Southampton on June 28, he booked a stateroom in first class not on a White Star liner but on the brand-new SS *Deutschland*, HAPAG's new flagship liner.

Deutschland was now the fastest ship on the North Atlantic, setting a westbound record of five days, twelve hours, and twenty-nine minutes the previous summer, with an average speed of just over 23 knots. Up until then, the fastest ship in the White Star fleet was the RMS *Oceanic*, with a top speed of only 19 knots. Maybe Morgan wanted to get home as fast as he could, but he no doubt took a close look at the flagship of his newest takeover target, which had financial ties to his foremost rival on Wall Street.

The key for Morgan's shipping trust to truly work was his network of American railroads, something Albert Ballin recognized early on. Every week, the ships of the growing HAPAG fleet tied up at the Hoboken piers, adjacent to three railroad terminals that could carry passengers and freight to Chicago, St. Louis, and other Midwestern cities with big immigrant populations. For steerage-class passengers, the spire of the Central Railroad of New Jersey Terminal less than a mile across New York Harbor from the Ellis Island reception hall beckoned. Passengers arriving on the British steamers, though they experienced the thrill of arriving in Manhattan, had to cross the Hudson River by ferry to get to the railroad terminals.

Jacob Schiff had his own ideas about what the railroads could do. New York, he feared, was becoming too crowded. The awful conditions on the Lower East Side, he felt, threatened the physical and moral health of his people. He began to encourage Jews to settle in other parts of the United States, away from the Eastern Seaboard to the smaller cities in the heartland. He was also afraid that the crowded conditions would empower aristocratic gentiles such as Senator Henry Cabot Lodge to stop the largely unchecked flow of Jews from Russia. That, Schiff knew, would be a virtual death sentence for hundreds of thousands of Jews still trapped there.

That same year, 1901, as J. P. Morgan and Clement Griscom planned to turn the North Atlantic shipping business into a trust, Jacob Schiff authorized the purchase of a few million shares in HAPAG for Kuhn, Loeb & Co.'s portfolio. The infusion of American capital was fortuitous, because Albert Ballin had just started construction of the *Auswandererhallen*. The company also needed capital to finance the expansion of its port facilities and maintain its fleet. Two years later, in October 1903, Adolph von

Hansemann, head of the Gesellschaft-Disconto and HAPAG's principal financier, dropped dead at his desk in Berlin. Ballin owed a great debt to Hansemann, as he had personally engineered the profit-sharing agreement with IMM that kept HAPAG out of Morgan's direct control.

Even with Schiff's money in hand, Albert Ballin needed additional funds. He decided he wanted more out of the relationship with Max Warburg than invitations to leisurely evenings at the Warburg family mansion overlooking the Elbe. Culturally and socially, Ballin felt at home with the Warburgs, and the friendship between Max and Albert deepened into a profound emotional bond. Max admired Ballin's fierce ambition, and was willing to help finance his dream of making HAPAG the preeminent shipping firm in the world.

While Schiff and Ballin planned, J. P. Morgan was focused on another endeavor. He was putting the finishing touches on U.S. Steel, the world's first billion-dollar corporation. In order to create a virtual monopoly on the production of the commodity used to build rail lines, skyscrapers, and steamships, he had to convince the wily Scottish immigrant Andrew Carnegie to sell the Pittsburgh-based steel manufacturing concern that he had started in 1874. Carnegie Steel Company ran fifteen steel plants in western Pennsylvania and was a major consumer of coal and coke. Its annual profits hovered in the $20 million range, making Carnegie one of the richest men in the country.

Despite Morgan's overtures, Carnegie was initially reluctant to sell his enterprise. An immigrant success story, he had created a steel behemoth from scratch. But Carnegie was in his mid-sixties and thinking about retirement. He had married late in life and had a four-year-old daughter whom he wanted to see grow up. Through Carnegie's intermediary Charles Schwab, Morgan and his partners finally made the Scot an offer he could not refuse: $492 million. Of this staggering sum, about $226 million would be paid directly to Carnegie. The press and the financial community were absolutely stunned by the deal.

The U.S. Steel purchase was revealed to the public on March 2, 1901. Carnegie became the first American corporation capitalized at over $1 billion. The corporation was a vertically and horizontally integrated marvel, able to churn out steel with such efficiency that its only real competitor was the Bethlehem Steel Company, controlled by the Wharton family of Philadelphia. Carnegie's share was delivered in the form of $226 million of 5 percent gold bonds, held in a steel bank vault in Hoboken, New Jersey. The body of his immense fortune, the largest in America, was only a stone's throw away from the main HAPAG shipping piers on the western bank of the Hudson River.

A pile the size of Andrew Carnegie's was within the realm of possibility for Albert Ballin, the poor Jewish boy from Hamburg. All he had to do was arrange for the sale of the company he had built to J. P. Morgan and cash out his managing director's shares.

Even after the Carnegie deal, Albert Ballin still wasn't interested. He couldn't betray his monarch or his country. He also had his own favorite banker, one who was of his own tribe.

* * *

Every morning, beginning in the 1890s, Albert Ballin would walk from the Rotherbaum to the HAPAG offices on the Alster Lake with Max Warburg. Dressed in top hats and tailored suits, the two of them chatted about politics, shipping, finance, and even matters of personal health. Their friendship had begun when Albert and his wife, Marianne, lived in the Rotherbaum. Albert shared a garden fence with Max's brother Paul, and the two enjoyed the over-the-hedge talks. Paul, recently married to the American-born Nina Loeb, decided that Ballin was a good person to know.

Jacob Schiff's daughter, Frieda Schiff Warburg, noted in her memoirs that the American and German branches of her family were close and constantly visited each other. Of her aunt Nina and uncle Paul, she wrote: "Paul and Nina lived for seven years in Hamburg and both their children, James Paul and Bettina, were born there. 'The Pauls' led a rather retired, quiet life in Hamburg, though they had many interesting friends." When Max assumed de facto leadership of M. M. Warburg in Germany, his brothers Paul and Felix couldn't resist the pull of America. They also knew that as younger sons, their prospects were better at Kuhn, Loeb & Co. in New York than with the family bank. Although Paul loved Hamburg, Nina missed New York and her extended family. In 1902, Paul and Nina moved to New York, where he almost instantly became a partner at Kuhn, Loeb, along with his brother Felix, while also retaining his position at M. M. Warburg.

Ballin surely knew that M. M. Warburg & Co. had unparalleled access to American capital markets through its sister firm, Kuhn, Loeb & Co. HAPAG was a mighty business concern, but Ballin, with no prominent relatives, understood that the Warburg firm had the power of family on its side. Nina Loeb Warburg was the daughter of Solomon Loeb and the sister of Jacob Schiff's wife, Therese. By "adopting" the Warburgs into his orbit, Ballin acquired the prominent Jewish family that he, of course, never had. Blood could be more powerful than a balance sheet.

And Ballin had something to offer in return: Max Warburg, who, despite professions of his Jewishness, still had a "*meschügge*" desire for acceptance in gentile society. Ballin gave Max entrée into the life he had created for himself in Hamburg and elsewhere. Max may have been a prince in Hamburg, but his world remained relatively circumscribed by the dictates and expectations of his family and the Hamburg Jewish community. Ballin, on the other hand, felt no such constraint.

When Paul Warburg sailed off to America, he left Max as the undisputed heir apparent, while older brother Aby buried himself in his book collection and father, Moritz, focused on Jewish philanthropy. Into the gap stepped Albert Ballin. Albert and Max became great friends. They were both Hamburg Jews, but there the similarities ended. The HAPAG general director might have been polished and genial, but he worked hard to hide a ferocious temper. Max, on the other hand, always kept a breezy, unflappable exterior.

On those morning walks, after reaching the stock exchange, Albert and Max would part ways, the former walking through the doors of the HAPAG headquarters at Alsterdamm and the latter going to the headquarters of M. M. Warburg & Co. at Ferdinandstrasse 75. There, both were greeted deferentially by dozens of employees as they strode to their respective offices and began their day's work.

Their morning chats were not enough. A private phone line connected their offices and the two could continue their conversations throughout the day without fear of eavesdroppers. But while Max knew how to relax at home, Ballin didn't and couldn't. He worked sixteen hours a day, often seven days a week. His worried colleagues persuaded him to work from his study at home on Sundays, rather than sit alone in his vast office at the HAPAG headquarters. Ballin always felt like he was on the brink of catastrophe. Perhaps he would be ousted in a corporate coup, tossed out of HAPAG forever, and forced to start over again. His being hard on others was rooted in the exacting standards he imposed on himself. According to biographer Peter Stubmann, he could, "while shaking physically, treat personalities to whom he normally attended with elevated manners with a sharpness that could lead to difficult situations." He then would regret his rage and try to repair the damage. "After such scenes the friendly and winning manner with which he attempted to lay differences aside could surprise the people he offended."

Whatever the stress at work, Ballin was devoted to his family, including his adopted one. In 1900, Max and Alice welcomed their son, Eric, into the world, and they asked Albert to be the baby's godfather, albeit in an unofficial capacity, as Judaism did not recognize the role. Then again, Max and Alice always ordered their butler to hide the German breakfast ham if Papa Moritz dropped by for an impromptu visit.

Albert doted on Eric the same way he did on his daughter, Irmgard. He and Marianne frequently visited the rambling Noah's Ark, the centerpiece of the Warburg family's "Kösterberg" country retreat in the fashionable Hamburg suburb of Blankenese. Max Warburg's relatives from New York were also frequent visitors, including Paul and Nina Warburg (known in the family as "Panina") and their children, Jimmy and Bettina. Felix and Frieda, known in the family as "Friedaflix," often visited as well.

"From our house," Max's nephew Jimmy Warburg would write later, "high on the hills overlooking the Elbe, I could watch an endless procession of ships of many nations going to or coming from every part of the world. . . . At the approach of the big Hamburg-America liners I would run up to the attic to dip the American flag, hoping for and sometimes getting a whistle-salute in reply from one of the captains who knew the family as frequent passengers."

But visits to Kösterberg did nothing to soothe Albert Ballin's nerves. He dealt with his stress-induced insomnia by taking sleeping pills, then more sleeping pills. He also made an increasing number of trips to fashionable spas, where he mixed recuperation with schmoozing and intelligence gathering.

Ballin was anxious but determined to protect HAPAG's interests.

"What was the secret of his personality?" Max Warburg would ask rhetorically about his friend. And his answer: "The harmonious tone of his voice, his good, firm handshake. His rare gift of being able to connect to everyone. His palpable desire to help, to console, and rarer yet, to celebrate in his heart with others [*sich innig mitzufreuen*]. The combination of these attributes gave him a power of attraction and produced an atmosphere that no one could escape. He had one more great gift—a robust sense of humor. His memory never failed and he knew well how to tell the many stories he had accumulated in his life."

Albert Ballin looked at Max and saw someone who had the self-confidence and optimism that he severely lacked. Max looked at Albert as someone who had overcome obstacles as a poor Jew to rise to the top of HAPAG and, hopefully, have the ear of Kaiser Wilhelm. Max was still a relative stranger to the larger world of German high society. Albert Ballin would be Max's guide to a whole new world, to the supposed center of the Wilhelmine power structure.

For all his outward confidence, Ballin's place in his nation's firmament was precarious, and he had to work hard to maintain it.

Perhaps he wondered if it was worth it. Soon, he would be presented with the opportunity to move to America himself, not as a poor immigrant but as a celebrated master of his profession. Maybe his position would be different there, though it would mean turning his back on his country and his homeland.

CHAPTER 10

Morgan's Big Offer

Anyone who saw Morgan going from the Clearing
House back to his office that day will never
forget the picture. With his coat unbuttoned
and flying open, a piece of paper clutched in
his right hand, he walked fast down Nassau
Street, his flat-topped derby set firmly down
on his head: his eyes fixed straight ahead.
He was the embodiment of power and purpose.

—HERBERT SATTERLEE ON HIS FATHER-
IN-LAW, J. P. MORGAN

After the Northern Pacific debacle in 1901, J. P. Morgan grudgingly admitted that Jacob Schiff was his equal in banking. Unhappy about being fought to a draw, Morgan would later privately snipe to Lord Revelstoke, head of Baring Brothers & Co., that "our firms and his were the only two companies composed of white men in New York." But Morgan would soon find himself up against another Jew who proved more than his equal in the shipping lanes of the North Atlantic.

Ballin had realized that if Morgan were able to create a completely integrated land and sea routing structure, HAPAG would find itself in trouble. The trick was to be part of the deal while retaining independence for his company. That thinking was the basis for the profit-sharing agreement that Morgan had accepted earlier that year. Morgan's shipping combination itself still wasn't, in his estimation, a danger to HAPAG or NDL. "The real danger, however," Ballin concluded, "threatens from the amalgamation of the American railway interests with those of American shipping."

In February 1902, Albert Ballin arrived in New York for a series of dinners and meetings with the directors of the soon-to-be-unveiled International Mercantile Marine to finalize the alliance between the Anglo-American and German lines. Accompanying him on this trip were Dr. Wiegand and President Georg Plate of NDL, as well as C. F. Tietgens, chairman of HAPAG's board of directors. It was Ballin who had convinced his rivals at NDL to meet with the Morgan people, arguing that the command they had over America's railroads was just too vast to ignore. During the entire crossing, Wiegand and Plate felt a bit like they were on a trip to the scaffold.

The meetings began on February 13, 1902. After Ballin met the executive team of the IMM in its Empire Building offices at 71 Broadway, the group adjourned for dinner at J. P. Morgan's townhouse at Thirty-Sixth Street and Madison Avenue. It was here, in the name of creating a community of interest on the North Atlantic, that J. P. Morgan cast aside his personal prejudices. Morgan felt it wise to present a strong, united front before the public. He was getting ready to take IMM public, and he couldn't afford an attack from his erstwhile rival Jacob Schiff over his budding transatlantic investment.

MORGAN'S HOUSE was a hulking brownstone, understated compared to some of the grand limestone French châteaux that were popping up to the west on Fifth Avenue. Ballin, never one to overlook beauty in art and architecture, was dazzled by the Louis Comfort Tiffany interiors, the shimmering electric lights (the first in a private residence in New York City), and the European art treasures that his host compulsively collected. Among them were three Gutenberg Bibles, touchstones of German high culture that Albert Ballin so loved.

There was more pageantry to come. Kaiser Wilhelm's younger brother Prince Heinrich of Prussia had arrived in New York City aboard the North German Lloyd flagship *Kronprinz Wilhelm*, as part of an official state visit to the United States. The timing with the meeting at Morgan's house was not a mere coincidence. The German steamship lines wanted to show the American financiers that Ballin and Wiegand had the full blessing of the government in Berlin to protect German interests. Also in port for the occasion was the imperial yacht *Hohenzollern*, dressed in flags and painted a gleaming white. Ballin would no doubt have preferred to have the royal party sail instead on his own flagship, SS *Deutschland*, but the spirit of cooperation meant more than jostling for position.

Even with Prince Heinrich on board, the *Kronprinz Wilhelm* was still on a regular commercial crossing. First class boasted a large coterie of reporters covering the voyage, as well as the usual group of affluent Americans and Germans who enjoyed seeing the Kaiser's brother in the dining saloon and strolling on deck. Not everyone got to rub elbows with the royals. Also aboard were seven hundred immigrants in steerage, many of them Russian Jews, who must have marveled when they saw Prince Heinrich standing on the bridge to salute the American fleet. After fleeing pogroms and enduring the indignities of the baths and border control stations, they might have wondered if the thundering guns, parade of ferry boats, and cheering crowds were there to welcome *them* to America!

When they did arrive, the prince greeted dignitaries on the royal yacht, and tenders pulled up alongside the big German liner to shuttle the immigrants to the new Ellis Island facility where, like hundreds of others that day, they would endure questioning, medical examinations, and hours of waiting. At the end of their stay in the Great Hall, they would be sorted by the infamous "stairs of separation": those walking down the left side of the staircase would be staying in New York, those on the right were going on by rail to other parts of the country, those in the center were being detained for further examination and possible deportation.

A public health official pulled each suspected case aside and marked their lapels or dresses with one or more of several abbreviations. Among them were:

- "EX" meant further examination.

- "X" meant potential insanity.

- "C" meant eye problems. Trachoma, a bacterial infection that led to blindness, meant automatic rejection.

- "S" meant senility.

Other conditions that were grounds for rejection included lameness, tuberculosis, cholera, epilepsy, and nail or scalp fungus.

It was the new immigration commissioner, William Williams, who implemented the "scientific" practices as part of processing the ever-growing number of people who arrived in New York every year. The facility was now operating at more than full capacity. In addition to the main processing hall, where the vast majority of immigrants passed without incident, there was a hospital, office space, several dormitories (which resembled the open steerage compartments on older transatlantic liners), baggage rooms, kitchens, and a big dining hall that was built for fifteen hundred, but often served over three thousand diners at a time.

About one in five new arrivals were detained for further examination. Only 2 percent of all twelve million arrivals at Ellis Island during its peak years of operation, or about 150,000 people, were sent back to their country of origin. But that statistic was no consolation to separated families, and terrifying to Russian Jews who knew that a return to the shtetl meant conscription in the czar's army, persecution, or even death at the hands of the Cossacks, or, at the very least, a life of poverty at the margins of an increasingly strife-ridden Russian Empire.

But these concerns of the immigrants were not discussed at J. P. Morgan's townhouse that night. Every man was likely focused on business: Morgan needed to placate Ballin so that he would keep his word about the profit-sharing agreement worked out with the Kaiser and the Gesellschaft-Disconto. Ballin's mission was to make sure HAPAG and NDL remained German companies, no matter what Morgan and his cronies threw at him. And both Schiff and Ballin knew that the immigrant business was the key to making money in the transatlantic trade, and they had it firmly in their pockets.

For their part, J. P. Morgan and Clement Griscom felt that the Germans had been contained. The International Mercantile Marine, crowned by the White Star Line, could proceed with its public offering. For Griscom, the goal was to secure a $40-million-a-year subsidy from Congress for the trust's operation, an amount that would make it more than competitive with its deep-pocketed European rivals.

Given Morgan's track record and his own history as a loyal Republican, Griscom hoped to win over White House support. His expanded fleet, he reasoned, would create jobs and transport even greater numbers of cheap immigrant labor to the United States. His prospects had improved in November 1901, when Theodore Roosevelt took the oath of office after William McKinley's assassination. A war hero and an imperialist, Roosevelt was also a major proponent of American naval expansion and overseas trade and was relatively friendly to immigration.

Although these men carefully plotted each part of their agreement around Morgan's glittering dinner table, things would not go as planned. A major conflict halfway around the globe would further destabilize the Russian government and cause even more Russian Jews to immigrate to America.

*   *   *

On February 4, 1902, the White Star Line agreed to the buyout from the Morgan interests. Shareholders would receive a total of $50 million, an astonishing amount of money for the shipping line. The American combine now was comprised of White Star (sailing out of Liverpool and Cherbourg, France) as the luxury line; Red Star (sailing out of Antwerp) as the immigrant line; American and Dominion as middle-market lines; and Leyland and Atlantic Transport as the freight carriers. IMM also had a controlling interest in the nominally independent Holland-America Line, which carried a substantial number of Russian Jewish immigrants out of Rotterdam, although nowhere close to the number sailing out of Bremen or Hamburg.

Throughout the negotiations, Albert Ballin and Heinrich Wiegand had preserved their profit-sharing agreement with IMM. At a meeting of the HAPAG stockholders in May 1902, when Albert Ballin and his fellow directors informed the public of the deal, the German press reacted gleefully. "[T]he blow to England is all the greater since the German companies have been able to keep out of the trust and maintain their independence," trumpeted the *National Zeitung*.

Following the agreement, Morgan and Griscom hoped that they could get the British government on board with the American combine. In the spring of 1902, while the German press hailed Ballin's triumph, Morgan met with Joseph Chamberlain, then the colonial secretary, to unveil the deal. Morgan thought his shipping alliance would be met with open arms. Instead, the typically suave Chamberlain exploded into a fury at a formal dinner. Britain's shipowners were selling out one of her most valuable assets, her colony-supporting merchant marine, to the highest bidder. Chamberlain couldn't stop the deal, but he could make life harder for Morgan and his backers by refusing to give the new company the government's blessing. Chamberlain asserted that the British-flagged ships, even if owned by an American firm, could still be requisitioned for wartime use should England need them. Above all, Chamberlain was incensed that Morgan had made a separate arrangement with Albert Ballin that kept the German lines independent, while buying up the British lines outright.

Chamberlain walked away from the dinner enraged, and the British papers turned against Morgan and his shipping trust.

The newly elected prime minister, Alfred James Balfour, decided to work with Parliament to maintain Cunard's independence, even if it couldn't block the White Star acquisition. Cunard's management saw what was happening as a golden opportunity: they might finally get a government subsidy to rebuild its transatlantic fleet to compete with the technologically superior German liners that were dominating the tourist and immigrant trades. Cunard also hoped to siphon off Jewish and Italian immigrants from HAPAG by expanding its Mediterranean service. Seeing that the British weren't willing to play along with this new "community of interest," Albert Ballin decided that Cunard had to be brought to heel.

Stung but still determined, Morgan sailed back to New York and then took the train to Washington to meet with Senator Mark Hanna, who had sponsored the bill to grant IMM a congressional subsidy. The Republican power broker gave the banker some bad news. The Senate had passed the bill and sent it to the House for approval, but with a new stipulation that ships built abroad were ineligible for congressional support. The main concern was that should war break out in Europe, the British government would commandeer the company's ships for military use, crippling America's merchant marine and endangering America's neutral status in any conflict to come. That had been exactly what Chamberlain had asserted.

Morgan was now looking at a major problem. The British government couldn't block the White Star acquisition, but without Cunard and an American subsidy, he was now saddled with a money-losing collection of ships that didn't have full control of the lucrative immigrant market. If he announced the deal was off, the Morgan bank would be out the $11 million he had fronted for the Leyland Line, as well as the money he had put up for Griscom's American companies to build expensive new ships in U.S. yards.

As Morgan sat in his study, smoking cigars and playing solitaire, he asked himself whether he should cut his losses and run or ram the deal through and make the best of it. If he could organize the chaotic American railroad system into an efficient and hierarchal system of corporations, surely he could make his new maritime venture pay off. He also harbored much bigger plans for Albert Ballin than the profit-sharing agreement that had been struck several months earlier. But Ballin didn't know that yet.

In June 1902, J. P. Morgan recrossed the Atlantic aboard his yacht *Corsair* to celebrate the unveiling of the shipping trust and to get the formal blessing of Kaiser Wilhelm II. For Albert Ballin, Morgan's visit required the most delicate hosting imaginable. Also aboard the *Corsair* was Clement Griscom, the new president of IMM, and Peter A. B. Widener, the Philadelphia streetcar tycoon who was among the biggest investors in the new venture.

The *Corsair* sailed from Dover on July 1 and arrived at Kiel the following night after enduring very rough weather. At daybreak, Albert Ballin, smiling and cordial, came aboard by launch, and greeted Morgan and everyone in his party. In the distance lay anchored a familiar sight: the imperial yacht *Hohenzollern*, herself the size of a small ocean liner, with two raked funnels and bedecked in festive signal flags. Now thrust into the dual role of HAPAG chief and royal host, Ballin informed Morgan that the Kaiser would receive him aboard the *Hohenzollern*.

The bulky Morgan, unaccustomed to any kind of physical exertion, clambered into a launch and soon found himself face-to-face with Kaiser Wilhelm. Wilhelm, as usual, did all the talking, as the two men strode up and down the deck. Despite his dislike of small talk, Morgan was impressed with the Kaiser, as he had clearly spent a lot of time thinking about what the "community of interest" on the North Atlantic meant for

Germany's stature in the world. The two men also enjoyed comparing notes on their yachts.

Ballin was delighted that the meeting went well. He knew that the House of Morgan connected British and French capital to American enterprise, and hoped that cordial relations between Morgan and the Kaiser would reduce the chances of a war in Europe. Although Theodore Roosevelt was president, Ballin knew that Morgan was more like a monarch. He had essentially bailed out a volatile American economy during multiple administrations. The House of Morgan was the equivalent of America's central bank.

Afterward, Ballin hosted Griscom, Morgan, and Widener at the Kiel Yacht Club. The party then left Kiel for Hamburg, where Ballin acted as master of ceremonies on a grand tour of his hometown. Anne Morgan, who accompanied her father on the German visit, found Albert Ballin's choreography over the top, and was more impressed with the Kaiser than the reputed self-made genius Albert Ballin. "You must have seen some account of it in the papers," Anne Morgan wrote to her mother about Ballin's tour of Hamburg, "but no description could half tell you how funny it was. All the party driving around Hamburg in about seven landaus—an enormous lunch of thirty at the smart restaurant."

After the lavish banquet at the Restaurant Pforde, Albert Ballin went the extra mile on the Fourth of July when he hosted a magnificent party at his home. The following day, Ballin chartered a small yacht and gave Morgan, Griscom, Widener, and their families an informal "review" of HAPAG's fleet. The next morning a special steamer took everyone around the harbor—"A brass band on board & all the Hamburg line boats dressed with flags." Among the vessels lined up in tribute to the Americans was the SS *Deutschland*, still the holder of the Blue Riband for the fastest crossing of the Atlantic and one of the largest vessels in the world.

For his part, J. P. Morgan was impressed with Ballin's display of pomp and pageantry. He also deeply appreciated how the HAPAG director arranged an introduction with the Kaiser. So after seeing the might of the HAPAG fleet, Morgan decided the time was right to make Ballin an offer he could not refuse. He would turn the so-called King of Steerage into the "King of the Atlantic."

Sometime during the visit, most likely during the Fourth of July festivities, the banker sat down with Ballin in his study. To the point, Morgan asked if Ballin would take the top job at International Mercantile Marine. If Ballin accepted the managing directorship, he would be personally in charge of hundreds of vessels, flying the flags of Great Britain, America, Holland, and Germany. He would no longer be responsible to HAPAG's other directors, nor would he have to deal with the hated Hamburg maritime unions.

The salary would be an astonishing $1 million a year, plus commissions and a bonus. Although Ballin was already quite wealthy, this offer would make him one of the richest men in the world. This would also almost certainly mean a move to New York City, headquarters of IMM.

Albert Ballin thought about it for a minute. "Neither he nor the HAPAG could be bought," he said.

Ballin stayed behind in Hamburg while Morgan and his coterie of plutocrats went on to Berlin, in a special saloon carriage that Albert had procured for the party. After bidding them adieu, Ballin went to his office to handle the day-to-day affairs of his company. Morgan, he hoped, would bask in the prestige of a private audience with the Kaiser. He would then, Albert also hoped, be distracted by another social affair back in London: the delayed coronation of Edward VII of Great Britain on August 9. The Morgan party then sailed home on a ship flying the flag of IMM's newest crown jewel: the White Star Line. There wouldn't be much time to spend thinking about Ballin's rejection.

The International Mercantile Marine was publicly unveiled in October 1902. In total, J. P. Morgan had raised $50 million in capital to support the creation and initial operation of the International Mercantile Marine. In return, he got to seat two of his firm's partners on the new company's board of directors, a fee of 5,000 shares of preferred stock valued at $85 per share, and 50,000 shares of common stock valued at $35 per share. This came to an expected value of about $2.2 million, not much considering the size of the deal. Morgan, Griscom, and Widener hoped there would be plenty of upside to the stock price. John Ellerman and Bruce Ismay, on the other hand, hedged their bets by demanding all or part of their buyouts in cash.

For his part in the negotiations, Albert Ballin got no compensation from J. P. Morgan & Co. or the trust organizers. His payoff was keeping HAPAG independent. Nor did his friend William Pirrie, principal owner of Harland & Wolff, get any stock or cash compensation. What he got came in the form of future shipbuilding contracts. IMM could not build any new vessels in Europe except at Harland & Wolff.

Albert Ballin had survived Morgan's visit, and achieved his—and his country's—aims. Privately, Ballin was gleeful at the howls of protest from the British public. "What makes the people in England feel most uncomfortable," he wrote in his diary, "is not the passing of the various shipping companies into American hands, but the fact that the German companies have done so well over the deal."

Albert Ballin knew that Kaiser Wilhelm had played a key role there too. He understood that the only way his shipping company HAPAG could flourish was to pay frequent homage to the Kaiser's whims and love of pomp. Kaiser Wilhelm II had real power. The chancellor, or *Reichskanzler*, the official head of the civilian government, reported directly to the monarch and served at his pleasure. In the words of Ballin's admirer, Chancellor Bernhard von Bülow, his role at the end of the day was to serve as "the executive tool of His Majesty, so to speak, his political Chief of Staff."

For now, Ballin treasured his relationship with Wilhelm and was a committed monarchist. Yet he knew Wilhelm had severe personality problems and needed constant guidance. And though Ballin needed men like the Kaiser or J. P. Morgan, he always kept in mind a lingering question: were the people on the other side of the table anti-Semites?

In America, Jewish religious leaders still didn't quite know what to make of the Kaiser or his relationship with Ballin and the shipping magnate's Jewishness. "The attitude of the Emperor continues to be as puzzling as ever," Rabbi Maximilian Heller of New Orleans observed in the fall of 1903, "with one hand he lavishes decorations on the great promoters of German commerce, such as Albert Ballin . . . wishing it to be understood that patriotic merit will be awarded regardless of race or faith; with the other he lightens the penalties of anti-Semites."

It was an attitude that would torment Ballin for years to come and eventually endanger all of Germany's Jewish population.

In the meantime, the immigrants who left Germany—and Russia, and other countries throughout Europe, who felt the threat of anti-Semitism more acutely—continued to stream across the Atlantic. Their steerage fares might have been pennies to the likes of Morgan and Ballin, but their plans were just as intricate, yet far more fragile and fraught. For these Jews, it was not a matter of profit and loss, but of life and death.

Part III

CHAPTER 11

The Weinsteins: One Journey of Many

For he shall give his angels charge over
thee, to keep thee in all thy ways.
    They shall bear thee up in their hands,
lest thou dash thy foot against a stone.

—PSALM 91

B y 1904, Max and Sophie Weinstein-Bacal made the difficult decision to leave everything they knew behind in Iași, Romania. Once a prosperous businessman, Max Weinstein-Bacal had been in the grain business, most likely as a middleman between the fields of Romania and the Russian city of Odessa, the closest major port to Iași. The economic unrest of the early 1900s, as well as frequent pogroms and boycotts, had, according to his granddaughter, wiped him out, and he "had turned over whatever silver and jewelry there was left to a sister for money enough to transport his family to the promised land—the new young world, America."

Iași was the city that the Weinstein-Bacals and their ancestors had lived in for centuries. Its population was about 40 percent Jewish, big enough to support several grand synagogues, vibrant Yiddish theater, sports clubs, and well-attended lectures by the likes of author Sholem Aleichem. There was also a thriving community of Jewish classical musicians and a small army of skilled craftsmen who made fancy clothes, watches, clocks, liquor, and furniture.

The Kishinev pogrom, touched off a year earlier in neighboring Moldova, was the tipping point for the Jews of Iași. Spurred on by their Russian neighbors, Romanian anti-Semitic newspapers and Orthodox clergy had emboldened gentile mobs to taunt and beat Jews in the streets. Students regularly vandalized Jewish-owned shops. The police stood by and did nothing. Now classed as "objectionable aliens" by the government in Bucharest, Jews were formally excluded from Romanian universities. In response to international protests, the Romanian government smugly responded that "whatever persecution they had endured they had fully deserved in consequence of their exploitation of the rural population."

Worse still, a politician named Alexander C. Cuza was gaining support among the peasants and the middle class for a new far-right party called the Democratic Nationalists. Among their planks was that Jews were systematically exploiting the average Romanian citizen.

According to *The Jewish Encyclopedia*, there were about 250,000 Jews living in Romania at the time. Of these, "it is admitted that at least 70 per cent would leave the country at any time if the necessary traveling expenses were furnished."

Early that year, Max and Sophie gathered their children—four-year-old Renee, three-year-old Natalie, two-year-old Albert, and one-year-old Nellie—and told them that they were leaving home for a new land. They could only bring what they could carry in their hand luggage. They would be boarding an enormous boat, bigger than Noah's Ark, that would take them across the sea to a new land, where they could live in peace. Above all, Max must have told his children, they must stick together and trust their parents. And they should be brave and avoid crying at all costs. Inspectors might mistake red eyes for trachoma, which meant certain rejection at the already-feared Ellis Island.

To get to Hamburg and America, the Weinstein-Bacals would have to sneak across the German border, like so many before them. If successful, they would then endure strip searches and fumigations, prodding by inspectors, fitful rest in flea-ridden guesthouses, and hours on the hard wooden benches of rattling railroad carriages. Some of the refugees would have papers, but many did not.

For Max and Sophie, the four-thousand-mile journey by land and sea would be choreographed like a military exercise. It was also extremely expensive. The total cost of obtaining passports (or, more likely, paying a smuggler), getting a medical exam at the Romania-Germany border control station, train fare, steamship tickets, food and lodging, and the $50 required by American authorities at Ellis Island amounted to $435 for an entire family, or about $8,878 today.

For the typical Russian Jewish tradesman, who only earned about $250 to $300 in a single year, this was a staggering sum. Sometimes a father like Max would travel alone to America, get a job, and send money home to Russia not just to support his wife and children but to save enough to buy steamship tickets for them. But Max and Sophie Weinstein made the difficult and expensive decision to stick together as a family. In the back of her mind, Sophie feared being *agunah*. It was not uncommon for the husband to travel to America alone, fall in love with someone else, start a new life, fail to send money home, and ultimately leave his wife and children destitute in the Old Country.

Most likely, Max purchased tickets for his family at a HAPAG agency in Iași run by one of Ballin's associates. Although the two big German lines, HAPAG and North German Lloyd, had agreed to form a cartel and share steerage passengers, that didn't stop either from employing agents who directed would-be immigrants toward favored lines. One of the most successful agents in Romania was Friedrich Missler, who was based in Bremen. Allied with North German Lloyd, he had a whole network of offices that displayed colorful posters boasting of the company's Four Flyers. By 1902, when the Weinstein-Bacals were planning their voyage, images of powerful-looking four-funneled liners had flooded the towns of Eastern Europe. To people who had never been to sea, a ship with four funnels conveyed power, speed, and safety.

Friedrich Missler also built and operated a group of barracks for steerage passengers in the Findorf district of Bremen, which he ran with North German Lloyd. They were modeled after Ballin's Emigrant Village in Hamburg. By subcontracting out much of the "dirty work" of emigrant processing, NDL's management reasoned, they could protect their image and shield themselves from liability.

Albert Ballin, for his part, hated using outside agents. Instead, he wanted a vertically integrated system that processed immigrants from the branch office in a city like Iași all the way to the immigrant barracks and the gangplank to the waiting vessel in Hamburg. Such a system would give Ballin control over the entire journey and allow him to make money at every stage. He directed HAPAG to employ ordinary Jews (and gentiles), who made some money on the side selling tickets. These included priests, rabbis, schoolteachers, and other members of the petite bourgeoisie throughout Eastern Europe.

After Max came home with the steamship tickets, Max and Sophie began to prepare for the twelve-hundred-mile rail journey to Hamburg. They would have to carefully pack whatever provisions they would need for the train, including a few changes of clothes for everyone in the family. And they would pack light because they could only bring what they could carry. Household furnishings and other cumbersome items would have to be sold or left behind.

From Iași, the Weinstein-Bacals' train either sped through the mountains of Austria-Hungary, or more likely through the flat fields and forests of the Russian province of Poland. As Romanian subjects, the Weinstein-Bacals were not subject to the same draft-dodging laws as their Russian counterparts, and thus were free to pass through Russian territory. The journey to Warsaw took at least two days, after which they changed trains and headed for one of the border control stations along the Russian-German border, most likely Tilsit.

It was here, in the chaos of the border-crossing towns like Tilsit, that the sorting of would-be immigrants to America began. Smuggling them across the border was done with a complicit wink and a smile. "It can easily be understood that several emigrants escape examination at the border stations," wrote O. W. Hellmrich, the American deputy consul-general in Hamburg, "for the reason that Russia does not approve of emigration, except for Hebrews and Mennonites, and all emigrants arriving from Russia are smuggled across the frontier."

When Max and Sophie Weinstein-Bacal got off their sealed train at the Emigrant Village (*Auswandererhallen*) on Veddel Island, their children would have been bleary-eyed and exhausted from sitting for hours on rattling, hard wood benches. But the family found themselves in the cleanest, best-kept village square they had ever seen in their lives. They heard a brass band playing tunes, the shrieks of seagulls over the brackish Elbe, and the whistle of distant steam. A church steeple towered above them, a pointed one, not the onion-domed type they knew from back in Romania. Beyond it were the cranes and warehouses of Hamburg.

Others disembarked from the train, which hissed steam as it rested at the platform. There were many other Jews, dressed in dark clothes and speaking Yiddish. There were also a smattering of Poles and Russians. And there were lots of children. Unlike many other immigrant groups, Jewish families tended to travel together as a unit even though many had to save for years to make the journey or sell almost everything they owned if they needed to leave in a hurry.

After the Weinstein-Bacals crossed the train platform at Veddel, they walked into a wide tiled hall, illuminated by large windows. Above the main doors was a clock and the motto "Mein Feld ist die Welt" in Gothic lettering. There was also a mural showing the four-funneled liner SS *Deutschland* running at full speed through a turbulent sea. HAPAG posters hung on the walls. The Weinstein-Bacals then approached a big oak counter, where several clerks in pressed blue uniforms sat in front of ledgers. Here, immigrants gave their names and intended destinations, and received their ship and berthing assignments.

Depending on the passenger flow, the Weinstein-Bacals could be booked on a westbound ship immediately or forced to wait up to two weeks until there was room aboard. Unlike first- and second-class passengers, immigrants traveling in steerage didn't really get much of a say about which ship they took across the Atlantic. HAPAG might have prided itself on the luxury of their most expensive quarters, but down in steerage, accommodations looked pretty much the same across the fleet.

They would stay nearby until the ship set sail. The station at Ruhleben, although controversial in the press, had drastically cut down on the number of immigrants who were turned away at Ellis Island. When Hamburg's Emigrant Village was opened for use, it ensured that all migrants boarding HAPAG ships were sequestered from the Hamburg population and in quarantine for up to two weeks before boarding. During the construction of the *Auswandererhallen*, the city of Hamburg had paid particular attention to the plans for the removal of sewage, by then suspected as one of the main carriers of cholera and other infectious diseases.

The Weinstein-Bacals had two choices about where to sleep. For steerage passengers with little to no money, there were the communal barracks, with tiered bunks for twenty-two people per pavilion, communal bathrooms, and almost no privacy for traveling families. For those with a little bit more money, there was the Hotel Nord et Sud, a modest hostelry in the village that offered simple yet clean private rooms and a restaurant. The whole complex could house up to five thousand people at a time. For those housed in the barracks, there were matching and segregated kosher and nonkosher dining halls, both at the center of the complex.

It is not known how many nights the Weinstein-Bacals stayed at the Emigrant Village. If their time there included a Friday night, they probably attended Sabbath services at the synagogue provided by HAPAG. The sight of the church spire might have frightened them some. In Romania, the family had lived in an almost exclusively Jewish neighborhood, as the Romanian government had imitated Russia's anti-Semitic policies. Still, pogroms spiked around Easter. But the sight of HAPAG-employed security guards inspired confidence, and the uniformed employees of the Emigrant Village were not there to harass or persecute.

The Weinstein-Bacals lucked out on their ship. Rather than an older, slower vessel, they were assigned to the SS *Deutschland*, the largest and fastest liner in the HAPAG fleet. They also must have been thrilled to learn that their vessel, which had four big smokestacks, looked just like the ones they had seen emblazoned on HAPAG brochures and posters.

The Weinstein-Bacals would not board the SS *Deutschland* at the Emigrant Village. As a hired brass band again played marches and polkas, the immigrants would board a special train that would take them to Cuxhaven, sixty miles down the Elbe River from Hamburg, where they would board their waiting ship. When they got off the train, they tightly grasped their suitcases for fear that they would lose them in the dockside melee of people. A large domed structure greeted them. Known as the Amerikabahnhof, the baroque revival structure served both as a shipping and railroad terminal. A pair of stone-faced sailors stood guard over the entrance, which of course was engraved with the ubiquitous HAPAG motto.

Looming above the western quay was the SS *Deutschland*, her hull painted in gleaming black, her upper decks in sparkling white, and wisps of black coal smoke coming from her four smokestacks. The main waiting rooms, lit by electric chandeliers and equipped with comfortable seating areas, were reserved for first- and second-class passengers. Steerage passengers were herded into another big shed, topped with a timber-trussed ceiling. They would have heard a babble of languages echoing from the rafters—Yiddish, German, Polish, and Russian—punctuated by the cries of confused, frightened children.

Finally, they were ordered out onto the quay. A sloping gangway, with "Hamburg Amerika Linie" embossed on its canvas sides, led up from the quay to the forward well deck of the *Deutschland*. Max and Sophie gripped their children's hands, all the while struggling with their luggage, and headed up the gangway. Now they were aboard, standing with hundreds of their fellow passengers amid a clutter of trunks, suitcases, and carpetbags. Looming above them were a set of booms, as the steerage deck area also doubled as the cargo loading area. A group of stewards yelled at them in German, telling them that single men had to go one way, single women another, and families yet another. The Weinstein-Bacals descended one set of stairs after another, down into the bowels of the ship. Dim amber-hued lightbulbs illuminated the spaces below, and the smell of bilgewater got stronger and stronger.

Finally, the Weinstein-Bacals and many other family groups found their new home aboard HAPAG's flagship: a low-ceilinged dormitory, crammed with two tiers of bunks, with two and a half feet of space between them. Six-feet-long by two-feet-wide mattresses were stuffed with straw and covered with gingham or canvas slips. Partitions separated each berth, which were labeled with stenciled numbers. Electric fans whirred from the bulkheads. Crammed between the bunks were tables and benches. The family would be eating in the same space in which they slept.

"Our compartment was subdivided into three sections," wrote one steerage passenger, who was actually traveling undercover as part of a congressional fact-finding mission, "one for the German women, which was completely boarded off from the rest; one for Hebrews; and one for all other creeds and nationalities together. The partition between these last two was merely a fence consisting of four horizontal 6-inch boards. This neither kept out odors nor cut off the view."

HAPAG separated Jewish passengers from non-Jews for two reasons. One was to facilitate the serving of kosher food, a service that Albert Ballin started in the early 1900s to attract more passengers. The other was to prevent a pogrom from taking place belowdecks.

The Weinstein-Bacals moved quickly to claim adjoining bunks, but then discovered a problem. There was no place to change clothes or diapers in privacy. To give herself and her family a modicum of privacy, Sophie probably hung up a spare shawl or shirt in front of her berth. White porcelain chamber pots sat underneath the rows of bunks. SS *Deutschland*, like most modern steamships, was equipped with communal flush toilets in steerage, but many passengers had never before used indoor plumbing. The hissing and gurgling terrified many of them, especially the children. Though there was indoor plumbing, there were no showers or tubs in which to bathe.

At the appointed hour, on June 24, 1904, the captain of the SS *Deutschland* blew her whistles and ordered the crew to slip the lines that held her to the quay. Steerage passengers crammed into the narrow forward well deck, their only open promenade area, and watched the banks of the Elbe fade into the distance. The *Deutschland* picked up speed as she entered the North Sea, her mighty engines causing her to shake violently, especially down in her lower decks. The ship's vibrations would have shaken Max's and Sophie's bunks, rattled the lightbulbs above them, and made their feet tremble. There was no escape from the constant vibration. And then the North Sea swells caused the big ship to roll and pitch sickeningly from side to side.

The portholes offered little respite from seasickness. "You could see a lot of water, but you couldn't see the sky," one steerage passenger recalled. There was little air circulation too. "On one line of steamers, where the blanket becomes the property of the passenger on leaving, it is far from adequate in size and weight," wrote the undercover government agent. "Generally, the passenger must retire almost fully dressed to keep warm."

The ship continued into the night, passing the coast of Holland and then crossing the English Channel. In the confines of the "Hebrew" section of steerage, Max and Sophie would have grabbed their dinner pail and lined up for their first meal. "A table without appointment and service means nothing," recalled an agent. "The food was brought into the dining room in large, galvanized tin cans. There were no serving plates, knives, or spoons. Each passenger had only his combination dinner pail, which is more convenient away from a table than at it. This he had to bring himself and wash when he had finished. Liquid food could not be easily served at the tables, so each must line up for his soup and coffee. On inquiring where the passengers were seated when the steerage was crowded, I was told by the Hebrew cook and several others of the crew that then there was no pretense made to seat them."

To procure kosher food for HAPAG ships, Albert Ballin had enlisted the services of Hamburg's Jewish community, which would provide a rabbi to inspect the galley when the ship was in port and to certify the Jewish cook on board. To remove all blood from chicken, liver, and beef, the meat had to be soaked for half an hour in water, thoroughly rinsed, then salted for another hour. Any dried blood left over from the slaughter had to be removed as well. Liver, because it contained a lot of blood, was not salted, but rather broiled over a fire. Pails, and if they were provided, plates, had to be labeled for meat and dairy dishes.

Within the cramped confines of the SS *Deutschland*'s service areas, the kosher kitchen required its own separate space, as the pork-based foods favored by the non-Jewish steerage passengers could not mingle with the food for Jews. How the Jewish passengers knew the food dished out to them was kosher remains a mystery, but they had to go on faith. In the past, some Jewish passengers brave enough to cross the Atlantic brought themselves to the brink of starvation rather than eat pork-based steerage fare.

The SS *Deutschland* dropped anchor for a few hours at Dover, where a tender brought out more passengers and mail. Most of the new arrivals were first- and second-class travelers, who had taken a special train from London for the chance to sail on the fastest ship on the Atlantic. There were also mazes of gates and barriers that kept first- and second-class travelers from steerage. In the bulletins posted in the foyers, these new passengers were told that they were not permitted to throw leftover food from their promenades down to the steerage-deck areas.

The voyage was in the summer so the weather was generally calmer than it was during the brutal winter months. Still, Max and Sophie found the ship's dormitory uncomfortable. There was constant talking and snoring, and the space was rank with the smells of body odor, vomit, and unwashed laundry. Narrow, fast ocean liners like *Deutschland* were also bad rollers. They corkscrewed violently in rough seas, sending plates, cutlery, baggage, and occasionally people flying into the air. And then there was the continuous thumping of the ship's powerful engines.

In calm weather, the Weinstein-Bacals ventured out as a family onto the cramped forward well deck for air. Here, they presented a curious sight for passengers in the upper two classes. Many turned up their noses at them. Yet others were fascinated. Photographer Alfred Stieglitz, a well-heeled German Jew traveling on the North German Lloyd luxury liner SS *Kaiser Wilhelm II*, was taken by a group of steerage passengers he saw from the forward first-class promenade. He rushed back to his stateroom, grabbed his 4x5 Auto-Graflex camera, and took a single photograph.

Stieglitz would later recall what he saw:

On the upper deck, looking over the railing, there was a young man with a straw hat. The shape of the hat was round. He was watching the men and women and children on the lower steerage deck. . . . A round straw hat, the funnel leaning left, the stairway leaning right, the white drawbridge with its railing made of circular chains—white suspenders crossing on the back of a man in the steerage below, round shapes of iron machinery, a mast cutting into the sky, making a triangular shape . . . I saw shapes related to each other. I was inspired by a picture of shapes and underlying that the feeling I had about life. There were men and women and children on the lower deck of the steerage. There was a narrow stairway leading to the upper deck of the steerage, a small deck right on the bow with the steamer.

The photograph depicted several mothers, their heads covered in shawls and kerchiefs, and many young men wearing worker's caps and bowler hats. The scene is cluttered with the machinery of a modern ocean liner: bollards, the base of the forward mast, railings, ladders, and a catwalk that connects the forward superstructure with the forecastle. The passengers are doing their best to create some semblance of domesticity in such a foreign setting: children playing, mothers holding babies, and a makeshift clothesline hanging between two deck stanchions.

Not a single person in the image is smiling.

Stieglitz titled his geometric image *The Steerage*, and it became an icon of modern photography.

The Weinstein-Bacals would spend a few more days in these conditions.

After a five-and-a-half-day passage from Dover, SS *Deutschland* sped past Ambrose Lightship and dropped anchor at the Staten Island Quarantine station sometime on July 28. Along with picking up the harbor pilot, the captain also greeted the U.S. health officials, who quickly screened all passengers for any contagious diseases.

Her papers in order, SS *Deutschland* then proceeded through the Narrows and into New York Harbor. Here, immigrants on board caught their first glance at the shores of America. In the far distance loomed the skyscrapers of Lower Manhattan, many times taller than any church spire they had known back home. And then, to port, stood a green-and-gold-hued statue of a woman, holding her torch aloft.

Hundreds of immigrants ran to the port-side rails of their cramped deck area, doing their best to get a good look at the symbol of Liberty that they had heard so much about. At her base was the plaque inscribed with Emma Lazarus's poem "The New Colossus."

"America, America!" they shouted in rolling waves. Children sat on parents' shoulders; babies were held high in the air. Tears mingled with the cheers.

"It appeared like in a fog," one immigrant boy recalled, "and everyone went over to the railing, just admiring."

Even though she was one of the largest ships in the world, SS *Deutschland* leaned slightly to one side as so many people scrambled to the rails.

Yet along with hope, there was also fear on the horizon. Just past the Statue of Liberty loomed the red-and-gray edifice at Ellis Island, where their admission to America would ultimately be decided.

Among the immigrants landing in New York, about 90 percent were allowed immediate entry. And because they had passed numerous inspections in HAPAG's system, Max and Sophie Weinstein-Bacal had good reason to hope that they would move through Ellis Island the day of arrival. The looming fear was that one or more family members would be turned away, and that they would have to make a chilling decision: to stay together and go back to Romania or to split up. That's how Ellis Island got its nickname: the Island of Tears.

SS *Deutschland* tied up at the HAPAG pier at Hoboken. First- and second-class passengers disembarked with minimal fuss. A ferry was waiting to transport the steerage passengers to Ellis Island for thorough examination, questioning, and possible detention.

The Weinstein-Bacal family were among the fortunate. They made it through the terrifying gauntlet that was the Island of Tears. But in the process, they dropped the second part of their last name and became simply the Weinsteins. For the four-thousand-mile journey over land and sea, and through Ellis Island, Max and Sophie had kept their family together.

They moved into an apartment in New York City's Lower East Side, "wretched" in the words of one family member. A desperate Max borrowed money from the United Hebrew Charities, purchased a pushcart and a selection of household goods, and spent long days hawking his wares on the streets of the Lower East Side. It was a miserable existence, one that left the family traumatized for years. For Max and Sophie's children and grandchildren, the word *pushcart* was uttered only in whispers.

But it was worth it. They were together, and safe.

Not every family could say the same. Certainly not the Jewish citizens of Kishinev, located just across the Russian border in Moldova. The previous year, the city had been the site of one of the most violent pogroms in the Russian Empire. The whole world took notice of Russia's atrocities. Some demanded that the czar's government be punished for its policies. Others cheered them on.

CHAPTER 12

The Most Infamous Pogrom

The Russian Jewish element defies analysis.
With its Lithuanian, Volhynian, Bessarabian,
and other constituents, and its Galician,
Polish, and Roumanian tributary streams, it
is more complex than either of the two [Se-
phardic and German]. . . . But to say what
the Russian Jew is and can be in America is to
prophesy the course of the twentieth century.

—*THE IMMIGRANT JEW IN AMERICA*, 1906

The 1903 Kishinev pogrom in the Russian province of Moldova was sparked by the death of two children: a young boy found murdered in the town of Dubasari and a young girl who died in a Jewish hospital after she attempted suicide.

Kishinev, Moldova's capital city, had a population of about 150,000, about one third of whom were Jewish. Anti-Semitism was a cultural norm in Kishinev; the newspaper *Bessarabian* frequently published headlines such as DEATH TO THE JEWS. But in the past, Christians and Jews had lived together fairly harmoniously, at least for the Russian Empire. The deaths of the two children, however, set off a firestorm in the anti-Semitic press and whipped up anger among the Orthodox population. It even reignited the old myth that Jews used the blood of Christian children to make their matzos for Passover.

The Jews of Kishinev were a crucial commercial link between the port of Odessa and the cities of the Austro-Hungarian Empire. Moldova/

Bessarabia was known for its fine wine, and Jewish merchants were leading exporters of the product, as well as of tobacco, lard, wool, hides, and
fruit. About a third of the Jews worked as tailors and seamstresses, and
as skilled artisans in other trades. Although not nearly as wealthy as the
Jews of Odessa or Vienna, the Jews of Kishinev had carved out comfortable middle- and working-class lives for themselves. It was this fragile
prosperity, though, that stoked the smoldering resentment of the Christian population, especially the peasantry. How could this heathen group
be so prosperous if they didn't recognize the supremacy of Christ and
czar? Despite this resentment, the Jews of Kishinev persisted.

But by 1903, the squeeze of official sanctions of the Jews by the government in St. Petersburg was choking off the fragile prosperity. Then
the fictitious reports about the dead children set off a powder keg. On
Easter Sunday, April 19 (in the old Orthodox calendar), parishioners filed
out of Kishinev's Orthodox churches consumed with rage. Groups of
teenage boys, many of them drunk, began looking for homes that did
not have a white Easter cross chalked on their front doors. They were
joined by groups of seminarians and students from the local universities.
Gangs dragged Jews out of their homes, bludgeoned them with clubs and
axes, and set houses and businesses on fire. Blood ran in the streets, and
pillars of smoke rose from the houses of the Jewish quarter. The chief of
the czar's secret police yelled gleefully at the crowd, cheering them on.
The Orthodox bishop, riding by in his carriage and resplendent in his
vestments, made the sign of the cross with his hand and blessed the mobs.
The military commander of Kishinev, General Beckmann, did not order
the five thousand troops stationed at the garrison to intervene.

A Russian Yiddish newspaper reported on the carnage. It was smuggled out of Russia and the report was reprinted in English in the *New York
Times*:

> *The mob was led by priests, and the general cry, "Kill the Jews," was taken-up
> all over the city. The Jews were taken wholly unaware and were slaughtered
> like sheep. The dead number 120 and the injured about 500. The scenes of
> horror attending this massacre are beyond description. Babes were literally
> torn to pieces by the frenzied and bloodthirsty mob. The local police made
> no attempt to check the reign of terror. At sunset the streets were piled with*

corpses and wounded. Those who could make their escape fled in terror, and the city is now practically deserted of Jews.

The death count was later revised downward to 49. The number of injured rose to 592. In addition, 700 homes were destroyed and 500 businesses looted.

That December, thirty-seven men who had participated in the riots were accused of murder and put on trial. Twenty-one of them were convicted and sentenced to periods of hard labor ranging from six months to two years. The rest were acquitted. When the Jewish witnesses were called to the stand, they were forbidden by the judge to characterize the riots as anti-Semitic or imply that they were instigated by the press, the clergy, and the police.

President Theodore Roosevelt was horrified by the atrocities. Though he was nervous about upsetting the tentative diplomatic cordiality between the United States and Russia, he forwarded a petition from B'nai B'rith to the Russian ambassador, demanding an answer. At a meeting at a synagogue on the Lower East Side, Samuel Dorf, the Grand Master of the Order Brith Abraham, declared that "he would not be surprised if the Government at Washington took cognizance of the outrage, since it was deplored by all Americans, without regard to creed or race."

Jacob Schiff congratulated President Roosevelt for standing up to the Russians about the Kishinev massacre. "I have your valued communication of the 1st inst., in reply to my telegram of December 31," he wrote, "and I beg to express appreciation of the prompt attention you have given the suggestion concerning the rumors and fears about further excesses in Russia."

The Russian ambassador, Count Cassini, refused to receive B'nai B'rith's petition, asserting that the Moldavian peasants had legitimate grievances against the Jews of Kishinev. The Jewish population, he argued, had lent the poor Christians large sums of money at outrageous rates of interest.

"The situation in Russia, so far as the Jews are concerned is just this: It is the peasant against the money lender, and not the Russians against the Jews," the ambassador said in a statement. "There is no feeling against the Jew in Russia because of religion. It is as I have said—the Jew ruins the peasants, with the result that conflicts occur when the latter have lost all their worldly possessions and have nothing to live upon."

Cassini then claimed that Russia valued the Jews and treated them as full citizens of the empire. "There are many good Jews in Russia, and they are respected," he continued. "Jewish genius is appreciated in Russia, and the Jewish artist honored. Jews also appear in the financial world in Russia. The Russian Government affords the same protection to the Jews that it does to any other of its citizens, and when a riot occurs and Jews are attacked the officials immediately take steps to apprehend those who began the riot, and visit severe punishment upon them."

President Roosevelt forwarded B'nai B'rith's petition to Nicholas II himself, who refused to receive it. Throwing up his hands, Roosevelt then asked his secretary of commerce Oscar Straus and several of his well-connected Jewish friends to deal with the matter. Privately, he told Secretary of State John Hay that "the Czar is a preposterous little creature as the autocrat of 150,000,000 people."

Despite claiming that he was not leading a movement to promote Jewish immigration, Schiff joined several other prominent members of New York's German Jewish community to support the Kishinev Relief Committee. Among the committee of notables were Oscar Straus (who was also the brother of Macy's owner Isidor Straus), attorney Louis Marshall, *New York Times* publisher Cyrus Sulzberger, and mining magnate Daniel Guggenheim. The committee's purpose was to raise money to send to the survivors so they could rebuild their homes and feed their families.

Across the Atlantic, the powerhouse behind Germany's relief efforts for the victims of the Kishinev pogrom was Paul Nathan, the well-respected head of the Hilfsverein der deutschen Juden, known in America as the Aid Organization of German Jews. It was headed by Paul Simon Lasker, and included Paul M. Warburg among its active members. Nathan's organization was the principal funnel for relief aid from Germany's prosperous Jewish community. Their aim was explicit: to send funds to destitute Jews that would allow them to buy railway and steamship tickets and to facilitate their transit out of Russia and Romania. Starting in late 1904, the Hilfsverein stepped up its efforts by distributing newsletters known as *Correspondenblätter* throughout Eastern Europe. Essentially travel guides for the migrants, they provided up-to-date information about immigration law, German train schedules, and other helpful information about life in the United States. Given its outsize role in Jewish immigration, Hamburg had its own chapter.

During the next several months, the Kishinev Relief Committee raised and distributed $500,000 to the city's beleaguered Jews. It is most likely that many of them used the money not to rebuild but to prepare for a journey out of Russia to America. Indeed, the numbers at Ellis Island reflected it. The United Hebrew Charities, to which Jacob Schiff and many of New York's German Jewish leaders were generous donors, noted in its annual report that "the year 1903–1904 will go down in history as the one in which the largest number of Jewish immigrants arrived at the port of New York since the opening of the Immigration Bureau. A total of 89,442 Jewish men, women, and children passed through Ellis Island from October, 1903 to September 30, 1904." Out of these, the vast majority, 66,536, were from Russia, followed by 16,507 from the Austro-Hungarian province of Galicia, and 4,856 from Romania.

The Kishinev pogrom confirmed two things for Schiff. First, it destroyed whatever hopes Schiff had of working with the czarist regime, both as an advocate for the Jewish people and as a financier. It was also clear to him that Russia was on the eve of war with Japan over control of the western Pacific. Once it started, Russian Jewish men and boys would be among the first to be drafted into the czarist army. And Jewish immigration to America would explode. The only solution to Russia's treatment of her Jews, Schiff declared in a fury, was revolution, and "with all the bitter experience that involves."

Jacob Schiff and his Jewish allies focused on their efforts to encourage mass migration to the United States. They weren't alone. A number of ecumenical organizations began to spring up to encourage immigration to the United States and to prevent more restrictive laws from being passed. Chief among them was the National Liberal Immigration League, which was formed in reaction to the increasingly determined lobbying of the Immigration Restriction League. Housed in offices at 150 Nassau Street in New York, its leadership was primarily Christian, but they presented themselves as allies of the Jews and all immigrant strangers. Among its influential board members were Charles W. Eliot, president of Harvard University; Woodrow Wilson, president of

Princeton University; Bishop H. C. Potter; and Andrew Carnegie, the steel tycoon.

"From the earliest days of our history," the league declared in its literature, "there have been persons, who, disregarding the teachings of religion that men should love their neighbor and welcome the stranger, inveighed against the admission of immigrants of a different church or nationality than their own. The victims of this prejudice have been in turn, the Quakers, the Germans, the Irish, and now the Italians and the races of Eastern Europe. At one time the spirit of intolerance displayed itself in mob riots, and later it gave rise to systematic persecution by means of magistrates and officials opposed to aliens, and the enactment of rigorous immigration laws."

In the meantime, a curious new document was circulating all over the Russian Empire. Titled *The Protocols of the Elders of Zion*, it first appeared in 1902, on the eve of the Kishinev pogroms, purporting to be the minutes of a Jewish congress that detailed a Jewish plot to take over the world by toppling existing monarchies and seizing control of the global financial apparatus. Serge Nilus, a minor czarist official who "unearthed it," claimed that he had smuggled it out of a library in France.

"Our motto is Power and Hypocrisy," the *Protocols* stated. "Only power can conquer in politics, especially if it is concealed in talents which are necessary to statesmen. Violence must be the principle; hypocrisy and cunning the rule of those governments which do not wish to lay down their crowns at the feet of the agents of some new power. This evil is the sole means of attaining the goal of good. For this reason we must not hesitate at bribery, fraud, and treason when these can help us to reach our end. In politics it is necessary to seize the property of others without hesitation if in so doing we attain submission and power."

The tract was taken to be "proof" of the assertions that the czarist government and the Orthodox Church had been making for years. Jews weren't just responsible for the murder of monarchs and the spread of radical ideas, but were planning world conquest, not through traditional war but through deception. The *Protocols* of course were a complete forgery, the hackwork of Russian anti-Semites with ties to the czarist regime. Yet the idea of a massive Jewish conspiracy, responsible for all the world's ills, became popular not just in Russia but in Germany, France, and even the United States, where it was endorsed by Henry Ford.

As the document spread, it placed every Jew, even Jacob Schiff and Albert Ballin, in the crosshairs of populist anger in Europe and to some extent in the United States.

Schiff, Ballin, and the Jews of Germany and the German Jews in the United States generally shrugged off the hatred stirred up by the *Protocols*. But a young Russian Jew named Chaim Weizmann, who left his home country to study chemistry at the Polytechnic Institute of Darmstadt, had no illusions about German tolerance of Jews in the early twentieth century. Weizmann observed trends more dangerous than Cossacks on horseback. "Anti-Semitism was eating deep into Germany in those days," he noted, "a heavy solid bookish anti-Semitism far more deadly, in the long run, than the mob anti-Semitism of Russian city hooligans and prelates. It worked itself into the texture of the national consciousness."

It was the same sort of scientific racism being developed in the United States, a school of thought that saw Jews not as contributors but as inferior beings, parasites, and beyond redemption. Or, as the president of MIT, Francis A. Walker, put it, "beaten men, from beaten races."

The Immigration Restriction League offered no public commentary on the *Protocols*, but it fell in line with their fears about Jews and other non-Nordics flooding into America. From the sequestered summer splendor of Nahant, Massachusetts, Senator Henry Cabot Lodge was lobbying hard to ram another literacy test for migrants through Congress, as well as a head tax of three dollars per person. Once again, Lodge found himself stymied by what he thought were dark forces.

"By all means have the press take the matter up," he telegrammed IRL president Prescott Hall on December 2, 1902. "Railroads and steamship companies very active here and by letter they are objecting chiefly to a reading test on the grounds that we need more cheap labor for which there is great demand. They say also they are opposing three dollar tax which is absolutely necessary to carry on work. Do all you can."

Hall sent out letters to newspapers throughout the country, asking their editorial boards if they were for or opposed to immigrants, and to indicate which nationalities they wanted to come and which nationalities they did not want. He then kept a careful notebook of which papers he felt were sympathetic to his cause and started to send them IRL literature.

Already, respectable publications such as *Leslie's Monthly Magazine* were publishing articles spelling out the dangers of unrestricted immigration to the United States. "Every American citizen knows that the American immigration system is faulty," *Leslie's* argued in 1904. "He knows that the designing steamship officials dump the refuse of the world on our shores, despite futile restrictions and laws too easy to evade. These immigrants are the sort that cannot, even in years, become assimilated. They will not make good citizens: they are paupers and outcasts in their own country, who will never be any better anywhere." The magazine went on to say that the border control stations, the Emigrant Village, and even Ellis Island did not provide protection from the ills these new arrivals brought with them to the United States. "A physical requirement was the only one exacted," *Leslie's* complained. "The officials are compelled to take the testimony of the immigrant and his friends, and you may be sure they have been properly coached on the voyage. The right place to learn the truth is the old country villages, where the commune records show who are paupers, insane, criminals, prostitutes, social malcontents."

The IRL's message was starting to gain traction outside of a small, elite circle. It was increasingly covered in the popular media. The message was clear: America would not uplift the immigrant. Instead, the immigrant would drag America down.

*   *   *

As Jewish immigration swelled in the wake of the Kishinev pogroms, Morgan focused on his shipping trust. He and his German allies found themselves facing two foes. Of the major transatlantic lines, only Britain's Cunard and France's Cie Generale Transatlantique (known as the French Line) stubbornly remained independent. The French Line was heavily subsidized by the central government and thus could operate at a loss. Cunard, despite its mail subsidy, could not. It was saddled with an aging fleet and was starting to see its profits slip.

Cunard's ability to resist the Morgan merger faded in 1902, when one of its four flagship transatlantic liners had an embarrassing accident at sea. On the evening of February 26, eastbound from New York, the twenty-year-old RMS *Etruria* fractured her single propeller shaft and was helplessly adrift for hours. Eventually, the crew was forced to hoist sail and slowly head for the Azores, where her passengers were transferred to other vessels. Cunard's transatlantic business was left in shambles.

After the *Etruria* broke down, J. P. Morgan and Albert Ballin decided to act as a team. Their two shipping companies would make a bid to purchase majority stakes in Cunard and the Rotterdam-based Holland-America Line, which had already been granted a 10 percent share of all eastbound traffic according to its original shipping pool. But it was here that the directors on HAPAG's board stymied Ballin. He proposed to buy Cunard shortly after his return from New York in the spring of 1902. But the supervisory board balked at the cost. Moreover, word about the deal had been leaked to the British press. When the public learned about what was about to happen, it was hardly amused at the prospect of American and German interests buying up one of Great Britain's most visible companies.

But Cunard did not have nearly the same government support enjoyed by HAPAG or North German Lloyd, and so Morgan and Ballin persisted. Ballin had decided to play hardball with Cunard. His ships were already technically superior to Cunard's, whose two flagship steamers, RMS *Campania* and RMS *Lucania*, were built back in 1892. The two ships had long been eclipsed by German liners in size, speed, luxury, and steerage-passenger capacity. Cunard's two other big liners, the RMS *Etruria* and RMS *Umbria*, dated from the early 1880s. The two were built to carry sails and were powered by a single propeller when new vessels used twin screws.

Not only was Cunard's fleet of liners getting old, but the flow of immigrants from the British Isles, notably Ireland, was rapidly dwindling. Ballin used this to bring the British company to heel. As HAPAG and NDL funneled Jewish and other Eastern European immigrants through German ports, with no stopover in Liverpool, Cunard found itself in a cash crunch, unable to build new ships to compete. What's more, a Russian Jew with a Cunard ticket had a hard time crossing at the border control stations in Germany under HAPAG's control. Ballin did all he could to cut Cunard out of the Eastern European immigrant trade.

But Lord Inverclyde, the head of Cunard, refused to concede defeat and accede to Morgan's or Ballin's entreaties. To stave off a takeover, Cunard built a trio of emigrant carriers along the lines of HAPAG's P-class of liners. *Carpathia*, *Ivernia*, and *Saxonia* were big ships for their era, each about 14,000 tons, but were slow, with a service speed of only 15 knots, and thus burned relatively little coal. Each would carry only a few hundred in first and second class, but over twenty-five hundred in steerage. To get around Ballin's border crossings, Cunard would have the ships sail out of Trieste, the principal port of the Austro-Hungarian Empire. That way, Cunard could get the best of both worlds, siphoning off Jewish emigrants from Russia and Austria-Hungary, and Italian migrants coming aboard in Naples. Cunard inaugurated its Mediterranean service in 1903, and it was an instant success.

At the same time, Lord Inverclyde started to secretly lobby the British government for an operational subsidy, arguing that the Cunard fleet would be indispensable should Great Britain ever find itself in a major conflict, with Germany especially in mind. Inverclyde's brilliant strategy left Albert Ballin and his fellow directors at HAPAG enraged. It also infuriated J. P. Morgan and Clement Griscom at International Mercantile Marine. Their dream of a unified (and lucrative) community of interest on the Atlantic was slipping from their grasp. The loss of Cunard signaled the beginning of the end of Ballin and Morgan's short alliance.

Since it was now too late to buy Cunard or force it into a passenger pool, Ballin decided to wage war on the stubborn British company. He ordered agents at the German border to deny safe passage to anyone holding a Cunard Line ticket. This aggressive move eventually panned out. In 1904, a pogrom in the Russian province of Bessarabia sent even more Jews looking to cross the Prussian border. HAPAG was ready. So was Cunard. They fought for each and every ticket.

At the same time, IMM's poor financial performance intensified that conflict. IMM had showed itself to be no maritime juggernaut, at least on Wall Street. When Morgan and Griscom had created their trust, they assumed that freight rates would stay as high as they were during the Boer War, when demand for moving men and matériel was high. But after the war ended in 1902, freight rates between America and Great Britain dropped precipitously. This was a disaster for IMM's freight divisions, Leyland and Atlantic Transport.

In response, IMM and Cunard started a vicious rate war, one that would last from 1903 to 1905. Steerage was the main battleground, but first- and second-class rates plunged too. This conflict damaged all the North Atlantic shipping lines, but Morgan's trust, which was only then getting off the ground, suffered the most. Albert Ballin of HAPAG and Heinrich Wiegand at NDL slashed their rates by 50 to 60 percent, something that White Star and the other IMM lines could ill afford but did anyway. Ballin figured that because of his greater passenger volume, he could make up what he thought would be short-term losses at some later point.

There were consequences, for both Ballin and Morgan. And then the shipping war became a real war, as Japan set its eyes on Russia.

CHAPTER 13

Gaming the Russo-Japanese War

Wednesday, March 28th is the great gala day
for me personally, the private audience with
the Mikado being set for half past eleven
o'clock, luncheon to be served right after
the audience, I am told it is the first time
that the Emperor has invited a foreign private
citizen to a repast at the palace, heretofore
only foreign princes have thus been honored.

—JACOB SCHIFF, *OUR JOURNEY TO JAPAN*

Albert and Marianne Ballin's magnificent summer villa was in the lake-dotted town of Hamfelde, just to the south of Hamburg. The purchase price was 160,000 marks, which Ballin raised by selling his personal stake in the Nordsee Line, a small steamship company that HAPAG had absorbed in 1905. Fittingly, Nordsee's fleet provided service between Hamburg and North Sea summer resorts. Thanks to his handsome salary at HAPAG and Max Warburg's investment advice, the HAPAG general director was well on the way to being a millionaire.

Ballin quickly set about remaking the property into what he thought a gentleman's country estate should be. Just as he brought the latest technological innovations to his ocean liners, Ballin did the same for his new villa. Among them was the installation of hundreds of electric lights around the grounds, which allowed the gardens and lawns to be brightly illuminated for social occasions.

Ballin posted the rules of the house in the foyer:

We ask our honoured guests in their movements and dispositions not to be restricted by considering us. We will strive to make our friends feel at home while staying with us by our avoiding pursuing them with a mother's loving care and treating them like children. What so often spoils German hospitality is the expectation that one has to stick together the entire day and be "sweet" to one another. We do not expect our dear guests to behave nicely to us because they were invited, nor do we expect them to seek our society more often than they would prefer. Please dispose freely of cars, wagons, racing horses and rowing boats (as long as the supply suffices). We ask guests to determine themselves the time for the first breakfast and to give servants all relevant instructions. The second breakfast is usually taken jointly at 1. Afternoon tea at 4. Dinner about 7. 15 minutes before the beginning of the second breakfast and dinner the bell is sounded and a second time as soon as it is served.

Such language reflected the spirit of the service first-class passengers received on board HAPAG's liners. It was a way of luxurious living taken for granted by wealthy Hamburg families like the Ballins.

Yet Albert Ballin made sure not to drink to excess, because he chose to be in control of himself at all times. One drunken misstep or wrong word, and his delicate place in Hamburg society would forever be destroyed. He was, despite his growing personal wealth and status as general director of HAPAG, still only a corporate manager, a hired man, not the scion of an old shipping family.

"To appreciate to the full the charm of his personality one must have been his guest at his beautiful home in Hamburg or at his beloved country seat near Hamfelde," wrote his secretary, Bernhard Huldermann, "and have listened to his conversation while sitting round the fire of an evening, or been his companion on his long walks and rambles through the neighboring Forest of Hahnheide. His conversation was always animated, his witty remarks were always to the point, and he was unsurpassed as a raconteur. . . . He was very fond of music and congenial company, and he knew how to appreciate the pleasures of a full and daintily arranged table."

Though many in the Hamburg business community respected Albert Ballin as a force to be reckoned with, behind his back, members of the Hamburg Exchange coined a new term for the man's ego: *Ballinismus*.

Grumblings from jealous businessmen were not a new occurrence. Besides, Ballin had reached the peak toward which he had always been climbing. He had won the general directorship, and retained HAPAG's independence, in spite of Morgan's efforts. He had secured his hold on the immigrant trade, despite Cunard's resistance. And more, he had built a beautiful estate, won powerful friends, and held the ear of the Kaiser. The Russo-Japanese War would lead Ballin to risk all this, and more.

*   *   *

In the meantime, Jacob Schiff was making several major financial deals with Russia's new enemy: Japan. An impending war between the two countries would complicate Schiff's business dealings, and Ballin's, and others'.

The Russo-Japanese War, which lasted between 1904 and 1905, was a turning point in world history. During the conflict, a rising Asian power decisively defeated an established European empire. The shock waves resulted in an attempted revolution in Russia, and an even greater surge of people trying to get out. Albert Ballin made sure his company would benefit from the faraway war, a gamble that risked compromising his reputation.

Beginning with the Meiji Restoration in 1868, Japan had embarked on a rapid program of industrialization. Like Great Britain, Japan was an island nation whose culture was defined by ships and the sea. To compete with the great Western powers, Japan needed resources from abroad, and that meant building a modern navy that could secure a sphere of influence in East Asia from which they could procure the coal, iron, and other raw materials needed to build factories and railroads. In 1887, Foreign Minister Inouye Kaoru declared that Japan had every right to annex land in Korea and Manchuria because, as he put it, "What we must do is to transform our empire and our people, make the empire like the countries of Europe and our people like the peoples of Europe." The goal, he declared, was to "Let us change our Empire into a European-style empire."

For Russia, this was a big red flag. The country's eastern empire on the

Pacific Ocean shared borders with China and Korea and was weakly defended. Siberia, despite its mineral riches, was a barren and frigid wasteland that for centuries had been the equivalent of a death sentence for thousands of political exiles. Vladivostok, its only major east coast port, was choked with ice during the winter, making its use as a naval base limited at best. The Russian port still irked the Japanese, however, because of its location about 575 miles across the Sea of Japan.

To achieve their foreign policy goals, Russia and Japan each wanted to control Port Arthur (or Lüshun City), a seaport located near China's border with Korea that possessed an excellent natural harbor. Whoever controlled Port Arthur effectively controlled the Yellow Sea, which was also accessible year-round.

Ballin presciently smelled a war coming between Russia and Japan. When it did, he would have three main challenges. First was Kaiser Wilhelm, who loved nothing more than military bluster. He egged on his cousin the czar to prosecute a war against the Japanese, who he felt were not worthy of being seen as racial equals. Next, he knew that if war should break out, Czar Nicholas II would need to drastically step up the draft. This meant more civil unrest, more pogroms, and more Jews trying to flee across the Prussian border to Hamburg, desperate to board ships to America. For the long-term interests of HAPAG, Albert Ballin knew he would have to find a way for his passengers-in-waiting to circumvent the czar's conscription machine. Finally, Ballin also needed capital to build a new fleet of ships to compete with the new vessels IMM was planning to construct. By the early 1900s, many ships in his fleet were getting on in years. Compared to the new luxury liners from White Star and Cunard, *Auguste Victoria* and her running mates were small and cramped. The company's flagship, SS *Deutschland*, was the fastest ship on the Atlantic, but she was plagued by mechanical problems, most notably severe vibrations put out by her enormous engines. HAPAG's transatlantic workhorses remained the big but slow P-class emigrant ships.

So whatever feelings he had as a Jew, and any misgivings he had toward the Russian government, Ballin, with the support of his fellow directors, decided to make an arrangement of convenience with the government of Czar Nicholas II. He hoped it would solve those problems and more.

As war clouds gathered, he realized that to protect HAPAG's interests, he also had to become a diplomat. By its very nature, the steamship business was international in scope. Steamships exchanged people, goods, and ideas. They also projected national power. His friendship with the Kaiser is what gave him diplomatic influence.

On Christmas Day 1903, Albert Ballin sent a group of HAPAG emissaries to St. Petersburg. Their mission was to convince Czar Nicholas II to buy several of HAPAG's aging liners and freighters for the Russian Navy. But the commander of Russia's Baltic Squadron, Admiral Zinovy Rozhestvensky, was more interested in how he could get his existing fleet to Vladivostok should the rather small Russian Pacific Squadron need help. It was an eighteen-thousand-mile journey from St. Petersburg to Vladivostok. No ship in the world could carry enough coal to make a journey of that distance nonstop.

Ballin's emissaries proposed a novel solution: HAPAG would transport coal to various ports along the route to supply the Russian battleships and cruisers along the way. The coal would come from Wales, which meant it would be of much higher quality than the fuel available in Russia. By using German-flagged ships, the Russians could avoid dealing with Great Britain, a nation suspicious of Russia's motives in South and East Asia.

As for HAPAG selling the Russian Navy several of the company's older steamships, Ballin found that the Russians were eager to listen. Because the Russian Navy was desperate to replace its depleted Pacific fleet, it found the chance to acquire HAPAG's outdated but well-built liners a good deal. "On Christmas Day I sent some representatives to Petrograd who were to approach the government in case it intended to acquire any merchant vessels for purposes of war," Ballin wrote in his diary. "These gentlemen are still staying at Petrograd, where they have been all the time with the exception of a few weeks, and we have carried on some extremely difficult negotiations by cable which so far have led to the definite sale of the *Fürst Bismarck* and the *Belgia*. The *Auguste Victoria*, which is still in dock until the necessary repairs have been executed, has also been sold to Russia, and the prospects that the *Columbia* will follow suit are extremely good."

War broke out, just as Ballin predicted. On February 8, 1904, the Jap-

The young Albert Ballin as a schoolboy in Hamburg. An undistinguished student, Albert would make up for lost time as an adult, mastering English and developing a fine appreciation for art and design as well as business. His downwardly mobile childhood haunted him. "I think you and I were never young," he told a friend. "This involves freedom from cares—and in this respect we are both badly burdened."

(Source unknown)

Czar Alexander III of Russia, who reigned from 1881 to 1894. Blaming the Jews for the assassination of his father, Alexander encouraged anti-Jewish violence across Russia and enacted a program of military conscription meant to separate young Jewish boys from their families and eradicate their culture. Konstantin Pobedonostsev, his supreme prosecutor of the Holy Synod, declared of Russia's Jews: "One third will die, one third will leave the country, and the last third will be completely assimilated within the Russian people." Portrait by Ivan Kramskoi.

(Universal Image Group via Getty Images)

Migrants gathering in the "village square" of the *Auswandererhallen* (Emigrant Village) on Veddel Island, off Hamburg. Built by HAPAG in the early 1900s, it was strategically segregated from the city center and could house up to five thousand emigrants at a time. It included dormitories, two dining halls (one kosher, one nonkosher), a church, a synagogue, fumigation facilities, and a medical clinic. When the migrants boarded ferries that would take them to their waiting liners, they would be serenaded by a brass band. During the peak years of its operation, 43 percent of the people who passed through *Auswandererhallen* were Jewish.

(Wikipedia Commons)

Ellis Island sparked fear and dread among all arrivals to New York. Immigrants were subjected to batteries of medical exams and questioning. HAPAG's border checkpoints and Emigrant Village ensured that as few people as possible would be rejected from America and returned to Germany at the steamship line's expense. In the peak immigration year of 1907, more than one million people passed through its doors.

(Bettmann via Getty Images)

Orchard Street on the Lower East Side, circa 1890. The hub of Jewish life in New York in the late nineteenth and early twentieth centuries, it was a beehive of tenement apartments, shops, pushcart peddlers, and garment factories. At its peak, the Lower East Side had a population of 500,000 people per square mile, making it the most crowded urban neighborhood on earth.

(Wikipedia Commons)

A formal portrait of Jacob Schiff at the height of his power and influence. As the leader of the German Jewish "Our Crowd," Schiff strongly believed that Jews could assimilate into mainstream American society while preserving their ancient faith.

(Public domain)

The young John Pierpont Morgan as a student at the University of Göttingen in 1856. The son of a prosperous banker from Hartford, Connecticut, young Pierpont was given an international education that few other Americans could access. He proved to be brilliant at mathematics but was socially awkward and volatile. After an apprenticeship with the Philadelphia banker Anthony J. Drexel, Morgan went on to combine Drexel's and his father's firm of J. S. Morgan & Co. into a single financial entity. The House of Morgan grew to become one of the most powerful investment banks in the world. Privately, Morgan disliked Jews, writing that his firm and Baring Brothers "were the only two companies composed of white men in New York." That didn't stop Morgan from extending to Albert Ballin a very generous job offer.

(Smith Archive/Alamy Stock Photo)

Albert and Marianne Ballin, with their adopted daughter, Irmgard, circa 1895. Albert doted on his daughter, whom he nicknamed "Peter."

(Collection of Heinz Hueber)

Albert Ballin and Heinrich Wiegand (general director of Norddeutscher-Lloyd) traveling to New York to meet with J. P. Morgan and Clement Griscom to hammer out the details of the International Mercantile Marine agreement. Although the two men were bitter rivals in the immigrant trade, they believed it best to present a unified face when dealing with the American threat to their shipping empires.

(Hamburg State Archives)

As one of Germany's leading businessmen, Albert Ballin gained many enemies, as illustrated by this cartoon. Left-wing trade unionists used the term *Ballinism* to describe what they saw as the cold, ruthless power of German big business. On the right, one anti-Semitic politician said of of Ballin, "The strangers from Palestine and America have gained access to the highest steps of the throne." *(Hamburg State Archives)*

The aftermath of the Kishinev pogrom of April 19, 1903. On Easter Sunday, rioters rampaged through the city's Jewish neighborhoods, killing 49 and injuring 592. The sheer brutality of this pogrom sparked outrage on both sides of the Atlantic, and accelerated Jewish migration out of the Russian Empire.

(Wikipedia Commons)

A 1905 cartoon from *Judge* depicting President Theodore Roosevelt ordering Czar Nicholas II to leave Russia's Jews alone. Roosevelt detested Czar Nicholas II, calling him "a preposterous little creature," and denounced Russia's anti-Semitic policies. Jacob Schiff counted Roosevelt as a friend. Privately, though, the president supported many of the immigration-restriction proposals championed by his friends Senator Henry Cabot Lodge, Owen Wister, and others in the Immigration Restriction League.

(Wikipedia Commons)

The SS *Deutschland* of 1900, the flagship of HAPAG and the holder for seven years of the transatlantic speed record. In spite of her swiftness and luxury, she was troubled by severe vibrations, and her limited steerage capacity hampered her profitability. In 1904, she carried Max and Sophie Weinstein-Bacal and their children to America.

(Wikipedia Commons)

Senator Henry Cabot Lodge of Massachusetts, a founding member and vocal supporter of the Immigration Restriction League in the halls of Congress. He declared, "The gates which admit men to the United States and to citizenship in the great republic should no longer be left unguarded."

(Library of Congress via Getty Images)

Prescott Farnsworth Hall, president of the Immigration Restriction League. A lawyer by training, Hall feared that southern and eastern European immigrants would degrade America's genetic stock. He detested the German steamship lines and the pro-immigrant lobby, declaring, "To hell with Jews, Jesuits, and steamships!"

(Wikipedia Commons)

The banker Max Warburg, head of the Hamburg-based M. M. Warburg & Co. investment bank. The leader of Hamburg's Jewish community, Max was Albert Ballin's closest friend and confidant. His firm was intimately involved in the financing of the Hamburg-American Line and other leading German firms, and had a close relationship with Kuhn, Loeb & Co. in New York. Max loved Albert, describing him as "more an artist than an engineer, and more a painter than a draftsman." An optimist and German patriot, Max would eventually find himself a refugee, fleeing the Nazi regime in 1938.

(Estate of Emil Bieber/Klaus Niermann via Getty Images)

The public saw Kaiser Wilhelm II and Albert Ballin as close friends. In reality, their relationship was more complicated and ambivalent. The monarch admired Ballin's enterprise and patriotism but in private disliked Jews as a group. Ballin appreciated the monarch's enthusiasm for Germany's shipping but knew that he would always be treated as an outsider by the militaristic clique that truly held power in Berlin. Behind the scenes, Ballin worked hard to prevent a catastrophic war between Great Britain and Germany.

(Ulstein Bild Dtl. via Getty Images)

Kaiser Wilhelm II greeting Albert Ballin at the entrance of the Villa Ballin in Hamburg. Because of the monarch's frequent visits, the house was known as "Little Potsdam."

(HAPAG Archives)

Felix Warburg, the fun-loving brother of Max Warburg and son-in-law of Jacob Schiff. Schiff initially had his doubts about the young man's seriousness and piety, but Felix and his wife, Frieda, proved to be stalwart supporters of Jewish philanthropies, especially of those benefiting refugees in war-torn Europe.

(Bettmann via Getty Images)

The mansion of Albert and Marianne Ballin at Feldbrünnenstrasse 58 in Hamburg. Completed in 1910, Villa Ballin reflected its owners' refined taste and love of grand entertaining. It is now the headquarters for the UNESCO Institute for Lifelong Learning.

(Ullstein Bild Dtl. via Getty Images)

J. P. Morgan dressed as the commodore of the New York Yacht Club, one of his many social organizations. A successful consolidator of many industries, Morgan partnered with the Philadelphia shipping tycoon Clement Griscom to buy up all the major transatlantic lines. Morgan, who disliked Jews, did try to hire Albert Ballin away from HAPAG to run his new shipping combine. Ballin tactfully declined. For years, J. P. Morgan & Co. was locked in a bitter professional rivalry with Jacob Schiff and the Kuhn, Loeb & Co. firm.

(Bettmann via Getty Images)

Jacob Schiff giving a speech at a groundbreaking ceremony, circa 1900. As one of the wealthiest Jews in America, Schiff adhered to the principle of *tzedakah* by founding or contributing to countless philanthropic organizations. Most were groups working to make America a welcoming place to Jews. Among them were the Henry Street Settlement House, the Montefiore Hospital, the Hebrew Emigrant Aid Society, the Jewish Theological Seminary, and the Galveston Project.

(Hulton Archive via Getty Images)

Isidor and Ida Straus. An immigrant from Bavaria, Isidor was a co-owner of Macy's department store and one of the leaders of the German Jewish community in New York. His brother Oscar was Theodore Roosevelt's secretary of labor and the first Jewish cabinet member. Close friends of Jacob Schiff, the Strauses perished together in the sinking of the *Titanic* and became martyrs for the entire American Jewish community.

(Wikipedia Commons)

The cover of a Yiddish penny song memorializing Isidor and Ida Straus as Jewish heroes of the *Titanic* disaster. After refusing to get into a lifeboat and be parted from her husband of forty years, Ida said, "As we have lived, so will we die, together."

(Wikipedia Commons)

J. Bruce Ismay, chairman of the White Star Line and president of the International Mercantile Marine, at the U.S. Senate inquiry into the *Titanic* disaster. Widely criticized for boarding the last lifeboat to leave the ship, Ismay defended his conduct, claiming "the officer called out asking if there were any more women, and there was no response, and there were no passengers left on the deck." The year after the disaster, he resigned from the White Star Line.

(Bettmann via Getty Images)

The brand-new HAPAG superliner SS *Imperator*, the largest vessel in the world, departing Hamburg in 1913, with a passenger-carrying zeppelin flying overhead. Grossing over 50,000 tons, *Imperator* was able to convey 4,500 passengers, most of them emigrants in third class and steerage. The construction of *Imperator* and her sisters signaled Albert Ballin's severing of his profit-sharing agreement with the Morgan trust.

(Public domain)

The third-class dining room on the SS *Imperator*. HAPAG pioneered "third class," which offered more-affluent immigrants private cabins rather than dormitories and meals served by waiters in formal dining rooms. Although austere compared with first and second class, it was a major improvement over the crowded steerage class, which offered no privacy and rudimentary passenger service. Other lines, including White Star, copied this approach.

(Süddeutsche Zeitung Photo/Alamy Stock Photo)

Immigrants gathered on the forward decks of the SS *Imperator* as she arrives at her pier in Hoboken, New Jersey, in 1913. First- and second-class passengers would be processed by immigration officials on board. Third-class and steerage passengers would be taken by ferry to Ellis Island for processing and possible quarantine.

(Everett Collection/Alamy Stock Photo)

The first-class winter garden aboard the SS *Vaterland*, one of many grand public rooms aboard the vessel. A man of exquisite taste, Albert Ballin brought new heights of seagoing luxury to the HAPAG fleet. This included a contract with the Ritz-Carlton company to operate specialty restaurants aboard his biggest liners. Aby Warburg, the art historian brother of his best friend, Max, mocked these period-revival interiors as "waiter chic."

(dpa/Alamy Stock Photo)

A brass band greeting steerage passengers as they board the SS *Vaterland* in 1914. Under Albert Ballin's direction, HAPAG made many efforts to enhance the previously stark steerage experience by providing better food and service than its competitors. Ballin hoped that satisfied immigrants would encourage their family and friends to book passage on HAPAG vessels to America.

(Scherl/Süddeutsche Zeitung Photo/Alamy Stock Photo)

Betty Joan Perske at the age of ten, in her first professional photograph. The daughter of the Romanian Jewish immigrant Natalie Weinstein-Bacal, she had a very close relationship to her maternal grandmother, Sophie. In the 1930s, she changed her name to Lauren Bacall and became one of the most celebrated actresses in America. She never forgot her family's immigrant struggles, recalling that the word *pushcart* was uttered only in whispers.

(Pictorial Parade via Getty Images)

Immigrants gazing on the Statue of Liberty as their ship arrives in New York Harbor. Originally conceived by its French donors as an allegorical representation of the spirit of liberty, the statue was reimagined by the poet Emma Lazarus as the "mother of exiles" welcoming newcomers to America. Her 1882 poem "The New Colossus" gave the statue a clarion voice that declared, "I lift my lamp beside the golden door!"

(Apic via Getty Images)

anese fleet, under the command of Admiral Togo, attacked the anchored Russian Pacific fleet guarding the entrance to Port Arthur. For the next few months, the Japanese Navy tried to dislodge the Russians from the strategic naval base. The fighting soon spread to the mainland, as the Russians and the Japanese battled for control of the Chinese province of Manchuria. The war went badly for Russia from the start, as its military suffered humiliating defeats delivered by the ascendant Japanese Empire.

To shore up their beleaguered Pacific naval squadron and the troops defending Port Arthur, the Russian Admiralty decided in May to send their Baltic fleet halfway around the world to do battle with Admiral Togo. That meant working out the details of its contract with Ballin and months of logistical planning. Ballin had taken a huge gamble and could not afford a misstep. The repercussions would be global.

So all the while, Albert Ballin continued to wine and dine the royals. In June 1904, HAPAG hosted the Kiel Regatta at Cuxhaven. The royal yacht *Hohenzollern*, the chartered flagship SS *Deutschland*, and the assorted other pleasure boats were ablaze with electric lights. Dulcet waltzes and peppy marches by Johann Strauss, Paul Lincke, and Franz Léhar wafted across the harbor. "Nowhere was the food so good, nowhere was hospitality given so much as a matter of course and without any swagger or ostentation," Theodor Wolff wrote, "nowhere was everything so brilliantly organized and thought out to the last detail." And if the Kaiser was aboard, even those who disliked Ballin, including the Kaiserin, were compelled to join in the party. "All the stars had hurried down from their skies to the deck of the hospitable ship, and usually there would shine in their center a warm, gracious radiance from the great Kaiserly constellation."

On June 19, 1904, Ballin learned that HAPAG's flagship liner had lost the eastbound transatlantic speed record to the North German Lloyd steamer *Kaiser Wilhelm II*, in consequence of her being equipped with larger propellers. If losing the speed record bothered Ballin, he didn't show it. The NDL ship's new record was still a win for Germany, and SS *Deutschland* still retained the record for the more difficult westbound passage. "Late at night the Kaiser asked me to see him on board the *Hohenzollern*," he wrote, "where he engaged me in a long discussion on the most varied subjects."

On June 21 the regatta took place at Cuxhaven. The Kaiser and Prince Heinrich were among the guests who were entertained at dinner on board the *Deutschland*. "The Kaiser was in the best of health and spirits," Ballin recorded in his diary. "Owing to the circumstance that Burgomaster Burchard—who generally engages the Kaiser in after-dinner conversation—was prevented by his illness from being present, I was enabled to introduce a number of Hamburg gentlemen to His Majesty."

To thank Ballin for his generosity, the Kaiser introduced him to his uncle, King Edward VII of Great Britain. "On June 27th my wife and I, and a number of other visitors from the *Prinzessin Victoria Luise*, were invited to take afternoon tea with the Kaiser and Kaiserin on board the *Hohenzollern*," Ballin continued, "and I had a lengthy conversation with King Edward."

In light of events abroad, it was important for Albert Ballin to stay in the good graces of both Kaiser Wilhelm and King Edward.

* * *

The negotiations between HAPAG and Russia remained secret until the summer of 1904. When the news was leaked to the press, many in the British Foreign Office wondered if the business move was a precursor to Germany forming a new and, for the British, dangerous alliance with imperial Russia. But Ballin felt the Russians simply were amenable dealmakers. "Our negotiations with the Russian Government have made good progress, and practically the whole of my time is taken up with these transactions, which have given us a very exciting time," he wrote in his diary. "They compel me to go to Berlin pretty frequently, as I consider it both fair to the Foreign Office and advisable in our own interests that the former should always be fully informed of all the steps I am taking. . . . In order to be in a position to carry out the coal contracts, we have been obliged to charter a large number of steamers, so that at times as many as 80 of these are employed in this Russian transaction."

As suspicious as it was of Albert Ballin, the Russian government was impressed with his savvy, even if the shipping company could profit from a huge surge of refugees trying to get out of Russia should war break out.

When Chancellor von Bülow first got wind of a deal between HAPAG and Russia, he angrily summoned Albert Ballin to the spa town of Bad Homburg von der Höhe, where the German court was on holiday. The chancellor, a longtime admirer of Ballin, nevertheless told him that he had gone well beyond his prerogatives as a private businessman by acting as a diplomat. The scolding may have had an unspoken subtext: Jews in Germany were barred from formal diplomatic service. But Ballin remained unruffled by the confrontation. The financial future of HAPAG hung on doing business with the devil, and as general director he was determined to retain the coal contract whatever the opposition. He explained to Bülow that the British knew all about the Russian coal contract, and that he was chartering British coal miners to supply the Russian Navy. He also pointed out that the Germans were more than happy to sell the Japanese armaments from Krupp. The HAPAG coal contract with the czar, Ballin said, would do nothing to jeopardize Germany's interests or standing in the world. In fact, it would benefit HAPAG, and thus would be good for Germany.

Charmed and consoled, the chancellor reported what happened at the meeting to the Kaiser, who decided to let the matter slide, and Ballin's unofficial naval diplomacy—and a lucrative contract—was left to proceed. The Kaiser then told his cousin the czar that he was in no position to intervene, and that he would let the mission to do battle with the Japanese fleet proceed. The czar, who felt he had gotten a good deal out of the whole affair, eagerly awaited the coming naval battle against Japan. So, too, did Ballin.

In October 1904, Ballin finalized the deal with the Russian government. HAPAG contracted with the St. Petersburg firm of C. Wachter & Co. to deliver 338,000 tons of Welsh coal to ports. Moreover, Ballin also sold the aging *Fürst Bismarck*, *Columbia*, and *Auguste Victoria* (which were hampered by high coal consumption and low steerage capacities) for conversion by the Russian Navy into fast cruisers or naval support vessels. As a bonus, HAPAG chartered around eighty of its cargo ships to deliver all of that coal to ports all the way from Denmark to the Chushan Archipelago, off the coast of China.

The sale of the old ships to Russia alone resulted in a 24.5 million mark windfall for HAPAG, or well over a quarter of a billion dollars in modern-day currency. This was more than enough for Albert Ballin to start rebuilding his fleet with more modern vessels. On top of that, the coaling logistics contract netted HAPAG another 13.5 million marks. The government in St. Petersburg also seemed pleased with the whole arrangement.

An article in HAPAG's newsletter by Ballin characterized the deal as a triumph of German nationalism and echoed a popular phrase about Germany's destiny: "England should learn to live with the fact that Germany cannot and will not renounce trying in honorable competition to conquer a place in the sun alongside it." What mattered above all else was the welfare of HAPAG. But working with Russia for the sake of HAPAG's bottom line would produce damaging repercussions in due course, though not for the German shipping giant.

*　*　*

In New York City, as Jacob Schiff directed the efforts of the Hebrew Emigrant Aid Society and his settlement houses on the Lower East Side, he looked for ways to stymie Russia at every turn. The czarist government was consistently short on funds and turned to the European capital markets to issue bonds to fund its war effort. As one of the most powerful investment bankers in the United States, Schiff argued passionately against Russian bond offerings, including those from J. P. Morgan & Co., and scorned Jewish bankers on the Continent who underwrote them. As a Republican, Schiff felt that he had an ally in President Theodore Roosevelt, who despite his patrician background was a friend of immigration to the United States, so long as the new arrivals did not overwhelm the existing Protestant majority.

Japan, meanwhile, solicited the support of the United States. The American ambassador in Tokyo was Lloyd Griscom, a polished Philadelphian who had gone into the foreign service shortly after his graduation from the University of Pennsylvania, and the son of Clement Griscom, president of the IMM. His job was to serve as Roosevelt's eyes and ears on Japan's plans for imperial expansion. Griscom grew to think favorably of Japan's expansion at the expense of Russia, so long as it didn't impinge on America's newly won possession in the Pacific, the Philippines.

The Japanese diplomat Baron Keneko Kentaro arrived in the United States a few months into the war to serve as a special envoy and public relations advocate for his nation's cause. A high-ranking nobleman, he had studied at Harvard when Roosevelt was an undergraduate there. Kentaro had made many friends in high places in America.

One of Kentaro's most ardent admirers, of course, was Ambassador Griscom, who provided an introduction to his father when the diplomat visited Philadelphia. Griscom entertained Kentaro at the Union League and introduced him to many of his industrialist friends, including Alexander Cassatt, president of the Pennsylvania Railroad and one of Jacob Schiff's most important clients.

"Philadelphia is a widely known shipbuilding place," Kentaro said, "and I am interested in ships." He added that "it delights me to find the sentiment of this country is apparently with Japan in this struggle, but I am rather disappointed at reading the flood of books and magazine articles that have so far been written about Japan. We know the power of Russia better perhaps than the world knows the power of Japan. Reverses will not dishearten the nation, and as I have said, Japan will fight until the last man is dead and the last bit of money is expended."

The two countries prepared for war.

The Russian fleet committed a massive blunder as soon as it sailed into the North Sea. On October 21, 1904, the commander of the supply ship *Kamchatka* radioed the rest of the fleet that he was under attack from Japanese torpedo boats that had steamed all the way from the East China Sea to preemptively engage them. Admiral Rozhestvensky ordered his ships to fire upon the group of small vessels, which turned out to be British fishing trawlers going about their business off Dogger Bank. One trawler, the *Crane*, sank, killing her captain and first mate. Four others were badly damaged by Russian gunfire. To make matters worse, two of Rozhestvensky's ships, the cruisers *Aurora* and *Dmitrii Donskoi*, opened fire on each other. The so-called Dogger Bank incident didn't bode well for the rest of the war.

"It is almost inconceivable that any men calling themselves seamen," the *Times* of London sneered, "however frightened they might be, could spend twenty minutes bombarding a fleet of fishing boats without discovering the nature of their target." Outraged by the loss of innocent lives, the British government considered declaring war on the Russian Empire, a move that would have been absolutely disastrous for Czar Nicholas. There was no way his small navy could have withstood an attack by the fearsome

Royal Navy. To placate the British, Rozhestvensky agreed to an inquiry at The Hague, put the officers deemed immediately responsible for the debacle to shore in Vigo, Spain, and sailed on to engage Togo's fleet.

What the Russian Navy did with his ships ultimately wasn't Ballin's business. The coal supply contract was. At the end of 1904, Albert Ballin concluded his fifth year as general director of HAPAG. When the company closed the books on the year, Ballin could proudly report to his shareholders that HAPAG had earned a profit of 27 million marks, up from 22 million the previous year, and could reward its shareholders with a 9 percent dividend. Much of that windfall came from the coffers of the Russian treasury. These funds carried over into the following year, with HAPAG earning a profit of an astonishing 38 million marks.

*   *   *

As the Russian fleet, fueled by Albert Ballin's logistical brilliance, steamed toward its rendezvous with the Japanese Navy in the Strait of Tsushima, between Japan and Korea, Russia had to face another problem closer to home. As winter settled in, residents in St. Petersburg frequently found themselves without heat. Families shivered as coal stoves went cold, just as strikers, unhappy about long working hours, shut down Russian factories.

On January 22, 1905, thousands of demonstrators, led by the Orthodox priest Father Gregor Gapon, marched on the Winter Palace in St. Petersburg. Carrying flags and patriotic banners, the crowd demanded an audience with Czar Nicholas II. The organization they represented, the Assembly of Russian Factory and Mill Workers of the City of St. Petersburg, desperately hoped to plead with the czar for better hours and pay for the nation's suffering working class. As they marched, they sang "God Save the Czar."

Czar Nicholas II and his family were not at the Winter Palace, where they almost never lived. They spent most of their time holed up in their country retreat at Czarskoe Selo, which of course had its own power plant and a staff that did their best to insulate the royal family from any bad news. Nicholas had been briefed about the march the previous evening and approved an order to send ten thousand troops to Palace Square to protect the official residence from looting.

At around 11:00 a.m., the czar's troops fired directly into the column of workers led by Father Gapon. In the melee that followed, soldiers slaughtered an estimated one thousand of the peaceful demonstrators in front of the Winter Palace. The city erupted in fury, as angry protesters looted homes and stores along the capital's grand boulevards. In the weeks to come, general strikes spread throughout other cities in the Russian Empire. The government's hope that the war would unify the Russian people in a nationalist cause was completely dashed.

The massacre would forever be known as "Bloody Sunday."

A month later, a socialist revolutionary tossed a bomb into the carriage of Grand Duke Sergei Alexandrovich, the czar's uncle. He was killed instantly.

Meanwhile, in the United States, Jacob Schiff continued to do everything in his power to undermine the Russian war effort by raising funds for the Japanese government. Unlike Albert Ballin, who was willing to cut a deal with the Russians for the sake of his company, Schiff would rather take a hit to Kuhn, Loeb's bottom line than float a Russian bond offering.

The czarist government's only hope was that Admiral Rozhestvensky would defeat the Japanese fleet, paving the way for Russian supremacy in the Far East, in a move that would hopefully quell unrest at home.

The war waged on with increasing fervor. On May 27, 1905, the Japanese and Russian fleets squared off against each other in the Strait of Tsushima. The Russian squadron was composed of eight battleships, three coastal battleships, nine cruisers, and nine destroyers. The ships were streaked with rust after the long voyage, and their crews were undermined by low morale. The Japanese squadron, freshly painted and well maintained, consisted of five battleships, twenty-three cruisers, twenty destroyers, and eighteen torpedo boats. Within the span of a day, Admiral Togo's ships utterly destroyed the Russian naval squadron. Ballin had given Russia the ships, and he had brought them coal to steam halfway around the world, but he could not and did not ensure a victory. Again, that was not his business.

Back in Hamburg, Ballin expressed no sadness at the Russian defeat. What mattered most were the vast profits the deal provided to HAPAG, and maintaining royal favor with the Kaiser. The Russian fleet's sinking, he wrote, "cannot, and does not, diminish the magnitude of the achievement; and the experiences we have gained by successfully carrying out our novel task will surely prove of great value to the Government. This whole coaling business has been a source of considerable profits to our company, although if due regard is paid to the exceptional character of the work and to the unusual risks we had to run, they cannot be called exorbitant."

There was something he did not say. There might have been another element in Ballin's business calculus, and a possible reason why his dealings with the Russian government did not attract the wrath of Jacob Schiff, who had so passionately worked on behalf of Japan. If Russia escalated the conflict with Japan, then more Russians, especially Jews, would try to leave for America rather than become cannon fodder. And after the Russian deal with HAPAG, perhaps the czar and his government would be happy to overlook lost military conscripts setting sail on Ballin's ships.

In any event, Schiff and Ballin met that fall, most likely in Hamburg. Perhaps they discussed this matter. No record of the meeting survives, but on November 11, 1905, Schiff sent Ballin the following cable, indicating the two of them had gotten along quite well:

Dear Friend:

I hope that when this letter reaches you, you and Frau Ballin will have been back at your own house for a long time, and that the Ocean, for which you are always doing so much, will have been kind to you on your return voyage.

My purpose in writing you these lines is chiefly to thank you for your kindness in sending us a Marconigram from the high seas. It is really touching that you always think so kindly of us, and it gives me pleasure to assure you how happy we are that you have become more intimate with my dear ones and with me. Certainly you know how cordial are the feelings which I cherish toward you.

I can only hope that no such great length of time will again elapse before we meet again. In the meantime, I beg you, if my firm or I personally can be of service to your interests in any way, to dispose of us without any hesitation.

With kindest assurances to Frau Ballin, as well as to yourself, in which my wife joins, I am

Yours etc.

RUSSIA, AFTER losing the war, was utterly humiliated on the world stage. To survive a revolution, the government needed a scapegoat, and it doubled down on its persecution of the Jews. Nicholas II's government tarred them as revolutionaries, subversives, and traitors. The general Russian population, impoverished by the war, was more than happy to turn on the Jews rather than blame the czar's incompetence. Jewish immigration surged in 1904 and continued to climb for the next three years.

Thanks to the 27-million-mark profit that year from his deal with Russia, Ballin was able to update his fleet with more passenger-carrying capacity. By 1906, the company boasted that its fleet of steamships "in one vast splendid armada of commerce would illustrate, as well anything could, the stupendous growth of the world's facility for transportation by water of passengers and freight." And unlike the International Mercantile Marine, HAPAG was not burdened by overcapitalization.

Albert Ballin continued to plow ahead with plans to cement his control of the immigrant business. One piece of mail that crossed Ballin's desk was a petition from a group of Jews marooned at the migrant holding camp of Ilowo, located on the border between Poland and Germany. This was purgatory for thousands of mostly Jewish families, whose hopes turned to despair as they faced a labyrinth of delay and paperwork. The migrants described the border crossing camp as a "wide net into which all of the fish of the immigration stream must swim," but didn't say these camps were a key component of a system that had made the German shipping lines dominant in the steerage trade.

Albert Ballin never appears to have responded, but he did find himself the target of a growing number of activists in the German Jewish community who viewed him not as a success story but as a sellout to capitalism, a supplicant to the Kaiser, and an exploiter of his own people—especially after his deal with Russia. Ballin, like Jacob Schiff and other German Jews, did his best to reconcile his own ethnic identity with his pride in being a German subject.

In the early 1900s, there was a growing movement in both Europe and the United States for the Jews to form their own homeland in Palestine, then under Ottoman rule. Jacob Schiff adamantly refused to support the idea. "I cannot for a moment concede that one can be at the same time a true American and an honest adherent of the Zionist movement," he declared. The Promised Land of the world's oppressed Jews, he believed, was the United States of America, where, with the power of uplift, one could remain both a devout Jew and a loyal American.

Schiff's real opinion of Albert Ballin remains somewhat of a mystery. His daughter, Frieda Warburg, always mindful of her father's approval, described Ballin as a genius in her memoirs, and that HAPAG under his management was a "great factor in German life not only as a business but as propaganda for Germany at its best." What is certain is that the banker viewed HAPAG's immigration business (and NDL's, to a lesser extent) as indispensable to the exodus of the Jewish people from the Russian Empire, especially after the Russo-Japanese War. Even if Schiff had thought that Ballin was not a good and observant Jew, no other steamship line had set up such a complex transportation network from Russia to the ports of Western Europe. Schiff needed him. The world needed him.

*　*　*

Ballin wasn't the only one with plans to rebuild his company's fleet. Cunard was building two new express liners, RMS *Lusitania* and *Mauretania*, scheduled to enter service in 1907. At 31,000 tons each and powered by 70,000-horsepower steam turbines, the twin four-funneled giants were bigger, faster, and far more luxurious than any German vessel. Both ships would use revolutionary new turbine engine technology to give them service speeds of 25 knots, a few knots faster than HAPAG's record-breaker SS *Deutschland*. Despite their tremendous coal consumption, a 2.6-million-pound subsidy from the British government ensured their profitability. In exchange, Cunard built the ships to British Admiralty specifications, which allowed them to be quickly transformed into Royal Navy heavy cruisers should war break out. Albert Ballin, on the other hand, knew that ocean liners were not practical as cruisers thanks to their high fuel consumption, so he built his ships with the German Navy nowhere in mind.

Cunard worked with naval architect Leonard Peskett to create a balanced passenger plan of 560 in first class, 464 in second class, and 1,338 in steerage for the sister vessels. The number of steerage berths in HAPAG's very profitable workhorse SS *Pennsylvania* of 1896 was 2,300, or about 1,000 more migrants than the Cunarders. By the mid-1900s, HAPAG and North German Lloyd had sufficiently eaten into the "indirect" immigration market to make the separate leg from a German port to Liverpool less competitive than a direct passage to New York.

But Cunard had another ace up its sleeve: its steerage revenue generators—the slow but capacious RMS *Carpathia*, *Saxonia*, and *Ivernia*—still carried Austro-Hungarian Jews and Italians to America, over 2,200 of both groups per voyage.

Cunard was now out of Ballin's and Morgan's grasp. What's more, J. P. Morgan knew that soon enough his large and sprawling IMM fleet would also be outdated. He would have to fund his fleet's modernization with profits from White Star.

Ballin worried about this, and more. Despite his healthy share of the immigrant market, he still fretted about competition from Cunard and others. He wrote Max Warburg that the Russian government might actually sponsor the creation of its own shipping line, and thus allow hundreds of thousands of Jews to bypass the Prussian border and sail directly out of the Baltic port of Libau. Max Warburg told Albert Ballin to stop worrying. The Russians had little to no experience in transatlantic shipping and could never compete with the well-oiled machine that was HAPAG.

Perhaps Albert Ballin still felt, despite his line's immense success, that he was just one mistake away from being booted from the general directorship of HAPAG. Like many assimilated German Jews of the time, he walked a fine line between two communities. He knew that helping Russia endeared him further to the Kaiser but made his standing even more precarious with his coreligionists.

Ballin's work, which always involved managing sensitive relationships, now played out on a world stage. He knew that to guarantee the future of his company, he needed to do everything he could to prevent war between Britain and Germany. The Dogger Bank incident showed how perilously close the major powers were to war, and that a simple misunderstanding could rapidly escalate.

Perhaps because of Ballin's growing anxiety about war in Europe, Max Warburg decided to introduce him to one of Great Britain's most powerful bankers and Jacob Schiff's close business partner and friend: Sir Ernest Cassel. By the early 1900s, Cassel had become the personal banker and trusted financial adviser to King Edward VII of Great Britain. As Warburg suspected, Cassel and Ballin got along famously. Both came from humble origins and had risen to become confidants of kings. Although Cassel had quietly converted to Catholicism decades earlier at the insistence of his wife, the general public still regarded him as a Jew. Both men also knew how it felt to be showered with royal favor, all while being sneered at by entitled and vindictive German and British aristocrats.

Cassel's relationship with King Edward VII was an interesting one. Although a libertine who indulged in food and mistresses, King Edward deeply believed in meritocracy, and was a great admirer of the Rothschilds and other assimilated Jewish families who had made major contributions to industry, learning, and the arts. Like Cassel's.

Cassel agreed with Ballin. He believed that with the right amount of tact and diplomacy, they could stave off war between Britain and Germany. How? By building a stronger community of business interests. They used their favor with their respective monarchs. Although the king had very little actual power domestically, he still had enormous clout among his relatives, including his nephew Kaiser Wilhelm II.

Albert Ballin lobbied to have the Kaiser and the king meet more regularly, even if the two men deeply disliked each other (the king thought the Kaiser was a raging egomaniac). "I hope that our respective monarchs may soon meet now," he wrote Sir Ernest. "There is nothing that we on our side would welcome more heartily than the establishment and the maintenance of the most friendly and most cordial relations between the two sovereigns and their peoples."

Shortly before the British king and the German Kaiser met at Friedrichshof Castle, Cassel wrote to Ballin: "I also feel that the meeting of their Majesties must produce a great deal of good, and, as I now hear, it will after all be possible to arrange for this meeting to take place on the outward journey of the King. I am still as convinced as ever that our side is animated by the same friendly sentiments as yours."

Ballin's business depended on that "friendly sentiment." Should England and Germany go to war, a blockade of Germany's ports would shut down his business.

Across the Atlantic, there were other threats. Voices in America lobbying for increased restrictions on Eastern European immigrants were growing louder. Jacob Schiff kept up his work. From his charities flowed money and resources that allowed Jews in the Russian Empire to buy steamship tickets, stay in lodging houses, and receive other forms of aid along the way to Hamburg or Bremen. According to the publication of the Hilfsverein der deutschen Juden, anywhere from seventy-five thousand to one hundred thousand Jews were leaving Russia, Romania, and Austria-Hungary every year, and the vast majority were headed for the United States. And so, for now, with the winds of war and revolution calming, his efforts to help the persecuted Jews through the Golden Door were bearing fruit.

Other loyalties, hard to reconcile, also pulled at Schiff. Despite his self-confidence, Schiff would find it very hard to strike a balance between his Judaism, his fondness for his native Germany, and his boundless faith in the United States of America. And in a conflict with fellow Jews, Ballin would be forced to choose, as one observer put it, between the religion into which he was born and his adopted "religion of the German flag." He would no longer be able to walk that fine line between two communities.

Until then, Ballin did what he could to stay his course. Oddly enough, Albert Ballin received a small token of recognition from the czar for his role in the Russo-Japanese War. On January 23, 1906, he received notice that Czar Nicholas II had bestowed upon him the Order of St. Stanislaus, Second Class with Stars, thus granting the German Jewish shipping magnate a knighthood in the officially anti-Semitic Romanov empire.

But his successful gambit into the sphere of *Weltpolitik* didn't stop him from making new enemies in his own country.

CHAPTER 14

Making Peace with the Aid Society

We have repeatedly pointed to the serious dilemma faced by our Russian brothers-in-faith
at the Prussian border. The Hilfsverein der
Deutschen Jüden, which took up negotiations
with the directors of the Hamburg-America
Line and the Norddeutsche Lloyd has now happily been able to bring the matter to a fe-
licitous conclusion.

—1904 ANNUAL REPORT OF THE
HILFSVEREIN DER DEUTSCHEN JUDEN

Sometime in 1904, a man dressed in rags showed up at one of the border control stations at the Russian border with Prussia. He said his
name was Joel Kalischer. The train ride through the flat meadows and
forests of Poland, he recalled, was not a beautiful or tranquil one. "As far
as the eye can see, one glimpses lonely country roads, lined by a gloomy
pine forest that blends into the grey horizon," Kalischer wrote of his journey to Tilsit. "Even nature reminds involuntarily of the nightmare that
weighs heavily on the large Czarist empire."

Kalischer claimed to be escaping conscription in the czar's army and
was looking for safe passage to London to join relatives. Before attempt-
ing to cross the border, he spent a night at a guesthouse popular with
Russian Jews. "A group of emigrants, brought together by fate, was sitting together by the dim light of a small lamp and conversing in lively

gibberish [*lebhaftes Kauderwelsch*] about their experiences at the border crossing and their worries about the upcoming journey."

Kalischer was not his real name. Nor was he a Russian immigrant, though he could speak Yiddish. His name was actually Julius Kaliski, a German Jewish journalist with the Social Democratic paper *Vorwärts*. For Kaliski, Jews at the border constituted a humanitarian crisis that needed to be addressed by government action and private philanthropy. The profit motive in what was, in his opinion, human trafficking, was disgusting. And he had gone undercover to show the world exactly that.

Kaliski had jumped into the maelstrom of a vicious rate war between Cunard and the German shipping companies over the immigrant trade. To stay independent and to capitalize on events, Britain's Cunard Line had decided to play hardball. Lord Inverclyde hit the German companies, and Morgan's trust, where it really hurt. He drastically cut Cunard's steerage rates to a mere eight dollars one-way on steamships sailing from France and the Mediterranean. What he hoped would happen was that Eastern European migrants would travel through Austria-Hungary to Trieste and sail from there to America.

Albert Ballin would have none of it. He had worked hard to gain the special border control privileges HAPAG and NDL received from the German government. To surrender to Cunard's pressures would put him in a very bad light in Berlin, especially with the Kaiser.

In 1904, Ballin appears to have told his agents at the border to refuse safe passage to immigrants holding a Cunard ticket. This move was part of his strategy to force his rival to the bargaining table. His swipe at his British rival angered many at Cunard's Liverpool headquarters, who felt he was unfairly using his power at the border crossings to destroy the competition. Ballin's tactics would go public if a journalist, like Kaliski, reported it in the left-wing German press. That would do tremendous damage to his carefully crafted public image.

Ballin knew that the Kaiserin and the Prussian conservatives in Berlin snickered behind his back that he was a *Kaiserjüde*. But as Theodor Wolff observed, Ballin "was sufficiently familiar, in any case, with court psychology to know that the lion must not be prodded with the end of a walking stick all the time." However, what really wounded Ballin was the Social Democratic movement, whose leaders attacked HAPAG as exemplifying the worst excesses of German capitalism. Jewish Social Democrats in particular saw him as exploiting the misery of his own people. Trade unionists called him a capitalist oppressor, coining the term *Ballinism* to describe the cold, ruthless power of German big business. Ballin certainly knew that in America, the term *Morganizing* connoted the same kind of unrestricted power. So even though more and more Jews escaped Russia through Ballin's efforts, as HAPAG piled up record profits Ballin found himself being depicted not as the savior of his people but as one of its greatest oppressors.

Kaliski's mission was to see if he would be denied passage to England, where presumably he could get a cheaper Cunard ticket from Liverpool to New York. Doing his best impression of a Russian Jew, Kaliski begged the border crossing agents to let him book a train to Hamburg, as he claimed he had family there who would take care of him. Kaliski had no passport. The agent refused him entry. The only way for him to cross the border, the agent said, was for him to book a steamship ticket to London, and from there sail on to America.

A fat, red-faced man named Klein, one of many "subagents" who worked for HAPAG, appeared. His job was to serve as backup to the border control agents, convincing reluctant Jewish refugees to either buy the steamship ticket or be deported back to Russia.

"We don't care about selling a ticket to you," Klein told Kaliski. "See for yourself how you can get to Hamburg."

Kaliski realized that he had run up hard against strict German immigration restrictions and paid for the steamship fare. It turned out that Kaliski was part of the share of Russian immigrant traffic that Albert Ballin had conceded to the Cunard Line. It wouldn't be Kaliski who would uncover the story about the rate war.

He tossed and turned all night in the barracks, kept awake by a bright electric light that burned continuously, as well as the snoring and chatter of the dozens crammed into the hall. At 6:00 a.m., an attendant burst into the room and barked that it was time to get up for inspection in the main hall of the border control station. There were hundreds more people who had arrived at Tilsit overnight, mostly by train. Kaliski now found himself waiting in line, holding a suitcase packed with the "typical belongings of a Russian Jew": a teakettle, clothes, a mug, and a pillow. All bags had to be opened and sent away to be fumigated.

After turning over his baggage, Kaliski moved into another room, this one crammed full of fifty or so people. All were told to undress. They all waited naked for a while ("the perfect place to contract and spread infectious diseases," Kaliski noted), and then were ordered into a room with ten showerheads. They then dried off and moved into yet another room. Here, the doctors were waiting for them. The would-be migrant would have his or her head examined for lice and their eyes for trachoma. The doctors would also look for signs of contagious diseases that could infect other immigrants and result in their rejection at Ellis Island. HAPAG and the other steamship companies could not afford another cholera fiasco like the one aboard the *Normannia* in 1892.

"Absolute silence reigned, and everyone waited for the vote of the doctor in breathtaking suspense," Kaliski wrote.

The following day, Kaliski and his fellow travelers boarded one of the special migrant trains that would take them to the great port city of Hamburg. As the train rolled through the flat Prussian countryside, the passengers took out the food they had brought with them. The smell of herring, stale bread, Russian tobacco, and sweat filled the poorly ventilated space. Kaliski heard a jumble of languages—Yiddish, Russian, Polish, and Lithuanian—above the clickety-clack of the wheels and the bright train whistle. There was the constant crying of small children, and their parents softly trying to comfort them. Yet despite the crammed conditions, everyone appeared to be pleased, even happy, that they had made it over the border, had passed the dreaded doctors' inspection, and were moving, slowly but surely, toward America.

Kaliski spoke to some of his fellow Jews, who now felt they could freely unload to a perfect stranger about their hatred of Czar Nicholas II. Among the single men, it was clear that a number had either deserted the Russian Army or were avoiding the draft altogether. "A flood of curses and imprecations about the Czar and his government gushed out in Polish, Russian, and Jewish [*jüdisch*]."

After making a few station stops for water and tea, the train rumbled through the great metropolis of Berlin. The passengers on the train stared at the twinkling lights, the great dome of the Domkirche, and the grand boulevards. Kaliski wrote:

> *The Alexanderplatz comes into sight and the light of the streetlights and of the many lamps in front of shops ablaze with light reaches our eyes sparkling, glittering. The blaze of light greeted us like the shine of a better future and, almost reverently, some of the Jews cry out: "Now it gets light!"*

Shortly after passing through Berlin, the train stopped at Ruhleben station, where travelers would be examined one more time before boarding the train for the nine-hour trip to Hamburg. Kaliski saw many families being reunited after having taken separate trains. He also overheard some of the conversations the Jewish migrants were having, most of which had to do with poverty and war.

"My wife stayed at home with one-and-a-half Rubles. Four children, may God keep them healthy, they want to eat," one Jewish immigrant lamented to another. "There's not a single Kopek in our house," others joined in, "but how is it different from when we were in the war?"

Finally, the sealed train arrived in Hamburg and deposited its passengers at Veddel. All continued to wait in the reception hall until sunset, when a dinner of black bread and syrup was served at 6:00 p.m. "We were still lingering in this gloomy place," Kaliski continued. "The adults were pondering, but several children between the age of three and six took up their games again after a long nap. They chase each other between boxes and baskets until their mother's holler calls them back. The women have aged prematurely, withered; hardship and work loom on their faces."

Before turning in for the night in the barracks, Kaliski begged the guards to let him into the city of Hamburg, as he claimed he had relatives he wanted to visit. His request was denied, but under cover of darkness, he managed to sneak out of the compound. Dressed in his overcoat and sporting an Orthodox-style beard, Kaliski had morphed from a German Jew into a Russian one. The residents of Hamburg did not welcome him.

The following morning, he walked back to the gate of the *Auswandererhallen* and explained to the guards that he wanted to stay in Hamburg rather than go on to America by sea. He then demanded that his money for the passage to London and his fumigation fee be returned.

The guards refused. "Report to the police commissioner that Joel Kalischer from Kyiv wants to stay in Hamburg," the department head Stellmacher of the *Auswandererhallen* responded curtly.

"As a matter of principle, sir!" Kaliski replied in fluent German, not Yiddish. He then handed Stellmacher his press card.

Kaliski's series in *Vorwärts* was released in six installments in December 1904 and January 1905, though word about it leaked out to German Jewish leaders before its publication. Among those who received advance notice was Dr. Georg Halpern, one of Germany's most prominent Zionist leaders and a close associate of fellow chemist Chaim Weizmann. Halpern was a native of Pinsk in the Russian province of Belarus. As one of the few Jews able to move from Russia to the German states, Halpern felt that the idea of America as the "Promised Land" was a capitalist chimera propped up by exploitative capitalists like Jacob Schiff and Albert Ballin. He didn't feel in any way rosy about Germany or Austria when it came to Jewish life, either, and felt that Jews should turn their thoughts toward establishing a foothold in the state of Palestine, then under Ottoman control.

An advance copy of Kaliski's exposé also appears to have landed on the desk of Paul Nathan, the founder of the Berlin-based Hilfsverein der deutschen Juden (Aid Organization of German Jews). Nathan had previously kept his mouth shut about any misgivings he had about HAPAG's operations. After all, it was Ballin's health measures and privately run border control stations that allowed so many Russian Jews to escape the Russian Empire in the first place.

The scion of a prosperous Berlin Jewish family, Nathan had eschewed going into business and had decided to become a journalist instead. He was then tapped by the Berlin tycoon James Simon to be the director of the Hilfsverein, which had been founded in 1901 as a more proactive alternative to the staid and cautious Alliance Israélite Universelle. Among its most powerful backers was Jacob Schiff, who used the Hilfsverein as a direct conduit for funds raised in the United States to aid Russian Jews trying to find passage to America.

A superb and well-connected organizer, Paul Nathan brought a deep sense of commitment to his fellow Jews in his work. He visited border communities to make sure that migrants were being treated well and were given funds to help pay their passage and feed their families along the way. He knew that without Albert Ballin's semilegal transportation system, most Jews would be unable to escape the clutches of the Russian Empire. Yet Nathan was continually troubled by what he saw: the steamship lines' treatment of Russian Jews as corporate revenue generators.

Ballin may have sympathized with the migrants, but he kept it well hidden under the guise of profit for HAPAG. Any display of his own Jewishness could potentially jeopardize HAPAG politically, because his company was a favorite target of the German far right, which encompassed not just rural conservatives but also members of the German aristocracy and the empress herself. Otto Böckler, a representative from the anti-Semitic Deutsche Reformpartei, pointed to Ballin as the head of a vast Jewish conspiracy, one to which he gave a new name on the floor of the Reichstag. "[T]he highest parts [of the state] have been *verballinisiert* [Ballinized]," he declared. "The strangers from Palestine and America have gained access to the highest steps of the throne."

It was Paul Nathan who went public with the news of the rate war and how it was affecting immigrants. He didn't attack North German Lloyd or HAPAG or go after Heinrich Wiegand, the most successful gentile shipping executive in Germany. Rather, he zeroed in on Albert Ballin, head of what was now the largest shipping company in the world and one of the most prominent Jews in Germany. Leaving the comfort of his Berlin office, Nathan traveled to the border towns to inspect conditions for himself. There, he listened to stories of Jews denied entry through the control stations because they held a Cunard ticket rather than a HAPAG or NDL one. They could either exchange their Cunard ticket for one of the German lines or go back to Russia. To Nathan, this was utterly inhumane.

In an October 1904 article in the *Geschäftsbericht des Hilfsverein der deutschen Juden*, the official organ of his aid society, Paul Nathan blamed Ballin "personally" for the terrible conditions at the border, as well as for the exploitation of his fellow Jews for the sake of HAPAG's profit.

The paper urged migrants to avoid taking German ships, and rather take Russian vessels sailing from Libau or Cunard steamers departing Fiume. "The conditions at the Prussian-Russian border had, thanks to the external occasion of a competitive battle between the English Cunard line and the German shipping concerns," Nathan wrote, "led to a great number of intolerable outcomes. In fact, the border was closed to all emigrants who could not travel on a German ship."

Other liberal Jewish publications, especially those sympathetic to Social Democrats, piled on. Ballin was used to such criticisms. The real surprise was when he opened the pages of the liberal but relatively mainstream *Berliner Tageblatt*. The paper reported on Paul Nathan's mission, stating that the "negotiations were stalled at the inception."

The editor in chief of the *Tageblatt* was Ballin's friend and admirer Theodor Wolff, himself a prominent member of Berlin's Jewish community. A savvy user of the press, Ballin had long employed a so-called literary bureau, a group of employees who wrote press releases and maintained relationships with friendly newspapers in major German cities. The *Tageblatt* was one of them.

For once, Ballin found himself backed into a corner. He was terrified by the anti-Semites on the right, but their bigotry was a known quantity. He railed against the Social Democrats because they threatened how his business worked and his view of the world. But Albert Ballin could not ignore a Jewish group singling him out as an exploiter of his own people. He also knew that James Simon, founder of the Hilfsverein, was an adviser to Kaiser Wilhelm II on Jewish affairs.

After months of avoiding Paul Nathan's entreaties, Albert Ballin agreed to sit down with him. James Simon also came to the meeting, which probably took place at the HAPAG headquarters on the Alster Lake in Hamburg. Nathan presented Ballin with a litany of complaints about the conditions on the border.

The so-called dossier of facts about the border crossings has been lost, but Nathan probably used language similar to what appeared in an undated petition signed by several Jews interned at the Ilowo migrants' camp at the Russian-Prussian border, who for one reason or another could not board ships to America.

The undersigned immigrants described Albert Ballin not as one of the most powerful business executives in Hamburg, not as the managing director of HAPAG, not as the friend of the emperor of Germany, but as a fellow Jew who had failed to take care of his people. It was not a petition for aid but a Yiddish version of Émile Zola's "J'accuse":

> *Do you know, Mr. Ballin, how the Jewish emigrants in the holding camps are being abused and harassed?*
>
> *Do you know, Mr. Ballin, that the holding camps (and) a wide network of agents in Russia support the trafficking of emigrants over the border with all the associated dangers to their lives?*
>
> *Do you know, Mr. Ballin, that this year at the holding camp Ilowo there were two suicides . . . ?*
>
> *Do you know, Mr. Ballin, that Jewish men, women, and children who were waiting to go to France were held in the holding camp for a long time living in filth until the children got lice, scabies, and scurvy?*
>
> *Have you ever, Mr. Ballin, seen a holding camp? Don't they call Castle Garden in New York the "island of tears"? So must one call your holding camps "the islands of the devil."*

"Yes, Mr. Ballin," they closed, "you know about all of this and must know about it all and being 'half-responsible' is a crime against humanity and your own people. Gather up the tears spilled in a single year on this demonic island and from them you will be able to make a long, wide stream on which you, Mr. Ballin, will be able to sail out on a nice yacht trip."

Paul Nathan knew that to get what he wanted—namely, the presence of Jewish aid organizations at the border control stations and the end of the rate war—he had to call out Ballin as a Jew. For all his love of Germany, Ballin had spent his life maintaining his identity as a Jew without practicing his religion or marrying within the faith.

To curtail more invective spilling into the mainstream press, Ballin had to ease up on Cunard and become more accommodating toward immigrants. As for Cunard, he regretted that he didn't act swiftly enough to buy them out two years earlier.

The *Berliner Tageblatt* reported that Nathan and Simon's negotiations with Ballin had proved successful in alleviating the sufferings of the Jewish refugees.

The agreement before us now thoroughly disposes of the evils that had transpired on the border and as a result we need no longer expect the unfortunate incidents that were once commonplace. Mister Ballin's point of view was happily revealed to be consonant with the demands that must be made in the interest of humanity and of Germany's good name. It is well known that only approximately 30 percent of emigrants from Russia are of the Jewish confession, while nearly 70 percent are Roman Catholics. The number of Greek Catholics is negligible. Though the Hilfsverein der deutschen Juden understandably initially entered into negotiations in the interest of their own coreligionists, it is clear that the arrangement will benefit all emigrants.

Paul Nathan received further concessions from Ballin, including the Hilfsverein running its own lodging house for Jewish emigrants in Tilsit that would also serve as a base for aid workers and interpreters. For its part, HAPAG realized it could live with Cunard ticket holders passing through the gates of its border control stations. The increased migrant flow of Russians, thanks to the Russo-Japanese War and political instability in St. Petersburg, meant that there were more than enough ticket buyers for all the shipping lines.

The agreement appears to have won over Theodor Wolff, who became Ballin's confidant in the years to come. Wolff could not help but notice that Ballin had to play many roles at once: the boss, the businessman, the patriot, the diplomat, the charmer, and, lastly and most reluctantly, the Jew.

In this, he differed from his best friend, Max Warburg. Max Warburg's father, Moritz, was one of the founders of the Hilfsverein. Max himself had served on HAPAG's board of directors since 1901, and although he played down his own Jewishness, he would never defy his father's wishes. Nor would he dare anger his brother Felix's autocratic father-in-law, Jacob Schiff, with whom M. M. Warburg & Co. enjoyed so many financial ties, by denying his faith.

Whatever complications existed between Albert Ballin and the War-burg family, especially as it concerned their Jewishness, they continued their productive personal and professional relationship. HAPAG would rise to even greater heights under Ballin's autocratic leadership. But the sacrifices Ballin made to achieve it would take a toll. Ballin's feeling of never feeling at home exacted a terrible personal cost.

CHAPTER 15

Revolution and Rebuilding

_____

_____

_____

In politics as well as in business he held
that "a lean compromise was preferable to a
fat lawsuit," as the German proverb puts it.

—BERNHARD HULDERMANN ON ALBERT BALLIN

The Russo-Japanese War was a disaster for Russia, but a bonanza for Albert Ballin and HAPAG. To avoid conscription into Nicholas II's army, hundreds of thousands of Russian subjects tried to get out of the czar's empire. Many who were sure to become conscripts sold everything to pay for a passage to the New World. Others already conscripted deserted their units. By train and by foot, all amassed at the Prussian border in ever greater numbers.

To stop the fighting and prevent the Japanese from dealing too great a blow to the Russian Empire, President Roosevelt called for a peace conference between the two warring nations at Portsmouth, New Hampshire. Roosevelt's policy goal was to curb, while also appeasing, Japan's expansionist impulses and to stabilize Russia. The resulting Treaty of Portsmouth, ratified by both nations in October 1905, recognized Japan's territorial claims on the Korean Peninsula and ceded Port Arthur to the rising Asian power. In return, the Russians avoided having to pay costly war reparations to Japan, since the defeated country's finances were on the brink of collapse.

The war was also good for Kuhn, Loeb & Co. in New York and M. M. Warburg & Co. in Hamburg. As a matter of principle, Jacob Schiff refused to underwrite any bond offerings to support the Russian government. But he did support the Japanese government. When Baron Korekiyo Takahashi, a high-ranking Japanese bureaucrat and financier, floated a proposal for a 10-million-pound bond issue to be offered to American and British investors to finance its war with Russia, Jacob Schiff enthusiastically volunteered to underwrite half the deal. So successful was the American offering that Kuhn, Loeb underwrote a second one. When Japan asked for a third loan, Schiff threw the deal to M. M. Warburg & Co., and it was ten times oversubscribed. All the more insulting to Czar Nicholas II was that his cousin Kaiser Wilhelm II, who had raged against the "yellow peril," gave the deal his royal blessing.

Jacob Schiff saw the war in religious terms, calling Russia "the Northern Goliath" and Japan "the Far Eastern David." As a Jew, Schiff felt underwriting the underdog was simply doing his part to "save the entire civilized world," just as he tithed 10 percent of his vast income to charity to uplift the civilized world.

The war, and the failed Revolution of 1905, had not changed "the Northern Goliath" in any meaningful way, especially for its Jews. Czar Nicholas II's autocratic regime grew increasingly isolated and out of touch. As part of a modest package of concessions to stave off further unrest, the czar had allowed the creation of a representative body known as the Duma, a watered-down version of Germany's Reichstag. It was largely the brainchild of Nicholas II's prime minister Serge Witte, the lead negotiator in the Portsmouth Conference and someone Jacob Schiff believed was the only man in the Russian government who had demonstrated any sort of goodwill toward the empire's Jews. Yet the very idea of a Duma still irked the czar, who felt it was a stepping stone toward constitutional monarchy. After the Duma went into session, a petulant Nicholas II issued the so-called Fundamental Laws, which reminded his subjects that he was still the "Supreme Autocrat" and retained the right to veto any measure passed by the new body. Kaiser Wilhelm II, himself irritated that he had to share any power with the Reichstag, cheered his cousin on, urging him to hold fast against the rabid radicals.

The first Duma, made up of five hundred or so deputies, convened in St. Petersburg on April 27, 1906. The far-left Socialist Revolutionary Party, which felt the elections were a sham, refused to participate.

Although it was heavily stocked with members of the moderate "Kadet" party, the Duma had a fair share of Social Democrat sympathizers. Even among the privileged sliver of the population granted the vote, the Duma's makeup made it clear that the czar's beliefs were unpopular. In response to leftists now having an official presence in his capital, Nicholas fired Serge Witte, replacing him with the staunch monarchist Ivan Goremkin.

Across the Atlantic, Jacob Schiff was deeply unhappy with the dismissal, calling Witte the only reasonable man in the whole czarist regime. With Witte gone, Schiff felt, all hopes of the Jews ever receiving any justice in Russia were also gone. Rather than bringing the Russian government to their senses, the Russo-Japanese War had made Nicholas II and his coterie even more intransigent. The attempted reforms did nothing to quell violence against Russia's Jews. Instead, reactionaries in the military, police, and the peasantry stepped up their activity. Between October and November 1905 alone, 690 pogroms erupted throughout the Russian Empire, and the czar did nothing to stop them. An estimated 900 Jews were murdered and 8,000 injured.

The bloodshed moved Jacob Schiff to despair, and he cried out to Sir Ernest Cassel: "One must alone lose one's faith in mankind if such horrors, beside which even a Bartholomew's night pales, can be perpetuated at this day. As sure as there is a God who looks down on all mankind, bitter vengeance will some day be wrought."

After just seventy days, Nicholas II dissolved the Duma. But the genie of representative government was out of the bottle, and political reality forced the czar to reconvene the Duma in 1907. This time, the Mensheviks and the Bolsheviks, the two branches of the Socialist Revolutionary Party, participated in the elections and won a significant number of seats. Horrified at the thought of Marxism at the gate, Nicholas dissolved the Duma again and ordered the election laws rewritten. When the Duma was once more reconvened, it was dominated by establishment elites, while the leftists had been banished from participating or, like so many before them, sent to Siberia.

Oddly enough, even while Nicholas II cherished the title of autocrat, he actually disliked the business of governing. He was not especially interested in making policy, or in policy details of any sort, that would make life better for his subjects. The existing system had lasted for four centuries and against all odds was Europe's sole surviving absolute monarchy. And so, Nicholas reasoned, his forebears and he himself must have been doing something right. Those who granted the revolutionaries any quarter, he believed, ended up either humiliated or assassinated. Those who bore him news about suffering and anger were liars and seditionists.

To Nicholas and Alexandra, the plight of the hated Jews and the civil unrest in the cities were trivial matters compared to the fate of Alexei, the son and heir to the Romanov throne. Born in 1904, their son was the only one of the royal couple's six children allowed to inherit the throne. Russia had had female rulers before. But after the death of Catherine the Great in 1796, Czar Paul I, who deeply hated his mother, forever barred women from holding the Russian throne. Alexei appeared healthy at birth, but as he grew older it was clear he had hemophilia, a disease that prevented his blood from clotting. The slightest bump or fall, or a simple nosebleed, could be fatal. It was a disease carried by mothers and passed on to male offspring, and had been endemic in the descendants of Queen Victoria. As Russia experienced further unrest and revolution, the royal couple focused more and more of their attention on keeping Alexei alive.

Nicholas and Alexandra consulted the best physicians in Russia, but eventually pinned their hopes for their son's survival on the prayerful intervention of a Russian peasant mystic named Grigori Rasputin. To the royal couple, Rasputin represented all that was good and earnest in their Russian subjects: obedient, religious, simple in dress and manner, and a fervent supporter of the monarchy. Yet to many of Nicholas's advisers, and to a growing number of his subjects, Rasputin was a cancer on the royal family. He was also a drunk and a lecher. But the czar waved off all concerns about the monk's presence in the royal household. For the czar, Rasputin was a good man, kept his son healthy, and warded off his wife's anxieties.

After a brief flicker of democratic hope, the Romanovs and the reactionaries regained control, curbed the power of the Duma, and continued to pursue the policies of the last four centuries.

What was bad news for Russia was good news for Albert Ballin. Although his reputation had been damaged by negative press, he still came out ahead. HAPAG continued to post record profits, all while maintaining relative independence from the floundering American shipping trust. The profit-sharing agreement with Morgan's IMM bought Ballin time to rebuild his fleet, and the Russian deal filled the company's coffers. He decided to play the German and British yards off against each other to determine which could build him the better ship of the future.

Nothing could stand in HAPAG's way, so long as the world didn't go to war.

Ballin deployed the proceeds from the Russian deal into the design and construction of two new passenger steamers that would be among the largest in the world. Ballin realized that SS *Deutschland*, despite her speed and good looks, had been a colossal mechanical and commercial failure. Not only did she have limited steerage capacity compared to the P-class liners but she burned too much coal to make her profitable.

Despite his efforts to build more ships in German yards, Ballin looked with envy at the White Star Line, which commissioned the first of a quartet of big liners that blended stability with economy of operation. RMS *Celtic*, the first of White Star's ships built under the auspices of J. P. Morgan's IMM, was the largest ship in the world when she made her maiden voyage from Liverpool to New York in July 1901. At over 20,000 tons and 705 feet long, she was able to carry 300 in first class, 160 in second class, and over 2,500 crammed into steerage.

But *Celtic*, which had a maximum service speed of only 16 knots, was much slower than HAPAG's SS *Deutschland*. Although she took several more days to cross the Atlantic than Ballin's record holder, she did not suffer from vibrations and did not corkscrew through the water at service speed. Comfort, her owners believed, was what rich and emigrant passengers wanted. With her smaller engines, which produced only 14,000 horsepower, White Star management also had to pay significantly less for coal per voyage, greatly increasing profit margins. Three similar ships, *Cedric*, *Baltic*, and *Adriatic*, all constructed at Harland & Wolff, would follow in the next six years. Together, they would be known as the White Star Line's "Big Four." Their first-class quarters were up to traditional White Star standards, something appreciated by the frequent customer J. P. Morgan, while their vast steerage capacities made the ships the most valuable assets in the company portfolio.

Ballin decided that to keep up with White Star, and to attract more immigrants, he had to build more ships like the *Celtic*. He knew exactly what to do. Harland & Wolff had built several HAPAG ships, and Ballin had been pleased with the results. One reason that the IMM trust built its new ships in British yards was that labor costs were significantly lower than at any American counterparts. Shortly after the Russian coal deal was made, Ballin approached Pirrie and asked him to build a ship in the manner of a "White Star liner" for HAPAG. Pirrie responded with designs for the SS *Amerika*, which at 22,500 tons was slightly larger than *Celtic*. But Ballin intervened in the ship's design, making sure she was sleeker and much better looking than her British rival. He also hoped that the ship's name would be an enticing advertising slogan for potential immigrants, and a nice counterpoint to the record-breaker SS *Deutschland*.

Ballin liked playing shipyards off against each other to see which of them produced the better liner. But he commissioned outright the AG Vulcan shipyard in Stettin, Germany, to construct a sister ship to the *Amerika*, which he intended to name *Europa*. He soon changed his mind to name the ship SS *Kaiserin Auguste Victoria*, nicknamed *KAV*. This time, Ballin made sure Auguste was spelled with an *e*, not an *a*. The empress still didn't like him.

As a result of Ballin's ship design ideas, Harland & Wolff produced a slimmer, more elegant-looking ship than did AG Vulcan. However, Ballin was not happy with its initial quality and insisted that Lord Pirrie follow HAPAG's strict safety standards, as well as those laid down by the German underwriters. Pirrie apparently balked, claiming that he built ships according to his own vision, not according to those prescribed by any other regulatory body. "The ships that Harlands built for us were therefore so disproportionately more expensive than the ones they built for the White Star Line," Ballin wrote to Warburg, "because we had strict specifications from German Lloyd and the Maritime Employers Liability Insurance Association [*See-Berufsgenossenschaft*], and our own company. For years, Lord Pirrie kept pointing out to me how much useless ballast we lug around with us [on the ships] due to [construction] material that is too strong and [due to] complicated safety precautions."

Both *Amerika* and *KAV* were equipped with luxurious quarters for about five hundred in first class and two hundred in second. Among the creature comforts Ballin installed were the first electric elevators on the high seas, as well as specialty restaurants whose offerings equaled the best cuisine ashore. And the restaurants wouldn't be managed by just any chef. During one of his visits to London, Albert had visited the brand-new Ritz Hotel. He admired its tasteful interiors, done up in the highest Louis XVI style, and its superb restaurant. So impressed was he that he approached the hotel's manager, Cesar Ritz, with a proposition: Would he be willing to run a concession aboard HAPAG's newest liners? Ritz agreed, and staffed the new "Ritz-Carlton" restaurants aboard the *KAV* and *Amerika* with the finest Escoffier-trained chefs.

For all the amenities in first class, both vessels had massive immigrant capacity, able to carry 250 in third class in separate cabins and 1,750 in steerage in traditional open dormitories. Revenues from the lower two classes, of course, subsidized the grandeur of first class and the comfort of second. HAPAG's introduction of the "third-class" category was a major leap forward for passenger comfort. For the fare of 180 marks, a third-class passenger got not only a separate cabin but also sit-down meals in a dining saloon, where they were served by white-jacketed stewards. Steerage passengers, who paid 160 marks, still had to sleep in open dormitories and collect their food from the ship's galley.

Amerika and *KAV* entered service in 1905 and 1906, respectively, and proved to be immensely profitable and popular vessels. The fast and fearsome-looking Cunard superliners *Lusitania* and *Mauretania* both debuted in 1907. Much to the delight of the British public, *Lusitania* snatched the westbound speed record away from HAPAG's *Deutschland*, rendering the troublesome German ship irrelevant. But Ballin decided that the Blue Riband wasn't worth the cost of keeping it, and let the British have it. The port of Hamburg and his company's possession of the border control stations was crucially important to the business. The Blue Riband was not.

By 1907, the steerage business had grown even larger and more profitable than Albert Ballin ever thought possible. The dark days of the Hamburg cholera epidemic were a distant memory. And by outsourcing the running of the border control stations to HAPAG and North German Lloyd, the German government had effectively granted the two lines a state-sanctioned monopoly.

Meanwhile, Ballin didn't forget the power of pageantry to demonstrate Germany's growing preeminence on the world stage. In June 1907, he pulled out all the stops by hosting a grand celebration that marked the twenty-fifth anniversary of the Kiel Regatta. This time, rather than using one of his transatlantic liners as the reception venue, he trotted out the brand-new HAPAG cruise vessel *Oceana*, a clipper-bowed beauty built to resemble a royal yacht. Ballin supervised all the proceedings, which included teas, dinners, and dancing on deck, as well as the customary speeches and toasts.

HAPAG could well afford such extravagances, as Ballin's investments in the *Auswandererhallen* and the two new flagship liners had paid off. In 1908, 115,982 immigrants passed through Hamburg on their way to America, and of these, 112,644 had passed through HAPAG's Emigrant Village. In its peak years, about 43 percent of the migrants who entered and left the village were Jewish, 55 percent Roman Catholic, and 2 percent Protestant.

By this time Ballin was well on the way to being a multimillionaire in control of the largest shipping fleet in the world. He had successfully fended off a takeover of his company by the Morgan trust. He had the ear of the Kaiser, and counted some of the most powerful men in Germany and Great Britain as his friends. But he was increasingly unhappy and anxiety ridden. Despite his apparent ease at social events, he found them exhausting, perhaps because, forever the outsider, he could never be fully comfortable among those who were not part of his life. His wife, Marianne, did not appear to take much joy in their burgeoning prosperity. She found all the pomp and pageantry draining, and photographs of her at events show her looking more resolute than happy. While providing Ballin with love in the privacy of their home, she performed her duties as HAPAG's official hostess more out of duty than pleasure.

Among the affluent elite of Hamburg and Berlin, extravagant entertaining had become the norm, and was seen as a business as well as a personal necessity and expense. Like his extravagant uncle King Edward VII of Great Britain, for whom the "Edwardian era" was named, Kaiser Wilhelm II set an example for ostentatious living. The nobility and the German bourgeoisie followed suit. This meant frequent dinner parties of a hundred people or more, and everyday evening offerings including caviar, pâté de foie gras, ice cream, and champagne. In order to play the game, one had to spend grandly.

Albert Ballin, an aesthete at heart, enjoyed everything from selecting the menus to arranging the seating charts and choosing the flowers. Marianne was happy to be in the background. Behind her back, society women sniped that Frau Ballin was good at folding napkins but overall was an uninspired hostess.

In addition to his constant party planning at his city house and at the Villa Ballin in Hamfelde, Ballin traveled ceaselessly, sometimes to London for business, often on cruises on his ships, which went as far afield as Spitsbergen, in Norway, China, and Japan. He even took his daughter, Irmgard, on a world cruise aboard the HAPAG liner *Cincinnati*. He also spent many weeks at German spas and sanitariums, accompanied frequently by Marianne. His favorite resort was Bad Kissingen, famed for its mineral waters. During his travels, Albert wrote Max Warburg that the stress of work and persistent anxiety about a war to come were consuming him even when he was taking the waters.

Ballin might have been the lord of HAPAG by dint of his own hard work and drive, but when it came to the country's governance and the future of his life's work, many things were spinning out of his control. After the Cunard battle, he focused on another issue. What worried him, at least as he wrote in his letters to Max, was not the plight of the Jewish people at the hands of the Russians but competition from Russian ports. He had heard rumors that the Russians were planning on establishing a rival steamship line that would carry emigrants from the Latvian port of Liepāja, bypassing Hamburg and the border control stations. After awarding him with coal contracts and a decoration, Ballin feared the Russians were about to take from him all he had built. "Very dire for us and Lloyd," he wrote Max Warburg. "Will also have corresponding impact on stock market. Best wishes and regards hope to travel tomorrow [to hotel] Stephanie in Baden-Baden."

The ever-breezy Max knew how to talk his close friend away from a cliff. "Just let the Russians sail from Liepāja to New York if they want to," he responded, "you'll survive that all right. In the worst case the shareholders will receive dividends that are 1 percent smaller."

EVEN THOUGH it enjoyed favored status in Berlin, HAPAG could build the three ships without a subsidy from the German government. In fact,

Ballin felt that direct government subsidies would make his company beholden to the interests of the Foreign Office and the Imperial Navy, and never pursued them. And despite the much-touted "patronage" of Kaiser Wilhelm II, HAPAG's only real subsidies came in the form of its contract to operate the Prussia-Russia border controls, as well as government fees to carry mail from Germany to the rest of the world. HAPAG's capital reserves were especially robust, plus his friendship with Max Warburg gave him ready access to any additional capital he might need.

While HAPAG prospered, its rival, North German Lloyd, stalled. HAPAG's emergence as the world's largest shipping line—with a fleet of 175 passenger and cargo vessels—had come at the expense of its longtime rival. Although Ballin and Wiegand professed to be allies in the interest of protecting German shipping from foreign influence, it was clear that the Bremen-based company was not making enough money to maintain the size of its fleet and therefore its share of the immigrant trade. There had been talk of a more formal alliance, possibly a merger. Wiegand wrote Albert Ballin, "That we have competed with each other and sought to reduce each other in particular areas, all annoyance and chagrin that now one and now the other of us has thereby experienced, has now, however, been forgotten in the end." But Ballin kept the so-called obstinate Frisian at arm's length. The general director decided that such a merger made no sense and that HAPAG would be best going it alone with a new class of superliners.

"He was more an artist than an engineer," Max Warburg said of Albert Ballin, "and more a painter than a draftsman. The richness of qualities with which he was blessed on life's path also generated a great many conflicts in him, through which he fought honorably." It was in the construction of three new superliners that Ballin went full-on artist, and was more than happy to do battle with the bean counters on the HAPAG board. He presented his plan to HAPAG's Board of Control not in the form of financial projections and blueprints but rather in a sketch on the back of an envelope, drawn by Bernhard Huldermann, his private secretary. Ballin estimated that the wonder ships would cost 25 million marks apiece, and that the seemingly endless stream of immigrants from Eastern Europe would easily pay for their size and grandeur.

Max von Schinkel, the head of the Board of Control and a frequent

Ballin critic, recoiled in horror. He felt that the new ships were ludicrous extravagances, a "general waste in the company's finances." Another board member, the penny-pinching banker Johannes Merck, snarled that the general director was "totally unbusinesslike" when he placed orders with shipbuilders, letting his emotions get in the way of practicality. Merck had approved of Ballin's construction program in the past, but now felt that he was so obsessed with outdoing Morgan's new fleet that he had lost all sense of what was practical. "Often, there were no extensive consultations with the various sections or a calculation about the feasibility of any project," Merck complained.

In truth, the new superliners would cost far more than anyone could have predicted. The first ran to 38 million marks and the second to 42 million marks. The third ship, bigger, grander, and more refined than the first two, would have cost even more, but would never sail under HAPAG's flag.

It was in the planning of the three new ships that the board was exposed to what Max Warburg once described as Albert Ballin's "demonic" side. Numbers didn't matter to him. He wanted to create floating showcases of German art, engineering, and decoration that also earned their keep as immigrant carriers. They would each be a *Gesamtkunstwerk*, a Wagnerian term for a "total work of art" that synthesized German engineering, technology, and art into a singular work of genius.

* * *

The work on the first of Ballin's new class of superliners started in 1909 at the Vulcan shipyard in Hamburg. Unlike other German liners, he made sure there were absolutely no provisions for wartime use included in her design. She would be a ship of peace, with no reinforced decking for the mounting of guns. Although her first-class quarters would be grander than anything afloat, Ballin focused particular attention on her third-class and steerage accommodations. Above all, the ship's vast scale would convey that feeling of safety that many frightened immigrants craved on a life-changing journey. Albert Ballin wanted to name her *Europa*, as a German gesture of peace and unity with the rest of the Continent.

A year later, the keel of her slightly larger sister ship was laid at the nearby Blöhm & Voss yards in Hamburg, whose cranes and gantries were visible from Ballin's desk at the HAPAG headquarters on the Alster Lake. Ballin hoped to christen it with a name that celebrated the German Empire. Once again, he wanted to see whether two competing shipyards— AG Vulcan or Blöhm & Voss—would provide the superior ship of the class.

Kaiser Wilhelm II got wind of the first new ship's construction and immediately suggested his own name: *Imperator*, or emperor, in Latin. After himself, of course. It was an extremely awkward choice. Norddeutscher-Lloyd already had a liner, the four-stacker *Kaiser Wilhelm II* of 1902. Moreover, an imperial moniker trumpeting German chauvinism wasn't good marketing for a ship meant to carry people from all over the European continent to the New World. Finally, there was a grammatical issue. Seafarers generally referred to ships by the feminine article, even those with masculine names. In the end, Albert Ballin felt he had no choice but to accede to the Kaiser's request and shelve the name *Europa*. The new flagship would be referred to by the masculine *der Imperator* rather than the traditional feminine *die*, a first for any ship in the German fleet.

By this time, if Jacob Schiff felt any ill will toward Ballin for helping the Russian fleet during the Russo-Japanese War, he abandoned it. As the work on the ships progressed, Ballin pursued new interests with Schiff. Although no direct correspondence survives between Ballin and Schiff during the early years of the twentieth century, the two men had some kind of business relationship brokered by Max Warburg and Sir Ernest Cassel, Jacob Schiff's man on the ground in Great Britain. Ballin now served as a mediator between German investors and Kuhn, Loeb & Co., which funneled German capital into American railroads.

In the meantime, Jacob Schiff was funneling his own substantial capital earned from advising *goyishe* railroad barons into his vision of American *tzedakah*. He helped more and more Russian Jews make their way to America. Schiff still maintained that the idea of a Jewish homeland in Palestine was a pipe dream. "A utopia . . . which I fear will only block the way of something practical," he scoffed.

America, Schiff believed, was destined to become the new Israel. And it needed more of his type of Jew. Less Emma Goldman, more Oscar Straus.

Unfortunately, calls for immigration restriction were now coming not just from the likes of Senator Henry Cabot Lodge and Prescott Farnsworth Hall but from the broader American public. And Congress was listening.

Schiff and his allies decided to fight them using new tactics. Their success would affect Ballin, Morgan, and everyone involved in the immigrant trade—particularly Jewish immigrants.

CHAPTER 16

Immigration Restriction Goes Mainstream

We would have been spared the curse of our
present flood of Lower East Side Jews if the
Hon. Grover Cleveland had not vetoed the il-
literacy test on account of the so-called
Corliss amendment many years ago.

—PRESCOTT FARNSWORTH HALL, PRESIDENT OF
THE IMMIGRATION RESTRICTION LEAGUE, TO
SENATOR ELIHU ROOT, MAY 10, 1912

As he fought against anti-immigration sentiment, Jacob Schiff felt that time was running out. He had become increasingly concerned that if Jews were too concentrated in cities along the East Coast, they could not assimilate themselves into the nation's fabric, which would inevitably lead to political backlash. The Immigration Restriction League, only a fringe movement twenty years earlier, now had broader appeal and was showing increasing political strength. Although Theodore Roosevelt had publicly endorsed immigration, he privately complained to his friend Henry Cabot Lodge about America's Protestant stock being bred out of existence.

Undeterred, Schiff funded a new venture in 1907. Its goal was to divert Jews away from settling in New York City and instead encourage them to spread out around the country. His plan was to turn the port of Galveston, Texas, into a southern Ellis Island, where Jews could settle as merchants and even as farmers. Jacob Schiff pitched in a substantial sum of $500,000 to fund the Galveston Plan. He didn't contract with

HAPAG, but with Norddeutscher-Lloyd, which already ran ships to the Texas port city. "If we had the ways and means to distribute the arrivals over the country," Schiff wrote, "I think it fair to say that the United States is in a position to absorb . . . between 1.5 and 2 million more Russian immigrants within the next ten or fifteen years." Schiff's choice of Galveston also probably came from a desire for Jewish arrivals to circumvent the increasingly strict and terrifying bureaucratic bottleneck at Ellis Island.

Israel Zangwill called the Galveston Plan "the only constructive idea my dear friend Schiff ever had." As he took charge of Schiff's initiative, he was also at work on a new play called *The Melting Pot*. Zangwill, himself a Russian immigrant, believed that the future of American Jews lay in intermarriage and assimilation into the mainstream. Schiff liked the play for the most part, but disagreed vehemently with one of its messages, that to survive as Americans, "we must here give up our identity and that the God of our Fathers and our God cannot be the God of our children."

Schiff grossly miscalculated. Zangwill was a better playwright than promoter. The pull of the big cities of the Eastern Seaboard, especially New York, Boston, and Philadelphia, was just too great. Immigrant Jews wanted to settle near family and where they could join communities. Small-town life and agriculture held no allure. "The port of Galveston invited entry," said one administrator of the program, "but to take the plunge into the Hinterlands where Yiddish may be an unknown tongue, kosher food an unknown thing, and labor opportunities limited, was left only to the most daring. . . . [The Russian] could make his wants known in his own language in New York and other Eastern cities; and if his wants were dire, his friends and fellow countrymen were ready to lend a helping hand." For a successful immigrant who valued family and community above all else, Schiff was remarkably tone deaf to the emotional needs of Russian Jewish immigrants in America.

Even while Schiff was embarrassed that not many Russian Jews chose to settle in Galveston, he continued to spar with the Zionist wing of the American Jewish community. In 1907, Schiff fired off a letter to Solomon Schechter, head of the Jewish Telegraphic Agency, about why the new Jewish arrivals should adapt to American life rather than see it as a staging area in a journey to a Jewish homeland:

> Speaking as an American, I cannot for a moment concede that one can be at the same time a true American and an honest adherent of the Zionist movement.... The Jew should not for a moment feel that he has only found "asylum" in this country; he must not feel that he is in exile and that his abode here is only a temporary or passing one.

In other words, American Jews should think about life more like the assimilated Jews of Germany, not the persecuted Jews of Russia.

Despite their shared faith, there were major, often insurmountable clashes of class and culture between the German and Russian Jews. The stately brownstone townhouses of the Upper West Side, furnished with Steinway pianos, dark carpets, and Germanic bric-a-brac, and often staffed with Irish cooks and German nannies, were worlds away from the apartments of the Lower East Side, with their airless rooms, straw mattresses, coal-fired stoves, and Singer sewing machines. Then, too, the atmosphere of a German Jewish synagogue was decorous and restrained, especially the Reform congregations. The men and women dressed in the fashionable clothes favored by the Episcopalians and Presbyterians. A few, including Temple Emanu-El, even employed a pipe organ, a distinctly gentile instrument, during worship.

The small Orthodox shuls of the Lower East Side were loud and bustling, full of men in prayer shawls, phylacteries and yarmulkes on their heads, bowing rhythmically and passionately reciting the Jewish prayers. Women, who had to keep their own hair covered, were seated in the upstairs gallery, shielded from the men by a screen. While on the Upper West Side Dr. Sachs prepared young men for Harvard, the boys of the Lower East Side learned their lessons about Judaism and Hebrew in crowded *cheder* schools, taught by harried, underpaid teachers known as *melamdim*. The lucky few would gain entry to City College, while most went to work in their teens.

Schiff, who kept meticulous track of all family expenses and scolded his children whenever they wasted any money, admired the thrift and grit he observed among the Yiddish-speaking shopkeepers and the pushcart peddlers, as well as the thrift and grit of their feisty customers looking to strike a bargain. He also noticed that the new Americans allowed themselves not a moment's rest as they worked to provide for their families. Most Jewish immigrant men had two choices, and both involved selling things. The first was operating a pushcart to sell groceries, baked goods, cloth, leather, or cigars. Most pushcart peddlers didn't bother to get a license from the city and were frequently harassed by less-than-friendly police officers. The second was to open a small brick-and-mortar store on one of the Lower East Side's congested commercial thoroughfares.

It was not unlike how Kuhn, Loeb & Co. and other banking houses got their start as purveyors of dry goods in the American Midwest half a century earlier. Even for the poorest immigrant, there was still the promise, however distant, of a better life for one's children, of someday achieving the "American dream," as Jacob Schiff and "Our Crowd" had done. They had arrived as immigrants and started out as peddlers and garment manufacturers, and their children had gone to college and become bankers, doctors, and academics.

That dream advanced, Schiff believed, through intellectual achievement. He was confident that the Jewish people could both keep their faith and partake of the rich tradition of higher education established by the nation's Protestant founders. Schiff believed that his people, like all Americans, would continue to improve and advance themselves. Other Harvard alumni, whose alma mater song declared that the school would endure "till the stock of the Puritan dies," weren't so sure. For the American establishment class, after all, Jewish immigrants also represented radical politics.

But over the past two decades, Schiff did his best to forge a Jewish alliance with the educational institutions of the gentile upper class. On May 13, 1891, Jacob Schiff delivered an address at Harvard University, the alma mater of Henry Cabot Lodge, to celebrate the installation of a new collection of Jewish artifacts, a project spearheaded by the Semitic Languages department. In a place that prided itself as one of the bastions of American Protestant culture, Jacob Schiff, the immigrant, had used his fortune and influence to establish a beachhead of Jewish culture. His friend Charles Eliot supported the venture. In his strong German accent, the five-foot-two Schiff reminded his audience that his faith, the Jewish faith, was the bedrock of monotheism.

"Indeed, the Jews, the modern representatives of the Semitic people, may well be proud of their origin and ancestry," Schiff said. "Anti-Semitism in Europe, social prejudice and ostracism in free America may for a time be rampant; posterity will shame and disgust these passions. To combat in the meantime these unsound currents in an efficient manner, opportunities should be created for a more thorough study and a better knowledge of Semitic history and civilization, so that the world shall better understand and acknowledge the debt it owes to the Jewish people."

*   *   *

Prescott Farnsworth Hall and his allies refused to acknowledge any debt that white Protestant Americans had to the Jewish people. Rather, they doubled down on exclusion. In 1906, the Immigration Restriction League tried again to flex its growing political muscle in Congress. At Hall's urging, Senator Henry Cabot Lodge and his allies in Congress decided to draft yet another bill that restricted immigration from Southern and Eastern Europe. This time, unlike their failed attempt under the Cleveland administration, they would convey their views to newspapers all over the country and garner the support of individuals thought to be respected scientists. Lodge and Hall might have been at ease in the private clubs of Boston, where their proclamations and screeds were met with nods of approval, but they were terrible public speakers and stilted wordsmiths.

Anti-Semitism looked different in Europe than it did in America, but it was still present. In 1906, at the beginning of his second term, President Roosevelt appointed Oscar Straus to the position of secretary of commerce and labor, making him the nation's first Jewish cabinet secretary. His brother Isidor served as a two-term Democratic congressman from New York. The two were the link between powerful gentile politicians and a growing and increasingly powerful Jewish constituency in New York and other big industrial cities. At a banquet hosted by Jacob Schiff, President Roosevelt declared, "When this country conferred upon me the honor of making me President of the United States, I of course at once called my good friend, Oscar Straus, to my side, and asked him to serve as Secretary of Commerce. It was not a question of religion, of politics, or of catering to any specific group. It was simply a matter of the best man for the job."

As soon as Prescott Farnsworth Hall learned that Oscar Straus had been appointed a cabinet secretary, he flew into one of his characteristic rages. Hall frequently wrote to the commissioner of immigration at Ellis Island, William Williams, to see if the first Jewish cabinet official in American history was enforcing the new Anarchist Exclusion Act and to see if more immigrants were being rejected for physical defects and mental deficiencies. Williams cooperated with Hall, who then passed along the data to Henry Cabot Lodge, who was plotting to introduce another round of restrictive legislation.

"From the above table," Hall wrote Lodge in 1907, "you will see that, after you tackled the Secretary on this subject in May or June, there was temporary improvement, since when [*sic*] things have been getting back to where they were before."

Hall claimed that Straus was being deceptive by failing to say that "immigration increased over 14 percent in the same period. By his method of statement he evidently wishes to convey the impression that his administration has been more stringent in this matter than in the proceeding one, whereas, in fact, the reverse is true."

He also sent Lodge statistics showing that between 1906 and 1907, the number of reversals of initial rejections under Secretary Straus's watch had gone up 25 percent. At a more granular level, the reversals on appeal of immigrants deemed to become public charges without bond had gone up 15 percent, and those with bond 142.2 percent.

Ever the paranoid conspiracist, Hall believed that a cunning cabal of Jewish bankers such as Jacob Schiff, steamship owners such as Albert Ballin, and activists in the Liberal Immigration League had captured the attention of President Roosevelt, a man Hall and Lodge believed was one of them.

Stymied at an attempt to exclude Jews and Southern Europeans because of their "poor physiques," Hall decided to go after the steamship companies and proposed to reduce their capacity in steerage under the guise of public health. The IRL wanted a new "Navigation Law" that would block the arrival of immigrants who landed on "rag ships," or vessels that had less than 200 feet of open space allotted to each immigrant in steerage. This would effectively cut the steerage capacity of ships such as HAPAG's immensely profitable P-class liners from twenty-one hundred to one thousand. But these efforts came to nothing. Since the cholera epidemic of 1893, Albert Ballin had worked very hard to enlarge his ships' third-class and steerage spaces, as well as the medical checks and fumigations at the border control stations and the *Auswandererhallen*. HAPAG's rivals, including the companies controlled by J. P. Morgan's International Mercantile Marine, had also enlarged spaces for steerage-class passengers.

In the end, Commissioner Williams did not impose any additional restrictions on the major steamship companies, including HAPAG, Cunard, and those controlled by Morgan. "There are many immigrant ships on the Ocean today with adequate quarters," he wrote to Hall, "and the above criticisms are directed against some, not all. The subject is a very important one, but it should be looked into carefully in all its details before the adoption of radical changes which might be unfair and, in addition, might or might not, remedy the real evils." What Williams meant by "the real evils" were the people being carried in the steamships, not the steamships themselves.

The new science of eugenics gave the IRL a way to identify those "real evils." Although the term *eugenics* was relatively new, Hall argued that improving the human race by segregating people into strict groups and selectively breeding among the "best" people was an ancient and noble cause. Hall felt that what he regarded as his race, the elite Protestants of the American Northeast, should perpetually lead and govern the country just as it always had. This meant controlling not only the institutions of government but also its schools, universities, and cultural organizations. "Since Christianity and civilization have emphasized the worth of the individual," Hall wrote in 1910, "the voluntary elimination of the unfit has been limited to the execution of the offenders against political and religious laws, and the forced segregation of certain other classes, like paupers, insane persons, idiots and leppers.

"The attempt to improve race stocks in recent times," he continued, "has therefore taken the form, not of killing off the least fit, but of preventing their coming into the State, either by being born into it or through migration. Eugenics includes, not only the prevention of the unfit but the conscious attempt to produce the more fit; indeed it is in the latter sense that the word is often used. Strictly speaking, however, it must include all attempts to improve the physical equipment of the individual in so far as he acquires it by heredity."

Hall and the IRL hoped not only to shut off immigration from Eastern Europe but to keep the new arrivals confined to their urban ghettos. There they could breed only among themselves, and not among the general population. This, in Hall's opinion, would serve the public interest. He also wouldn't have to endure prosperous Jewish merchants and bankers moving anywhere close to his secluded Brookline, Massachusetts, estate. For Hall, a successful Jew was in no way an example of survival of the fittest, but rather a perversion of natural law.

Soon enough, Hall would find his ideal Nordic specimen who would codify these beliefs into literary propaganda. In 1907, his mind consumed by satanic images of conspiring Jews and smoke-belching HAPAG steamships, Hall wrote the New York attorney Madison Grant asking for a favor, one that involved some paid espionage on his pro-immigration opponents. "Something has occurred to me in which I think you could be of considerable use to the cause of restricting immigration," he wrote to Grant. "One (Mrs.) Florence Brooks (Hiley) has been doing some investigating in New Jersey for the Liberal Immigration League, which you probably know is fighting all legislation, and is even trying to have the present law made weaker. I believe it is backed by the Jews and the steamship companies."

Madison Grant was more than happy to help. "I will talk to Mrs. Brooks if you care to send her to me," he replied. He also added that he was working his own connections in Congress, namely Speaker Joseph Cannon of Illinois, who "is the main factor in preventing the restriction of immigration. He is hopelessly behind the times and does not appreciate the conditions we have here in the East."

Born in 1865, Grant was a generation younger than Henry Cabot Lodge, and, like him and Prescott Hall, never had to work a day in his life. After graduating from Yale and Columbia Law School, Grant dabbled in zoology. His study of evolution led him into the realm of eugenics, a "scientific" belief that the human race could be improved by selective breeding. Grant came up with the idea of the "Nordic race," a group of people who supposedly originated in Germany and Scandinavia and who possessed superior intellectual and physical traits. It was pseudoscientific nonsense, but the Nordic ideal caught on among those inclined to believe such notions. Grant's fear was that immigration would destroy the primarily "Nordic" character of the country's pre–Civil War inhabitants. And so he proposed that "undesirable types," particularly Jews and Southern Europeans, be segregated from the rest of the population in ghettos to prevent them from interbreeding with "Old Stock" Americans.

The IRL lobby introduced yet another bill to require a literacy test requirement for new arrivals to the United States. When the bill came up for a vote in 1906, Speaker Joseph G. Cannon, a conservative Illinois Republican who controlled the House with an iron fist, made sure it died on the floor. Cannon felt it reeked of anti-Americanism and bigotry. No admirer of the president and his upper-crust patrician cronies, Cannon had once declared that Roosevelt had "no more use for the Constitution than a tomcat has for a marriage license." But Cannon had to cover himself politically, and called for the creation of a congressional commission, headed by Representative William P. Dillingham, to study the effects of unrestricted immigration on the United States, particularly from Southern and Eastern Europe. It would be composed of three senators, three congressmen, and three experts selected by President Roosevelt.

The IRL decided to hitch its wagon to the work of the Dillingham Commission. The league hoped to influence the commission's report in a way that would in the future help to create a political environment amenable to imposing tough restrictions. In the meantime, Hall, who had the fervor of a zealot but the charisma of a mortician, kept a meticulous collection of the proceedings of groups that opposed him. To get the documents, the IRL almost certainly planted spies at their meetings. Among the papers were reports of the United Hebrew Charities of the City of New York, whose donors and board members included Solomon Loeb, Jacob Schiff, and the Liberal Immigration League.

The more Hall read, the more his hatred of the Jews and their allies grew. He learned that the steamship companies were building bigger and faster liners that could carry ever more immigrants into the country from Southern and Eastern Europe. International Mercantile Marine, even if its mastermind J. P. Morgan disliked Jews, depended on immigration to make money.

While being cordial to Jacob Schiff, Theodore Roosevelt still considered Senator Henry Cabot Lodge of Massachusetts his best friend. No matter what Cabot said or wrote, the deep tie that bound the two men together—Harvard's exclusive Porcellian Club and their sense of belonging to a kind of American aristocracy—could not be undone. To Lodge and the Immigration Restriction League, America's growing Jewish population was not something to be celebrated. In 1907, Lodge was appointed, with Roosevelt's blessing, to serve on the Dillingham Commission.

At the same time, the drumbeat of anti-Semitism became increasingly strident. Among the most vociferous new commentators was Poultney Bigelow, a graduate of Yale University, and like Senator Henry Cabot Lodge and Prescott Hall, a man of independent wealth who fancied himself a member of the Anglo-American elite. Trained as a lawyer, Bigelow retired from private practice at a young age to take up newspaper work. He eventually got a column at the *New York Herald*, arguably the city's most patrician daily paper. Like Lodge, Bigelow felt that Eastern European Jews were mongrelizing the nation's gene pool, and in his columns, he trained his fury at the "Jew-German" lobby, Jewish philanthropic organizations, and steamship lines.

He had special ire for the Baron de Hirsch Fund, the enormous philanthropic foundation started by Jacob Schiff's old mentor, which encouraged Jewish emigration from Russia. Jacob Schiff had served as vice president of the organization's American branch, which managed a $2.5 million bequest to set up Jewish agricultural and trade schools in the United States. Rather than a charity, Bigelow saw the fund as a Jewish plot to replace Old Stock Americans with outsiders. In one of his columns, Bigelow wrote:

Today the United States has probably more Jews than all the rest of the world—thanks to the Hirsch fund, and its able political committee in Washington. Our immigration agents may with impunity turn back families of Norwegian, Danish, English or Scotch extraction, and the matter ends there. But let the most undesirable Jew from the Russian border be excluded, and the American Press makes flaming articles about race prejudice. The best lawyers are employed; the best lobbyists invade the capital;

Congressmen are cajoled or bullied; a Hebrew senator leads an influential deputation to the White House; the Secretary of State is inundated with Jew-German rhetoric; and in the end a cable instructs the immigrant agent abroad to pass that particular Jew because Congressman Rosenbaum and Senator Pfeilchenblum have an interest in the matter. The Jew wants no farm in Palestine or anywhere else—he wants New York, where he can underbid and undersell, and play with our legal paragraphs.

Bigelow didn't dare mention Jacob Schiff by name, but his readers picked up the unmistakable cues as they read the polemicist's columns over morning coffee in their dark-paneled Upper East Side townhouses.

Once the domain of a small sliver of true believers, Bigelow's conspiratorial rhetoric and Henry Cabot Lodge's policy goals were becoming acceptable in the upper echelons of American society. Three decades earlier, the decision by Judge Henry Hilton to refuse giving a room to Joseph Seligman in the Grand Union Hotel had outraged the public. Now anti-Semitism had become completely and broadly socially acceptable.

Madison Grant was now hard at work on a new book, one he claimed used science to prove that the so-called Nordic race was superior to all others but was under threat of being overrun and outbred by inferior races. These were the "Alpines" and "Mediterraneans," categories he had invented whole cloth. He postulated that the only way the Mediterraneans who built the civilizations of Greece and Rome achieved greatness was because they had "intermingled with the Nordic race" and were essentially Nordic in character. The Alpines were the Slavs of Central Europe.

His views, Grant asserted, were not racist, but were based on science, although they stemmed from the virulently racist work of earlier self-styled European "social scientists" like Count Arthur de Gobineau and Francis Galton. To protect America's Nordic character, Grant argued, America needed to institute the restrictions and quotas based on national origin that the IRL had been pushing since the 1890s.

One of the most powerful voices speaking against the views of the Immigration Restriction League was the anthropologist Franz Boas. Unlike the self-styled gentlemen dilettante lawyers and anthropologists of the IRL, Franz Boas had received a rigorous academic education. Born in 1858 into a cultured and assimilated Prussian Jewish family, Boas had studied physics at the universities of Heidelberg, Berlin, and Kiel, but then decided to move into the nascent field of anthropology. Boas traveled to the American Pacific Northwest and Canada's Baffin Island, where he immersed himself in the study of the native populations. It was while studying the Inuits that he had a life-changing revelation about the human race, one that made him an avowed enemy of the so-called scientific racism that was becoming increasingly fashionable in the cosseted university faculty clubs in Europe and America. His revelation concerned human empathy.

"I often ask myself what advantages our 'good society' possesses over that of the 'savages' and find, the more I see of their customs," he wrote in his journal during a visit to Baffin Island in the early 1880s, "that we have no right to look down upon them. . . . We have no right to blame them for their forms and superstitions which may seem ridiculous to us. We 'highly educated people' are much worse, relatively speaking."

Franz Boas moved to the United States, where he was appointed curator of the American Museum of Natural History in 1893, and professor of anthropology at Columbia University a few years later. Like Albert Ballin, he felt culturally German and was thoroughly secular in his outlook. Yet he could not in good conscience erase his Jewish identity, and saw the confluence of anti-Semitic forces both in Europe and America as extremely dangerous not just for science but for all of humanity.

Despite Boas's work to counter Grant's own, anti-Semitism swirled and intensified in American institutions. Jacob Schiff, now in his sixties and pushing himself hard in both his investment banking and charitable activities, doubled down on his assimilationist efforts. He paid particular attention to the Henry Street Settlement on the Lower East Side and gave generously to Montefiore Hospital in New York, which provided advanced medical care to the city's poorest residents, with a focus on Jewish patients.

And then Schiff lost a friend in a high place. In 1909, President Eliot of Harvard stepped down. His replacement was another Boston patrician, but one decidedly less accepting of Jews than his predecessor. A lawyer by training, Abbott Lawrence Lowell was an active member of the Immigration Restriction League, and was concerned about not only the growing number of Italians and Jews settling in Boston but about the growing number of sons of immigrants applying for admission to Harvard.

President Lowell found Schiff's entreaties annoying, but he tolerated him and other members of the German Jewish elite, such as the banker's son-in-law, Felix Warburg, because of their financial generosity. Warburg, it turned out, proved to be a much better philanthropist and Jewish cultural ambassador than a banker. He gave large sums to Harvard's Fogg Museum of Art, run by the curator Edward Forbes, who gradually amassed a first-rate collection of paintings and established a world-class art history program. Such an atmosphere made Harvard a welcoming and comfortable place for culturally sophisticated and intellectually curious Jewish students of both German and Russian origin. Lowell put up with the art museum only because it stood on its own financial feet and needed no help from university coffers. The museum was one thing; the college another. From the start, Lowell was developing plans to exclude Jews should they make up more than 10 percent of the student population.

Lowell's concerns—and Schiff's, Boas's, Grant's, and Lodge's, too— would soon intensify. War loomed in Europe, and that threat encouraged more and more refugees from Eastern Europe to seek safety in America. Despite the hard work of many pacifists, Europe was still moving slowly toward conflict. In 1908, Austria-Hungary annexed Bosnia-Herzegovina, a tiny country with a large population of ethnic Serbians. Serbia, an Orthodox country and longtime ally of Russia, was indignant at this move and started to supply insurgents with weapons to fight against the Catholic intruders. From the sidelines, Germany cheered on Austria-Hungary in its fight to subdue the Serbian upstarts.

In the meantime, Russia grew outraged at Austria-Hungary's persecution of its Slavic brethren.

As Bismarck predicted, the mixture of Pan-Slavism and Pan-Germanism in the tinderbox of the Balkan Peninsula would one day ignite the whole continent of Europe.

CHAPTER 17

Halting the March to Armageddon

No Bismarck was needed to prevent *this* war.

—ALBERT BALLIN

As the Immigration Restriction League (and Lodge's allies in Washington) worked to restrict immigration, Albert Ballin worried about the potential of war in Europe. Great Britain, as the established power and the holder of the world's reserve currency, was allied with France and Russia in an agreement known as the Triple Entente. Germany, a rising power and crucible of science and industry, was allied with Austria-Hungary and Italy in an agreement called the Triple Alliance. An attack on one country would trigger war with all the others.

Some thought this alliance mechanism was a powerful deterrent to war. Ballin did not. He knew the Kaiser and his circle had dreams of further expansion into the rich agricultural lands of the east, including parts of the Pale of Settlement, and would be willing to go to war for it. France was still bitter about its defeat by Prussia in the Franco-Prussian War forty years earlier, and Great Britain found Germany's growing naval strength and colonial ambitions a threat to its imperial supremacy.

And then there were the simmering ethnic tensions over Bosnia-Herzegovina between the Austrians and the Serbs. As a committed Slavophile, Czar Nicholas II of Russia was more than happy to help support the ethnic Serbs (and fellow Orthodox coreligionists) in their quest for a unified nation-state. Russia's support of Bosnian Serbian rebels greatly irritated the government in Vienna, which was struggling to keep its ancient, multiethnic empire together. Meanwhile, Berlin took secret delight in these machinations, hoping they would give Germany the chance for a major European land grab should war break out.

Albert Ballin fervently believed that England and Germany should be friendly rivals, not military enemies. He also knew that a war on the Continent, no matter how small, could completely disrupt the intricate and fragile transportation web that made HAPAG's lucrative immigration business viable. At a personal level, he also hated the idea of war, and had no romantic illusions of glory in combat.

As an advocate for his company and his nation, Albert Ballin felt the use of corporate diplomacy was an effective way to keep war from breaking out in Europe. North German Lloyd prepared itself in other ways. The leadership of the Bremen company had no problem working with the German Admiralty to integrate military capabilities into their ships. This meant they could easily be converted from ocean liners into speedy raiders of commercial traffic should war break out. All NDL captains of the Four Flyers were prepared to transform their vessels into warships in short order.

By contrast, HAPAG's ships had virtually no capacity for wartime use as part of their design. They were built and designed to be big, comfortable, and moderately powered people movers, not swift birds of prey. What united Germany's shipping executives was the recognition that the lucrative business of moving immigrants from the Russian Empire to the United States had to be protected. And the biggest guarantor of that business was peaceful coexistence between Germany and Great Britain.

In 1908, after the introduction from Max Warburg, Albert Ballin began a long correspondence with Jacob Schiff's friend Sir Ernest Cassel. Cassel's royal client, unlike his nephew Kaiser Wilhelm, had no problem with Jews at all. In fact, he embraced them as valuable subjects, especially if they were well educated and successful. Poking fun at the banker's large girth and grand tastes, journalists had dubbed him "Windsor Cassel." Edward visited Sir Ernest's London mansion almost every day for a running bridge game. As tensions mounted, Cassel, who felt affinity for both his native Germany and his adopted country, thought that Ballin would make the ideal Berlin-to-London intermediary in any negotiation to prevent a naval arms race.

Comfortable in London society, Albert Ballin was happy to become that go-between. Ballin, like Germany's Grand Admiral Alfred von Tirpitz, knew that if Great Britain joined Russia and France in a war against Germany, the Royal Navy would blockade entry to the North Sea and starve the Fatherland into submission. A British blockade would also trap the HAPAG fleet in port and end mass emigration to the United States.

Thanks to Cassel, Ballin got to know Prime Minister Sir Herbert Asquith and a rising MP named Winston Churchill.

In his meetings with the Kaiser, Albert Ballin conveyed Sir Ernest Cassel's thinking about a war on the Continent: It would be a disaster. Ballin also posited how such a war could be avoided. Just as HAPAG, NDL, and IMM could share the passenger and freight business through controlled competition, Germany could expand and modernize its navy while making sure not to threaten Britain if both belonged to the same cartel. In short, Germany and Britain could become members of a business alliance with shared interests.

The proposition was sound, but whether or not the governments, and the people, of these countries would agree to it was less clear. Ballin and Cassel blamed anti-German feeling in Great Britain on "an unscrupulous press and fostered by foolish politicians." But there was plenty of bad blood for the press to exploit. In October 1908, the *Daily Telegraph* ran a story that purported to be an interview with Kaiser Wilhelm II about his feelings toward Great Britain. Rather than using words of restraint and conciliation, the Kaiser was bellicose and petulant, sounding more like a victim than a monarch:

> *You English are mad, mad, mad as March hares. What has come over you that you are so completely given over to suspicions quite unworthy of a great nation? What more can I do than I have done? I declared with all the emphasis at my command, in my speech at Guildhall, that my heart is set upon peace, and that it is one of my dearest wishes to live on the best of terms with England. Have I ever been false to my word? Falsehood and prevarication are alien to my nature. My actions ought to speak for themselves, but you listen not to them but to those who misinterpret and distort them. That is a personal insult which I feel and resent.*

The interview came from a set of notes taken by a prominent British Army officer who had interviewed the Kaiser a year before the story ran. As a courtesy, the *Telegraph* sent the story to the Kaiser for review, but the lazy, distractible Wilhelm passed it off to Chancellor Bernhard von Bülow. The overworked chancellor, worried about upsetting his boss, sent the story along to the Foreign Office for comment. The ministry didn't say or do anything until after the interview was published.

The reaction in Germany and Great Britain was catastrophic. The British public saw the Kaiser not as someone to be feared but as a mentally disturbed megalomaniac. Many Germans, especially on the left, concluded that the Kaiser, who loved to bedeck himself in gleaming uniforms and eagle-topped helmets, was a buffoon who was taking the whole nation toward war.

"A dark foreboding ran through many Germans," Chancellor von Bülow wrote, "that such . . . stupid, even puerile speech and action on the part of the Supreme Head of State could lead to only one thing—catastrophe."

The Kaiser hid from public view for a time, embarrassed and angry at his diminished standing in the world. But rather than apologize, he found a scapegoat. He sacked Chancellor von Bülow and looked for someone servile to replace him. Whereupon Kaiser Wilhelm II approached Albert Ballin with a remarkable proposition, one that made J. P. Morgan's offer of the chairmanship of IMM seem insignificant.

Would Albert Ballin be interested in serving as chancellor of Germany? After the Kaiser, the position would make Ballin, a poor Jewish boy from Hamburg, the most powerful man in Germany.

To accept the post, Ballin would have to make three sacrifices, each extremely difficult. First, he would have to give up his top post at HAPAG and resign as its general director. He had been with the shipping company for twenty years but in charge for less than ten. Second, he would have to move to Berlin, a city he didn't like and in which he didn't feel comfortable. The move would be especially hard on his wife, Marianne, who was shy and retiring, and his teenage daughter, Irmgard. Third, he would have to convert to Lutheranism, because Jews were formally barred from performing any diplomatic work, let alone serving as chancellor. Albert Ballin knew full well that even converted Jews were hardly welcomed in the highest ranks of Berlin society, and that his appointment as chancellor would not be well received by the conservative Prussian elite. And then there was the matter of principle: Despite having married a Christian woman and raising his adopted daughter as a Lutheran, Ballin felt that becoming a Christian would dishonor the memory of his father, Samuel Joel Ballin.

As brilliant as he was, and as much as he loved his Fatherland, Ballin knew his limits, and the game in Berlin was not one he wanted to play. Shipping was an arena of numbers and brutal honesty. At HAPAG, he could rule. In Berlin, he would be playing second fiddle to the monarch and his courtiers, and life would be about flattery and kissing the rings of people he didn't respect.

Ballin declined.

Perhaps he wondered, for a moment, if this position would have brought him the acceptance he so longed for in German society. There were some rich German Jews who were pushing for patents of nobility, especially in Berlin. In the waning days of von Bülow's term, the industrialist Fritz Friedländer-Fuld said if the chancellor could get the monarch to bestow a "von" on his family, he would contribute 500,000 marks to a charity of the Kaiser's choice. Bülow responded by saying that the industrialist would have to double his gift to guarantee the "von." Friedländer-Fuld agreed. Upon hearing the news, the Kaiser responded gleefully, "You don't have more of this kind of people?"

For all of his fame, Albert Ballin never gained an honorific "von" before his surname, but he did win the coveted designation of "hoffäig," meaning acceptable to be presented at court. This was an honor few German businessmen, and even fewer German Jews, could dream of receiving. The Hamburg Senate, still proud of the city's independence, forbade its members to accept titles like "von" from "foreign" monarchs, including the German emperor. Even if Ballin had received a knighthood, it would have made little difference in Hamburg society. As one mayor snorted, "a merchant could not rise any further in status than he already is." Even the Jewish bankers of Berlin who had garnered "von" were still not welcome at court.

Outgoing Chancellor von Bülow praised Albert Ballin and intimated he might have been too good a man for the position of chancellor. "There were few people who I liked so well, there were few people for whom I felt such an honest respect," he said. "Ballin was very smart, but he had not only a sharp mind, he had a mind full of resources, which is exceptionally rare in Germany. He sought and usually found a path of escape. He was thoroughly practical, but he had—thoroughly the autodidact—a deep understanding for culture. Above all he had a golden heart, and the number he, absent any expectation of recompense, helped with his advice or with his deeds was great indeed. His error was perhaps a certain tendency to try to do right by everyone."

Theobald von Bethmann Hollweg, the former Prussian interior minister who succeeded von Bülow as *Reichskanzler* that same July, was no friend of Ballin's. A Junker aristocrat of the old order, he, too, wanted to avert war with Great Britain, but disapproved of backdoor diplomacy practiced by financiers and businessmen. The focus of Bethmann Hollweg's foreign policy was making Central Europe, known in German as *Mitteleuropa*, a sphere of German and Austrian economic domination, at the expense of Russia and the Slavic states.

Ballin feared that Bethmann Hollweg's narrow-minded nationalism could lead Germany into war. The chancellor took the time to meet with Ballin, but his entreaties at the Foreign Office in Berlin and to the Imperial German Navy were ignored, and he grew disgusted with Bethmann Hollweg. While the HAPAG director wanted Germany to become cosmopolitan and global, the chancellor was a deeply conservative nationalist. In the end, he was at the beck and call of the landed Prussian military establishment, which wanted war and agrarian expansion to counter the growing political power of cities and industry.

If war was not yet certain, this was: German military expansion into Poland and other parts of the Russian Empire would destroy the carefully choreographed system of border control stations and railroads that funneled Jewish migrants into Hamburg and Bremen. For all its financial success and business might, HAPAG was a fragile creation at the mercy of forces beyond its control, forces that included the provincial and often stupid men in the Kaiser's inner circle. And no one was more aware of the danger that threatened Albert Ballin than the man himself.

Although Bethmann Hollweg did not like HAPAG's general director, the Kaiser maintained his friendship with Ballin. Unlike many of the archconservatives in Berlin, the Kaiser strongly believed that the shipping man was a German patriot. Yet even while Ballin retained the Kaiser's backing, he nevertheless felt a growing sense of dread about German politics.

Ballin declined a position of political power. But his friend Sir Ernest Cassel did not. When Cassel was sworn into King Edward VII's Privy Council, many in the audience, especially his Jewish friends, were shocked when he placed his hand not on the Old Testament but on a Catholic version of the Bible.

* * *

As the Prussian nationalists planned for war, Albert Ballin continued to plan for peace and prosperity, even if the effort caused him anxiety. In 1910, he and Marianne arrived at the front gates of a grand villa at Feldbrünnenstrasse 58, in the heart of the patrician Rotherbaum district. There to meet the couple were Max and Alice Warburg, as well as their five children. As the Ballins went from room to room, they were greeted by each of the Warburg children, who recited poems welcoming them to their new home.

Modeled on the Petit Trianon at Versailles, the "Villa Ballin" was built of golden-hued limestone and topped by a hipped roof. The house had a porte-cochere suited to receive dignitaries in their chauffeured cars. Inside, family and guests were greeted with the same grace, grandeur, and service found aboard the newest HAPAG vessels. The villa's interiors were cool and classical, accented with marble and gilt. The heart of the house was Ballin's office, which was cluttered with paintings, heavy draperies, and leather-bound books. The centerpiece of the room was a white marble bust of Kaiser Wilhelm II, given to Ballin by the monarch himself.

For all his love of the maritime cutting edge, Albert Ballin's taste in art and design remained conservative, in line with Kaiser Wilhelm II's. Unlike many Jews of his class, Ballin did not patronize avant-garde artistic movements that were flourishing in Germany and Austria in the early 1900s. There were no paintings by Viennese Secessionists such as Gustav Klimt or Expressionists such as Ernst Ludwig Kirchner hanging on the walls of the Villa Ballin. Heavily influenced by Cubism and African art, such works were thought by many traditionalists to be too bold, too abstract, too critical of the Wilhelmine establishment to be on display.

Kaiser Wilhelm, who took an interest in art, decried almost all modern painting as gutter trash.

Now in his fifties, Albert Ballin doted on the children in his life, giving them all that was denied him when he was a poor boy. He had a playhouse built for the Warburg children, and gave them a stable of little Swedish ponies for riding lessons. Lola, the prettiest of the girls, was the apple of Max's eye, but she endured constant verbal abuse from her demanding mother, who would shout out "Stupid Lola" for all to hear. Alice had so little confidence in Lola's academic abilities that she was the only daughter not to receive formal schooling. Ballin, sensing the poor child's misery, once slipped her six books to read while she was ill. Lola Warburg never forgot the kindness of her father's odd-looking friend. In time, she would prove herself to be anything but stupid.

On several occasions when he was in Hamburg for the Lower Elbe Regatta, Ballin and Marianne entertained the monarch, Kaiser Wilhelm, at their city home. As the relationship deepened publicly, they got together more often. The two men discussed shipping policy, Germany's growing preeminence on the seas, and her relationship with Great Britain. However, they apparently never talked about the condition of the tens of thousands of Jewish migrants who poured into Hamburg each year on their way to New York.

Social observers nicknamed the Villa Ballin "Little Potsdam." Like the term *Kaiserjüde*, it could be interpreted as a compliment or an insult. Ballin knew that to appeal to the Kaiser's taste for grandeur, and to position HAPAG as the "official" royal line of imperial Germany, he needed to build a new house that would impress Kaiser Wilhelm. Especially since he came to visit so often.

Ballin was equally invested in creating haute design on the three new giant ships. He hired Charles Mèwes, fresh from his triumph at the Ritz Hotel in London. Ballin insisted that the first-class interiors be just as splendid as the neoclassical edifice on Pall Mall. Among the highlights were a grand staircase adorned with a massive portrait of the Kaiser, a giant social hall in the Louis XVI style, a three-story dining room, and a Roman-style indoor swimming pool complete with marble fountains and mosaic columns. Second- and third-class interiors were simpler and more modern in style, while steerage was spartan as usual, with exposed steel bulkheads and functional, durable furniture.

Ballin had initially hired Max's brother Aby, by now a well-known historian, to advise him on art and decoration. Aby hoped that *Imperator* would be a floating showcase for modern German interiors, featuring contemporary trends such as the Art Nouveau "Jugendstil" and the Viennese minimalism of Josef Hoffmann. Ballin, thinking of what the Kaiser would like, overruled him at almost every turn. Max also disapproved of his brother's choices. Aby, who was as neurotic as his brother Max was unflappable, was furious. He claimed that Ballin was wasting a tremendous opportunity to show the world that Germany was looking to the future, not catering to the whims of rich, self-important travelers. Aby Warburg walked away, calling Albert Ballin a philistine and his taste "Kellner-Eleganz" (waiter chic).

Ballin responded that the business of HAPAG was making money, not building floating modern-art galleries. "Naturally, you take us for philistines," he snapped at Aby, "but you shouldn't forget that at least 90% of our passengers will be just as uneducated in these matters as we. Consequently, it is necessary either to hang paintings that are merely decorative and arouse no criticism, or purchase works by Rembrandt."

For all his love of the beautiful, Albert Ballin knew that most travelers on his ships, whether in first class or steerage, were too preoccupied with their own affairs to spend much time taking in the ship's décor. What they wanted was comfort and security, and for the trip to be smooth, not transcendent. Especially when it came to immigrants, referrals to friends and family were key to the company's survival. The most magical part of the trip came at the end, when they crowded the rails and cheered as the ship passed the Statue of Liberty.

At the same time, Ballin worked with architect Martin Haller on a new Renaissance revival headquarters for HAPAG at Alsterdamm 25, smack in the center of Hamburg's commercial district. The three-story structure was crowned with a seven-meter-high copper statue of Neptune carrying his trident and riding a chariot. Inscribed above the main entrance was the slogan "Mein Feld ist die Welt." Miles away from the teeming *Auswandererhallen* on Veddel Island, HAPAG's wealthier passengers could book first- and second-class tickets on ships bound for destinations around the world in a grand, marble-clad main hall.

There was new décor, and there were new contracts too. HAPAG became the exclusive booking agent for the world's first airliners, Count Ferdinand von Zeppelin's new lighter-than-air aircraft. Founded in 1909, the airships of the Deutsche Luftschiffahrts-Aktiengesellschaft (DELAG) offered sightseeing trips throughout Germany. One day, DELAG's founders dreamed, zeppelins would be able to offer swift passenger service across the North Atlantic. Never would he have imagined that the German military was already thinking about how these massive airships could be used as long-distance bombers in a future conflict.

Though Ballin still planned for peace and prosperity, the German military's presence found a surprising way into the Villa Ballin. In 1910, Marianne and Albert Ballin announced the engagement of their eighteen-year-old daughter, Irmgard, to a handsome young German naval officer named Heinz Bielfeld. The religious ceremony took place at the St. Johanneskirche in Harvesthüde on October 29, 1910, a civil ceremony at home, and a grand reception at the Hotel Esplanade. Among the hundred people who sent the newlyweds congratulatory telegrams were Kaiser Wilhelm II from Berlin, Sir Ernest Cassel in London, and Jacob and Therese Schiff in New York. Albert Ballin was sick with the flu, but he mustered the energy to give his daughter away at the ceremony.

Soon afterward, Albert Ballin wrote to his daughter:

Dearest Mrs. Bielfeld,

My warmest thanks for your letter. I'm doing fine. The pleurisy has healed, but I still can't sleep.

But I was never a virtuoso at that.

You should stay on vacation. You'll be able to land at the Düvelsbekerweg long enough.

Is Heinz still nice to you and are you happy, or do you want to go back to your father?

Greetings to both of you,
Your Dearest Pap

Family always came first for him, and his daughter's wedding brought him tremendous joy, but by the early 1910s, the constant demands at work made his battles with depression and insomnia worse. As a child, he had grown up with his father working late nights in the same space in which his family lived, and Ballin never could quite separate his professional from his personal life. Among his worries was an ongoing fight with the board to build megaships that could each carry twenty-five hundred steerage passengers across the Atlantic. And though Ballin had made peace with the Jewish community, he was still hated by the trade unions and by the anti-Semitic right-wing press. A cruel cartoon appeared showing a leering Ballin, arms folded and dressed in an officer's uniform, standing at the crest of a wave that was about to engulf a German sailor in a rowboat.

Marianne was not an especially warm or affectionate person in public. But in private, she kept Albert on a mostly even keel emotionally. The banker Carl Fürstenberg observed that Marianne frequently read to him late at night to soothe his nerves. "While reading," he recalled, "she held his hand until it slipped out of her own and she could tell that he had fallen asleep. Albert's devoted wife then took her shoes off and left the room as quietly as possible so as not to wake her husband who had finally drifted off."

As Ballin worked feverishly for world peace, he struggled even harder to find peace within himself.

* * *

In 1910, as Albert Ballin moved into "Little Potsdam," J. P. Morgan was putting the finishing touches on a new library addition to his townhouse at Thirty-Sixth Street and Madison Avenue in New York. Designed by McKim, Mead & White, Morgan's library wing was also classical and restrained on the outside, yet sumptuous on the inside. It contained three principal rooms: a grand entrance foyer, a two-story-high library room for his collection of rare books and manuscripts, and a red damask-draped office where he could meet with other bankers or take refuge in games of solitaire.

J. P. Morgan continued to prosper, as evidenced by that new addition. Even though the International Mercantile Marine was a losing financial proposition, companies in his other trusts were doing handsomely. IMM was just a small part of a financial empire that included de facto control of the American sugar, steel, coal, and rubber industries, as well as a major share in the nation's railroads. With millions at his disposal, Morgan had the means to collect great works of art. And like Ballin, Morgan used art and architecture to charm and intimidate people into doing his will. The library made a beautiful, and fearsome, backdrop to business meetings.

When a series of bank failures triggered a financial panic that rocked Wall Street in 1907, Morgan called together several of America's leading bankers. He urged them to come up with enough money to bail out crucial financial institutions and inject liquidity into the country's economy. This time, Jacob Schiff was forced to cooperate with Morgan to help keep his own investment bank from being pulled down into the maelstrom. Morgan might by now accord Jacob Schiff grudging respect, but he was especially impressed with Kuhn, Loeb partner Paul Warburg. An intellectual and good on his feet, he had attracted Morgan's interest with a compelling argument for the creation of a central bank for the United States. Morgan was unhappy with the chaos produced by unchecked boom-and-bust business cycles in the country. Instead, he wanted the kind of order a central bank would offer the entire American economy.

IMM, meanwhile, continued to disappoint its shareholders in the American stock market. Besides being grossly overcapitalized, its decentralized management structure produced poor decision making and its sailing schedules were badly coordinated with Morgan-controlled railroads. When the congressional subsidy for its operations didn't materialize, investors saw it more as a bailout of Clement Griscom's American-based operations than a shipping monopoly that controlled the immigrant market.

*　　*　　*

Farther north on upper Fifth Avenue, Jacob Schiff remained the unofficial patriarch of the American Jewish community. He tried to control not only the image of the Russian Jewish immigrant but also that of his own family. He had strong opinions on everything from religion to morality. For Jews to hold their own in America, they had to be genteel, strict, devout, and disciplined. They also had to demonstrate love of learning, art, and culture. He expected the same of his children. Schiff's belief in external restraint even went so far as to encompass his daughter's taste in architecture.

It took a while for Felix and Frieda Warburg to convince Frieda's father, Jacob, to come to their house at 1109 Fifth Avenue. The five-story mansion, built in the Gothic revival style by the fashionable architect C. P. H. Gilbert, was finished at the same time as the Villa Ballin in Hamburg and J. P. Morgan's library addition. It boasted an art gallery, squash courts, and every modern convenience. Jacob told his daughter and son-in-law that where they lived was too ostentatious for a partner of Kuhn, Loeb & Co., and that a mansion like theirs only provokes the ire and jealousy of the *goyim*.

But the real reason for Schiff's anger was that the mansion challenged his own supremacy in the German Jewish world of business and philanthropy. Schiff felt that Felix Warburg was a great friend and father, but unlike his brothers Paul and Max, was not an especially talented banker or dealmaker. Nor was he a deep thinker. Instead, he was a lover of beautiful things, including having more than a few girlfriends on the side. However, he began to notice that Felix was beginning to take his religion and Jewish philanthropy seriously. He also had a common touch and a personal warmth that his father-in-law lacked.

For its part, the downtown Eastern European Jewish community was growing tired of Schiff's stern dictates. The Galveston Plan had been a dismal failure, and most immigrants continued to flock to the big cities of the Eastern Seaboard, with New York the most popular destination. By the early 1900s, the Jews of the Lower East Side had created their own unique culture. Thanks to their ingenuity and hard work, as well as the generous (if sometimes condescending) philanthropy of Jacob Schiff and other wealthy uptown Jews, they had formed civic aid organizations and successful small businesses. In the same way that many of their German antecedents had gotten their start peddling dry goods door to door, business-minded Russian Jews proved to be remarkably enterprising. The needle trade was only one of many ways poor but savvy Jewish entrepreneurs started to climb the ladder into the American middle class. Some got into the food business, selling butter and eggs to individual households and eventually to hotels in Midtown and HAPAG ocean liners docked on the Hudson River. Others became leather dealers, bakers, and liquor store operators. Some Jews also began to get involved in organized crime, especially prostitution and extortion from legitimate business owners.

Many small-business owners received seed capital from benevolent societies such as the Schiff-backed Hebrew Emigrant Aid Society, as well as small banks that were springing up all over the Lower East Side and Brooklyn. As more downtown Jews achieved a certain level of success, they, too, began to contribute to benevolent societies and charities. The core of social life for many a hardworking Jewish father still remained the *landsmanshaft* mutual aid societies for Jewish immigrants who came from the same village, town, or city in the Russian Empire.

Life remained hard for most first- and second-generation Jewish immigrants to America. Tuberculosis and other infectious diseases continued to ravage tenement dwellers. The death of the family breadwinner could plunge a Jewish woman and her children from surviving and making do into abject destitution. The deep poverty and privation psychologically scarred many families even after they achieved some level of material comfort in their new lives. But however much they suffered in the tenements, there was always the hope that little by little life would get better. And America had no secret police, no marauding Cossacks, no May Laws, no pogroms to fear on Easter, and no twenty-five-year draft into Czar Nicholas II's army.

The Russian government looked on the increasingly thriving Jewish community in the United States with misgiving. To retaliate against Russian Jews who left the czar's empire, the Russian government passed a new series of laws in 1904 that banned Jews with American passports from reentering the country, even if they had previously been issued a visa. This was mostly empty political posturing: few Jews wanted to return permanently to Russia, and not many American Jews traveled there for business or personal reasons. The real motivation behind the so-called Passport Question was to send a clear message to Jews wanting to immigrate to America that they would never again be able to visit family back in the Old Country.

Jacob Schiff was outraged at the latest Russian insult, because it relegated even American Jews to second-class status in Russia. Roosevelt, for all his personal warmth toward Schiff, had refused to engage the Russian government about the issue. He had already spent his diplomatic capital with Russia at the Portsmouth Conference, and the best he could offer was to counter efforts by his friend Senator Henry Cabot Lodge to restrict Russian immigration to the United States. Having promised at his second inauguration in 1904 that he would not run for a third term, Roosevelt knew that his influence was on the wane. Already, European far-right publications sniggered that he was in the pocket of the Jews. Roosevelt also feared backlash from anti-Semites, populist and patrician alike, in his own country.

Undeterred by his friend's noncommittal stance, Jacob Schiff continued to lobby publicly to build broad support against Russia on the Passport Question. In August, the Alliance Israélite Universelle's American branch, one of Schiff's favorite charities, issued a broadside calling on the world's Jewish community to protest Russia's singling out of American Jews for humiliation:

> *If the Jews of America, England, France, Germany, Italy, etc., could reside or travel in Russia the same as all Russians can do in the aforementioned countries, Russian officials would find themselves curbed in their abuse of Jews. . . . Will our influential English brethren take up the cause? Will they remember England's humiliation when some of her best citizens were driven away from Russia simply because they were Jews?*

Schiff's efforts, however, came to nothing. Most of the world looked the other way. And Jews in Russia continued to leave for America, preferring the trials of immigration to the pain of perhaps never again seeing loved ones.

For a growing number, it was a race to get out of Europe before war or revolution came.

Part IV

CHAPTER 18

Betraying the Morgan Trust

[A]s far as it is possible to do so, these
two wonderful vessels are designed to be unsinkable.

—WHITE STAR LINE PUBLICITY LEAFLET FOR
THE RMS *TITANIC* AND RMS *OLYMPIC*, 1910

L ord William Pirrie and IMM chairman J. Bruce Ismay supposedly
came up with the idea for White Star's new class of ships over
brandy and cigars at the former's magnificent townhouse on London's
Belgrave Square. The keel of the first of White Star's trio of ships, the
RMS *Olympic*, was laid down at the Harland & Wolff shipyards in Belfast on December 16, 1908. Several months later, the keel of her sister
ship, the RMS *Titanic*, was laid down on the neighboring Belfast slip-
way. A third ship, to be named RMS *Gigantic*, would follow a few years
later. When completed, they would be the biggest, most luxurious, but
not the fastest, ocean liners in the world. The sister ships would be 882
feet long, weigh 45,000 gross tons, and would steam at a service speed of
21 knots.

It was rumored that J. P. Morgan was using the vast resources of his
bank and the International Mercantile Marine trust to finance the construction of these three ships. In fact, the reverse was true. During the
previous ten years, White Star had proved to be immensely profitable
and was able to raise the capital to build the new liners from its own revenue streams. It was the other shipping companies, most notably Clement

Griscom's troublesome American Line, that were the great drags on the trust's finances.

Albert Ballin had predicted that Morgan's IMM had been a paper tiger from the start. But he took great interest in the new White Star Line ships that were rising on the stocks at Harland & Wolff. Ismay had plans for steerage. He hoped to make up for less capacity by providing immigrants with better service and more privacy than the German ships offered. In a nod to a big segment of its intended clientele, White Star made sure the RMS *Olympic* was equipped with kosher cooking facilities, as well as many sets of kosher dishes.

Across the North Sea in Hamburg, Ballin sized up his new adversary and found him wanting. His decision to turn down the top job at IMM (and its million-dollar-a-year salary) had been the right one. To be sure, Morgan's trust was a fearsome-looking agglomeration of British and American shipping lines. But once the company went public, its securities flopped. A few years later, Albert Ballin told reporters that he didn't need to start another war with White Star and J. P. Morgan's trust. "The German lines have come to an agreement with White Star Line that eliminates all frictions between them," he said, "as the company has chosen Southampton as port of departure."

Shut out of the indirect migration business by HAPAG's control of the border stations and Cunard's service out of the Mediterranean, White Star continued to rely on the shrinking pool of immigrants from Western Europe and the British Isles. The Red Star Line, which sailed out of Antwerp, Belgium, still provided IMM with a steady stream of Russian steerage passengers, but its operations by now paled in comparison with HAPAG's. Much of the diminution came from Clement Griscom withdrawing from the day-to-day operations of the combine two years after his appointment, in 1904, due to poor health. His successor, J. Bruce Ismay, quickly moved operations from New York to Liverpool.

Nevertheless, White Star hoped to fill its steerage berths when its ships called at Cherbourg, France, and at Queenstown, Ireland. Moreover, RMS *Olympic* was equipped to carry only 1,000 passengers in third class. By comparison, HAPAG's SS *Amerika*, about half the size, could carry 222 emigrants in third class and 1,750 in steerage. Ismay hoped that grander first- and second-class facilities would partially make up the difference in steerage revenue. Ismay also wagered that emigrants would pay a premium for upgraded accommodations. This meant separate cabins housing eight to ten people, which were much more friendly to traveling families than the open-berth arrangements found on the German ships.

To attract both first-class and steerage passengers, White Star proclaimed that its new class of ships was built to be "practically unsinkable." As initially designed, the ships were supposed to have forty-eight lifeboats, enough to carry almost all thirty-two hundred passengers and crew on board when booked to capacity. Ismay intervened, arguing that all those lifeboats would clutter the decks and detract from sports and promenading. After all, no other ship on the Atlantic carried enough lifeboats for everyone on board. They were meant to ferry people from one ship to another in the event of an emergency. And even in the worst case, a ship like *Titanic* should stay afloat long enough for rescue ships to arrive, especially in the crowded North Atlantic sea lanes. Lord Pirrie acquiesced, and the number of lifeboats was reduced to sixteen wood boats and four canvas-sided collapsible rafts. This meant seats for twelve hundred people.

Back in Hamburg, Albert Ballin thought the time had finally come to get out of his profit-sharing agreement with White Star and IMM. RMS *Olympic* and *Titanic*, scheduled to enter service in 1911 and 1912, would make his lead vessels *Amerika* and *Kaiserin Auguste Victoria* functionally obsolete. This meant he would have to raise significant capital to compete with White Star, made easier because the immigrant business was picking up nicely after the Panic of 1907. On March 9, 1912, as the finishing touches were put on RMS *Titanic* in Belfast and *Imperator* was readied for her launch in Hamburg, Norddeutscher-Lloyd sent a letter to HAPAG confirming that the pooling agreement between the German lines and IMM was now void:

> In accordance with the wish of the International Mercantile Marine Company expressed to you, we have declared to them today that we agree to the annulment of the Morgan Agreement of January 1, 1912.

Although its White Star division was still earning hefty profits, IMM itself had proved to be a colossal flop. The profit-sharing agreement was detrimental to HAPAG, as the annual dividend payments it paid to the Morgan trust always surpassed the fixed sum it got in return for its conditional independence. By withdrawing from the agreement, Albert Ballin felt he could wage commercial war with Cunard and the Morgan trust.

Yet ocean liners, no matter how big or grand, were insignificant compared to the competition between the two powers to build bigger and more lethal warships. By 1912, the chances of avoiding armed conflict seemed to be slipping away. Great Britain felt gravely threatened by Germany's growing fleet of battleships and U-boats. Earlier, Ballin had made enemies at the British Admiralty for his covert and profitable coal deal with the Russian Navy. And in Berlin, if Ballin was the Kaiser's genial Neptune, Grand Admiral Alfred von Tirpitz was the Kaiser's belligerent Neptune. Tirpitz, sporting an array of medals, had expanded the Imperial German Navy into a formidable fleet that included seventeen modern "dreadnought" battleships, five battle cruisers, twenty-five "predreadnought" older battleships, and forty technologically advanced submarines.

Should war break out, Tirpitz thought that a strong navy could help protect Germany's overseas possessions in Africa and the South Pacific, as well as do battle with the British fleet if it tried to blockade her North Sea and Baltic ports, principally Hamburg and Bremen. This was crucial. Without food and supplies from overseas and from the United States in particular, Germany would be starved into submission.

Critics on the left felt that Tirpitz's naval expansionism was just another way the Kaiser's government was using jingoistic German nationalism and dreams of empire to paper over the severe social and economic grievances of the country's working classes. According to German historian Volker R. Berghahn:

> *Tirpitz believed that the fleet's impact on the economy, its attractions for the liberal, anglophilic, commercial, bourgeoisie, the extension of the kaiser's powers of command of the world's oceans, and its ultimate effect on the international balance of power would provide a domestic cement for a*

crumbling regime and a foreign political lever to heave Germany into the front rank of imperialist states.

As much as Albert Ballin detested militarism, the Tirpitz Plan was simply a heavily armed version of the HAPAG slogan "My Field Is the World." As a businessman, Ballin shared his nation's global ambitions. Nonetheless, Ballin's support of naval expansion was more to stay in the good graces of the Kaiser than to provide protection for his fleet of merchant ships, which needed peace to sail on the seas. "I do not need the protection of the German fleet for my ships," he asserted, "and I should have said so more forcefully to the Kaiser, but I was never able to work myself up to it. We were all weak when faced with the Kaiser. No one wanted to darken his cheerful, childlike optimism, which tipped into a nearly endless depression if his favorite topics were criticized. And the expansion of the fleet was the first of them. Now we have the results of a lack of courage!"

The Tirpitz Plan dovetailed neatly with the financial goals of M. M. Warburg & Co., which in addition to funneling money into German industry also served as a financial conduit to its overseas imperial expansion. As one of the lead financiers of German adventures in Southwest Africa, Max Warburg had no qualms about colonialism and the subjugation of the native population. He was supremely confident, publicly at least, about his place in the world. It did not register to Max that Germany's exploitation of the Namibians and Rwandans mirrored the czar's subjugation of the Jews. All the while, Max continued in his role of aiding the oppressed of his own faith.

Across the Atlantic, Schiff felt similarly about his own duty to his fellow Jews. Yet his position as supreme leader of the Jewish community was being challenged on several fronts. He was aging, and starting to turn over more of his philanthropic responsibilities to his son-in-law, Felix Warburg, who was becoming more interested in Jewish affairs than in his yachts and paintings. At Kuhn, Loeb & Co., Schiff slowly gave more control of the firm's banking operations to the gifted and disciplined Otto Kahn. Although Otto and Adele Wolff Kahn never converted, they raised their children as Episcopalians. "It is said that as a man may be judged by the company he keeps," Kahn said to Schiff's son, Mortimer, "so a company may be judged by the men it keeps."

Schiff also was being challenged by the Russian Jewish community, who chafed under the patronizing condescension of the German Jewish grandees. Some of them were committed Marxists, who saw men like Schiff as capitalist stooges who were doing their best to stave off the workers' revolution. Once, when Felix and Frieda Warburg hosted a Jewish charitable event, two Russian Jewish guests not wearing dinner jackets said, as they were admiring their host's fine collection of Old Master paintings, "When Communism comes and there's a division of property, I hope to draw this house."

Felix overheard the exchange, walked over, and said, "When Communism does come, and there's a redistribution of goods, I hope that if you get my house, you will also invite me to be your guest, because I have always enjoyed it."

Other rebels were rising members of the new Russian Jewish middle class, first- and second-generation Americans who had moved out of the Lower East Side and into more prosperous quarters in Brooklyn, Queens, and the Upper West Side. They were small-business owners, lawyers, doctors, and others who had become the thrifty Americans Schiff had hoped they would become. They sent their children to private high schools and to the Ivy League, sat on the boards of their own synagogues, and attended the symphony rather than the Yiddish theater. They were now tired of being treated like unruly, unwashed children. And like Tevye in *Fiddler on the Roof*, they dreamed of being a rich man who lived in a "big tall house with rooms by the dozen" on Fifth Avenue, just like Felix Warburg and Jacob Schiff.

And then there were the Zionists, who held out hope for a Jewish homeland in Palestine.

*   *   *

Albert Ballin's work on behalf of the Jewish community was, in public, strictly commercial. Though it benefited them, it also benefited him. So he laid out plans for his new ships—the greatest people haulers of all time—on the grandest scale. The trio featured a three-funnel silhouette, rather than the four stacks of the White Star Line ships. Three stacks still looked quite imposing on travel posters and advertisements. And they were all being built in German yards. Above all, the Kaiser wanted a ship bigger and better than Morgan's White Star vessels.

What set the HAPAG ships apart from the *Olympic* class, however, was their enormous immigrant capacity. They were also built of the finest materials and designed to last three or more decades. Each of the three ships would make about six round trips per year. If war was averted, the emigration business would remain strong and HAPAG would continue to prosper.

The peak year for European immigration to the United States was 1907, when over one million new arrivals walked up the stairs to the main reception hall at Ellis Island. According to the *American Jewish Year Book*, 131,910 Jews arrived on the island between September 1, 1906, and June 30, 1908. The sheer number of American Jews was increasing rapidly, thanks to a combination of heavy immigration and high birthrates in the tenement districts of New York, Philadelphia, Boston, Chicago, Baltimore, and other large cities. Between 1907 and 1914, the American Jewish population almost doubled, from 1.7 million to 2.9 million.

Non-Jewish immigration also continued to be robust. Between 1900 and 1914, an estimated ten million people—a human tide of Russians, Poles, Germans, Lithuanians, Austrians, Bohemians, Italians, Slovaks, Greeks, Turks, French, Irish, and British—traveled across the Atlantic in steerage to America. Of these, about one third went back to their native countries. Some had come to make enough money to go back home better off financially, some found that life in America was too fraught with hardship to stay, and others found the pain of being separated from family and friends in the home country was simply too great to endure.

So the steerage quarters on HAPAG's ships were partially occupied on eastbound voyages, making it possible for Ballin to rebuild his new fleet without a subsidy from the German government. Few Russian Jews returned, however. Conditions were terrible for any Jew in Russia, particularly those who may have made a fortune in America. A successful returnee Jew was an especially inviting target for the czarist police, the army draft board, or the garden-variety Russian anti-Semite.

But even as Morgan and Ballin's giant new vessels took shape in Belfast, Hamburg, and Stettin, war between the great powers of Europe was looking more and more likely. To Jacob Schiff, a war would mean the Golden Door would slam shut, and the Jews of Eastern Europe would find themselves victims of the German and Russian war machines. Schiff felt that Kaiser Wilhelm II could keep a war from happening, and he believed he could convince the Kaiser of that if only he could get access to the palace in Berlin. That meant using Albert Ballin and Sir Ernest Cassel as emissaries between London and Berlin.

He investigated all possible avenues of influence. At home among New York's German Jews, Schiff was used to wielding autocratic authority. So he was shocked to find himself frozen out of access in Washington, D.C. He had believed that the Republican Party—the party of Lincoln, emancipation, and the business establishment—was the party that stood for the rights of the American Jew. He turned out to be wrong. As the Jews of the Lower East Side became naturalized citizens, they voted overwhelmingly for candidates of the Democratic Party, the party of Tammany Hall, organized labor, and, paradoxically, of Southern segregationists.

After his friend Theodore Roosevelt left the White House in 1909, Schiff tried to convince his successor, President William Taft, to issue sanctions against the Russian Empire for its actions in the Passport Question. Taft did nothing. He found Schiff annoying and strident, and didn't have much interest in courting the Jewish vote. What mattered to Taft was staying on Russia's good side.

Schiff accused Taft's ambassador to Russia, William Rockhill, of working with a commercial agent of the czar to finance the construction of American-owned factories in the empire. The factories would, Schiff asserted, "form the nucleus of a big export trade and bring Russia into closer touch with the United States." Schiff was afraid that the United States was being inexorably drawn into a financial relationship with the Triple Entente. Even if Schiff had positive feelings toward Britain and France, their entanglement with Russia poisoned everything for him. The last straw was Taft's refusal to recommend Schiff's friend Louis Marshall to the Supreme Court. When Taft invited Schiff and the leadership of the American Jewish Congress to a private meeting at the White House, he refused to shake the president's hand.

Trembling in anger, his blue eyes blazing, Schiff lit into President Taft.

"Mr. President," Schiff said, "you have said that you are not prepared to admit the commercial interest of ninety-eight million of the American people to suffer because two million feel their rights are being infringed upon. My own opinion has always been that it was the privilege of the head of this nation that, if only a single American citizen was made to suffer injury, the entire power of this great Government should be exercised to procure redress for such injury . . . you would not do anything to protect two million American citizens in the rights vouchsafed to them under our Constitution and laws."

Schiff then compared Russia's treatment of the Jews to America's treatment of African American slaves. "In 1861," he said, "public opinion insisted that the slave must be freed and the Union remain supreme at any cost; the war for the right was thereupon fought and won. . . . To this same public opinion, Mr. President, we shall now turn, and we have no fear of the results."

A longtime believer in the goodwill of his adopted land, Schiff realized that hatred of his own people had crept into the highest levels of American government. Upon leaving the White House, one American Jewish Committee member lamented, "*Wir sind in Golus*." ("We are in exile.") Infuriated, Schiff responded in English, "This means war."

Worse was to come for Schiff and the supporters of a liberal immigration policy. In 1911, the bipartisan group of senators and congressmen released the Dillingham Commission's forty-one-volume report to the public. Senator Lodge's fingerprints could be found on every page. Its conclusion was that immigrants from Eastern and Southern Europe, as well as those from Asia, were to be discouraged from coming to the United States. Immigrants from Great Britain, Ireland, Germany, and Scandinavia, on the other hand, were acceptable. The latter were from the most progressive sections of Europe, the report stated, "and assimilated quickly. . . . On the other hand, the new immigrants have come from the less progressive countries of Europe and congregated separately from native Americans and the older immigrants to such an extent that assimilation has been slow." The report went on to say that there should be a "limitation of the number of each race arriving each year to a certain percentage of that race arriving during a given period of years."

It would take another ten years, and much political warfare, to hammer out a quota system, but the Dillingham Commission had set the political wheels in motion to close Emma Lazarus's "golden door" forever.

Even Roosevelt, the self-proclaimed friend of the immigrant (as long as he assimilated to American life), was starting to echo some of the nativist rhetoric coming from Congress and the media campaigns of the Immigration Restriction League. Turning against his old friend William Howard Taft, Roosevelt left the Republican Party and ran for president as the candidate of his own political party, the newly formed Bull Moose Party. Roosevelt's campaign plunked for some of the left-wing goals of many Jewish socialists on the Lower East Side. Among them were women's suffrage, old-age pensions, workmen's compensation, an inheritance tax on the rich, and an eight-hour workday.

But Roosevelt started to tilt more to the right when it came to American nationalism. In true messianic spirit, Roosevelt chose as his party's battle song the explicitly non-Jewish "Onward Christian Soldiers." Despite his break with the Republicans, Roosevelt remained close to Senator Henry Cabot Lodge, even as their political views grew increasingly divergent. On the Passport Question, Lodge wrote to Roosevelt, "There is a distinction, of course, between our people who go to Russia with passports and Asiatic immigrations, but at the same time I think there is some danger in our going too far in forcing any class of citizens upon another country."

And Roosevelt was dead set against moving toward any kind of social democracy favored by the Jewish left. In the tenements of the Lower East Side, leftist Jews dreamed that one day a revolution would come to Russia that would overturn Nicholas II's hapless autocratic government and replace it with a socialist regime. Abraham Cahan, who became editor of the *Jewish Daily Forward* in 1903, was America's greatest public critic of the Russian regime. A self-proclaimed Social Democrat, he saw socialism as the salvation of the Jewish people in Russia. Other newspapers, such as the ultra-far-left *Di Freiheit*, advocated for a Communist revolution, in which the czar would be overthrown and replaced by a "Dictatorship of the Proletariat" that would abolish all private property and place the means of production into the hands of all the people.

The world was changing. New ideas had outgrown old alliances, for

Ballin and the IMM trust, for Schiff and his friends in high places, for countries around the globe. Although outwardly serene, the Old World order—one built on economic growth, royal privileges and bourgeois prosperity, and peace in Europe—was coming apart.

A great maritime disaster would shatter the era's outward serenity.

CHAPTER 19

The Martyrs of the *Titanic*

```
Man, you are no match,
For the cold ocean's power.
It is a wet and deep grave . . .
Shed tears for all the lives lost.
And for her noble courage,
All should honor and remember,
The name of Ida Straus.
```

—SOLOMON SHMULEWITZ, "THE *TITANIC'S*
DESTRUCTION, THE WATERY GRAVE"

The Triangle Shirtwaist Company was located on the top three floors of a ten-story building near Washington Square, which some fifty years earlier was part of the most fashionable residential neighborhood in New York. And it was known in literary circles as the setting for some of Henry James's genteel novels of manners. But by 1911, the rich had moved farther north to upper Fifth Avenue. Their townhomes were turned into tenements for the working poor, or demolished and replaced with factories housing light industry.

Triangle's owners, Isaac Harris and Max Blanck, were Russian Jewish immigrants. They rose from humble tailors to successful entrepreneurs. They, too, had moved farther north. Both lived in grand townhouses on the Upper West Side, employed several servants, and were driven to work in chauffeured cars. Their company employed five hundred or so workers, mostly teenage Italian and Jewish girls, who worked ten to twelve hours a day hunched over sewing machines, churning out hundreds of shirtwaists, the upper portion of a woman's blouse. The raw shirtwaists, made of cotton or linen fabric, were then dispatched to other shops, where embroidery, rhinestones, or other decorations would be added. The finished products would then be displayed at Macy's, Bloomingdale's, and other department stores that catered to rich and middle-class women. The entire women's garment industry employed about thirty thousand learners (apprentices), operators, cutters, patternmakers, and supervisors, and generated about $50 million in annual revenue.

The young women who labored at Triangle were supporting not just themselves but also their families back in the tenements of the Lower East Side. They earned between seven and twelve dollars a week, the modern-day equivalent of between $191 and $327. Many of the women also set aside a portion of their meager wages to help relatives back home purchase steamship tickets, often on a HAPAG vessel.

Harris and Blanck believed their wages were fair enough. After all, they, too, had come up the hard way and had resisted all attempts by the workers to join the International Ladies' Garment Workers Union. To them, profit margins were just too thin to pay more, or to comply with proposed regulations such as fire exits, shorter workdays, and adequate ventilation.

The women disagreed. Two years earlier, the employees of the Triangle Shirtwaist Company had walked off the job in protest of the terrible working conditions, which included verbal abuse and sexual harassment from male supervisors. At a meeting of activists at Cooper Union in November 1909, the largely male labor leadership, including AFL president Samuel Gompers, dithered about whether or not to call a general strike.

Frustrated, the twenty-three-year-old socialist Clara Lemlich demanded to speak. She and her family had fled the Kishinev pogroms six years earlier and emigrated to New York. Clara quickly got a job in a garment factory, like countless young Jewish women. Yet she wasn't willing to endure the long hours, dehumanizing work, and dangerous working conditions just to bring home money to help her family pay tenement rent. She wanted to improve the lot of all workers. She dreamed of a day when the garment workers would take matters into their own hands, perhaps influenced by the novels of Tolstoy and Gorky, which she secretly read against the wishes of her religious, Yiddish-speaking parents.

The young firebrand quickly earned a reputation as a troublemaker. A few months before the meeting at Cooper Union, hired thugs had beaten Clara and other picketers. Despite the agony of several broken ribs, she summoned the strength to get up to the podium, where she shouted in Yiddish:

> I have listened to all the speakers, and I have no further patience for talk. I am a working girl, one of those striking against intolerable conditions. I am tired of listening to speakers who talk in generalities. What we are here for is to decide whether or not to strike. I make a motion that we go out in a general strike.

The crowd rose cheering, and everyone in the hall agreed to a general strike. In all, twenty thousand garment workers walked off their jobs. As winter fell upon New York, the women marched in picket lines and held up signs in Yiddish, Italian, and English demanding higher wages and better working conditions.

Photographs of the brave women strikers electrified the city. But the business establishment, including J. P. Morgan, brushed off their demands as mere socialist troublemaking. Jacob Schiff, who had given so much of his fortune to the Educational Alliance and the Henry Street Settlement House, from which many of these women must have benefited, also appears to have said nothing about the strike. Although his fortune came from financing railroads, he supported labor unions in principle. "I believe the proper organization of employees for their own benefit," he declared before Congress, "which is the benefit of the State, ought to be encouraged in every way." Yet if Schiff did support the "Uprising of the 20,000," it was in no way public. However, Anne Morgan, J. P. Morgan's daughter, was deeply moved by what was happening. She and several other wealthy suffragettes donated to the strikers' support fund and even joined them on the picket lines, dressed in mink coats and feathered hats.

By the winter of 1910, the society women withdrew their support of the socialist-backed strike, and the shirtwaist makers, exhausted and out of money, went back to their sewing machines, shivering in the unheated lofts and surrounded by months' worth of fabric scraps. The Triangle Shirtwaist Company was one of the manufacturers that refused to grant any of the protesters' demands for better working conditions. In fact, Harris and Blanck had hired goons to terrorize the striking women into submission.

In the late afternoon of March 25, 1911, the women of the Triangle Shirtwaist Company were rushing to fill their quotas for the day before heading home. Sometime around 4:40 p.m., smoke began billowing from a pile of fabric scraps on the eighth floor. Within minutes, flames spread to the rest of the floor. Dozens of terrified workers swarmed for the exits, but managers had locked the doors from the outside to make sure no one left early or took a cigarette break. Soon, the fire spread to the upper two floors of the building.

Some of the women managed to escape the inferno using a rickety fire escape, but it soon gave way, crashing to the street below. Others were helped into an adjoining building by students from New York University. By 5:00 p.m., dozens of people were still trapped on the upper floors. The fire department arrived within minutes, but its ladders couldn't get high enough to reach the fire. The best it could do was train its hoses upward onto the building. From the street below, observers saw figures standing on the windowsills, flames and smoke billowing behind them. They had two choices: burn or jump. In all, 123 women and 23 men perished in the tragedy. Some lay dead in the streets; others were at their sewing machines or pressed up against the locked exits.

A jury acquitted Max Blanck and Isaac Harris on state charges of manslaughter, but their reputations were permanently ruined. It was the Triangle Shirtwaist fire that finally led to tighter government regulation of the garment industry. The dead would also become martyrs of the Jewish labor movement. At the public memorial for the victims, which took place at the packed and incongruously splendid Metropolitan Opera House, ILGWU leader Rose Schneiderman compared the machinery of American capitalism to that of the Spanish Inquisition:

I would be a traitor to these poor burned bodies if I came here to talk good fellowship. We have tried you good people of the public and we have found you wanting. The old Inquisition had its rack and its thumbscrews and its instruments of torture with iron teeth. We know what these things are to-day; the iron teeth are our necessities, the thumbscrews are the high-powered

*and swift machinery close to which we must work, and the rack is here in the
firetrap structures that will destroy us the minute they catch on fire.*

Within a year, hundreds more immigrants would become martyrs to
the American Dream, not by fire in the midst of the city, but by ice in the
midst of the ocean.

And the public would place the blame on Anne Morgan's father.

* * *

A few months after the Triangle Shirtwaist fire, Paul Warburg booked
first-class passage aboard the new White Star liner RMS *Olympic*. The
ship had debuted in June 1911. *Olympic* had attracted the admiration of
the press and the traveling public. IMM's new flagship was broad, spacious, and elegant in profile, with four towering black-and-buff funnels
that signaled safety and size to rich travelers and immigrants alike. Ad-
vertisers called her bright and spacious immigrant quarters "the new
steerage." It was modeled on the "third class" that Ballin had pioneered
aboard SS *Amerika* and SS *Kaiserin Auguste Victoria*.

After his arrival in New York, Paul gave a full report of his thoughts
on the new ship to his brother Max, who then passed along his assessment
to Albert Ballin. Paul thought the new ship was wonderful. But he still
maintained that HAPAG could surpass it with their "superior service and
taste."

Albert Ballin refused to believe that emigration could come to an end
and felt a bright future awaited HAPAG and himself. His name appeared
in a new, beautifully bound volume titled *Jahrbuch des Vermögens und Ein-
kommens der Millionäre des Königsreich Sachsen* (Yearbook of the Wealth
and Income of the Millionaires of the Kingdom of Saxony), which listed
the incomes and net worth of the richest German citizens. Its publisher,
Rudolf Martin, wrote that the secrecy surrounding wealth in the past was
an antiquated practice, and that "the social, economic and political struggles of the present call for education about the wealth and incomes of
the rich." The 1912 volume was dedicated to the three Hanseatic cities
(Hamburg, Bremen, and Lübeck). Martin calculated that Albert Ballin
had a personal fortune of 5 million marks, and an annual compensation
of 500,000 marks. The rough modern-day equivalent is about $55 million

net worth, and about $5 million a year in compensation. His best friend, Max Warburg, head of M. M. Warburg & Co., one of the German Empire's leading investment banks, was listed as having the same net worth and a salary of 400,000 marks.

As one of about five hundred millionaires in Germany, HAPAG's general director was a very rich man by any standard. He was not in the top tier of Wilhelmine German society, but still, it was an astonishing rise for Albert Ballin, who seemed to have few roadblocks on his way to the highest echelons of German society and on the world stage.

Max Warburg, who had helped finance so many of HAPAG's ambitions, and those of many other German capitalists, was in awe of what his friend had accomplished. "The economic boom times of the last thirty years are unimaginable without Albert Ballin," he declared. "His age knows what he, supported by Germany's economic success, made out of the Hamburg-America Line. But not only out of it, but also out of all of the other lines that worked together with the Hamburg-America Line. Leading colleagues from other countries recognized his superiority."

That spring, Ballin played host to an important guest, Jacob Schiff. He and his wife, Therese, traveled to Germany that May, and through Ballin made a request to see the Kaiser. "His Majesty wishes to receive you but is prevented from doing so before June third, twelve o'clock noon," Kaiser Wilhelm's secretary wrote to Schiff. "Please advise whether you are able to prolong your stay in Berlin to June third." Schiff of course did just that. He got his audience with Kaiser Wilhelm II aboard the imperial yacht *Hohenzollern* at Kiel. It is safe to surmise that the banker brought up his frustration with Russia over its relentless persecution of Jews, his love for Germany, as well as his firm's financial support of HAPAG.

Perhaps at Lord Pirrie's urging, Albert Ballin may have considered booking passage on the inaugural voyage of the second and newest of the White Star Line's superliners, the RMS *Titanic*, to check out the competition and see how the *Titanic* compared to the *Imperator* class now on the stocks. For Ballin, a trip on the *Titanic* would be the perfect working vacation. But according to Ballin's great-grandson Heinz Hueber, he declined the opportunity because of the impending launch of HAPAG's new giant *Imperator* at the AG Vulcan yard in Hamburg.

J. P. Morgan attended the launch of *Titanic* on May 31, 1911, along with IMM chairman J. Bruce Ismay and the ship's supervising naval architect, Thomas Andrews. Unlike Ballin's festive launches, which were full of speeches, dinners, and royal visitors, *Titanic*'s launch was a plain affair. No bottle of champagne was smashed against the bow before the empty hull slid into the water, and no brass bands played "Rule, Britannia." The only festive adornments were two enormous flags—the American and the British—stretched out over the launching ways.

The completion of the RMS *Titanic* had been delayed twice because of two accidents suffered by her sister ship. During her first season, *Olympic* had dropped a propeller blade and had been rammed by a British Navy cruiser, which meant construction crews and parts had to be diverted from *Titanic* at the Harland & Wolff yard on two occasions.

On April 10, 1912, RMS *Titanic* departed Southampton, England, on her maiden voyage to New York. Although the largest liner afloat (barely edging out *Olympic*), the new vessel didn't attract world headlines. What really caught the interest of the press was the aggregate wealth of the first-class passengers, which totaled over $500 million. The richest man on the ship, real estate heir Colonel John Jacob Astor, was alone worth $87 million. Close behind him was George Dunton Widener, son of IMM director Peter A. B. Widener, who was traveling home to Philadelphia with his wife, Eleanor, and son Harry, a recent graduate of Harvard College. Also aboard was J. Bruce Ismay, who had booked one of the two grandest suites on board even though he was traveling alone.

Along with the gentile rich, several of America's most prominent German Jews were also on board the *Titanic*. Benjamin Guggenheim, the youngest and least motivated of Meyer Guggenheim's sons, was coming home from France accompanied by his mistress, Léontine Aubart, his valet, Victor Giglio, and chauffeur Rene Pernot. Also aboard were the much more straitlaced Isidor and Ida Straus, who were returning to their mansion on the Upper West Side after wintering in Cape Martin, France. They had also visited Isidor's brother Nathan in Palestine. Nathan had done everything he could to convince Isidor to stay longer and help Jews in need there. This could be, he argued, the home of a future Jewish state.

After a week in Palestine, the cofounder of the American Jewish Congress had had enough and wanted to return to America. "How many camels, hovels, and yeshivas can you see?" Isidor allegedly said. "It's time to go." Nathan Straus and his wife stayed behind in Palestine. Isidor and Ida booked the *Titanic* for home.

Also traveling first class were Dr. Henry Frauenthal, a prominent orthopedic surgeon and head of the Jewish Hospital for Deformities and Joint Diseases in New York. He was returning with his wife, Clara, whom he had recently married in France, as well as his bachelor brother Isaac. Then there was Abraham Lincoln Salomon, another Upper West Side resident and owner of a successful stationery business. Abraham's wife, Hattie, was waiting for him in New York.

When Isidor and Ida Straus arrived in their suite on C deck, they found themselves in a space more luxurious than most land-based hotels. The suite consisted of a private bath, a trunk room, a Louis XV–style sitting room paneled in dark wood with gilt carvings, and an Empire-style bedroom with a double and a single bed. A large electric fireplace helped complete the illusion they were ashore.

The biggest name missing from the roster of first-class passengers was John Pierpont Morgan himself. He had planned to sail on the ship's maiden voyage, an event that in itself would have made the *Titanic* launch much more newsworthy than she proved to be that April. It might have been at his personal instruction that two special suites were added to the ship's original first-class B-deck plans. Morgan remained in France, supposedly because of ill health, but in fact he was spending some more time with one of his many mistresses. Lord Pirrie, Albert Ballin's good friend and head of Harland & Wolff, also canceled for health reasons.

RMS *Titanic* departed Southampton at noon. Her maiden voyage almost came to an end within a few minutes of casting off. When she passed the American Line steamship SS *New York*, suction from her three gigantic propellers yanked the much smaller liner free from her moorings. Just before *New York* slammed into *Titanic*'s side, a group of tugboats pushed her away from the big liner and back toward her wharf.

Regal and yacht-like, the giant vessel sailed across the English Channel and dropped anchor off Cherbourg, France, at sunset. There, 142 first-class, 30 second-class, and 102 third-class passengers came aboard, transported from the mainland by two steam tenders. The following day, *Titanic* stopped at Queenstown, Ireland, her last port of call, where another 123 passengers came aboard, 110 of whom were Irish emigrants traveling in third class.

When *Titanic* sailed out of Queenstown on the afternoon of April 11, 1912, her steerage quarters held 708 people, which was about 70 percent capacity. According to surviving records, the passengers skewed heavily toward immigrants from Great Britain, Ireland, Sweden, Finland, and Norway. There were 44 passengers from Austria-Hungary and 18 from Russia. The group that had traveled the farthest were 83 Syrians, who boarded the ship at Cherbourg.

Although the number is unclear, there were probably only about fifty Jews in *Titanic*'s third-class quarters, a small number compared to the hundreds typically in the berths of HAPAG or NDL ships. By 1912, Jewish immigration out of the Russian Empire had rebounded after a short drop-off that resulted from the financial panic of 1907. Conditions at the *Auswandererhallen* grew so crowded that HAPAG considered renovating and expanding them even further. A worried Hamburg physician named Dr. Sannemann wrote to the city's immigration administration:

> The influx of foreign emigrants, especially from Russia, has been so large lately that the sleeping accommodations in the emigration halls of Hamburg America Line are no longer sufficient. For that reason, some of the dining halls are being used as accommodations, where emigrants find their place for the night on mattresses on the floor.

Albert Ballin's three new ships, scheduled to enter service between 1913 and 1915, would greatly relieve the backlog at the *Auswandererhallen*. Any overflow passengers who stayed longer than two weeks could be sent on to Liverpool, Cherbourg, Antwerp, or Southampton, where White Star liners or other competition could take them across the Atlantic. Maybe even on the *Titanic*.

Even on grand new ships like the *Titanic*, passengers were largely expected to entertain themselves over the course of the weeklong voyage. For most passengers, the main entertainment of the day was the food, and this applied to all three classes, as the meals served were both prodigious and of very high quality. *Titanic*'s galleys were capable of churning out ten thousand meals a day. Among the army of chefs, waiters, and dishwashers, thirty-year-old Charles Kennel had the most specialized job. He was the designated "Hebrew cook," the one person aboard who was allowed to prepare kosher meals for the ship's third-class passengers. In accordance with kosher law, Kennel kept separate sets of china and silverware for meat and dairy. He also allowed his kitchen to be inspected by a rabbi before every sailing. According to the ship's plans, Kennel's workspace was tiny, not much bigger than a small closet. When he was done for the day, he slept in a bunk space adjoining the third-class dining saloon on F deck.

Many of the luxuries that dazzled the ship's first-class passengers—staterooms fitted out with period décor, public rooms resembling those in grand hotels on land, and an extra-tariff specialty restaurant—had been pioneered by Albert Ballin on his HAPAG liners many years earlier. First-class passengers also had access to an indoor swimming pool, a barbershop, Turkish baths, and a regulation-size squash court. She was in every respect a floating city, having borrowed many of the innovations HAPAG had pioneered.

And like every big liner afloat, the class tension aboard was palpable. Gates, railings, and barricades prevented one class from mingling with the others. For White Star, keeping third-class passengers out of first- and second-class spaces was a matter of U.S. immigration regulation. That there were fewer third-class passengers than expected didn't matter.

The fact that *Titanic*, the biggest and newest ship in the world, was sailing only half full spoke volumes about the company's larger problems. A coal strike in Great Britain made procuring the 5,000 tons of fuel for the new ship a major headache. Rather than cancel the voyage, White Star commandeered the coal of the smaller *Oceanic* and *Adriatic* and dumped it in the *Titanic*'s bunkers. Along with the coal, *Titanic* also got the two ships' passengers, along with those from the SS *Philadelphia*, another IMM vessel.

There was another big problem: a fire had broken out in coal bunker 6, deep in the bowels of the vessel, and continued to rage as the ship departed Southampton and called at Cherbourg and Queenstown. As the passengers dined and relaxed and the *Titanic* sped across the Atlantic at a brisk 22 knots, the crew fought for days to shovel the burning coal out of the bunkers and into the boilers, which was the only way to put it out.

The passengers didn't notice.

In first-class suite C 55-57, Isidor and Ida Straus looked forward to seeing their children in New York. The first-class menu offered the couple no specifically kosher options, but like most German Jews (and unlike Jacob Schiff), they did not observe strict dietary laws. The dining room's menu offered such *traif* Edwardian delights as *canapés à l'amiral* and filets mignons topped with truffles and foie gras.

In the comfortable but not grand second-class section of the ship, the Russian Jewish couple Sinai and Miriam Kantor looked forward to skipping the dreaded inspections at Ellis Island. Originally from Vitebsk, Sinai and Miriam were university graduates who planned to study medicine in the United States. Along with their personal belongings, the Kantors had trunks of furs they intended to sell to help finance their studies.

In steerage, the small group of Jewish passengers enjoyed the simple but hearty kosher cuisine. The third-class dining saloon was located deep amidships, with small portholes overlooking the ocean. The room was painted white and filled with long tables and hundreds of swivel chairs bolted to the floor. The space was divided into small sections by water-tight bulkhead doors that would slam shut in an emergency. They were visible reminders that *Titanic* was built, the newspapers said, to be "practically unsinkable."

Among the single men who unpacked their belongings in the forward third-class cabins was twenty-two-year-old Eliezer Gilinski, who was originally from a small shtetl in the Russian province of Lithuania but had moved to England to escape conscription in the czar's army. He made a decent living as a locksmith, but his family back in Russia hoped that he could make a better one in America. Eliezer was not only the youngest child, but he was also unmarried, which meant it was relatively cheap to send him to Chicago to establish a family beachhead. After a few years, his parents hoped, they, along with his brothers, David and Louis, and their wives and children, would all join him.

There was no rabbi on board to conduct Sabbath services, so observant Jewish passengers probably gathered in one of the third-class public rooms for a short service on the night of Friday, April 12. Isidor and Ida Straus were longtime members of New York's Temple Emanu-El, the same congregation dominated by Jacob Schiff and his coterie. Chances are the Strauses said a short prayer in the parlor of their suite before putting on their evening clothes and descending the grand staircase for dinner.

No third-class menu survives from the *Titanic*, but a third-class bill of fare from her sister ship RMS *Olympic* indicates plain but hearty fare:

Breakfast: Oatmeal Porridge and Milk, Stewed Beefsteaks and Onions, Irish Stew, Bread and Butter, Preserves, Swedish Bread, Tea and Coffee

Dinner: Barley Broth, Caper Sauce, Lima Beans, Boiled Potatoes, Cabin Biscuits, Fresh Bread, Stewed Apricots and Rice

Tea: Rabbit Pie, Baked Jacket Potatoes, Bread and Butter, Swedish Bread, Rhubarb and Ginger Jam

Supper: Cabin Biscuits, Cheese, Coffee, Gruel

Fresh Fish served as substitute for Salt Fish as opportunity offers.

Kosher Meat supplied and cooked for Jewish passengers as required.

Sunday on the *Titanic* was a thoroughly Christian affair. Captain Edward Smith presided over Protestant services in the white-paneled, Jacobean-style first-class dining room. Down in the third-class general room, Father Francis Byles conducted a Roman Catholic Mass. That evening, as the sun set on the western horizon and the temperature outside fell below freezing, Reverend Ernest Courtenay Carter, an Anglican priest, led a hymn-sing in the second-class dining room. Among the hymns sung by the hundred or so attendees was "Eternal Father, Strong to Save," also known as "For Those in Peril on the Sea."

Later that night, at 11:40 p.m., *Titanic* grazed an iceberg while traveling at full speed. The conditions were calm, the skies clear, the night moonless. In a matter of seconds, the ice cut a series of gashes into the ship's starboard side, opening up five of her sixteen watertight compartments to the sea. Passengers in first and second class, most of whom were asleep high up in the ship, barely noticed the impact. Those deep down in third class, however, felt a jolt and heard the screeching and grinding of hard ice against buckling steel plates. Within minutes, seawater was seeping into the forward steerage cabins that housed the single men, as well as the mail room, cargo holds, and the squash court.

Over the next hour, hundreds of bleary-eyed third-class passengers gathered in the enclosed open space on D deck and in the general room or smoking room at the stern, awaiting instructions about what to do. Many were carrying boxes and bags containing all their worldly possessions. Stewards stood at the doorways, telling them to stay in place. The third-class deck areas—the forward and aft well decks, and the poop deck— had no lifeboats. Small groups of passengers, fed up with the inaction and feeling the decks sloping under their feet, decided to find their way to the upper decks on their own. They were confronted by a maze of barriers and locked gates blocking their way.

Meanwhile, the ship's officers had a hard time convincing first- and second-class passengers to board the lifeboats. The brightly lit ship seemed safe and steady. The first several lifeboats, each able to carry sixty-five people, left the ship less than half full. It wasn't until 1:00 a.m. or so, with the ship seriously down by the head and listing to port, that people took the "women and children first" order seriously.

Clara Frauenthal boarded lifeboat number 5. As it was being lowered, her husband, Henry, jumped in, landing with a thud onto fellow passenger Annie May Stengel, breaking several of her ribs. His brother Isaac also managed to find a place in a boat.

Abraham Salomon stuffed a copy of that evening's first-class menu and a Turkish bath ticket into his coat pocket. He got into lifeboat number 1, which contained only eleven other people, among them Sir Cosmo and Lady Duff Gordon.

After seeing his French mistress Léontine Aubart off in a lifeboat, Benjamin Guggenheim took off his lifejacket and put on his evening clothes. He then told one survivor that he and his valet, Victor Giglio, had dressed in their best, "and were prepared to go down like gentlemen."

In front of lifeboat number 8, an officer urged Isidor Straus to climb aboard. He refused, saying it was not appropriate for him to leave the ship while there were still younger men on board. Then his wife, Ida, refused to leave the ship. According to one eyewitness, she turned to her husband and said: "We have been living together for many years. Where you go, I go. I will not be separated from my husband. As we have lived, so will we die, together." Miriam Kantor boarded a lifeboat, but her husband, Sinai, stayed behind, along with the vast majority of the 155 second-class male passengers.

At around 2:05 in the morning on April 15, *Titanic*'s bow was awash. To the hundreds stranded on board, it was now undeniable that the "unsinkable" ship was going down, and fast. J. Bruce Ismay, the chairman of the International Mercantile Marine, climbed into the last lifeboat to be launched from the ship that night.

First-class passenger Colonel Archibald Gracie IV, who had spent the past two hours helping women and children into the boats, thought he had done his duty. Seeing the water surging up the deck, he and his friend Clinch Smith decided to head to the stern, which was rising higher and higher in the air.

"We had taken but a few steps in the direction indicated," he said, "when there arose before us from the decks below, a mass of humanity several lines deep, covering the Boat Deck, facing us, and completely blocking our passage to the stern. There were women in the crowd, as well as men, and they seemed to be steerage passengers who had just come up from the decks below. Even among these people there was no hysterical cry, or evidence of panic, but oh, the agony of it!"

At 2:20 a.m., April 15, 1912, the ship split in two and plunged into the North Atlantic. Among the 1,523 people left thrashing about in the freezing water were Captain Edward J. Smith, chief designer Thomas Andrews, IMM shareholder George D. Widener and his son Harry, John Jacob Astor, Benjamin Guggenheim, Isidor and Ida Straus, Sinai Kantor, and kosher chef Charles Kennel.

The two halves of the *Titanic* crashed onto the ocean floor about ten minutes after leaving the surface. Deep in her holds, along with a Renault limousine, fifteen cases of cognac, and thirty-four cases of Spalding athletic goods, were the boxes of Russian furs that Sinai and Miriam Kantor had hoped would finance their medical school studies.

Seven hundred twelve people survived the disaster. Eighteen of the ship's twenty lifeboats were launched before the ship sank, and two floated off as she went down. More first-class men (57 out of 118) survived the disaster than third-class children (27 out of 59).

The widowed Miriam Kantor arrived in New York aboard the rescue ship RMS *Carpathia* on the rainy evening of April 18, 1912. Without the support of their husbands, many of the women and their children who survived the *Titanic* disaster decided to return to their home countries. But not Miriam. Despite the loss of her husband, she was determined never to go back to Russia. She moved in with cousins, and accepted a gift from the Red Cross to help cover her dentistry school tuition. As the Red Cross reported, "After she learns the language, she will carry out her intention of learning and practicing dentistry . . . at the end of which she expects to be self-supporting. The money has been placed in charge of the Council of Jewish Women, who will keep supervision of her plans (2,600 dollars)."

On April 20, two days after RMS *Carpathia*'s arrival, Albert Ballin sat down at his desk in Hamburg to put together his thoughts about the disaster to Max Warburg. Albert couldn't help but think that White Star had skimped on construction quality to save on weight and fuel costs. The greatest loss of life aboard a HAPAG vessel had been the cholera outbreaks on *Normannia* twenty years earlier. Since then, the company, for all of its commercial success, had an impeccable safety record.

"According to telegraphic reports from New York up to now, the *Titanic* disaster has only become more baffling to me," Ballin wrote. "In light of the reports, which are only preliminary, after all, I can't help but think that the material [i.e., of the ship] was too soft and that its construction was too lightweight. Lord Pirrie was always proud that he was able to build the White Star ships solely according to his own ideas, without regard for the regulations of the Classification Societies. The ships that Harland's built for us were therefore so disproportionately more expensive than the ones they built for the White Star Line, because we had strict specifications from German Lloyd and the Maritime Employer's Liability Insurance Association, and our own company. For years he [i.e., Lord Pirrie] kept pointing out to me how much useless ballast we lug around with us due to material that is too strong and complicated safety precautions. Today, I fear, he will have a completely different opinion."

Albert Ballin then did something he appears never to have done before: made a 20,000-mark donation to the German Jewish Aid Society.

The same day Albert Ballin wrote his letter to Max, the cable ship *Mackay-Bennett* arrived at the scene of the disaster from Halifax. The

White Star Line had chartered the vessel to recover as many bodies as possible and bring them back to land so they could be claimed by relatives. There was a practical reason as well. The area was busy with passenger ships, and the last thing shipping companies wanted their passengers to see were scores of decomposing corpses floating past.

The ship's hold carried one hundred coffins, one hundred tons of ice, and copious amounts of embalming fluid. *Mackay-Bennett*'s crew was quickly overwhelmed by the number of bodies floating in the icy seas. All were wearing life jackets and floating feetfirst. Some appeared to be only asleep. Others were battered, discolored, and eaten by marine life. For the *Mackay-Bennett*'s crew, it was a ghoulish ordeal, especially when they retrieved the bodies of children.

The head undertaker, John R. Snow, took careful notes on every body retrieved, noting hair color, tattoos, personal effects, and information in a record book.

The forty-seventh body to be retrieved was a dark-haired man in his twenties or early thirties.

NO. 47.—MALE.—ESTIMATED AGE, 30.—HAIR, DARK.

CLOTHING—Grey coat, vest and pants; green shirt.

EFFECTS—Photographs; tickets; $5 bill; baggage insurance, No. 73941 (B. Ins. Ass., Ltd.; £12 in gold; 60c; 4 pence; keys; purse; primer on English language).

THIRD CLASS TICKET No. 14973

Eliezer Gilinski's body was wrapped in a canvas sack, with large lumps of coal placed at his feet. Reverend Kenneth Cameron Hind then read the burial at sea prayer from the Anglican Book of Common Prayer: "We therefore commit his body to the deep, to be turned into corruption, looking for the resurrection of the body, when the Sea shall give up her dead."

Down he sank, two miles to the bottom of the Atlantic, along with the recovered remains of 115 other third-class passengers and crew.

The ninety-sixth body recovered was of an older man with gray hair and a mustache. Snow noted:

NO. 96.—MALE—ESTIMATED AGE, 65—FRONT GOLD TOOTH (PARTLY)—GREY HAIR AND MOUSTACHE

CLOTHING—Fur-lined overcoat, grey trousers, coat and vest; soft striped shirt; brown boots; black silk socks.

EFFECTS—Pocketbook; gold watch, platinum and pearl chain; gold pencil case; silver flask; silver salts bottle; £40 in notes; £4 2s 3d in silver.

Like other bodies believed to be those of first-class passengers, Isidor Straus's remains were embalmed and stored in a coffin on deck.

Among the last bodies to be pulled from the sea by *Mackay-Bennett*'s crew was a light-haired male in his thirties. Snow noted:

NO. 283. MALE.—ESTIMATED AGE, 36. VERY FAIR HAIR AND MOUS-TACHE

CLOTHING—Grey and green suit; green overcoat; blue shirt; check front marked "F"; black boots; "C" on singlet.

EFFECTS—Pocket telescope; silver watch; Pocketbook with foreign notes; letter case; empty purse; purse; £1 10s. in gold; ten shillings in silver and other coins.

Sinai Kantor's remains were packed in ice, placed in a canvas bag, and lowered into the hold. The face of his silver watch was marked with Hebrew letters in place of Roman numerals, the back with a miniature scene of Moses receiving the Ten Commandments.

Her work done, *Mackay-Bennett* left the site on April 26, 1912, with 190 bodies on board. She arrived in Halifax four days later, where most identified bodies were claimed by relatives and shipped home for burial. Those unclaimed were laid to rest in Halifax. Among them were ten victims believed to be Jewish, who were buried at the Baron de Hirsch Cemetery.

Twelve hundred others found their final rest in the North Atlantic. Among them was Ida Straus.

On May 12, 1912, a public memorial service for Isidor and Ida Straus took place at Carnegie Hall. Six thousand dignitaries and guests crammed into the elegant yet austere main auditorium. Outside, in the pouring rain, stood several thousand other well-wishers who could not gain entry. Among them were many Lower East Side Jews wearing their prayer shawls and mourning clothes.

Onto the stage filed the official delegation of mourners, among them Andrew Carnegie, Mayor William Jay Gaynor, Louis Marshall, Felix Warburg, and Jacob Schiff, who all took their seats. As Schiff glanced up at the boxes, he could see other representatives of the German Jewish community of which he was the uncrowned leader, including the Strauses' six children and Isidor's brother (and former secretary of commerce) Oscar Straus. There were also representatives of the nation's Protestant elite, including Episcopal bishop Thomas H. Gailor and City College president John H. Finley.

J. P. Morgan, Jacob Schiff's great adversary, was not listed among the attendees. He was still in France, in shock that he had so narrowly escaped traveling on the doomed liner.

Andrew Carnegie, the immigrant Scotsman whom Morgan had made "the richest man in the world," spoke first. He touched on both Christian and Jewish themes in his eulogy.

"Women and children first for the boats was the order," Carnegie said, his voice breaking, "and not a man wavered. The rule is strictly observed: the ship sinks, the band plays 'Nearer, My God, to Thee.' We imagine the figures of our two beloved friends, in whose memory we meet today, in the appalling scene, shining before us, two angels of light, clasping each other, united in life, resolved to remain united in death, braving together the watery grave, with all of its terrors."

Jacob Schiff then took the podium. Just over five feet tall, he seemed dwarfed by the size of the stage and the cavernous auditorium. Yet he stood proud and erect. He knew that the American Jewish community—Russian and German alike—was listening.

"What made Isidor Straus so valued as an adviser and a friend was not alone his clear mind," Schiff said, "it was more the warmth of his great heart. He never considered himself, and he was ever ready to place himself at the service of any good cause. As it was with him, so it was with his devoted wife, ever his most trusted adviser and coworker. These two great souls are no longer here on earth, but the examples of their noble lives move on to strengthen and inspire us."

The Straus couple, although not traveling as immigrants on the *Titanic*, became proxies for the fear and hope that so many Jews experienced on their voyages across the Atlantic. In Yiddish theaters, singers performed a new song by Morris Rund called "Di korbones fun der shif *Titanik*" ("The Victims of the *Titanic*"). The sheet music cover featured busts of Isidor and Ida Straus. An angel crowns the couple with a pair of laurel wreaths. Beneath the busts were the following inscriptions:

> *Isidor Straus: a noble example [of] the bravery of Jewish man.*
> *"Women and children must be saved first. There's time for me later, later."*
> *Ida Straus: a noble example of the love of the Jewish wife.*
> *"Where you are, that's where I'll be. If we must die, we should die together."*

The song lamented not just the Straus couple but the immigrant Jews who died in the disaster:

> *Children's fathers sank in the sea*
> *The orphans and widows brought to this.*
> *Hundreds of corpses sank there to the bottom*
> *and cannot have proper Jewish burials.*
> *Oy, such a terrible death!*
> *The ocean made no distinction and swallowed everyone the same way*
> *No exception. Christian or Jew,*
> *Poor or rich,*
> *All were taken together*
> *The catastrophe was so terribly immense*
> *Hundreds of bodies have now been found*
> *Among them, oy, Isidor Straus.*
> *He fell, a victim, along with his wife.*
> *"Save the children first," they said.*
> *Weep and lament, Jews, at such a destruction.*
> *The ocean robbed you of the pride you earned.*

For this brief moment, the Straus funeral bridged the yawning chasm between the haughty yet philanthropic German Jews and the impoverished yet enterprising Russian Jews. Long suspicious yet dependent on each other, they were now united, not just by their shared faith but by the fact they had all, at one point or another, braved the North Atlantic as immigrants to a land that would be their new home, free from the persecution of the Old World.

While New York and the nation lionized the Straus couple, they crucified J. P. Morgan, J. Bruce Ismay, and the White Star Line for being reckless with the lives of the passengers in their care, rich and poor alike. Already in bad financial straits, International Mercantile Marine was forced to spend large amounts of money updating its ships with more lifeboats and other safety features, including the RMS *Olympic*, which was pulled out of service for a complete structural rebuild that allowed her to survive the same damage that sank her sister. This included extending the watertight bulkheads up several decks, allowing the ship to stay afloat if any six of her sixteen watertight compartments were breached. The double bottom was also extended up to the sides of the vessel. Most importantly, White Star added enough lifeboats for everyone on board to have a place. This only occurred because shortly after the *Titanic* disaster, the entire crew of RMS *Olympic* walked off the ship and refused to come back to work until lifeboats to save every man, woman, and child on board were installed.

But the traveling public, especially immigrants, lost their faith in White Star. The "improvements" made to *Titanic*'s third-class accommodation—private cabins for families, table service in the dining room, and well-appointed public rooms—paled when compared to lack of access to a few lifeboats. The fact that more first-class men survived the disaster than third-class children showed what the company valued. IMM was soon besieged with lawsuits from angry survivors and families of the deceased, who demanded compensation for lives and property lost.

On December 31, 1912, J. Bruce Ismay submitted his resignation as chairman of the IMM to J. P. Morgan. "At the time that the *Titanic* was lost," the *Times* of London noted, "Mr. Ismay was subjected to some criticism for not waiting on board until the vessel foundered, but with this criticism Lord Mersey [the lead investigator of the British wreck inquiry], in the course of his report on the loss of the vessel, expressed his complete disagreement." Harold Sanderson, Ismay's replacement at the head of IMM, found himself faced with a floundering, disorganized conglomerate of shipping lines without reliable sources of revenue. The rich boycotted the White Star ships, and the immigrants were flocking to the German lines, especially HAPAG.

Three months later, on March 31, 1913, J. P. Morgan died in his sleep at the Grand Hotel Plaza in Rome. Accompanied by his daughter Louisa and her husband, Herbert Satterlee, the financier's body was brought back to America on the brand-new SS *France*, the flagship of the French Line. Along with HAPAG, the French Line was one of the few companies that had successfully fended off IMM's advances. Following a service at St. George's Church in New York, he was buried in Cedar Hill Cemetery in his native Hartford, Connecticut.

"The king is dead. All New York is at half-mast," Frank Vanderlip, president of the National City Bank, wrote to his friend James Stillman. "There are no cries of 'Long live the king,' for the general verdict seems to be that there will be no other king: that Mr. Morgan, typical of the time in which he lived, can have no successor, for we are facing other days."

There was scant mention of his involvement with the *Titanic*. The *Wall Street Journal*, however, did offer a laconic verdict on the International Mercantile Marine, his only business failure: "The ocean was too big for the old man."

Forces were gathering to shut down the business model that made possible the RMS *Titanic*, the International Mercantile Marine, and the Hamburg-America Line.

CHAPTER 20

My Field Is the World

One is forced to think of the contrast between the front of a great house with a palace façade and proletarian tenements, and it
is difficult to comprehend why there are not
specially built transport ships for immigrants and luxury ships for those on pleasure
cruises.

—OPEN LETTER FROM KARL SCHEFFLER, ART
HISTORIAN, TO ALBERT BALLIN, 1913

In November 1912, as the shock of the *Titanic* disaster faded, forty-six-
year-old Sophia Fuko and her six-year-old son Kalman boarded the
HAPAG flagship *Kaiserin Auguste Victoria* at Hamburg. Kalman was a
common Yiddish name in the Austro-Hungarian Empire; it is likely that
mother and son were Jews. The widowed Sophia had no surviving relatives left in Hungary, but she did have family waiting for her in America.
Her adult sons, Bela and Laszlo, had done well enough to pay for two
second-class berths, sparing Sophia and Kalman the cramped steerage
quarters aboard the vessel. On top of that, Bela's wife and child were due
to arrive in America soon on another ship, again most likely in second
class. Traveling in second class also almost certainly exempted the Fukos
from staying at the Emigrant Village upon their arrival in Hamburg.

When *Kaiserin Auguste Victoria* arrived at her Hoboken pier, third-
class and steerage passengers disembarked onto ferries that carried them
to Ellis Island. Sophia must have breathed a sigh of relief—she and her

boy were being spared the "Island of Tears." The former housekeeper had the required twenty dollars in cash. Her adult children were prepared to take Kalman and her under their care, and had already rented and furnished an apartment for them.

The medical examination of immigrants traveling in first and second class was almost always conducted by officials who came aboard the liner, and it was typically a perfunctory affair. Since the cholera epidemic twenty years before, HAPAG prided itself on doing thorough screenings of all potential immigrants to avoid families being separated, as well as carrying rejects back to Europe at company expense. Even so, immigrants still needed to be examined by officials on Ellis Island.

Sophia's optimism was short-lived. She and her boy were put on the boat to Ellis Island, where, like so many before them, they climbed the stairs and filed into the vast, echoing Great Hall, all under the watchful eyes of Williams's "scientifically trained" employees. The doctors then started their examinations. They determined that Sophia Fuko was "practically blind in one eye," and that her son Kalman was a deaf mute. They would be denied admission to America on the grounds that they were likely to become public charges.

As was her right, a distraught Sophia appealed to President Taft's secretary of commerce, the Texas native Charles Nagel. She claimed that her son was not a deaf mute, and that she had family support in the United States. If necessary, she could sell her property back in Austria-Hungary to raise additional cash.

As Nagel's office weighed her appeal, a letter from Ellis Island arrived from Commissioner William Williams, who felt he needed to intervene in this case to make a point. For Williams, rules were rules, and the Anarchist Exclusion Act of 1903, signed by President Roosevelt and still in full effect, barred the entry of "anarchists, epileptics, beggars, and importers of prostitutes."

Williams argued that Sophia Fuko's child "will always be physically defective, and it would be improper to admit merely because of her relatives here." Another letter then arrived from the commissioner general of the Bureau of Immigration, who seconded his colleague's opinion. The Taft administration refused to intervene in Sophia Fuko's case. On December 21, she and Kalman boarded the HAPAG steamer SS *Pennsylvania*, bound for Hamburg.

Sophia may have stood at the rail, watching the gray New York skyline and the Statue of Liberty recede into the distance. The New World, and the home of her two older sons, vanished like a dream behind the ship's slow-churning wake. As with all would-be immigrants rejected from America, the cost of their passage was borne by the shipping line, so chances were she was not placed in second class, but rather steerage. As one of the P-class liners of the 1890s, *Pennsylvania* could carry up to 2,382 in steerage class on westbound crossings. Eastbound, most of the berths were broken down and the open dormitories were converted into cargo space. There, among crated-up American-made farm equipment and automobiles, Sophia and Kalman may have slept with a handful of other steerage passengers. Some were so-called birds of passage, people who had made some money in America and were on their way back to the Old Country for good. Others were visiting relatives back home. But many were bleary-eyed, terrified rejects from Ellis Island.

SS *Pennsylvania* arrived in Hamburg after a two-week journey. When Sophia and Kalman disembarked at the pier, there was no brass band to welcome them, only the spires and dormers of the Emigrant Village, and the throngs of hopeful people preparing to depart on *Pennsylvania*'s next crossing. The Fukos would be two of about forty-eight thousand returning immigrants who passed through Hamburg each year. Because of pogroms and the czar's stubborn refusal to recognize the passports of American Jews, few of these reverse migrants by choice were Jews.

From his office on Ellis Island, Williams found himself facing two opposing tides of opinion: those who wanted to keep the gates of immigration open and those who didn't. From the latter, he found himself forever looking at piles of letters from the persistent Prescott Hall, who took a fiendish delight reading about the number of people rejected at Ellis Island. Hall thought of Williams as his kind of man, one of the elite crowd and a defender of America against the thousands of impoverished, genetically inferior invaders arriving on her shores each day.

But as Williams and Hall both knew, the ships arriving each day were becoming not only more numerous, but also larger and more capacious.

The steamship lines had tapped into an ever-growing demand of Europeans seeking a better life in America. So they were selling not just a voyage, but a dream. And no matter how much the immigrants feared Ellis Island, no matter how harsh the sweatshops or filthy the tenements were, they still came.

Albert Ballin was not fazed by the machinations of William Williams and the Immigration Restriction League. In 1913, 192,733 emigrants, the vast majority of whom were headed for New York, passed through the port of Hamburg. With the Morgan trust still reeling from the *Titanic* disaster, Albert Ballin's dream of transatlantic domination of the immigrant trade was coming to fruition. He would deal with Cunard and its ports of call on the Mediterranean later, even though Ballin knew it had recently launched its new superliner *Aquitania*, which along with *Lusitania* and *Mauretania* provided weekly service between Liverpool and New York.

Across the North Atlantic, Jacob Schiff took these machinations more seriously. But at the moment, he and his partners Paul and Felix Warburg were preparing an exciting new public offering for the New York Stock Exchange: the first American issue of stock in the Hamburg-America Line. With IMM flailing (the NYSE had denied its listing) and immigration rates still rising, the timing was perfect to raise more capital for the biggest shipping company in the world.

On June 11, 1913, SS *Imperator* departed Hamburg on her maiden voyage for New York City, with stopovers in Southampton and Cherbourg. Albert Ballin was not aboard. Under the command of Commodore Hans Ruser and four subcaptains, the giantess sped past Land's End and headed into the North Atlantic. Yet as the ship hit rough seas, it became clear to everyone on board, no matter how much they paid for the trip, that *Imperator* was top-heavy and had a frightening tendency to roll. Upon her arrival at HAPAG's Hoboken, New Jersey, pier, the new imperial German flagship had a noticeable list to starboard. On a later voyage, a giant wave struck the vessel and sheared off most of her nine-foot bronze figurehead: a screaming crowned eagle holding a globe in its talons. A ribbon wrapped around the globe proclaimed: "Mein Feld ist die Welt."

Despite the problems, the public loved the new ship. On a trip in September, *Imperator* was almost fully booked, with 859 in first class, 647 in second class, 648 in third class, and 1,495 crammed into steerage. "Never

before were there so many persons on one ship as there are on *Imperator*,"
a *New York Times* reporter radioed from the ship. "There has been fairly
good weather on the voyage. A great undercurrent caused heavy swells
on the first day and the big ship had its severest test so far. It pitched
steadily, but did not roll."

The ship's performance was hardly good enough for Ballin. Harbor
pilots had already given her the nickname "Limperator." That October,
Ballin ordered *Imperator* taken out of service for modifications. Workers
poured 2,000 tons of cement into her bilge, trimmed 9 feet from her three
funnels, and carted away crates of marble bathroom fixtures and heavy
wood paneling and furniture from her upper decks. What was left of
the figurehead was removed from the bow and replaced with decorative
scrollwork. AG Vulcan covered the 200,000-pound cost, because the ship
was still under her builder's warranty.

In May 1914, SS *Vaterland*, the second ship in the trio, set sail on her
maiden voyage from Cuxhaven to New York. Unlike her sister ship *Imperator*, the grand liner operated smoothly and handled the rough North
Atlantic with grace. Albert Ballin had every reason to be proud of his new
vessel. If the first ship of the class was problematic, Ballin made sure the
next two were as perfect as he and his engineers could make them. They
would be faster than *Imperator*, able to sail at 23 knots and cross the Atlantic in only five days, and steadier in rough seas.

HAPAG used Wagnerian language to promote its two new ships, even
if no military features—such as gun mounts—were incorporated in their
designs. "The Hamburg-Amerika Line has forged two fiery weapons
of highly-tempered steel, two sharp, gigantic, gleaming swords," read a
company press release. "[L]ife is conflict, and a strong man must always
be armed for battle, either in order to ward off aught that might hinder
him in his course, or in order to advance victoriously along hitherto untrodden paths and thus attain his goal. This is the duty of the strong."
War, after all, was still in the air.

Many of his fellow directors at HAPAG, however, were still not so
sure if the new class of vessels made business sense, and wondered if Ballin was building them simply to thumb his nose at J. P. Morgan. But the
numbers made sense for now. One of his big new ships—able to carry
about two thousand immigrants in third class and steerage—could

make twelve round trips between Hamburg and New York a year. At full capacity, this meant the combined trio of *Imperator*, *Vaterland*, and *Bismarck* could carry a total of 72,000 migrants per year on westbound trips.

Based on 1913 numbers, that would leave 120,000 immigrants who were booking passage on other HAPAG ships or who were leaving for ports other than New York. Based on steerage fares of 160 marks, the three ships combined could produce about 11,520,000 marks in annual revenue, in a best-case scenario, assuming war didn't break out. Accordingly, first- and second-class fares were almost incidental to the overall profitability of the three ships. As maritime historian Frank Braynard aptly said about them, "First class got two-thirds of the ship, but four-fifths of the people were crammed into one-fifth of the space as immigrants. They paid for those great liners."

A month after *Vaterland*'s maiden voyage, on June 2, 1914, Countess Hanna von Bismarck, granddaughter of the Iron Chancellor, christened the third and final ship of HAPAG's new class of people carriers. Or she tried to. The countess and the Kaiser mounted the platform at Hamburg's Blöhm & Voss and waved to the crowds below. She took in hand the bottle of champagne that was attached to the ship with a long cord.

The countess swung the bottle too late, missing the ship's bow as the mammoth vessel began its slide into the Elbe River. The people watching gasped. A bad omen, perhaps? The bottle swung back toward the platform. Resplendent as always in his admiral's uniform, Kaiser Wilhelm caught the bottle with his good arm, and swung it back toward the bow. This time, the bottle struck the huge ship, shattering on the prow and spraying its golden, bubbling contents into the sunlight.

The largest ship in the world, she stretched 950 feet long, and when complete, she would register at 56,000 tons. No passenger liner would surpass *Bismarck* in size for the next twenty years.

By all appearances, 1914 was gearing up to be a banner year for the emigration business. Some 878,000 new arrivals would pass through Ellis Island, a large percentage of them on HAPAG vessels. Powering the renewed tidal wave was increasing fear about war in Europe between Russia and Germany. The several million Jews who were still living in Poland, Ukraine, Belarus, and the Austro-Hungarian province of Galicia knew they would be caught between the maws of two armies should war break out. The Jews of Galicia, although granted full citizenship rights, were relatively poor. Although facing discrimination of all sorts, they, unlike the Russian Jews, didn't have the Cossacks hounding and killing them. Still, there was impending fear that should the Russians invade Galicia, their towns and villages would be burned to the ground and they would be slaughtered.

Finally, the simmering fight over the fate of Bosnia-Herzegovina claimed a member of the royal House of Habsburg. On June 28, 1914, Archduke Franz Ferdinand, heir to the Austro-Hungarian throne and nephew of the aging Emperor Franz Joseph I (who had granted his nation's Jews full citizenship rights back in 1867), was shot to death while riding in his car in Sarajevo. The assassin was Serbian nationalist Gavrilo Princip. Also killed was the archduke's wife, Sophie, Duchess of Hohenberg. Princip had hoped the assassination would make the Austrian government think seriously about leaving the occupied province of Bosnia-Herzegovina and returning it to Serbia.

Instead, Ferdinand's death drew the nations of the Triple Alliance (Germany, Austria-Hungary, and Italy) and the Triple Entente (England, France, and Russia) into military action. In its ultimatum, Austria-Hungary demanded an inquiry into the assassination on Serbian soil, and that the Serbian government in Belgrade help suppress Serbian independence factions in Bosnia-Herzegovina. Sensing opportunity for war, Germany encouraged Austria-Hungary by promising its "faithful support" should it go to war with Serbia.

Serbia rejected the ultimatum outright, and Austria-Hungary declared war on its Slavic neighbor. Russia was furious.

Several hundred miles away in Hamburg, Albert Ballin, who had celebrated the launch of the *Bismarck* only eight days before the assassination, prayed that the fighting would be confined to Austria and Serbia. He also hoped desperately that Kaiser Wilhelm II would understand how disastrous a war would be for Germany's place in the world, her empire, her industrial economy, and her status as a civilized European power.

Ballin sailed for Great Britain. On July 24, he had an emergency dinner meeting with Winston Churchill, First Lord of the Admiralty. At this critical moment, Churchill hoped that Ballin could work his business-diplomatic magic with the Kaiser. "My dear friend," Churchill tearfully told Ballin, "don't let us go to war."

But in Berlin, the Prussian reactionaries who actually ran the country, people whom Albert Ballin had dismissed as office boys, had been planning for the moment of war to begin for years. Now was their chance to put their expansionist military ideas into action, and the Kaiser gleefully went along.

On August 1, 1914, Germany and Austria-Hungary declared war on Russia, Serbia's longtime ally. In response, Great Britain and France, allied to Russia, entered the war. German troops then circumvented France's Maginot defensive line and marched through Belgium and toward Paris. German and Russian armies clashed in Poland and Galicia, creating an eastern front.

The timing could not have been worse for Germany's mighty commercial fleet. SS *Vaterland* was at her pier in Hoboken, as was the SS *Amerika* and several other of the company's finest and most valuable ships. Several of rival Norddeutscher-Lloyd's biggest ships were also stranded in American ports. Both companies decided it was safer to leave their ships in the neutral United States than risk sending them back to Germany across the Atlantic, which was now crawling with British and French warships. Many other HAPAG vessels, including *Imperator* and *Kaiserin Auguste Victoria*, were moored in Cuxhaven, but were now marooned and financially crippled.

Thousands of passengers were now stranded in Hamburg's hotels and at the *Auswandererhallen*. On August 2, the German military seized the facility and transformed it into a military hospital. The German immigrant commissioner coldly wrote:

> . . . *the unmarried Russians, male and female, were . . . transported to Pomerania to be listed for work on the harvest there. In addition, 49 persons had to stay in Hamburg because they had relatives in hospitals. . . . The last member of this Russian family did not recover until 19 November, since when the family have been treated as prisoners of war.*

These unfortunate Russian Jews, hoping to escape pogroms and conscription, now found themselves little more than serfs, laboring on Prussian estates to feed the German Army. Wanting desperately to become Americans, they were now without a country, caught in a war.

On the other side of the Atlantic, HAPAG's New York operations ground to a halt. With no way to get money from Germany to the United States, the American directors of the company composed a desperate cable to the headquarters in Hamburg:

> We will be compelled to make large refunds of passage money *Vaterland, Amerika,* [*President*] *Grant*. Also monies already paid for passage tickets for vessels advertised but which cannot make their departures. Cessation of our business causes very little inflow of money. Could you please arrange through Mr. Warburg that Kuhn, Loeb finance us temporarily. Matter urgent.

Watching his once-profitable company bleeding money, Albert Ballin leaned on Max Warburg to use his influence with his brothers Felix and Paul to help keep HAPAG afloat. "I received your cable," Max wrote his friend on August 28, "and am delighted to have succeeded in lending HAPAG 1,750,000 marks before my taking leave of Kuhn, Loeb and Company and we have combined as a group. This is against deposit of ships as a guarantee at the same time a guaranteed minimum commission for their possible sale. This is a costly transaction for HAPAG but everything is so stuck here and nobody will release his money and in addition the trend against Germany is so stormy that it was only possible to bring the people to cooperate under the said conditions.

"It is a shame that Paul is based in Washington and not in New York," Max added. Ballin's old neighbor already had enough on his plate, because he had just been sworn in as vice governor of the newly created Federal Reserve Bank of the United States. For years, Paul Warburg and J. P. Morgan had dreamed of creating the central bank to flatten the ups and downs of the business cycle, to better control the American money supply, and to regulate private banks. After Taft, and under President Woodrow Wilson, the bank had finally been created. But now, at his moment of greatest triumph, Paul Warburg was under scrutiny for his and his firm's close ties to Germany.

The first loan of 1.75 million marks wasn't enough to keep HAPAG's

American operations going without passenger and cargo receipts. On September 14, 1914, HAPAG's finance department wrote a panicked memo to Kuhn, Loeb & Co. pleading for more money to pay staff and marooned crews. "We will need $300,000 if more sailings are canceled," the letter read. "We will need $600,000 for current costs during the two weeks. Cash at the banks of $100,000 along with the $150,000 authorized by Alsterferd at Kuhn, Loeb will give us $250,000.00 so that you should transfer $650,000 in order to enable us to meet our commitments during the next two weeks. As we cabled on the 30th of July, as a result of a complete cessation of our business, we have been unable to receive any money. Can you remit another $1 million?"

In desperation, Albert Ballin offered collateral in exchange for more liquidity in New York. "[C]ould possibly offer property there in the form of land and property as security," another memo read. "The need does not seem to be gross if spread over a longer period and no longer than a precautionary ruling."

Meanwhile, across the Atlantic, Max Warburg pleaded with the German Admiralty for funds to keep HAPAG going at home. He was rebuffed.

Soon the British Navy began to lay mines in the North Sea, cutting off Germany's access to anything coming in from overseas. The British government wanted the blockade to starve Germany's military and civilian population into submission. Although America was officially neutral, public bias leaned toward Great Britain, France, and Russia. As a result, Albert Ballin realized he could no longer rely on Kuhn, Loeb & Co. for bridge financing. HAPAG's ships sat idle and rusting in Hoboken, maintained by paid skeleton crews.

William G. Sickel, the vice director of HAPAG, insisted to a Senate subcommittee that Kuhn, Loeb was not financing the company's American interests. He admitted that HAPAG had gone to the investment banking firm to ask for a $2.5 million loan but had been turned down because of hostilities in Europe.

"Why did you go to Kuhn, Loeb and Company at the outset?" demanded one senator.

"Our company had never had anything to do with Kuhn, Loeb and

Company," Sickel responded, "but one of our Hamburg directors had a brother in that company, making a connecting link between our two concerns, and we were unable to communicate with the Foreign Office and needed a large amount of money for temporary use and thought we might get it there. I refer to Max Warburg, our director, who is a brother of Felix Warburg of Kuhn, Loeb & Co."

Clearly under duress, Sickel then pleaded, "Peace does not want to find the company without ships."

The British blockade did not produce mass starvation in Germany. But within months, trench warfare on both the eastern and western fronts exacted a devastating toll. Germany's invasions of France had been halted just thirty miles east of Paris. In the fall of 1914, 500,000 soldiers died in the First Battles of the Marne and over 200,000 at Ypres. In Poland, the Germans smashed the Russian Army at Tannenberg, with 45,000 casualties on both sides. The figures were staggering. Over the next four years, mechanized trench warfare would decimate an entire generation of Europe's men and lay waste to the Continent.

Some businesses profited. Germany's wartime industries such as Krupp boomed, but HAPAG, the world's biggest and most profitable shipping company, had effectively ceased to exist. HAPAG canceled all future sailings. So did Norddeutscher-Lloyd and all other German shipping lines. Thousands of people were stranded in Hamburg and Bremen. The control stations along the Prussian-Russian border, through which thousands of Jewish migrants passed every year, closed their doors.

There was no escape left for the Jews of Russia. Nicholas II drafted every last man into his army to fight the Germans, and military conscription turned into a full-scale draft. Soon enough, the czar himself would travel to the eastern front and personally command his troops. Nicholas II was already ill equipped to be a ruler, but he proved more hapless still as a commander in chief.

In February 1915, Albert Ballin begged Kuhn, Loeb & Co. to buy all or some of HAPAG's ships stranded in American ports, including *Vaterland*, and hold them until the war ended. Kuhn, Loeb refused. That fall, the German government stepped in and promised HAPAG a loan for

12 million marks, at 4 percent interest, should the war end by the first of the next month. The promise, of course, came to nothing, as the war continued to rage on.

The war may have been a disaster for HAPAG, but it saved the ailing International Mercantile Marine. Undeterred by Germany's fleet of U-boats that prowled English waters, the company's ships carried vast quantities of food and supplies to Great Britain. IMM went into receivership in 1915, but high wartime freight rates and the astute management of its new president (and former receiver), Philip Franklin, made it profitable.

J. P. Morgan Jr., who took his father's place at the helm of the bank, was unapologetic about his desire to help finance and supply England and her allies, including Russia, over Germany. Unlike his father, who kept his dislike of Jews close to his vest, J. P. Morgan Jr. was flagrantly anti-Semitic. During one transatlantic voyage, before the war, Jack Morgan cabled his mother saying: "this is only a line to tell you we are all right and having a really delightful voyage with <u>no</u> Jews and no one on board traveling with anyone else's wife." The war hardened his disdain for Jews and Jewish bankers in particular, whom he believed were allied with the Kaiser.

Declaring Czar Nicholas II "the enemy of mankind," Jacob Schiff refused to condemn Germany's march into Belgium or endorse the Allies. Perhaps it was out of loyalty for his home country. Instead, he went into high gear raising funds for the four million Jews trapped in Eastern Europe and suffering from hunger and persecution behind the eastern front.

Egged on by nationalist propaganda, many of the czar's subjects viewed the empire's Yiddish-speaking Jews as German spies, even while 450,000 Russian Jews were fighting for Mother Russia. Cossacks forcibly expelled Jews from villages and towns in the Pale of Settlement, and an estimated 30,000 to 100,000 Russian Jews died at the hands of the military and ordinary Russians during the course of the war. Countless more were raped, beaten, and maimed. Now there was no way out, legal or illegal, by land or by sea.

Working late into the night, Jacob Schiff cast about for ways to get some Jews out of Russia without the use of the German shipping lines. His efforts came to nothing. "The world will never be the same again," he said about the war that raged.

In early 1915, Germany struck at Britain's lifeline by declaring unrestricted submarine warfare. This meant that any commercial vessel could be torpedoed and sunk without warning or time for the passengers and crew to escape. On May 7, 1915, the submarine U-20 torpedoed the Cunard Line's RMS *Lusitania* off the southwest coast of Ireland. One of the few commercial liners left in regular service, *Lusitania* was returning to Liverpool from New York City carrying 1,959 passengers and crew, as well as 4,200 cases of Remington small-arms ammunition. The giant ship sank in just twenty minutes, taking 1,198 people with her. As *Lusitania* was traveling eastbound, there were no immigrants in steerage, but the terrific loss of civilian lives infuriated the American public, who felt that Kaiser Wilhelm II was not just a megalomaniac but a murderer.

Horrified by the disaster, Jacob Schiff left his office at 52 William Street and walked over to J. P. Morgan & Co.'s new headquarters, a squat limestone bunker at 15 Broad Street. There he found J. P. Morgan Jr. fuming in his office. A portrait of his father stared imperiously down from the wall. A shaken Jacob Schiff offered his sincerest apologies for Germany's barbaric killing of civilians, including 128 Americans. Jack Morgan exploded in a fury and told Schiff to get out of his office. Realizing that Wall Street was still a small world, Morgan rethought what he did and walked over to Kuhn, Loeb & Co. to apologize to Schiff for the outburst.

Even after the *Lusitania* was sunk, Jacob Schiff found it hard to turn against Germany and support a possible American alliance with Russia. He still refused to let Kuhn, Loeb & Co. make and underwrite loans to the Allied powers, not just out of principle but also because it would endanger the umbilically linked M. M. Warburg & Co.'s position with the German government. In a June 1915 letter published in the *New York Times*, Schiff declared, "I would just as little think of turning against [Germany] in this hour of its struggle and peril as I would turn against my own parents were their existence endangered." Stung by the response to his letter and knowing that American entry into the war was imminent, Schiff concluded that the time had come to publicly declare his allegiance not just to America, but to the Allied cause. This meant severing or concealing his firm's many ties to Germany and whatever financial aid it was providing to HAPAG.

Otto Kahn, by now the firm's senior partner, and Schiff's own son,

Mortimer, met with special envoy Lord Rufus Reading later that year to discuss Kuhn, Loeb & Co. joining a consortium of Wall Street banks to make available a $500 million loan to the Allied war effort. Schiff snapped that his bank would participate in the loan as long as "not one cent of the proceeds be given to Russia." The younger Schiff and Kahn were aghast. At a meeting in the Kuhn, Loeb & Co. boardroom, Schiff listened as best he could (he was by now growing deaf) to what was going on.

After Lord Reading made his pitch for the loan, Schiff got up, looked the British aristocrat in the eye, and repeated his demands. "I cannot stultify myself by aiding those who in bitter enmity have tortured my people and will continue to do so," he said, "whatever fine professions they make in their hour of need. I cannot sacrifice my profoundest convictions. This is a matter between me and my conscience."

Everyone in the partners' room gasped. But Schiff held firm. Lord Reading walked out. The following day, the newspaper headlines read: KUHN, LOEB, GERMAN BANKERS, REFUSE AID TO ALLIES.

As part of damage control, Otto Kahn and Mortimer Schiff decided to make loans to the Allies from their own personal funds. It was too little, too late. The firm, once second only to J. P. Morgan & Co., would never fully recover from the public relations disaster, even though Felix Warburg and Otto Kahn spent the next few years stumping for the Allied cause.

Sir Cecil Spring-Rice, the British ambassador to the United States and a close friend of J. P. Morgan Jr., snarled that the "German Jewish Bankers are toiling in a solid phalanx to compass our destruction . . . and the principal Jew is now Schiff."

Jacob Schiff, so used to being obeyed, was losing control not just of his bank but his own family. He paid a giant price as he took on not only the czar but the Allied cause to help his people. A deeply moved Otto Kahn declared that "the old man was magnificent this morning," but felt along with others at the bank that he had hardened with old age. That year, the younger, more suave, nonpracticing Jew Otto Kahn took over most of the managerial duties at Kuhn, Loeb & Co. Kahn promptly changed his citizenship from British to American, and did his best to distance himself from all things German.

Schiff's son-in-law, Felix Warburg, who the old man had once felt was frivolous and non-pious, took the helm of the newly created American Jewish Joint Distribution Committee of American Funds for the Relief of Jewish War Sufferers. Donations poured in from German and Russian Jews who wanted to help Jews who were now unable to get themselves to America. Soon, the "Joint" was collecting and distributing $16.4 million a year to the four million Jews trapped in Central and Eastern Europe. Under Felix Warburg's charismatic leadership, the AJJDC gave America's three million Jews a unifying cause, regardless of ethnic origin, class, or belief in Zionism. But the most radical (and secular) minority of American Jews hoped for something other than salvation for their suffering coreligionists: a worldwide Communist revolution.

As a capitalist who had become hugely wealthy by financing railroads, Schiff was now openly attacked by the Yiddish press, which mocked him not as a savior but as a patronizing dictator. One thing he said attracted particular ire: "It has occurred to me—and it is considerable thought that I have given to this—that if the Jews of Russia and the Jews of Poland would not have been kept as a separate people by themselves, by discriminatory laws, the prejudices of persecution to which they have been subjected, would not have reached the stage to which we all regret it has unfortunately come."

At a 1916 meeting of the Kehillah of New York City,* many in the audience called on Schiff to answer for what he said, blaming the persecuted for their plight. Furious and his eyes full of tears, the humbled Schiff took the podium and defended himself. "The Russian Government will rejoice," he shouted, "because you are battering down the man who has stood between persecution, between anti-Semitism as far as his power goes, and the Russian Government."

The audience stood spellbound, and as Schiff walked off the stage, everyone broke into applause. The assembled body then called for a vote of confidence in Schiff's leadership of the American Jewish Congress. When the votes were tallied, Schiff received only one vote of no confidence. Even the socialist *Forward* endorsed him. But rather than renewing Jacob Schiff's leadership of the American Jewish community, the 1916

---

* The official Jewish community organization of New York City, incorporated in 1914.

Kehillah proved to be his curtain call. He was sixty-nine, and his health was rapidly failing. His daily sixty-block walk from his Fifth Avenue townhouse to his office in Lower Manhattan and back again had become far too much for him.

As America's entry into the war on the side of the Allies grew more certain, the German Jewish elite turned their attentions to supporting the efforts of the American Jewish Joint Distribution Committee rather than the old Fatherland. In November 1916, a group of wealthy German Americans threw a gala ball aboard the SS *Vaterland* to raise money for charities back home. Among the 650 attendees who milled about the ship's grand salons was the publisher William Randolph Hearst, whose pro-German and anti-Russian editorial pages made him popular with Eastern European Jewish readers and with the Jewish operatic tenor Jacques Urlus in particular. Schiff was wise to avoid the gala. Soon enough, public opinion in America had turned so strongly against Germany that such events were never held again.

For Albert Ballin, it seemed only a matter of time before America entered the war on the side of Great Britain, and most of his marooned ships would become prizes of war. With Germany at war and his fleet stranded, Ballin was now officially out of favor in Berlin. He found himself blocked from all further audiences with the Kaiser. After years of frigid civility, the leadership of the Foreign Office now openly mocked Ballin: "Weakling! Ungerman pacifist! Greedy anglophilic shipping magnate!"

That summer, Ballin wrote Arndt von Holtzendorff, HAPAG's well-connected representative in Berlin. In the letter, he urged von Holtzendorff to make the case to the government that Field Marshal Paul von Hindenburg, the hero of the Battle of Tannenberg, be put in charge of the army. He was, Ballin said, the last best hope for Germany to stave off total defeat. He then predicted that if Germany lost the war, the Kaiser would lose his throne.

Albert Ballin would prove to be right. But if the letter was intercepted by wartime censors, he could find himself arrested as a traitor. Worse was to come for him and his beloved HAPAG.

CHAPTER 21

A Life's Work Ruined

The evolution of higher and of lower forms of
life is as well and as soundly established as
the eternal hills. It has long since ceased
to be a theory; it is a law of Nature as
universal in living things as is the law of
gravitation in material things and in the mo-
tions of the heavenly spheres.

—HENRY FAIRFIELD OSBORN, DIRECTOR OF THE
AMERICAN MUSEUM OF NATURAL HISTORY

The deafening silence in the once-bustling Great Hall at Ellis Island was music to Prescott Farnsworth Hall's ears. The great ships that landed nearly a million immigrants a year on America's shores now lay idle at their berths in Hoboken, Bremen, and Hamburg, or had been pressed into service as warships. Meanwhile, an estimated 500,000 to 700,000 Jews fled the fighting in Poland and the Baltic States. Some found their way across the German border, but most remained stuck in refugee limbo. No country would take them.

The suffering of Jews in Europe in no way moved Prescott Hall and his friends at the Immigration Restriction League. What really excited them was the publication in 1916 of a new book by their resident gentleman scholar, Madison Grant. He had been hard at work on it for many years, to the dismay of Franz Boas and others.

Unlike previous racist works, *The Passing of the Great Race* provided a scientific gloss and attracted broad popular appeal to the eugenics movement. Promotional materials released by publisher Charles Scribner's Sons described Grant as a "scientist, savant, traveler, and trained observer [who] is exceptionally qualified for this work." Grant's book was a breezy and smug reply to the broad humanism of anthropologists like Boas.

Grant divided whites into three distinct racial groups, ranked in order of genetic and mental superiority.

Of the Nordics, he wrote:

The Nordics are, all over the world, a race of soldiers, sailors, adventurers, and explorers, but above all, of rulers, organizers, and aristocrats in sharp contrast to the essentially peasant character of the Alpines. Chivalry and knighthood, and their still surviving but greatly impaired counterparts, are peculiarly Nordic traits, and feudalism, class distinctions, and race pride among Europeans are traceable for the most part to the north.

Of the Mediterraneans, he gave credit for their supposed intellectual and artistic prowess:

The mental characteristics of the Mediterranean race are well known, and this race, while inferior in bodily stamina to both the Nordic and the Alpine, is probably the superior of both, certainly of the Alpines, in intellectual attainments. In the field of art its superiority to both the other European races is unquestioned.

In the end, Grant argued, the great civilizations of Greece and Rome did not originate from the people of Southern Europe and Northern Africa but rather from the Nordics. He reserved his greatest contempt for the so-called Alpines of Eastern Europe and Asia, a peasant class that included the Ashkenazi Jews and Slavs. In the same way Louis Agassiz postulated that Black Africans were a distinct subspecies to justify their enslavement by whites, Grant felt that subjugation was the Alpines' natural lot. "The process of conquering and assimilating these Alpines must have gone on for long centuries before our first historic records," he wrote, "and the work was so thoroughly done that the very existence of this Alpine race as a separate subspecies of man was actually forgotten for thousands of years by themselves and by the world at large, until it was revealed in our own day by the science of skull measurements."

Grant then turned his attention to the United States, which he felt was the cultural heir to Greece and Rome. He argued that America, and the world, was in a great struggle to stop the superior Nordic race being bred out of existence by the inferior ones. For the Jews, he reserved special hatred and disgust. He saw them not as refugees but as chameleons, as cultural thieves, as usurpers. Assimilation was not a goal but a crime against the Nordic race.

Grant then echoed Senator Henry Cabot Lodge's declaration that those of lesser races could never aspire to be the equal of the Nordics, no matter how well educated or physically fit they were. The solution to the preservation of the Nordic race in America and Europe, Grant argued, was a rigid system of sterilization and segregation. And barring non-Nordics from American shores.

The Passing of the Great Race was a bestseller and spawned a host of imitators. The shift in American public opinion toward England and the Allies helped the author's stature. Grant was a self-declared Nordic of British descent, and a rich and rakish one at that, while his archenemy Boas was a well-educated German Jew.

Former president Theodore Roosevelt, who had long positioned himself as a friend of the immigrant, loved Madison Grant's views and wrote to him, saying, "The book is a capital book, in purpose, in vision, in grasp of the facts our people need to realize. It shows an extraordinary range of reading and wide scholarship . . . and all Americans should be sincerely grateful to you for writing it." By the time of *The Passing*'s release, Roosevelt had launched full-scale attacks on German Americans for not being sufficiently patriotic, and on President Woodrow Wilson—who had not yet declared America's entry into the war—for being a coward. Many years before, Roosevelt had stated:

> *The worst deed that any man can do here, so far as the national life is concerned, is to try to keep himself apart from his fellow Americans, and to perpetuate Old World differences, whether of race, of speech, of religion, or of religious hatred, or on the other hand to try to discriminate against his fellow Americans because they may come of a different race stock from his.*

Now, even an intelligent man like Theodore Roosevelt was flirting with the very bigotry he had once condemned.

Armed with impending war against Germany, the public success of *The Passing of the Great Race*, and the Dillingham Commission Report, Senator Henry Cabot Lodge felt the time was finally right to push for strict immigration quotas that would legally bar almost all Southern and Eastern Europeans from American shores. The war at sea had given the United States a temporary reprieve from unrestricted immigration, and much of the American public appeared to like it.

On April 17, 1917, President Wilson asked Congress to declare war on Germany. Within hours, U.S. troops seized every single German ship in Hoboken and other American ports, including the SS *Vaterland*. She, along with dozens of other HAPAG vessels, were stripped of their fittings, painted gray, and pressed into service as troop transports carrying American soldiers to the western front. At Woodrow Wilson's request, the biggest ship in the world, *Vaterland*, got a new name: the USS *Leviathan*.

Most of HAPAG's ships were now prizes of war. With America now fighting on the side of the Allies, it was clear that Germany was going to lose the war. Casting about for hope, Albert Ballin sat down in his study and composed a letter to Admiral von Müller, head of the German Naval Cabinet, one of his very few allies in the military establishment now in control. "I am writing to you now after the start of the war that my life's work has been destroyed," Ballin wrote. "One would have to be able to give me back my youth if one were to entrust me with the task of reaching the position in international ship travel that I once possessed."

Even if HAPAG got its ships back at the end of the war, the passenger market to the United States looked increasingly grim. In February 1917, Congress passed a new bill that banned from American shores all immigrants over the age of thirty deemed illiterate, as well as all new arrivals from East Asia, Southeast Asia, and India. Worse still for the steamship companies, the new bill also added an eight-dollar head tax per immigrant, cutting into their profit margin and increasing the cost of steerage fare. To make things harder for migrants at the border crossings and at Ellis Island, the bill barred all "idiots, imbeciles, and feeble-minded persons"; persons of "constitutional psychopathic inferiority"; "mentally or physically defective persons; the insane; alcoholics; persons with epilepsy, tuberculosis, or contagious diseases; paupers and vagrants; criminals; prostitutes; anarchists; polygamists; political radicals; and contract laborers." President Wilson angrily vetoed the measure, but Congress overrode him.

It was only a matter of time, Henry Cabot Lodge reasoned, before Congress would have the votes needed to pass strict quotas based on national origin.

A month after the United States passed its new immigration bill, the starving and exhausted Russian people finally rose up en masse against their government. Strikes ground the war effort to a halt, and rioters tore through the streets of all the major cities. Czar Nicholas II left the eastern front and tried to return to St. Petersburg, but found his train blocked by his own soldiers. The army, who he expected to back him, had lost all confidence in the man who thought of himself as "Autocrat of All the Russias." On March 16, 1917, Nicholas abdicated the throne both for himself and his son, Alexei.

Three hundred years of Romanov rule in Russia had come to an end. For now, Russia was ruled by a democratically elected government.

Jacob Schiff rejoiced at the overthrow of the czar, calling it a "miracle." He hoped that Russia would one day become an enlightened democracy, just like the United States, in which all people, Jew and gentile, would enjoy equal rights under the law. Writing to Paul Milyukov, foreign minister of the new Provisional Government, Schiff could barely contain his happiness. He declared himself "a persistent foe of the tyrannical autocracy, the merciless persecutors of my co-religionists. . . . Just as before I hated most intensely the Russian government, so now I love deeply the new Russia."

But in its fragile state, Russia was still at war with Germany, and for many Russians, the so-called February Revolution wasn't enough. They wanted "peace, land, and bread," and Vladimir Ilych Lenin was more than happy to promise all three to all who would join him. In October 1917, with help from the Germans, Lenin's Bolshevik party overthrew the Russian Provisional Government and announced plans to turn the former Russian Empire into the world's first Communist nation. Lenin kept his promise about peace. He withdrew Russia from the war and gave away vast swaths of territory to Germany in the Treaty of Brest-Litovsk.

According to its terms, Russia ceded the three Baltic States—Latvia, Lithuania, and Estonia—and a big chunk of the province of Belarus to Germany, and granted Ukraine its independence.

This put the remaining Jews in much of the old Pale of Settlement under German control, at least for a while. Lenin also declared that organized religion in the new Soviet Union was dead, and that atheism was the official state policy. "It is not the Jews who are the enemies of the working people," Lenin declared. "The enemies of the workers are the capitalists of all countries. Among the Jews there are working people, and they form the majority. Shame on the accursed Czarism which tortured and persecuted the Jews."

On the Lower East Side of New York, Communist Jews danced in the streets and even talked of returning to Russia to fight for Lenin's Red Army. But Jacob Schiff feared that nothing good would come out of the new regime. Conspiracy theories were already circulating in far-right American publications that Schiff and other Jewish leaders had engineered the Bolshevik revolution and that Judaism and Bolshevism were inextricably linked. No matter that Jacob Schiff was an avowed capitalist and ardent admirer of American constitutionalism.

The tumult of the revolution in Russia, and the false hopes it aroused in America, finally convinced Jacob Schiff that perhaps Zionism was not such a bad idea after all. He also realized that the United States, after thirty years of unrestricted immigration, was on the verge of being a much less welcoming place for the Jews. Germany, too, had proved itself to be an unreliable and increasingly hostile home. On April 22, in a speech in front of the League of the Jewish Youth in America, Schiff declared that he hoped that Palestine would become, if not a country, a center of Jewish culture:

It has come to me, while thinking over the events of recent weeks—and the statement may surprise many—that the Jewish people should at last have a homeland of their own. I do not mean by that there should be a Jewish nation. I am not a believer in a Jewish nation built on all kinds of isms, with egotism as the first, and agnosticism and atheism among the others. But I am a believer in the Jewish people and in the mission of the Jew, and I believe that somewhere there should be a great reservoir of Jewish learn-

*ing in which Jewish culture might be furthered and developed, unhampered
by the materialism of the world, and might spread its most beautiful ideals over the world. And naturally, that land will be Palestine. If that ever
develops—and the present war may bring in the development of this ideal
nearer—it will not be accomplished in a day or a year, and in the meantime it is our duty to keep the flame of Judaism burning brightly.*

Schiff's hopes for a new and kinder Russia did not come true. A provisional democratic government was one thing. A Communist one was
another. Lenin's new regime did not treat its dissenters with mercy. On
July 17, 1918, at Vladimir Lenin's direct orders, Nicholas, Alexandra,
and their five children were lined up in a basement near the Ural Mountains and shot to death.

Russia's withdrawal from the eastern front wasn't enough to save Germany from defeat. In Berlin, the military closed ranks around a feeble
and increasingly delusional Kaiser Wilhelm II, doing their best to shield
him from bad news, even as fresh American troops pummeled his armies.
German soldiers were deserting and civilians were starving in the streets.

On the Hamburg waterfront, the mighty SS *Imperator* sat rusting, idle,
and decrepit. The half-completed hulk of the SS *Bismarck* was tied up at
the fitting-out* pier at Blöhm & Voss, her paint faded and her superstructure a haven for nesting birds. Downriver at Veddel, the *Auswandererhallen* were filled not with hopeful immigrants but with twenty-five hundred
wounded and dying soldiers brought in from the front. Its synagogue
sat silent, as did the kosher kitchens. HAPAG's prewar twenty thousand
employees were idle, fighting in the trenches, or dead.

Albert Ballin still showed up to work at the company's offices on the
Alsterdamm and talked to Max Warburg every day on their private telephone line. But the grandeur and pageantry that had defined so much of
his meteoric career was gone, as was much of his fortune. There were no
more regatta dinners or breakfasts with the Kaiser at the "Little Potsdam"
villa. The proud slogan "Mein Feld ist die Welt," carved in stone or emblazoned in gold above nearly every HAPAG doorway and ticket office,
now seemed a mockery. The once-proud Fatherland was humiliated.

---

* The installation of a ship's interior decoration, electrical systems, and machinery.

"I want nothing more for myself," Albert Ballin despaired, "but when I think about my HAPAG, then it is hard, very hard, not to cry."

As Albert thought about how HAPAG could rise again from the catastrophe of war, he paid a social visit to the home of Max and Alice Warburg. In walked their eighteen-year-old son, Eric, striking and resplendent in his German military uniform. He had just been drafted. Many years earlier, his father, Max, had dreamed of a romantic career as a cavalry officer. Now such ambitions seemed like a joke in an age of mechanized warfare and mass slaughter.

Ballin could barely stand the sight of his godson in uniform.

"When Ballin saw me in my uniform, he broke out in tears," Eric Warburg later recalled, "because he knew that all was lost and feared that my generation would be the last to be sacrificed."

On September 5, 1918, Albert Ballin boarded the southbound train to meet the Kaiser for the first time in four years. The meeting was at the Wilhelmshöhe palace in Hesse. This time, the monarch's handlers made sure that Albert Ballin would be having a supervised audience, not a private meeting. Ballin arrived at the palace and found that the Head of the House Cabinet, a stalwart conservative named Herr von Berg, stood at the monarch's side and refused to leave.

The Kaiser asked his old friend to take a walk around the gardens with him. Von Berg was a step or two behind them the whole time.

"I found the Kaiser badly misinformed," Ballin recalled, "and in the high spirits he likes to show in the presence of a third party. It is all being served up to the poor monarch in such a way that he has not the slightest idea how disastrous it is."

During a pause in the Kaiser's ramblings, Ballin took the opening to suggest that Germany open up separate peace negotiations with President Wilson, saying the American was an idealist who wanted the best for all parties after the devastation the war produced.

Furious, von Berg stepped between the two men, pulled Ballin aside, and snapped that the Kaiser "must not be made too pessimistic."

Realizing that he was "getting too outspoken," Ballin said goodbye to the Kaiser and returned to Hamburg. Here he could find solace in the company of his wife, Marianne, his beloved daughter, Irmgard, and his grandchildren Albert (age seven), Harald (age five), and Ursula (age three). All were alive and safe. Irmgard's husband, Heinz Bielfeld, was away at sea on the battleship *Seydlitz*.

At that point in the war, Ballin confided to his diary that the institution of the monarchy had to survive the war to keep Germany stable, but Kaiser Wilhelm II himself had to go. Over the past four years, 4 million soldiers had died and 750,000 civilians had starved to death. To what end? When Gottlieb von Jagow, state secretary of the Foreign Office, wrote Ballin requesting a meeting, he no longer had the energy to be polite.

"I too have more to do than wait around until it suits you," he snapped. "And secondly, I wish to have nothing more to do with a man who is guilty of this terrible catastrophe and of the deaths of hundreds of thousands."

A month later Albert Ballin met his old friend, *Berliner Tageblatt* editor Theodor Wolff, for lunch at Hiller's restaurant in Hamburg, even though wartime rations and food shortages reduced its once lavish menu to the basics. Wolff, who deeply loved his old friend and fellow Jew, was shocked at what he saw. The sparkling humor, those kind "speaking eyes," the witty repartee were gone. "The conversation, skirting this subject yet unable to get away from it, could only drag along," he wrote. "Nobody was equal to the old brisk exchanges. Ballin was filled with incurable melancholy. He looked ill; the fresh bronzed color of old had long disappeared, now that he was no longer able to travel through the sea breezes; his face was deeply lined."

But Wolff still saw great internal strength. "But amid all the weariness and depression he remained gallant and chivalrous." Throughout the entire course of the meal, Albert Ballin sipped his cherished French cognac and clenched his favorite cigar between his teeth.

Albert Ballin knew that a revolution was coming, and had given up all hope for the restoration of the old order. When a member of the General Staff approached Ballin about leading the peace negotiations with the Allied powers, he wrote, "I let him know that I would not back down, but would prefer to allow anyone else to do it."

On November 8, 1918, the starving and decimated German people demanded an end to the war. As a new variant of influenza, known as the Spanish flu, was killing hundreds of thousands on both sides of the Atlantic, a full-fledged revolution broke out all over Germany. Protesters clashed with police in the streets of Hamburg, Berlin, and other major cities. The Social Democrats and a coalition of left-wing activists took over the Hamburg city government and triumphantly raised the red flag above the Art Nouveau Dammtor station.

An angry group of sailors and dockworkers—representatives of the Hamburg Workers' and Soldiers' Council—stormed and ransacked the HAPAG building and entered Ballin's office, where he was working. "Rough sailors with red nooses and cockades threatened the sensitive and ill old man with physical harm," the former prime minster Bernhard von Bülow wrote later. "They screamed at him. A new age was starting, a wonderful time that would see his end, the end of capitalism, and the end of the HAPAG." Even as the mob milled about his office, Albert Ballin didn't lose his composure, telling them his company would be organizing efforts to feed the thousands of hungry citizens of Hamburg. Amazed at his calm, the rioters left.

Ballin then attended an emergency meeting of the Association of Hamburg Shippers, after which he walked to his home on the Feldbrünnenstrasse, where Marianne, pale and shocked, greeted him at the door. She told him that Villa Potsdam had also been ransacked, but Irmgard and the children had escaped to the relative safety of the country house at Hamfelde. Leaving Marianne downstairs, Albert Ballin went into his second-floor study and watched the sun set over the Alster Lake and the spires of his beloved Hamburg. In the distance he could see the laid-up, rusting SS *Imperator* and the half-finished hull of the SS *Bismarck*. He summoned his servant Karl Fischer to bring him a glass of water. Albert then opened up his desk drawer, took out some of his sleeping medications, and swallowed them. Shortly after taking the pills, he doubled over in agony. Gasping for breath, Albert reached for his phone and called his beloved friend Max Warburg, asking him to send for a doctor.

The medication was thought to have caused his numerous gastric ulcers to burst.

His servant and a physician carried the still-conscious Ballin to a nearby private clinic, where his stomach was pumped. It was too late. Albert fell into a coma. At 1:15 p.m., on November 9, 1918, Albert Ballin died. He was sixty-one years old. His death certificate stated that the cause of death was "bleeding of the stomach caused by gastric ulcers."

That same day, Kaiser Wilhelm II abdicated the throne of Germany and fled to Holland. Shortly after getting there, he blamed the fall of the German Empire on the Jews. The proper retribution for this betrayal, he wrote, was a "regular international all-worlds pogrom à la Russe . . . I believe the best thing would be gas." When stripped of his crown and titles, Wilhelm the man was no friend of the Jews. Rather, he called for what became known as the Final Solution.

After the Kaiser fled, a jubilant crowd assembled in front of the Reichstag in Berlin. "Workers and Soldiers," shouted Philipp Scheidemann, a member of the new Social Democratic government, from one of the windows, "the unfortunate war has come to an end! The murdering is over!"

Albert Ballin was Jewish out of pride rather than out of belief, but in accordance with that tradition, there was no autopsy on his body. Irmgard Ballin Bielfeld got word of her father's death. Distraught, she rushed from Hamfelde to the morgue to identify his body. Because of the influenza epidemic, she had to receive a special pass to enter the city. On her pass, she used her birth name: Emma Auguste Kirchheim. What she encountered at the morgue brought her to tears. "I was with my father again yesterday—he isn't reposing here," Irmgard wrote her husband, Heinz. "The place those guys took him is so terrible. For two nights he lay in the mortuary across from the prison, surrounded by criminals! When I finally went yesterday, ½ an hour before he was supposed to be put into the coffin, I saw this disgraceful treatment. They wrapped him in paper!"

To make things right, she decorated the coffin cover with flowers, green tendrils, and a wreath, "which we had acquired in a rush so that he need not travel to Ohlsdorf [cemetery] completely without adornment." Despite her grief, Irmgard also saw that her father was at rest. "I see him lying there so still and peaceful," she continued, "and with a blissful face and I can't be sad, but think instead that he's finally well. My beloved father. I will miss him very, very much."

The memorial service took place at the hastily cleaned-up Villa Ballin on November 12, 1918. No members of the Hamburg Senate or City Council were there, as both municipal bodies had been dissolved as of that day. "I had father's picture on the table in front of the couch in the smoking room," Irmgard wrote Heinz, who was unable to get away from naval duty. "It was surrounded by flowers and wreaths, and was made as pretty as it could possibly be. Day after day, I say that it is such a blessing for father that he need not live through this terrible time."

In front of a small group of mourners, Max Warburg gave the eulogy for his friend, fellow Jew, and honorary member of his family.

"The night before the burial of my good friend Albert Ballin," Max said, "I'd like to try to put the feelings I am experiencing into words. The pain of his wife—a true companion throughout life—as well as of his daughter, son-in-law, and grandchildren is too sacred for me to discuss."

Warburg then touched on Albert Ballin's drive, and his struggle to balance his German patriotism and professional ambition with his Judaism. "Restless, always striving forward, he set his goals ever higher. His own advantage was uninteresting to him. How often did he turn down positions that could have brought him even more power—he always stayed faithful to his original task and to his faith, which he never denied, despite—or more properly said because of—the hostility he encountered. The way that he fought for the position of the Hamburg-America line for Germany and for Hamburg's benefit can only be described as fearless and he faced every difficulty in the process. He saw the unhappy ending of this war in advance.

"His motto was: 'In serviendo consumer.' Nothing made him sadder over the last four years of his life than the fact that he was unable to fully sacrifice himself to the service of his profession and his *Vaterland*. It was not injured vanity, but the impossibility of making his warnings heard that troubled him. More and more he saw that that which he had helped to build up—the old German *Reich* and its free ship travel—was disappearing and he had to complain of the loss of many true friends. He felt increasingly alone and his worries about how the future of the German people could be erected on the ruins of the war bore heavily on him."

Of Ballin's supposed friendship with Kaiser Wilhelm II, Max was guarded and qualified. "His relationship to the Kaiser," he said, "was based on the honorable wish to awaken an awareness of economic topics in the appropriate places. Here, too, he was never afraid to share his opinion, though he encountered resistance that he was not able to overcome."

As he ended his eulogy, Max Warburg did not directly say that Albert Ballin's company had rescued hundreds of thousands of Jews from war and persecution. But the leader of Hamburg's Jewish community did declare: "Navigare necesse est, vivere non necesse est." Ship travel is necessary. Life is not.

Albert Ballin was not a self-proclaimed savior of his people. He catered to all immigrants, no matter their background or religious beliefs, and cared above all for the well-being of his HAPAG. But the intricate transportation system he devised—with its safe ships, border control stations, health inspections, and kosher food—directly led to the salvation of hundreds of thousands of people. Between 1881 and 1914 in the Second Jewish Exodus, an estimated 1.5 million Jews fled czarist Russia for the United States of America. Several hundred thousand more left Romania and the Austro-Hungarian Empire. It is difficult to calculate exact numbers, but it is safe to assume that HAPAG ships had carried at least half of them—between 750,000 and 1 million people—to new lives across the Atlantic, most of them in New York City. The rest of the fleeing Jews found passage on the North German Lloyd, Red Star, Cunard, and White Star liners.

"We live in a time of great death," Max Warburg concluded, his eyes welling up with tears. "The right to mourn a single individual has nearly been taken from us. Albert Ballin's departure has affected us so deeply and painfully, however, that we wish to keep his picture close in gratitude despite the tremendous events in Germany. In memory, we wish to hold his powerfully creative [*schaffensstarke*] and life-affirming figure alive, spurring us on to new activity in a new time!"

Albert Ballin was laid to rest at Ohlsdorf Cemetery. His grave was marked by a giant boulder that simply read: Albert Ballin.

For the rest of his life, Max Warburg insisted that his friend's death was an accident.

Shortly after the funeral, Irmgard Ballin fell ill with the Spanish flu. She died on December 7, 1918, aged twenty-six, leaving three small children behind. She was buried next to her beloved adoptive father under another granite boulder.

Albert Ballin's estate was probated around the time of Irmgard's death. Despite the ruined German economy, Ballin had still died a wealthy man. In his will, he left 300,000 marks to his wife, Marianne, and another 300,000 marks in trust for her to administer for the benefit of Irmgard and her three children. He also left his wife the title to the Villa Ballin and the country house at Hamfelde, worth a combined total of 600,000 marks. In addition to his salary from HAPAG, he also received substantial income from his board seats. The last year of his life, Albert Ballin had earned a total of 114,303.72 marks from his various corporate directorships, which included the Gesellschaft-Disconto in Berlin, the AG Vulcan shipyard, and German-American Petroleum Corporation. The record is incomplete, but Albert Ballin died worth at least 1.2 million marks, well below his estimated prewar 5-million-mark fortune, but more than enough to comfortably provide for his loved ones. Germany's economy was already in shambles, and the years ahead would bring even more financial hardship to its people.

The Treaty of Versailles, formalized in 1919, did more than impose crushing financial burdens on Germany. It also stripped HAPAG of almost all its 175 ships. Of its three new superliners, *Imperator* would go to Cunard, which renamed her *Berengaria*. *Leviathan* would go to the newly formed United States Lines, becoming America's largest liner. *Bismarck* would be ceded to the White Star Line, which completed her and renamed her *Majestic*. The rest, including the *Amerika* and the *Kaiserin Auguste Victoria*, would be shared by the Americans and the British. Only the mechanically faulty cruise ship SS *Victoria Luise* (formerly the SS *Deutschland*) would remain under HAPAG's flag. She was renamed *Hansa*, converted into a bare-bones immigrant carrier, and sent to the ship-breakers in 1925.

Germany would eventually rebuild its fleet but would never again be a major player in the immigration business. And after years of debate, the United States government finally enacted quota-based immigration restrictions that closed Emma Lazarus's "golden door" for good.

CHAPTER 22

He Who Saves One Life,
Saves the World Entire

He who carries out one good deed acquires one
advocate in his own behalf, and he who com-
mits one transgression acquires one accuser
against himself. Repentance and good works
are like a shield against calamity.

—THE TALMUD, MISHNAH, ABOT 4:13

At the end of the war, Jacob Schiff was in his mid-seventies, but he remained active. Throwing himself into the humanitarian cause, he donated many hours and large sums of money to war refugees. The Great War and the Russian Revolution left millions of displaced and impoverished Jews who wanted to come to America from Eastern Europe. But in 1919, there were few ships to take them across the Atlantic. Most of the great transatlantic liners were being used as troop and hospital ships, rusting dockside, or had been sunk by German U-boats. Although Poland was granted independence, the border stations between Russia and the rest of Europe were now either closed or had been pulverized by the fighting.

Jacob Schiff suggested that Russian Jews who wanted to escape the civil war raging between the Red Communists and the White royalists should board the Trans-Siberian Railroad for Vladivostok, get themselves to Shanghai or Yokohama, and then board ships for the American West Coast. Like the 1907 Galveston Plan, it worked on a small scale, but was in no way a major new immigration channel to America. For Jacob Schiff, however, the Talmud verse held true that no matter how small the deed: "Whoever saves a single life saves the world entire."

In the spring of 1920, after Jacob Schiff fell gravely ill, his doctors advised him to spend time in the countryside to recover. After his seasonal visit to Bar Harbor, Schiff spent August in the White Mountains of New Hampshire, away from the countless telegrams and telephone calls from Jewish groups seeking his advice and asking for help taking care of refugees. Rejuvenated, he returned to New York City on September 15, but fell ill again and was confined to bed at 965 Fifth Avenue. "He took to his bed then with the knowledge that his illness was extremely serious," the *New York Times* reported, "but with an expression of determination soon to be up again." Despite his illness, he insisted on fasting for Yom Kippur. After making it through the Day of Atonement, he fell into a deep sleep.

For the next several days, he lay semi-comatose, with his son, Mortimer, and his daughter, Frieda, at his bedside. At 6:30 p.m. on September 25, 1920, Jacob Schiff died, surrounded by his extended family. The cause of death was heart disease.

Jacob Schiff—who had left Germany in 1865 with $500, a few references, and a packet of kosher meat—was worth about $50 million at his death. His fortune would have been much larger had he not given away many millions to charities, including the Montefiore Home for the Incurables, the Henry Street Settlement House, the Hebrew Emigrant Aid Society, the Alliance Israélite Universelle, the Hilfsverein der deutschen Juden, the Semitic Museum at Harvard, the American Jewish Joint Distribution Committee, Hebrew Union College, and many other groups that benefited his fellow Jews on two continents. Unlike his rival J. P. Morgan, he lived grandly, but derived no satisfaction from collecting works of art and rare books. For Schiff, giving money away was his pleasure. On his seventieth birthday alone, Schiff had written checks worth over $500,000 to his favorite charities, big and small. Most of his gifts were anonymous. No official numbers survive, but it can be safely estimated that Jacob Schiff gave between $20 million and $30 million to charity over his lifetime, or the modern-day equivalent of half a billion dollars. The vast majority of this largesse went to Jewish aid organizations, both at home and in Europe.

The funeral took place at Temple Emanu-El at Forty-Third Street and Fifth Avenue on September 28. Two thousand people filled the pews of the dark, Moorish-revival edifice, among them Mayor John F. Hylan, Louis Marshall, and many other leading citizens, Jew and gentile, of New York City. The service was Orthodox, the tradition that Schiff knew as a boy in Frankfurt. But there were no eulogies. In his last wishes, Jacob Schiff had forbidden them on principle. He felt his deeds spoke for themselves. "Happy is the man who like Mr. Schiff can forbid any praise at his funeral," said journalist Arthur Brisbane. "He needs none."

An estimated ten thousand mourners stood outside. These poor Jews wore black coats, prayer shawls, and kerchiefs, and they kneeled, wept, and murmured in the Yiddish of the Old Country. The funeral fell on the Jewish festival of Sukkoth, so these men, women, and children had walked all the way from the Lower East Side, Brownsville, and other Jewish neighborhoods to pay their respects to the man who had made America, in spite of its many failings, a welcoming place for them. If not for his strength of will and determination to stand up to bigotry, many of them would still be trapped, if not dead, in the former Russian Empire.

And if not for Jacob Schiff, America would not have become *das goldene Land* for his people. He was autocratic and imperious, and failed to reconcile his love of American democracy with his native Germany's militarism. But at his death, the American Jewish community realized Jacob Schiff was a new Moses of the Second Exodus, who had helped to lead almost two million of his fellow Jews to the Promised Land.

The pallbearers carried the plain wooden coffin out of the synagogue. As rain pelted down and the wind howled along Fifth Avenue, the thousands of mourners standing outside bowed their heads and recited the Mourner's Kaddish. Not in English, German, or Yiddish, but in Aramaic, the language originally spoken by the Israelites before the Diaspora. It was a prayer that united Jews—Sephardic, German, and Russian—across the world.

The death of Jacob Schiff marked the end not just of his reign over the American Jewish community but also of the immense lobbying effort that kept America's immigration system relatively open. Between 1900 and 1920, the American Jewish population had grown from about 1.2 million (1.4 percent of the American population) to 3.6 million (3.4 percent of the American population). Much of this explosion was due to migration from Russia, Romania, and Austria-Hungary. But no other proponent of liberal immigration laws—Andrew Carnegie, Nathan Straus, Charles W. Eliot, Louis Marshall—could stop the tidal wave of bigotry that the Great War had unleashed, though the bigotry had been steadily building for years.

The crackdown on immigration went hand in glove with the rounding up of political radicals. For President Wilson, making the world safe for democracy meant rooting out anarchists and Communists at home. Upon America's entry into the First World War, Emma Goldman had been arrested for speaking out against the draft. She, along with her former lover Alexander Berkman and 248 other political radicals, were deported to Russia several months before Schiff's death. "Today so-called aliens are deported," she declared. "Tomorrow native Americans will be banished. Already some patrioteers are suggesting that native American sons to whom democracy is a sacred ideal should be exiled."

In 1921, Congress passed the so-called Emergency Quota Act, which restricted the number of immigrants from any given country to 3 percent of the number of people from that country living in the United States in the 1910 census. The quotas meant that only 24,405 people from the former Russian Empire (now the Soviet Union), 31,146 from Poland, and 42,057 from Italy could legally enter the United States each year. Northern and Western European nations were heavily favored at the expense of Poland, Romania, the Soviet Union, and Italy. Total legal immigration was capped at 357,803, or only about one-third of its 1907 peak. The impact of Madison Grant's *The Passing of the Great Race*, as well as many other "scientific" eugenicists, had much to do with the passage of the Emergency Quota Act.

But the quotas weren't enough for the dyspeptic and now terminally ill Prescott Farnsworth Hall. Shortly before his death, Hall published an article in the *North Atlantic Review* about the human tide on its way to America after the devastation of the Great War. The battered steamship companies, he wrote, were getting ready to move that tide across the Atlantic. Even though Albert Ballin was dead, Hall was convinced others like him would emerge.

"Great Britain and this country will have an enormous tonnage for commercial purposes," Hall wrote, "and Germany has already taken steps to restore her merchant marine and compete for her former place in transportation. Never have the steamship companies been more active at Washington than at present. . . . Although there has been legislation both here and abroad to check misrepresentation and fraud, there has been an emigration propaganda carried on by thousands of steamship agents reaching into the most remote hamlets of Europe and Western Asia."

Even from beyond the grave, the specter of Jacob Schiff tormented Hall. "Mr. Schiff, who was as well informed as anyone," he said, "expected three million Jews to come to this country after the war. Russia contains more Jews than any other European country, and most of those millions will come from there.

"The best plan in sight for cutting down the total number of immigrants," he concluded, "and at the same time favoring the kindred Nordic races, is that based on natural capacity of the alien for assimilation. . . . If the United States is to continue to stand for that which it has always represented, not only within its borders, but to the world at large; if it is to be protected from those who are foreigners, not only in name but in character, which as Le Bon says destroys a nation's soul, some such legislation should be speedily enacted."

Prescott Hall got his dying wish. Three years later, Congress went a step further to cement its ethnic quota system by passing the Immigration Act of 1924, also known as the Johnson-Reed Act. This time, total yearly immigration would be limited to 164,667, or a little more than a tenth of its prewar peak. The number of immigrants allowed from any one country was restricted to a mere 2 percent of the foreign-born population in the 1890 census. This meant quotas of only 2,248 from the former Russian Empire, 6,524 from Poland, 295 from Romania, and 5,802 from Italy. In contrast, nations that Madison Grant deemed Nordic were given much higher quotas. Great Britain was allotted 66,521 spots, Germany 25,957, and Ireland 17,853. One of Ballin's three superliners could carry the entire quota from Russia on a single voyage. The law also barred all immigrants from Japan and other Asian nations not covered by the Chinese Exclusion Act of 1882. Among the supporters of the 1924 bill was American Federation of Labor president Samuel Gompers, himself a Jewish immigrant from Great Britain.

Its mission complete, the gentlemen of the Immigration Restriction League dissolved the organization.

Senator Henry Cabot Lodge died on November 9, 1924, shortly after the passage of the Johnson-Reed Act. At his funeral at Christ Church in Cambridge, Massachusetts, the choir sang the hymn "The Strife Is O'er, the Battle Won." The *New York Times* observed that "these services were as simple as the ritual of the Episcopal Church would permit."

Max and Sophie Weinstein-Bacal, who immigrated to America aboard the SS *Deutschland* in 1902, had settled in the Bronx, where they opened a candy store. But the trauma of the early years of trying to feed his family from pushcart earnings proved too much for Max. "Grandpa did the best he could," his granddaughter Betty Joan Perske recalled. "Two more children—Charlie and Jack—were born in America. Grandma worked in the candy store, Renee, the oldest, helped after school; Natalie, my mother, was still too young. Grandpa suffered with a goiter for years and was given much medication for it—heart-weakening medication. One afternoon, he went to a movie, came home, lay down for a while, and died. He was fifty-five."

Max and Sophie's daughter Natalie, who was only a year-old baby when she arrived in America, became a secretary and married William Perske in 1923. His parents were immigrants from the Russian province of Belarus. Their daughter, Betty Joan Perske, was born the following year, but the marriage was tumultuous. Natalie divorced William in 1929, and changed her name to the Romanian form of her mother's maiden name: Bacal.

Natalie moved to the Upper West Side to live with her mother, Sophie, and brother Charlie. This allowed her daughter, Betty Joan, to attend the well-regarded Julia Richman High School. The old woman sang songs in German, Romanian, and Yiddish, and told Betty Joan stories about the Old Country. "I remember watching her sit in her chair reading book after book," she wrote, "each in a different language. Her telling me how I must always help my mother—how hard my mother worked. Grandma was quite religious. A candle was lit every Friday for my grandfather. She would comb her long hair, wind it round into a bun (never looking in a mirror), put on her coat and hat, and go to Temple. Dishes were changed for the proper holidays. She had a fierce temper—not too often, but when it was, it was wild. All those years of frustration, hard work, and worry had to come out some way."

Sophie wanted the best possible life for her granddaughter, as a way to validate the decision to leave all that she knew in Romania behind. "She was not demonstrative," Betty Joan recalled, "but I never doubted her love and her total dedication to me." Like so many American Jews who came of age during the Great Depression, Betty Joan wanted desperately to be American, but could not fully escape the powerful orbit of her immigrant grandparents, Jews who had sacrificed so much to give their descendants a better life, free from the poverty, bigotry, and fear of the Old Country, whether it was Russia, Romania, Poland, or Austria-Hungary.

She applied to the American Academy of Dramatic Arts and was accepted. Betty Joan Perske then gave herself a new stage name and an all-American identity: Lauren Bacall.

Epilogue: Kaddish for Those Left Behind

For the Jews left behind in the Old World, the struggle to survive would prove more harrowing than any immigrant's hardships in America. Ultimately, the stakes were life and death.

The Russian Revolution quickly soured from an idealistic, experimental dream to a bloody, authoritarian nightmare far worse than any czar's rule. After Lenin's death in 1924, his successor, Joseph Stalin, resumed persecution of the Jews within the Soviet Union, especially Zionists. He also forced Lenin's Jewish right-hand man, Leon Trotsky, into exile, obliterated the memory of his contributions to the revolution, and had him assassinated. Over the course of Stalin's nearly thirty-year rule, an estimated forty million Soviets of all ethnicities died in his brutal purges and labor camps.

Germany's own postwar experiment in democracy proved fragile and doomed to fail. In 1923, the Hamburg-America Line launched its first new ship built since the war. A small, elegant combination of cargo and passenger liner, a symbol of German maritime rebirth, she was christened the SS *Albert Ballin*. Able to carry 1,650 passengers, she would successfully sail the Hamburg–New York route for the next sixteen years.

Following Adolf Hitler's rise to power in 1933, Max Warburg was forced to resign from the HAPAG board. Before leaving, he gave a fiery speech to the management in the very room in which he had spent so many happy hours with his late friend. "The steamship line which a brave Jew, Albert Ballin, built up with all his patriotism and energy, now flies the Nazis' swastika on the yardarm," he said. "And what irony of fate that the ship called after Albert Ballin should be so decorated."

In response, HAPAG gave the SS *Albert Ballin* a new Aryan moniker: SS *Hansa*.

Soon after the death of her husband, Marianne Ballin sold the Villa Ballin and all its contents. She died many years later, in 1936, and was laid to rest next to Albert and Irmgard. By that time, the Nazis had been in power for three years, and HAPAG's management was busy eradicating all traces of Albert Ballin's legacy in Hamburg. And Germany's Jews, who once thought themselves safe from the sort of persecution meted out by the czar, were facing violence from a populist dictator who blamed them for all the nation's postwar humiliations.

Across the Atlantic, Madison Grant giddily wrote, "It seems strange that after a silence of about seven years, there should be this sudden excitement in Germany over my book." One of the most prominent admirers of *The Passing of the Great Race* was none other than Hitler himself.

Despite his best efforts, Max Warburg lost control of M. M. Warburg & Co. after 150 years of family ownership. Soon after, following Kristallnacht in 1938, Max and Alice Warburg fled Germany. They escaped to America and took up residence with Frieda Warburg's family in New York. Felix had died the previous year, celebrated by the Jewish community as a banker but "better known for his countless benefactions which succored Jews in many parts of the world, and which helped to foster numerous branches of the arts, sciences, and education." He proved more than worthy of his demanding and devout father-in-law, Jacob Schiff.

Out of Germany's five hundred thousand Jews, three hundred thousand emigrated to the United States, Canada, South America, and other European countries between 1933 and 1939. Because of the strict quotas against Jewish immigrants, now law thanks to Henry Cabot Lodge and the Immigration Restriction League, only a scant number of German Jews were able to find asylum in America in spite of three hundred thousand applications. Because of their influential connections and because their son, Eric, was an American citizen, Max and Alice Warburg were among the lucky ones. Most of the remaining two hundred thousand German Jews, along with those who lived in European nations occupied by the Nazis, perished in the Holocaust.

Before the Warburgs fled for the New World, a friend named Bertha Ehrenberg visited Kösterberg and recorded what she saw:

Everything in that twilit evening was so remote and as already forgotten by the world. Enormous, unreal trees, such as those that only in Hamburg or England take root in the landscape, afforded glimpses of a distance in which the broad, still river flowered toward the horizon opposite. Everything was quiet and almost unreal—another world—and in this quiet and remoteness I met the men whom I had met years before at the height of their power, their influence, their prestige intact. They sat there together, the Warburgs, Erich, Hans Meyer from Paris, Spiegelberg and Liebmann, once the heads of the bank, now stripped of their rights, denounced as "rogues" and "scum," their estate no longer cheerful and the only thoughts in their minds, how to get out of this captivity. . . . Outwardly everything calm and friendly and cheerful, "composed," but I sensed intensely the dreadful and tragic tension which lay over these uprooted, obliterated people.

The proud Jewish merchant princes had become the oppressed, "tempest-tost" migrants. The once sunny Max Warburg died a broken man in New York in 1946, a refugee from a world that no longer existed.

Max's daughter Lola and her husband, Rudolf Hahn, sought refuge in England. There, the woman derided by her mother as "Stupid Lola" masterminded *Kindertransport*, a carefully planned humanitarian mission that brought 669 Jewish children to England from Nazi-occupied Czechoslovakia. In her later years, Lola Hahn-Warburg was a fierce advocate and supporter of the new nation of Israel.

The year after Max and Alice left for America, a HAPAG liner named MS *St. Louis* left Hamburg carrying 937 German Jewish passengers seeking refuge in Havana, Cuba. The ship was under the command of Captain Gustav Schröder, who insisted on treating the Jewish passengers with courtesy and respect, even though the vessel was flying the swastika flag. Upon her arrival in Havana, the Cuban authorities refused the ship entry. Captain Schröder then radioed the U.S. State Department, requesting permission to land his passengers in America. President Franklin Delano Roosevelt refused. Anti-immigration feelings were too potent in America. *St. Louis* recrossed the Atlantic. Rather than docking in Hamburg, where the Jewish passengers would face certain imprisonment, Schröder docked his ship in Antwerp, Belgium. From there, various European countries granted the ship's passengers asylum in a deal brokered by the

American Jewish Joint Distribution Committee. Tragically, 254 of *St. Louis*'s passengers would eventually perish in the Holocaust.

For his heroism, Captain Schröder would be honored by Yad Vashem as one of the "Righteous Among the Nations." As a young sailor aboard the SS *Deutschland* in 1902, Schröder never forgot the great kindness HAPAG general director Albert Ballin showed to him on one of his many shipboard inspections.

As an old man living in exile in Holland, the former Kaiser wrote in his memoirs that he never knew Albert Ballin was a Jew. This was a lie. In these ramblings, the deposed monarch also claimed that Jesus of Nazareth could never have been a Jew. Although he expressed early support for the Nazi regime, he changed his mind after the horrors of the 1938 Kristallnacht pogroms. His son, Prince August, did not. "For the first time," Wilhelm told August, "I am ashamed to be German." Wilhelm also realized that Adolf Hitler had no plans to restore the Hohenzollerns to the throne. He died in 1941. In violation of his last wishes, the occupying German forces gave Wilhelm a full Nazi funeral.

When the Nazis invaded the independent nation of Poland in 1939 and the Soviet Union two years later, the Reich captured not just territory, but millions of Jews. In the summer of 1941, Nazi and Romanian soldiers massacred most of Iași's thirty thousand Jews. Thousands were packed into sealed trains and sent from one station to another, until their occupants died of thirst or suffocation. In the words of one survivor of the Iași pogrom: "They piled us into the train . . . we did not know what was going to happen . . . we thought that they would not want to set the cars ablaze only because they did not want to destroy the locomotive itself. . . . For five days we suffocated in that crowded train. Most of the people died in the car . . . we slept on dead bodies."

At the Wannsee Conference of January 20, 1942, fifteen high-ranking members of the Nazi Party and the SS decided to implement the so-called Final Solution, the extermination of all of Europe's Jews. Before Germany's surrender on May 8, 1945, over six million Jews died at the hands of the Nazis and their collaborators, the majority of them from Poland and the former Russian Pale of Settlement. Stripped of their homes, possessions, loved ones, nationhood, and their very humanity, they perished in the gas chambers of Auschwitz, Dachau, and Treblinka; or from overwork, starvation, and disease in scores of forced labor camps throughout the Third Reich.

It was a fate neither Albert Ballin nor Jacob Schiff could ever have imagined for the Jews of Europe. The Final Solution was planned by the German elite, but it was implemented by everyday people. Not just in the old "Fatherland," and not just in "Mother Russia," but in Austria, Czechoslovakia, Hungary, Poland, Holland, Belgium, and France. "Monsters exist," wrote Holocaust survivor Primo Levi, "but they are too few in number to be truly dangerous. More dangerous are the common men, the functionaries ready to believe and to act without asking questions."

The Bielfeld family, fiercely protective of Albert Ballin's legacy, knew that being related to a prominent Jew, even by adoption, was dangerous. They packed his letters, photographs, and other memorabilia into old steamer trunks, scraped away his stenciled name (except for the letters *A* and *B*), and hid them in the attic of granddaughter Ursula Bielfeld Hueber's home in Hamburg. Miraculously, despite the Allied firebombing and searches by the Nazis, these papers survived. All the while, Heinz Bielfeld and his son Harald served Germany in the Kriegsmarine.

When America entered World War II, Albert Ballin's godson, Eric Warburg, joined the U.S. Army. In 1945, he interrogated top Nazis, including Hermann Göring, for war crimes. He and his wife, Dorothea, herself a Jewish refugee from Vienna, reclaimed the family estate at Kösterberg and divided their time between New York and Hamburg. But not before they opened the estate up to hundreds of orphaned Jewish children who had survived the Bergen-Belsen concentration camp.

All three of Albert Ballin's grand superliners remained in service until the late 1930s, when they were outclassed by new ships like Cunard's RMS *Queen Mary*, the first transatlantic liner with a permanent synagogue on board. Ballin's giants were then sold for scrap and melted down into shot and shell to fight the Nazis. U.S. immigration laws greatly reduced the liners' third-class capacities and the ships were never profitable as a result. The SS *Hansa*, once the SS *Albert Ballin*, was sunk by a mine off Swinemünde. She was raised by the Russians, rebuilt as a cruise liner, renamed *Sovetskiy Soyuz*, and sailed between Vladivostok and ports in the Far East until she was scrapped in the early 1960s.

In 1944, Felix Warburg's widow, Frieda, donated their neo-Gothic

New York mansion to the Jewish Museum. The structure that her father once derided as *goyishe* continues to serve as the museum's home. Continuing her father and husband's tradition of *tzedakah*, Frieda gave generously to the YWHA, the Hadassah Hospital in Jerusalem, the American Jewish Joint Distribution Committee, and the Jewish Welfare Board. She also housed numerous refugees, including her in-laws, Max and Alice Warburg, at her country estate in White Plains. At her death in 1958, she bequeathed her $9 million estate to her children, grandchildren, and numerous Jewish causes. The village of K'far Warburg in Israel is named in the Warburg family's honor.

The descendants of Max Warburg still live at Kösterberg and have resumed their leadership of Germany's Jewish community. Today, the Villa Warburg and Noah's Ark stand watch over the placid, slow-moving Elbe River. A bronze sundial keeps time on the lawn where Jacob Schiff, Max Warburg, Albert Ballin, and their families once watched the HAPAG ships steam by more than a century ago. A red wooden playhouse—a gift by Albert Ballin to Eric, Renate, Gisela, and Lola Warburg—sits a stone's throw away from the main house.

The neoclassical HAPAG headquarters on the Alster Lake survives as the headquarters of HAPAG-Lloyd, a corporation that resulted from the merger of Hamburg-America and North German Lloyd in 1974. The street in front of the building has been renamed Ballindamm in Albert Ballin's honor.

The Villa Ballin, where Albert and Marianne Ballin entertained so lavishly and where they raised their beloved daughter, Irmgard, is no longer a private residence. It still, however, contributes to Ballin's vision of global peace and understanding. The villa now serves as the headquarters of the UNESCO Institute for Lifelong Learning. "I'm sure he would be very pleased that his house is now being put to such use," said Albert's great-grandson Heinz Hueber.

Miraculously, the Ballin family plot escaped desecration by the Nazis. Albert Ballin, Marianne, Irmgard, grandchildren Harald and Albert, and son-in-law Heinz Bielfeld rest eternally under a cluster of massive boulder headstones in Hamburg's Ohlsdorfer Friedhof cemetery.

"Albert Ballin would never have gained the commanding position he held if the keenness of his intellect and the force of his character had not been supplemented by that pleasing amiability which distinguishes all really good men," his friend Bernhard Huldermann wrote in his biography. "To him was given a large measure of that noble courtesy which springs from the heart. He who could be hard and unyielding where the business interests entrusted to his care were at stake, was full of generosity and sympathy towards the members of his family circle and his friends. Nothing delighted him more than the happiness of others."

The *Auswandererhallen* on Veddel Island was used as a prison camp during the Second World War. After years of postwar neglect and abuse, most of the complex was demolished in 1962. A few barracks have survived, and now form the core of the Immigration Museum at Ballinstadt. A white marble bust of Albert Ballin greets the thousands of people who visit Ballinstadt each year. Many of them are descendants of the "tempest-tost" immigrants who passed through the *Auswandererhallen* on their way to America.

The exit from the Ballinstadt museum bears not a slogan, but a blessing: *Das güte Leben wartet auf Dich.*

"The good life waits for you."

A good life was the good fortune of most of the estimated 1.2 million European migrants, Jew and gentile, Albert Ballin helped to bring through the Golden Door. Their living descendants, now numbering in the tens of millions, have in turn helped to make the United States of America a richer, stronger, and better place.

Acknowledgments

As a nation, we began by declaring that "all
men are created equal." We now practically
read it "all men are created equal, except
negroes." When the Know-Nothings get control,
it will read "all men are created equal,
except negroes, and foreigners, and Catholics." When it comes to this I should prefer
emigrating to some country where they make
no pretense of loving liberty—to Russia, for
instance, where despotism can be taken pure,
and without the base alloy of hypocrisy.

—ABRAHAM LINCOLN

The idea for this book started at the intersection of Forty-Third Street and Baltimore Avenue in Philadelphia back in the summer of 2018. My wife, young son, and I were enjoying outdoor pizza and beer at Clarkville. We started chatting with two women at the table next to us. Both taught at Swarthmore College. One was originally from Hamburg. I mentioned to her that my specialty was maritime history and that I had long been intrigued by Albert Ballin, the genius who had turned the Hamburg-America Line into the world's largest shipping company on the eve of World War I. Immediately, she explained how her native city was on a campaign to restore Ballin's prominence after his name had been virtually erased by the Nazis. I also talked about his role in immigration. After dinner, my wife, Alexandra, turned to me and said, "Albert Ballin should be the subject of your next book!"

I'm glad I took her sage advice. What followed was a four-year-long journey to learn more about the life of a man who is little known in the United States but who helped mastermind the greatest human exodus in history, from the Old World to the New, between 1881 and 1914. I realized that the subject touched on so many issues now so relevant in today's climate: immigration, refugees, nationalism versus globalism, authoritarian versus democratic governance, "scientific racism," and anti-Semitism.

HarperCollins accepted the proposal in the spring of 2019, and a few months later, we went as a family to Hamburg. The language barrier was daunting. I spoke no German, aside from snippets I had picked up singing church music in college. Thankfully, my wife is fluent from her time as an exchange student. Also daunting was access to archival sources. The Hamburg-America Line archives are closed to outside researchers. I also needed special access to the Warburg Archive at the family's Kösterberg estate. Howard McMorris II, a friend of mine from the Orpheus Club of Philadelphia, offered to help. He had spent much of his career working as a banker in Hamburg, and offered to put me in touch with Claus Budelmann, the former chairman of Joh. Berenberg, Gossler & Co. KG. Claus was also the honorary British consul in Hamburg. After our introduction, Claus picked up the phone and called his friend Michael Behrendt, the chairman of HAPAG-Lloyd, and Dorothea Hauser, the Warburg family archivist, asking if I could be granted research access.

Without the assistance of Howard and Claus, this book would not have been possible.

I made contact with Heinz Hueber, the great-grandson of Albert Ballin, and we agreed to meet at his home in Austria. Then, in March 2020, COVID struck, and I could no longer travel for research. Our second son was born that May. For the next two years, it seemed that we were reliving so much of the disease, civil unrest, and violence that characterized life in czarist Russia. Yet thanks to the support of my wife, friends, family, editor, and agent, I was able to press on, despite all the uncertainty and fear around us. As my late grandmother Judy used to say, when it comes to daily life in tough times, "You have to do what you have to do."

I am also grateful to my three professional translators—Peter Alexander, Ryan Dahn, and Peter Kuras—for helping me organize and translate a massive number of documents, many of them handwritten, and some never used before by an American historian.

I was fortunate to have three wonderful outside editors look over the manuscript before I submitted it to HarperCollins. Thanks to Terry Dunkle, Vivien Ravdin, and Elena Serocki for your helpful suggestions regarding structure and storyline.

In October 2021, I traveled to Austria and finally met with Heinz Hueber and his wife, Ingrid, who spent much of the pandemic transcribing the papers of Albert Ballin and his daughter, Irmgard (his grandmother). They graciously allowed me to use these precious archival sources, which miraculously survived the Nazi regime and the firebombing of World War II. I'll forever be grateful to Heinz and Ingrid for their generosity—and for the homemade Sacher torte! In Vienna, I also had the pleasure of meeting Georg Geigusch, owner of the historic clothing store Wilhelm Jungmann und Neffe and a leading authority on Jewish genealogical research. Thanks to him, I was able to learn more about Albert Ballin's place in Germany's economic firmament.

Many years ago, I met Jonathan Warburg, a great-great-grandson of Jacob Schiff and great-grandson of Felix Warburg, at an event between our two rowing clubs. I reached out to him regarding my current project, and I'm glad he pointed me toward his grandmother Frieda Schiff Warburg's privately printed memoir *Reminiscences of a Long Life*.

Also thanks to the American Jewish Archives at the Theological Seminary in Cincinnati, Ohio, which have preserved many of Jacob Schiff's surviving papers, including the sprawling manuscript of a biography of the banker by his friend Cyrus Adler.

In the fall of 2020, I was the second researcher admitted to the reading room of the J. P. Morgan Library since it had closed for COVID. There, I found some documents related to Anne Morgan and the International Mercantile Marine, but most of the IMM-related material appears to have been lost. Fortuitously, past historians such as Lamar Cecil, Jean Strouse, and Ron Chernow have done a wonderful job reconstructing what they could of IMM's inner workings.

I am also grateful for the assistance of Tobias Brinkmann at Penn State, who has specialized in Albert Ballin's role in Jewish immigration.

Special thanks to a small band of intrepid writers whom I've been privileged to have as sounding boards: Travis Logan, Timothy Sohn, Darrell Hartman, Dr. Charles Edel, Dr. Robert Richard, Dana Vachon, and Joe Flood. I'm also grateful to my fellow members of the Orpheus Club of Philadelphia and the Union Club of the City of New York for their comradeship and support.

My agent, Becky Sweren, at Aevitas Creative felt that the story of Albert Ballin had to be told. She pitched the proposal to Gail Winston, the then executive editor at HarperCollins, who accepted it with enthusiasm. She and my editor, Emily Graff, helped shepherd the manuscript into its final form, making crucial narrative suggestions. Thank you so much to everyone at Aevitas and HarperCollins for all of your faith in me and the project.

My wife and I owe a tremendous debt of gratitude to our fabulous nanny, Adriana Sostre, who cared for our two boys for five years and stayed with us all during COVID. Without her, this book would not have been possible.

Finally, this book would not have been possible without the love and support of my family, especially during these very trying times, when the very foundations of American democracy seemed to be shaking under our feet. To my wife, Dr. Alexandra Vinograd; my sons, Isaac and Max; and my parents, Grant and Amy Ujifusa; I love you all from the depths of my heart.

Notes

CHAPTER 1: THE JEW BOY OF MORRIS & CO.

7   "One needed to have seen the wonderous eyes": Susanne Wiborg, *Albert Ballin*, trans. Peter Kuras (Hamburg: Ellert & Richter Verlag, 2000), 5.

8   so-called kaiserly constellation: Theodor Wolff, *Through Two Decades*, trans. Ernest Walter Dickes (London: William Heinemann, 1936), 181.

8   "based on the honorable wish": Max Warburg, "Eulogy for Albert Ballin," November 13, 1918, in Heinz and Ingrid Hueber, *Mein Urgroßvater Albert Ballin* (Privately printed, 2021), 408–11.

9   Albert Ballin was an unlikely mastermind: Wolff, *Through Two Decades*, 174.

9   "I think you and I were never young": Johannes Gerhardt, *Albert Ballin* (Hamburg: Hamburg University Press, 2009), 11.

10   "Why shall Israelites be inferior": Samuel Ballin to Landherrenschaft der Marschlande, December 6–9, 1836, Folder *Staatsarchiv Hamburg Archiv der Landherrenschaft der Marschlande* [administrative district that was later incorporated into Hamburg] *XXII. Grundeigentum und Hypotheken—Billwärder* [property and mortages—Billwerder], Nr. 2427.

10   a Christian Mendelssohn was no more possible than a Jewish Confucius: Abraham Mendelssohn to Felix Mendelssohn, July 8, 1829, in Eric Werner, *Mendelssohn: A New Image of the Composer and His Age* (New York: Free Press of Glencoe, 1963), 33–38.

11   "Mendelssohn has shown us that a Jew": Adrian Mourby, "Can We Forgive Him?," *Guardian*, July 21, 2000, https://www.theguardian.com/friday_review/story/0,3605,345459,00.html.

11   "alien, Asiatic people": Alfred Apsler, "Herder and the Jews," *Monatshefte für Deutschen Unterricht* 35, no. 1 (1943): 3, www.jstor.org/stable/30169949.

12   Friedrich Trump of Kallstadt: The grandfather of President Donald Trump.

13   But by the 1860s: Tobias Brinkmann, "Why Paul Nathan Attacked Albert Ballin: The Transatlantic Mass Migration and the Privatization of Prussia's Eastern Border Inspection, 1886–1914," *Central European History* 43 (2010): 52.

14   "subject to all sorts of maladies": Bernhard Huldermann, *Albert Ballin*, trans. W. J. Eggers (London: Cassell & Co., 1922), http://www.gutenberg.org/files/44135/44135-h/44135-h.htm.

15   In 1872, the year after German unification: Fritz Stern, *Gold and Iron: Bismarck, Bleichroder, and the Building of the German Empire* (New York: Vintage Books, 1979), Kindle edition, location 182 of 17,726.

16   There was an exception made: Dolores L. Augustine, "The Business Elites of Hamburg and Berlin," *Central European History* 24, no. 2 (1991): 137, http://www.jstor.org/stable/4546199.

17   In 1881, the first year of their partnership: Huldermann, *Albert Ballin*, 12.

18   Ballin managed the ticketing side of the business: Brinkmann, "Why Paul Nathan Attacked Albert Ballin," 53.

18   One night, over a game of billiards: Huldermann, *Albert Ballin*, 12.

20   "Many scions of the old Hamburg families": Wolff, *Through Two Decades*, 176.

20   Whether Ballin's mother, Amalia, objected to the marriage: Gerhardt, *Albert Ballin*, 16.

21   The same was true for Great Britain and Ireland: Brinkmann, "Why Paul Nathan Attacked Albert Ballin," 40.

CHAPTER 2: CONVERT, EMIGRATE, OR DISAPPEAR

22   "Thinking he was merely wounded heavily": Edvard Radzinsky, *Alexander II: The Last Great Czar* (New York: Free Press, 2005), 413.
26   "the exploitation of Christians": "Odessa," Jewish Virtual Library, https://www.jewish virtuallibrary.org/odessa.
27   This meant learning Russian instead of Yiddish: Yohanan Petrovsky-Shtern, "Military Service in Russia," Yivo Encyclopedia of Jews in Eastern Europe, 2010, https://yivo encyclopedia.org/article.aspx/Military_Service_in_Russia.
28   The May Laws: Herman Rosenthal, "May Laws," JewishEncyclopedia.com, http://www .jewishencyclopedia.com/articles/10508-may-laws.
28   "Jews may be admitted as members:" Rosenthal, "May Laws."
28   "One-third will die": "Konstantin Petrovich Pobedonostsev (1827–1907)," Jewish Virtual Library, https://www.jewishvirtuallibrary.org/pobedonostsev-konstantin-petrovich-x00b0.
29   "The Jewish artisans are not really artisans": Arnold White, "The Jewish Question: How to Solve It," *North American Review* (New York: Franklin Square, 1904), 14.

CHAPTER 3: SCHIFF, THE IMMIGRANT SUCCESS STORY

30   "The surplus wealth we have gained": Naomi W. Cohen, *Jacob H. Schiff: A Study in American Jewish Leadership* (Hanover, NH: Brandeis University Press, 1999), 60.
30   "Herr Doktor Sachs was a stern Old World schoolmaster": James Loeb, *A Memorial: Our Father, 1829–1929* (Munich: privately printed, June 1929), 13, 22.
31   "We never forgave Sir Ernest": Frieda Schiff Warburg, *Reminiscences of a Long Life* (New York: privately printed, 1956), 46.
31   "I drastically became aware of its great temptations": Cohen, *Jacob H. Schiff*, 5.
32   "I have, for a long time, made it a rule": Jacob Schiff to Thomas Jefferson Coolidge, January 9, 1899, in Cyrus Adler, unpublished manuscript of a biography of Jacob Schiff, Jacob H. Schiff Papers, Series B, Manuscript Collection No. 456, American Jewish Archives, 938–39.
32   "Of course, there are liars, thieves, and swindlers": Bishop H. C. Potter to Jacob Schiff, January 11, 1898, Jacob Schiff Papers, Hebrew Union College.
32   "I am told that it is the only race on Wall Street whose word": Bishop H. C. Potter to Jacob Schiff, January 11, 1898, Jacob Schiff Papers, Hebrew Union College.
32   "Strange to say": Jacob Schiff to Bishop H. C. Potter, January 10, 1898, Jacob Schiff Papers, Hebrew Union College.
33   mansion at 965 Fifth Avenue: The modern-day equivalent is about $14 million.
33   "Mr. Schiff looked at the property": "When Rich Men Buy Their Homes," *New York Times*, February 28, 1904.
34   "I spent the years of my apprenticeship": Jacob Schiff to R. L. Strauss, June 12, 1865, Cyrus Adler, ed., *Jacob H. Schiff: His Life and Letters*, vol. 1 (Garden City, NY: Doubleday, Doran & Co., 1928), 26.
36   "The opportunity is enormous here": Jacob Schiff to Clara Schiff, January 1, 1875, Cohen, *Jacob H. Schiff*, 5.
37   "*Das war Musik!*": Stephen Birmingham, *Our Crowd: The Great Jewish Families of New York* (New York: Harper & Row, 1967), 188.
37   "I know you haven't any clear conception": Birmingham, *Our Crowd*, 190.
37   "A word spoken hastily in anger": Birmingham, *Our Crowd*, 190.
39   Over the course of his career, his work for the Pennsylvania: Cyrus Adler, unpublished manuscript of a biography of Jacob Schiff, Jacob H. Schiff Papers, 938.

39 In his memos, he told his clients: Birmingham, *Our Crowd*, 193.

41 "the deceitful race": Extract from a certain letter from Director Pieter Stuyvesant to the Amsterdam Chamber, dated September 22, 1654, Manhattan, quoted in Samuel Oppenheim, "The Early History of the Jews in New York, 1654–1664. Some New Matter on the Subject," *Publications of the American Jewish Historical Society* 18 (1909): 1–91, 5.

42 "perfectly conscious that . . . contempt": Katie Mettler, "Give Me Your Tired, Your Poor: The Story of Poet and Refugee Advocate Emma Lazarus," *Washington Post*, February 1, 2017.

43 "As [yet] the law . . . permits a man to use his property": Birmingham, *Our Crowd*, 144.

44 "It represents the habitual light": Emma Lazarus to Philip Cowen, ca. 1883, Jewish Women's Archive, https://jwa.org/media/transcription-of-letter-from-emma-lazarus-to -philip-cowen-c1883.

46 Fifteen years later, that number was approaching five hundred thousand: Paul Ritterband, "Counting the Jews of New York, 1900–1991: An Essay of Substance and Method," *Papers in Jewish Demography*, January 1, 1997, 202, Berman Jewish Policy Archive (BJPA), Stanford University, https://www.bjpa.org/content/upload/bjpa/ritt/Ritterband-Jewish PopulationStudies29.pdf.

48 "As to your surprise at the resentment which Hebrews show": Jacob Schiff to Bishop H. C. Potter, January 10, 1898, Jacob Schiff Papers, Hebrew Union College.

48 Kahn might have been a nonobservant dandy: "Otto Hermann Kahn," *The Cyclopedia of American Biography*, ed. James E. Homans (New York: The Press Association Compilers, Inc., 1918), 50.

49 "The charm of the Warburgs": Schiff Warburg, *Reminiscences of a Long Life*, 61.

49 Charlotte and Moritz Warburg led Hamburg's sixteen-thousand-strong: Ron Chernow, *The Warburgs* (New York: Vintage Books, 1993), 25.

49 Sara Warburg sent her famous Passover buttercakes: Chernow, *The Warburgs*, 25.

49 "The Jews are and remain a people within a people": *American Anthropology, 1971–1995, Papers from the American Anthropologist*, ed. Regna Darnell (Lincoln: University of Nebraska Press, 2022), 349.

50 "Either we succeed in this": Leonard B. Glick, "Types Distinct from Our Own: Franz Boas on Jewish Identity and Assimilation," *American Anthropologist* 84, no. 3 (1982): 550, https:// anthrosource.onlinelibrary.wiley.com/doi/pdfdirect/10.1525/aa.1982.84.3.02a00020.

51 "*du*" rather than the formal "*sie*": Chernow, *The Warburgs*, 51–52.

CHAPTER 4: ALBERT BALLIN TAKES OVER HAPAG

54 "Really, when those Hamburg magnates": Theodor Wolff, *Through Two Decades*, trans. Ernest Walter Dickes (London: William Heinemann, 1936), 180.

54 And so for running its flailing passenger division: Johannes Gerhardt, *Albert Ballin* (Hamburg: Hamburg University Press, 2009), 15.

55 Laiesz admired Ballin so much: Frank Broeze, "Albert Ballin, the Hamburg-America Line and Hamburg," *Deutsches Schiffahrtsarchiv* 15 (1992): 138, https://d-nb.info/11865 07853/34.

55 "Young man, according to paragraph 1 of our bylaws": Susanne Wiborg, *Albert Ballin*, trans. Peter Kuras (Hamburg: Ellert & Richter Verlag, 2000), 11.

56 "You are the ones who connect our fatherland with invisible ties": Matthew Jefferies, *Hamburg: A Cultural and Literary History* (Oxford: Oxford University Press, 2011), 181.

59 "If there is ever another war in Europe": Otto von Bismarck, as quoted in Tony Judt, *Postwar: A History of Europe Since 1945* (New York: Penguin, 2006), 665.

60 appeared like a "meteor on the bridge": Wiborg, *Albert Ballin*, 16.

60 "He received the honour of a decoration": Bernhard Huldermann, *Albert Ballin*, trans. W. J. Eggers (London: Cassell, 1922), http://www.gutenberg.org/files/44135/44135-h /44135-h.htm.

60 "Let us, here at the boundary of two parts of the earth": Wiborg, *Albert Ballin*, 17.

62   "the civil rights and the country's policy": "Franz Josef I (1830–1916)," Jewish Virtual Library, https://www.jewishvirtuallibrary.org/franz-joseph-i.

62   Tens of thousands more: Tobias Brinkmann, "Why Paul Nathan Attacked Albert Ballin: The Transatlantic Mass Migration and the Privatization of Prussia's Eastern Border Inspection, 1886–1914," *Central European History* 42 (2010): 57.

63   Although Bismarck relied on Bleichröder: Fritz Stern, *Gold and Iron: Bismarck, Bleichröder, and the Building of the German Empire* (New York: Vintage Books, 1979), vii.

64   "You know what I see now": Charles Guggenheim, *Island of Hope, Island of Tears* (1989, New York, Guggenheim Productions), film, https://www.youtube.com/watch?v=qh5CWbTDsuQ.

67   Ballin liked Emil Boas's work: "Emil Leopold Boas," Immigrant Entrepreneurship, 1702 to the Present, https://www.immigrantentrepreneurship.org/entries/emil-leopold-boas/.

67   Boas joined numerous upper-class Protestant clubs: "Emil Leopold Boas," Immigrant Entrepreneurship, 1702 to the Present.

68   "Without steerage passengers": Hans-Hermann Groppe and Ursula Wost, *Über Hamburg in die Welt. Von den Auswandererhallen zur Ballinstadt* (Hamburg: Ellert & Richter Verlag, 2007), 21, quoted in Mark A. Russell, *Steamship Nationalism: Ocean Liners and National Identity in Imperial Germany and the Atlantic World* (Milton Park, UK: Routledge, 2020), 45.

CHAPTER 5: IMMIGRANTS AND "ASIA'S FEARFUL SCOURGE"

69   "With the cholera killing people": *New York Times*, August 29, 1892, in Howard Markel, "'Knocking Out the Cholera': Cholera, Class, and Quarantines in New York City, 1892," *Bulletin of the History of Medicine* 69, no. 3 (1995): 430, http://www.jstor.org/stable/44451706.

70   "With the danger of cholera in question": *New York Times*, August 29, 1892, in Howard Markel, *Quarantine! East European Jewish Immigrants and the New York City Epidemics of 1892* (Baltimore: Johns Hopkins University Press, 1997), 88.

71   Among them were the Hornishes: The *New York Times* lists the casualties from the voyage as being either from the Horn or Hornisch family. Rudolph Hornish is listed as the same age as Ottlie Hornish, so it is almost certain they were twins.

71   "Little Ottlie Hornish died": "Report of a Health Officer," *New York Herald*, September 4, 1892, in Markel, *Quarantine!*, 103.

71   Over the next few days, as *Normannia*: "Two More Cholera Ships." *New York Times*, September 4, 1892.

72   A small group of stewards: "Two More Cholera Ships."

73   "It is a very hard thing to get news": "Two More Cholera Ships."

73   "cabin passengers seemed to feel the gravity": "Two More Cholera Ships."

73   "To have three cholera-scourged ships arrive": "Downhearted Agents," *New York Times*, September 4, 1892, 2.

74   "The wealthy gentlemen, poor things": *Arbeiter Zeitung* (New York), September 16, 1892, in Markel, *Quarantine!*, 115.

74   "there are two water closets near the stern": Report of the Advisory Committee on Quarantine, 1892, 39, Markel, *Quarantine!*, 129.

75   "He has made a marvelous fight in this world": Mark Twain, "Concerning the Jews," *Harper's Magazine*, March 1898.

76   The company's chief executive: Susanne Wiborg, *Albert Ballin*, trans. Peter Kuras (Hamburg: Ellert & Richter Verlag, 2000), 42.

76   "Occasional explosions of temper": Wiborg, *Albert Ballin*, 42.

77   Others, like those aboard *Bohemia*: Markel, *Quarantine!*, 89.

77   Between 1890 and 1900, 776,000 people departed Bremen: Dick Hoerder, "The Traffic of Emigration via Bremen/Bremerhaven: Merchants' Interests, Protective Legislation, and Migrants' Experiences," *Journal of American Ethnic History* 13, no. 1 (Fall 1993): 70.

79   Some of the nation's leading medical and public health officials: Markel, "'Knocking Out the Cholera,'" 430.

CHAPTER 6: THE ARISTOCRATS MOBILIZE

80   "The danger has begun": "The Restriction of Immigration," speech of Hon. Henry Cabot Lodge, of Massachusetts, in the Senate of the United States, March 16, 1896.

81   "our history, our victories, our future": Henry Cabot Lodge, "The Great Peril of Unrestricted Immigration," in *The New Century Speaker for School and College*, ed. Henry Allyn Frink (Boston: Ginn & Co., 1898), 177–78.

81   "with the careless elegance that only comes with habit": Theodor Wolff, *Through Two Decades*, trans. Ernest Walter Dickes (London: William Heinemann, 1936), 174.

82   "spoiled child": Warren Zimmerman, *The First Great Triumph: How Five Americans Made Their Country a Great Power* (New York: Farrar, Straus and Giroux, 2004), 343.

83   "The older men in congress": Prescott Farnsworth Hall, "Present Status of Immigration Restriction," *Gunton's Magazine*, vol. 27, April 1900, 380, https://archive.org/details /guntonsmagazine18guntuoft/page/308/mode/2up?view=theater.

84   "If genius and talent are inherited": Adam S. Cohen, "Harvard's Eugenics Era," *Harvard Magazine*, March–April 2016, https://www.harvardmagazine.com/2016/03/harvards -eugenics-era.

84   "German steamship companies making great effort": Neil Swidey, "Trump's Anti-Immigration Playbook Was Written 100 Years Ago. In Boston," *Boston Globe Magazine*, January 2017, https://apps.bostonglobe.com/magazine/graphics/2017/01/im migration/.

84   "radical departure from our national policy": Henry Pratt Fairchild, "The Literacy Test and Its Making," *Quarterly Journal of Economics* 31, no. 3 (May 1917): 454, https://www .jstor.org/stable/pdf/1883384.pdf.

84   "To hell with Jews, Jesuits, and steamships!": Swidey, "Trump's Anti-Immigration Playbook Was Written 100 Years Ago. In Boston."

84   "I do heartily sympathize with this bill": Theodore Roosevelt to Prescott Hall, March 26, 1896, Theodore Roosevelt Center, https://www.theodorerooseveltcenter.org/Research /Digital-Library/Record?libID=o283261.

85   "I had become instantly naturalized": Mark Twain, "3,000 Years Among the Microbes," in *The Devil's Race Track: Mark Twain's Great Dark Writings*, ed. John S. Tuckey (Berkeley: University of California Press, 1980), 163.

86   "They have none of the ideas and aptitudes": Francis A. Walker, "Restriction of Immigration," *The Atlantic*, June 1896, https://www.theatlantic.com/magazine/archive /1896/06/restriction-of-immigration/6011/.

87   The cost for an overnight stay: Mark A. Russell, *Steamship Nationalism: Ocean Liners and National Identity in Imperial Germany and the Atlantic World* (Milton Park, UK: Routledge, 2020), 46.

88   "had some kind of a heart": Peter Butt, *The Liners: Ships of Destiny* (1997, Australian Broadcasting Corporation).

88   By 1899, that number had grown: Georg Halpern, *Freistatt: Süddeutsche Wochenschrift für Politik, Literatur und Kunst* [South German Weekly for Politics, Literature, and Art] 6, no. 41 (October 8, 1904): 812–13.

89   The Prussian government expelled thirty thousand: Tobias Brinkmann, "Why Paul Nathan Attacked Albert Ballin: The Transatlantic Mass Migration and the Privatization of Prussia's Eastern Border Inspection, 1886–1914," *Central European History* 42 (2010): 54.

89   All others seeking asylum: Brinkmann, "Why Paul Nathan Attacked Albert Ballin," 56.

90   Halpern had no problems calling: Halpern, *Freistatt: Süddeutsche Wochenschrift für Politik, Literatur und Kunst*, 812–13.

92   "As you are now sure to be hanged from the Brandenburger Tor": Bernhard Huldermann,

Albert Ballin, trans. W. J. Eggers (London: Cassell & Co., 1922), http://www.gutenberg .org/files/44135/44135-h/44135-h.htm.

92   "The Empress did not begrudge her husband": Susanne Wiborg, *Albert Ballin*, trans. Peter Kuras (Hamburg: Ellert & Richter Verlag, 2000), 45.

93   "I was taught Hebrew, not the mongrel language": Samuel Gompers, *Seventy Years of Life and Labor*, vol. 1 (New York: E. P. Dutton and Company, 1925), 6.

95   "extremely seaworthy, and were capable": Huldermann, *Albert Ballin*.

96   By contrast, the twelve-year-old *Auguste Victoria*: Annual balance sheets of HAPAG as of December 31, 1901–1912, HAPAG Reederei, 1651, Band 3, 8, Hamburg State Archives.

96   This was significantly less than the *Deutschland*: Annual balance sheets of HAPAG as of December 31, 1901–1912.

CHAPTER 7: A BANKER'S CHARITY

101   "Forget your past": G. M. Price, as quoted in Ric Burns and James Sanders, *New York: An Illustrated History* (New York: Alfred A. Knopf, 2021), 246.

101   "Our God and Father": Frieda Schiff Warburg, *Reminiscences of a Long Life* (New York: privately printed, 1956), 43.

104   "Money is their God": Jacob Riis, *How the Other Half Lives: Studies Among the Tenements of New York* (New York: Charles Scribner's Sons, 1890), https://www.gutenberg.org /files/45502/45502-h/45502-h.htm.

105   In 1897, 60 percent of the Jewish workforce labored: Howard Sachar, "Jewish Immigrants in the Garment Industry," My Jewish Learning, http://www.myjewishlearning.com /article/jewish-garment-workers/.

108   "In the philanthropic institutions of our aristocratic German Jews": *Yiddische Gazette*, April 1894, in Harold Silver, "Some Attitudes of the Eastern European Jewish Immigrants Toward Organized Jewish Charity, 1890–1910" (M.A. thesis, Graduate School of Jewish Social Work, 1934), 219, quoted in Moses Rischin, *The Promised City: New York's Jews, 1870–1914* (Cambridge, MA: Harvard University Press, 1977), 104.

109   "beat in responsive sympathy": Samuel Greenbaum, "Isidor Straus," *Publications of the American Jewish Historical Society* 22 (1914): 238, http://www.jstor.org/stable/43057958.

110   "It may interest you to know": William Williams to Prescott Hall, Papers of the Immigration Restriction League, Houghton Library, Harvard University, bMS AM 2245 (999), Box 11, Folder 1.

111   "as if we attempted to play": Naomi W. Cohen, *Jacob H. Schiff: A Study in American Jewish Leadership* (Hanover, NH: Brandeis University Press, 1999), 14.

CHAPTER 8: MORGANIZING THE ATLANTIC

112   "Millionaires operating with the unnumbered millions": Benjamin Taylor, "British and American Shipping," *Nineteenth Century and After: A Monthly Review* 52 (July–December 1902): 28.

112   headlights of an onrushing train: John Steele Gordon, quoted in Ric Burns, *New York*, episode 3 (1999, Steeplechase Productions/WGHB Boston).

113   Morgan's group also promised to supply: Rob Wile, "The True Story of the Time JP Morgan Saved America from Default by Using an Obscure Coin Loophole," *Business Insider*, January 13, 2013, https://www.businessinsider.com/morgan-1895-crisis-and-1862 -gold-loophole-2013-1.

116   "had close contact with gentile bankers": Evyatar Friesel, "Jacob Schiff and the Leadership of the American Jewish Community," *Jewish Social Studies* 8 (Winter–Spring 2002): 63.

119   "You could not have a better reason": Lloyd Griscom, *Diplomatically Speaking* (New York: Literary Guild, 1940), 10, quoted in William Henry Flayhart III, *The American Line 1871–1902* (New York: W. W. Norton and Company, 2000), 85.

120   He had counted on receiving a $750,000 annual subsidy: John J. Clark and Margaret T. Clark, "The International Mercantile Marine Company: A Financial Analysis," *American Neptune* 57, no. 2 (1997): 137.

121   A small but still significant portion of Jewish immigration: "Yiddish Advertisement," Red Star Line Museum, https://www.redstarline.be/en/page/yiddish-advertisement.

121   It also printed Yiddish advertisements: "Yiddish Advertisement," Red Star Line Museum.

121   In the agreement, which would expire in five years: Bernhard Huldermann, *Albert Ballin*, trans. W. J. Eggers (London: Cassell & Co., 1922), http://www.gutenberg.org /files/44135/44135-h/44135-h.htm.

122   "In this way, mails would go forward": Herbert L. Satterlee, *J. Pierpont Morgan: An Intimate Portrait* (New York: Macmillan and Company, 1939), 373, as quoted in Flayhart III, *The American Line 1871–1902*, 318.

124   It earned 50 percent more per ship: Thomas R. Navin and Marian V. Sears, "A Study in Merger: Formation of the International Mercantile Marine Company," *Business History Review* 28, no. 4 (1954): 291–328, https://doi.org/10.2307/3111799, 303.

124   Partners Schwabe and Wolff: Michael S. Moss, "Wolff, Gustav Wilhelm (1834–1913)," *Oxford Dictionary of National Biography* (Oxford: Oxford University Press, 2020), https://www.oxforddnb.com/view/10.1093/ref:odnb/9780198614128.001.0001/odnb -9780198614128-e-38146;jsessionid=1FD07C910B60EB3E61DD6A0F5E52598A.

125   the same "cost-plus" arrangement: Cost-plus meant that the shipyard would not quote a direct price to the steamship company for the construction of a new vessel. Rather, the shipyard would build the new vessel to the customer's satisfaction, and then add their profit margin to the final cost.

CHAPTER 9: THE KAISER'S JEWS

127   "Theatrical superficiality": Ron Chernow, *The Warburgs* (New York: Vintage Books, 1993), 106.

127   "Darling, everything a person can become!": Susanne Wiborg, *Albert Ballin*, trans. Peter Kuras (Hamburg: Ellert & Richter Verlag, 2000), 37.

130   In return, the German lines would pay the trust: Lamar Cecil, *Albert Ballin: Business and Politics in Imperial Germany, 1888–1918* (Princeton, NJ: Princeton University Press, 1967), 52.

132   Northern Pacific's stock price rose: Jean Strouse, *Morgan: American Financier* (New York: Random House, 2014), 424.

132   "the rest of your stay abroad be pleasant": Strouse, *Morgan: American Financier*, 425.

132   When Morgan set sail: Strouse, *Morgan: American Financier*, 421–24.

133   Every week, the ships of the growing HAPAG fleet: "Hamburg-America Line Piers in Hoboken, NJ, ca. 1905," Immigrant Entrepreneurship, 1720 to the Present, https://www.imm igrantentrepreneurship.org/images/Hamburg-America-line-piers-in-hoboken-nj-ca-1905/.

133   Jacob Schiff authorized the purchase of a few million shares in HAPAG: Chernow, *The Warburgs*, 105.

135    $226 million of 5 percent gold bonds: Matthew McCreary, "How Andrew Carnegie Went from $1.20 a Week to 309 Billion . . . Then Gave It All Away," *Entrepreneur*, August 14, 2018, https://www.entrepreneur.com/money-finance/how-andrew-carnegie-went-from-120 -a-week-to-309-billion/317827.

135   "Paul and Nina lived for seven years": Frieda Schiff Warburg, *Reminiscences of a Long Life* (New York: privately printed, 1956), 35.

137   "while shaking physically": Peter Stubmann, as quoted in Wiborg, *Albert Ballin*, 25–26.

137   to hide the German breakfast ham: Chernow, *The Warburgs*, 72.

137   "From our house": James P. Warburg, *The Long Road Home: The Autobiography of a Maverick* (New York: Doubleday & Co., 1964), 17.

138   "The harmonious tone of his voice": Max Warburg, "Eulogy for Albert Ballin," November 13, 1918, as quoted in Heinz and Ingrid Hueber, *Mein Urgroßvater Albert Ballin* (Privately printed, 2021), 408–11.

CHAPTER 10: MORGAN'S BIG OFFER

139   "Anyone who saw Morgan going": Cass Canfield, *The Incredible Mr. Morgan* (New York: Harper & Row, 1974), 93.

139   "our firms and his were the only two companies": Jean Strouse, *Morgan: American Financier* (New York: Random House, 2014), 537–38.

139   "The real danger, however": Bernhard Huldermann, *Albert Ballin*, trans. W. J. Eggers (London: Cassell, 1922), http://www.gutenberg.org/files/44135/44135-h/44135-h.htm.

141   "stairs of separation": "Stairs of Separation," Ellis Island, Part of Statue of Liberty National Monument, National Park Service, https://www.nps.gov/places/000/stairs-of-separation.htm.

141   "EX" meant further examination: Alison Bateman-House and Amy Fairchild, "Medical Examination of Immigrants at Ellis Island," *AMA Journal of Ethics, Virtual Mentor* 10, no. 4 (2008): 235–41, doi: 10.1001/virtualmentor.2008.10.4.mhst1-0804, https://journalofethics.ama-assn.org/article/medical-examination-immigrants-ellis-island/2008-04.

142   Only 2 percent of all twelve million arrivals: "Immigration and Deportation at Ellis Island," PBS, *American Experience*, "Emma Goldman," May 21, 2019.

142   the goal was to secure a $40-million-a-year subsidy: Vivian Vale, *The American Peril: Challenge to Britain on the North Atlantic, 1901–1904* (Dover, NH: Manchester University Press, 1984), 47.

143   "[T]he blow to England is all the greater": Lamar Cecil, *Albert Ballin: Business and Politics in Imperial Germany, 1888–1918* (Princeton, NJ: Princeton University Press, 1967), 56.

144   Morgan had made a separate arrangement with Albert Ballin: Strouse, *Morgan: American Financier*, 465.

144   The main concern was that should war break out in Europe: Thomas R. Navin and Marian V. Sears, "A Study in Merger: Formation of the International Mercantile Marine Company," *Business History Review* 28, no. 4 (1954): 316, https://doi.org/10.2307/3111799.

145   the Morgan bank would be out the $11 million: Navin and Sears, "A Study in Merger: Formation of the International Mercantile Marine Company."

146   "You must have seen some account of it in the papers": Anne Morgan to Frances Morgan, July 7, 1902, Anne Tracy Morgan Papers, Box 37, Folder 7, J. P. Morgan Library, New York.

146   "A brass band on board": Anne Morgan to Frances Morgan, July 7, 1902.

147   "Neither he nor the HAPAG could be bought": Susanne Wiborg, *Albert Ballin*, trans. Peter Kuras (Hamburg: Ellert & Richter Verlag, 2000), 47.

147   The Morgan party then sailed home: Strouse, *Morgan: American Financier*, 471.

147   a fee of 5,000 shares of preferred stock: Navin and Sears, "A Study in Merger: Formation of the International Mercantile Marine Company."

148   "What makes the people in England feel most uncomfortable": Albert Ballin, June 5, 1902, as quoted in Vale, *The American Peril: Challenge to Britain on the North Atlantic, 1901–1904*, 104.

148   "the executive tool of His Majesty": Bernhard von Bülow, as quoted in review of John Röhl, *The Kaiser and His Court: Wilhelm II and the Government of Germany*, by Dr. Alan Sked, Reviews in History, January 1998, https://reviews.history.ac.uk/review/47.

148   were the people on the other side of the table anti-Semites?: Wiborg, *Albert Ballin*, 30.

CHAPTER 11: THE WEINSTEINS: ONE JOURNEY OF MANY

153   "had turned over whatever silver and jewelry there was left": Lauren Bacall, *By Myself and Then Some* (New York: Harper, 1978), 3.

153   Its population was about 40 percent Jewish: "Iași," YIVO Encyclopedia of Jews in Eastern Europe, https://yivoencyclopedia.org/article.aspx/iasi.

154   "whatever persecution they had endured": Cyrus Adler, *The Jewish Encyclopedia: A Descriptive Record of the History, Religion, Literature, and Customs of the Jewish People from the*

Earliest Times to the Present Day, vol. 10 (Columbus: The Ohio State University Press, 1909), 515.

154   "it is admitted that at least 70 per cent": Adler, *The Jewish Encyclopedia*, 515.

155   who only earned about $250 to $300 in a single year: Guy Alroey, *Bread to Eat & Clothes to Wear: Letters from Jewish Migrants in the Early Twentieth Century* (Detroit: Wayne State University Press, 2011), 64–65.

155   feared being *agunah*: A "chained woman," whose husband had disappeared. Under Jewish law, an *agunah* could not remarry until proof of her husband's death had been provided.

156   These included priests, rabbis, schoolteachers: Daniel Okrent, *The Guarded Gate: Bigotry, Eugenics, and the Law That Kept Two Generations of Jews, Italians, and Other European Immigrants Out of America* (New York: Scribner, 1970), 70.

156   "It can easily be understood that several emigrants": O. W. Hellmrich to John Hay, October 8, 1903, Gjenvick-Gjønvik Archives, https://www.gjenvick.com/Immigration/Emigration/1903-10-08-EmigrationToTheUnitedStatesViaHamburgGermany.html.

158   house up to five thousand people at a time: Johannes Gerhardt, *Albert Ballin* (Hamburg: Hamburg University Press, 2009), 50.

159   "Our compartment was subdivided into three sections": United States Senate, "Importing Women for Immoral Purposes: A Partial Report from the Immigration Commission on the Importation and Harboring of Women for Immoral Purposes," Senate Documents, vol. 63 (Washington, DC: Government Printing Office, 1910), 12.

160   At the appointed hour on June 24, 1904: "Max Weinstein in the Hamburg Passenger Lists, 1850–1934," Ancestry.com, https://www.ancestry.com/discoveryui-content/view/1347777:1068.

160   "You could see a lot of water": Charles Guggenheim, *Island of Hope, Island of Tears* (1989, New York, Guggenheim Productions), film, https://www.youtube.com/watch?v=qh5CWbTDsuQ.

160   "On one line of steamers": U.S. Immigration Report on Steerage Conditions, 1911, https://www.gjenvick.com/Immigration/Steerage/USImmigrationReportOnSteerageConditions-1911.html.

161   "A table without appointment and service means nothing": United States Senate, "Importing Women for Immoral Purposes," 17.

161   To remove all blood from chicken, liver, and beef: "Making Meat Kosher: Between Slaughtering and Cooking," My Jewish Learning, https://www.myjewishlearning.com/article/making-meat-kosher-between-slaughtering-and-cooking/.

162   "On the upper deck, looking over the railing": Alfred Stieglitz, "How *The Steerage* Happened," *Twice a Year*, no. 8–9 (1942): 175–78.

162   The photograph depicted several mothers: Alfred Stieglitz, "The Steerage," Metropolitan Museum of Art, https://www.metmuseum.org/art/collection/search/267836.

163   "It appeared like in a fog": Guggenheim, *Island of Hope, Island of Tears*.

164   Island of Tears: "Historic Immigration Station," National Park Service, https://www.nps.gov/elis/learn/historyculture/index.htm.

164   the word *pushcart* was uttered: Bacall, *By Myself and Then Some*, 4.

CHAPTER 12: THE MOST INFAMOUS POGROM

165   "The Russian Jewish element defies analysis": Edmund J. James, Oscar R. Flynn, Dr. J. R. Pauling, Charlotte Kimball, and Walter Scott Andrews, *The Immigrant Jew in America* (New York: B. F. Buck & Co., 1906), 14.

166   The Orthodox bishop, riding by in his carriage: Monty Noam Penkower, "The Kishinev Pogrom of 1903: A Turning Point in Jewish History," *Modern Judaism* 24, no. 3 (October 2004): 187, https://www.jstor.org/stable/1396539#.

166   The military commander of Kishinev, General Beckmann: Herman Rosenthal and Max Rosenthal, "Kishinef (Kishinev)," JewishEncyclopedia.com, https://www.jewishencyclopedia.com/articles/9350-kishinef-kishinev.

166   "The mob was led by priests": "Jewish Massacre Denounced," *New York Times*, April 28, 1903, 6.

167   The death count was later revised downward to 49: Rosenthal and Rosenthal, "Kishinef (Kishinev)."

167   That December, thirty-seven men who had participated: Rosenthal and Rosenthal, "Kishinef (Kishinev)."

167   "he would not be surprised if the Government": "Jewish Massacre Denounced."

167   "I have your valued communication of the 1st inst.": Theodore Roosevelt Center, Dickinson State University, Dickinson, North Dakota, https://www.theodorerooseveltcenter.org/Research/Digital-Library/Record/ImageViewer?libID=o43475&imageNo=1.

168   "There are many good Jews in Russia": Cyrus Adler, ed., *The Voice of America on Kishineff* (Philadelphia: Jewish Publication Society, 1904), xiii.

168   Throwing up his hands, Roosevelt then asked: Stuart E. Knee, "The Diplomacy of Neutrality: Theodore Roosevelt and the Russian Pogroms of 1903–1906," *Presidential Studies Quarterly* 19, no. 1, Part I: American Foreign Policy for the 1990s and Part II: T. R., Wilson and the Progressive Era, 1901–1919 (Winter 1989): 73, http://www.jstor.org/stable/40574565.

168   "the Czar is a preposterous little creature": Knee, "The Diplomacy of Neutrality."

168   Essentially travel guides for the migrants: David Hamann, "From Hamburg Out into the World—Jewish Emigration and the Aid Organization of German Jews," Key Documents of German-Jewish History, Institut für die Geschichte der Deutsche Juden, Jewish History Online, https://jewish-history-online.net/article/hamann-aid-organization#section-1.

169   "the year 1903–1904 will go down in history": Twenty-Seventh Annual Report of the United Hebrew Charities of the City of New York (New York: Stettiner Brothers, 1902), 30, Records of the Immigration Restriction League, Houghton Library, Harvard University, bMS AM 2245 (1331), Box 20, Folder 5.

169   "with all the bitter experience that involves": Jacob Schiff to Paul Nathan, December 29, 1905, Jacob Schiff Papers, Box 25, Jewish Theological Seminary, as quoted in Zosa Szajkowski, "Paul Nathan, Lucien Wolf, Jacob H. Schiff, and the Jewish Revolutionary Movements in Eastern Europe 1903–1917," *Jewish Social Studies* 29, no. 1 (January 1967): 6.

170   "From the earliest days of our history": "An Appeal to American Citizens" (New York: Liberal Immigration League, 1906), Records of the Immigration Restriction League, Houghton Library, Harvard University, bMS AM 2245 (1124), Box 19.

170   Serge Nilus, a minor czarist official: "A Hoax of Hate: The Protocols of the Learned Elders of Zion," Anti-Defamation League, https://www.adl.org/resources/backgrounders/a-hoax-of-hate-the-protocols-of-the-learned-elders-of-zion.

170   "Our motto is Power and Hypocrisy": Sergei Aleksandrovich Nilus, Natalie de Bogory, and Boris Leo Brasol, trans., *The Protocols and World Revolution*, Project Gutenberg, https://www.gutenberg.org/files/64977/64977-h/64977-h.htm.

171   "Anti-Semitism was eating deep into Germany": Chaim Weizmann, *Trial and Error: The Autobiography of Chaim Weizmann*, vol. 1 (New York: Harper Brothers, 1949), 21.

171   "beaten men, from beaten races": Francis A. Walker, "Restriction of Immigration," *The Atlantic*, June 1896, https://www.theatlantic.com/magazine/archive/1896/06/restriction-of-immigration/6011/.

171   "By all means have the press take the matter up": Henry Cabot Lodge to Prescott Hall, December 6, 1902, Records of the Immigration Restriction League, Houghton Library, Harvard University, MS AM 2245, Box 7.

172   "Every American citizen knows that the American immigration system is faulty": "Leslie's Magazine Takes a Stand on Immigration—1904," GG Archives, https://www.gjenvick.com/Immigration/Steerage/LesliesMagazinesStandOnImmigration-1904.html.

174   It also infuriated J. P. Morgan: Vivian Vale, *The American Peril: Challenge to Britain on the North Atlantic, 1901–1904* (Dover, NH: Manchester University Press, 1984), 38–39.

175   NDL slashed their rates by 50 to 60 percent: Vale, *The American Peril: Challenge to Britain on the North Atlantic*, 210.

CHAPTER 13: GAMING THE RUSSO-JAPANESE WAR

176   "Wednesday, March 28th is the great gala day": Cyrus Adler, "Jacob Henry Schiff: A Biographical Sketch," *American Jewish Year Book* 23 (1921): 27, http://www.jstor.org/stable/23601039.

177   "We ask our honoured guests in their movements and dispositions": As quoted in Johannes Gerhardt, *Albert Ballin* (Hamburg: Hamburg University Press, 2009), 73.

177   "To appreciate to the full the charm of his personality": Bernhard Huldermann, *Albert Ballin*, trans. W. J. Eggers (London: Cassell & Co., 1922), http://www.gutenberg.org/files/44135/44135-h/44135-h.htm.

178   coined a new term: Frank Broeze, "Albert Ballin, the Hamburg-America Line and Hamburg," *Deutsches Schiffahrtsarchiv* 15 (1992): 159, https://d-nb.info/1186507853/34.

178   "What we must do is to transform our empire": Donald H. Shively, *Tradition and Modernization in Japanese Culture* (Princeton, NJ: Princeton University Press, 2015), 91.

180   "On Christmas Day I sent some representatives to Petrograd": Huldermann, *Albert Ballin*.

181   "Nowhere was the food so good": Theodor Wolff, *Through Two Decades*, trans. Ernest Walter Dickes (London: William Heinemann, 1936), 181.

182   "On June 27th my wife and I": Huldermann, *Albert Ballin*.

182   "Our negotiations with the Russian Government have made good progress": Huldermann, *Albert Ballin*.

182   the Russian government was impressed with his savvy: Lamar J. R. Cecil, "Coal for the Fleet That Had to Die," *American Historical Review* 69, no. 4 (July 1964): 993, https://doi.org/10.2307/1842932.

183   The Kaiser then told his cousin the czar: Cecil, "Coal for the Fleet That Had to Die," 995–96.

184   The sale of the old ships to Russia alone: Cecil, "Coal for the Fleet That Had to Die," 995.

184   "England should learn to live with the fact": *Zeitschrift der Hamburg-Amerika Linie*, III, Jg. (October 5, 1904), 148–149, archive of the Hamburg-America Line, as quoted in Cecil, "Coal for the Fleet That Had to Die," 995.

185   "Philadelphia is a widely known shipbuilding place": "Jap Statesman Here on Errand Full of Mystery," *Philadelphia Inquirer*, May 17, 1904, 1–2.

185   "It is almost inconceivable that any men": Richard Michael Connaughton, *The War of the Rising Sun and the Tumbling Bear* (New York: Routledge, 1991), 247, 250, 259.

186   These funds carried over into the following year: Gerhardt, *Albert Ballin*, 34.

188   "cannot, and does not, diminish the magnitude of the achievement": Huldermann, *Albert Ballin*.

189   "in one vast splendid armada": HAPAG, *Sixty Years of Ocean Navigation and the Half Century Anniversary of the Establishment of the First Line of Steamships Flying a German Flag* (New York: n.p., 1906), 6, as quoted in Mark A. Russell, *Steamship Nationalism: Ocean Liners and National Identity in Imperial Germany and the Atlantic World* (New York: Routledge, 2020), 48.

190   "I cannot for a moment concede": Jacob Schiff, as quoted in Ron Chernow, *The Warburgs* (New York: Vintage Books, 1993), 248.

190   "great factor in German life": Frieda Schiff Warburg, *Reminiscences of a Long Life* (New York: privately printed, 1956), 30.

191   He wrote Max Warburg that the Russian government: Albert Ballin to Max Warburg, May 25, 1906, Warburg Archive, Hamburg, Germany.

192   "I hope that our respective monarchs may soon meet now": Huldermann, *Albert Ballin*.

192   "I also feel that the meeting of their Majesties": Huldermann, *Albert Ballin*.

193   "religion of the German flag": Theodor Wolff, as quoted in Susanne Wiborg, *Albert Ballin*, trans. Peter Kuras (Hamburg: Ellert & Richter Verlag, 2000), 48.

193   the Order of St. Stanislaus, Second Class with Stars: Max Warburg, as quoted in Heinz and Ingrid Hueber, *Mein Urgroßvater Albert Ballin* (Privately printed, 2021), 88.

CHAPTER 14: MAKING PEACE WITH THE AID SOCIETY

194   "We have repeatedly pointed to the serious dilemma": *Geschäftsbericht (1904) des Hilfsvereins der deutschen Juden* (Berlin, 1905), 30–35, as quoted in Tobias Brinkmann, "Why Paul Nathan Attacked Albert Ballin: The Transatlantic Mass Migration and the Privatization of Prussia's Eastern Border Inspection, 1886–1914," *Central European History* 42 (2010): 70.

194   "A group of emigrants, brought together by fate": Julius Kaliski, "On the Road with Ballin: Experiences of a Russian Emigrant," *Vorwärts*, December 20, 1905, trans. Matthias Mueller.

195   *lebhaftes Kauderwelsch*: In this context, the term might refer to Yiddish. Note by trans. Matthias Mueller.

195   "was sufficiently familiar . . . with court psychology to know that the lion": Theodor Wolff, *Through Two Decades*, trans. Ernest Walter Dickes (London: William Heinemann, 1936), 187.

196   "We don't care": There are two inextricable ambiguities in this passage. The first one relates to the German phrase "*Uns liegt nichts daran Ihnen ein Billet zu verkaufen*" (which is translated as "We don't care about selling a ticket to you"). In German, the phrase can be interpreted in two opposite ways: as "We don't mind selling a ticket to you" or "We are not interested in selling a ticket to you." The second problem concerns the verb that describes Herr Klein's action: "Herr Klein beugte vor." *Vorbeugen* is a separable prefix verb that means "to prevent," but it doesn't really make sense in the context (unless it means that Herr Klein prepared the speaker for something to happen later). The verb can also mean "to lean over," though it is usually used with a reflexive pronoun, *sich vorbeugen*, and it would indicate that Herr Klein leaned in to tell the narrator quietly that he should no longer bother him. Note by trans. Matthias Mueller.

197   "and Jewish [*jüdisch*]": The author uses the term "Jewish language" here, not "Yiddish." Note by trans. Peter Kuras.

198   "The Alexanderplatz comes into sight": The translator has chosen to translate the German word *Schein* as "shine" in this context as it is ambiguous here. The German noun *der Schein* has several different meanings, but the two competing here are (1) glow, flash, gleam, light (like a blaze of light), and (2) appearance. Both meanings are at play here, I think. (Heidegger makes a big fuss about it too.) Note by trans. Peter Kuras.

200   "[T]he highest parts": Brinkmann, "Why Paul Nathan Attacked Albert Ballin," 70.

200   Paul Nathan blamed Ballin: Brinkmann, "Why Paul Nathan Attacked Albert Ballin," 70.

201   "The conditions at the Prussian-Russian border": Paul Nathan, "Organisation der jüdischen Auswanderung aus Ostereuropa," *Geschäftsbericht (1904) des Hilfsvereins der deutschen Juden* (Berlin, 1905), 30–35, trans. Peter Kuras.

201   "negotiations were stalled": *Berliner Tageblatt*, October 23, 1904, trans. Peter Kuras.

202   "Do you know, Mr. Ballin, how the Jewish emigrants": "Open Letter to Mr. Ballin," Central Zionist Archives, A36/3, as quoted in Gur Alroey, *Bread to Eat & Clothes to Wear: Letters from Jewish Migrants in the Early Twentieth Century* (Detroit, MI: Wayne State University Press, 2011), 99–102.

203   "The agreement before us now thoroughly disposes": *Berliner Tageblatt*, October 23, 1904, trans. Peter Kuras.

203   Max himself had served on HAPAG's board of directors: Ron Chernow, *The Warburgs* (New York: Vintage Books, 1993), 106.

CHAPTER 15: REVOLUTION AND REBUILDING

205   "In politics as well as in business": Bernhard Huldermann, *Albert Ballin*, trans. W. J. Eggers (London: Cassell & Co., 1922), http://www.gutenberg.org/files/44135/44135-h/44135-h.htm.

206 When Japan asked for a third loan: Ron Chernow, *The Warburgs* (New York: Vintage Books, 1993), 110.

206 "the Northern Goliath": Jacob H. Schiff, "Japan After the War," 161–68, as quoted in Adam Gower, *Jacob Schiff and the Art of Risk* (New York: Springer, 2018), 82–83.

206 "save the entire civilized world": Jacob H. Schiff, "Peace and Friendship with Japan," *Advocate of Peace* 72, no. 11 (1910): 268.

207 690 pogroms erupted throughout the Russian Empire: Naomi W. Cohen, *Jacob H. Schiff: A Study in American Jewish Leadership* (Hanover, NH: Brandeis University Press, 1999), 140.

207 "One must alone lose one's faith in mankind": Jacob Schiff to E. Cassel, November 23, 1905, as quoted in Cohen, *Jacob H. Schiff*, 140.

210 "The ships that Harlands built for us": Albert Ballin to Max Warburg, April 20, 1912, Warburg Archive, Hamburg, Germany.

211 Steerage passengers, who paid 160 marks: Hans-Hermann Groppe and Ursula Wost, *Über Hamburg in die Welt. Von den Auswandererhallen zur Ballinstadt* (Hamburg: Ellert & Richter, 2007), 64.

212 In 1908, 115,982 immigrants: Groppe and Wost, *Über Hamburg in die Welt*, 64.

212 In its peak years, about 43 percent of the migrants: Groppe and Wost, *Über Hamburg in die Welt*, 55.

212 offerings including caviar, pâté de foie gras, ice cream, and champagne: Dolores L. Augustine, "The Business Elites of Hamburg and Berlin," *Central European History* 24, no. 2 (1991): 132–46, http://www.jstor.org/stable/4546199.

213 good at folding napkins: Susanne Wiborg, *Albert Ballin*, trans. Peter Kuras (Hamburg: Ellert & Richter Verlag, 2000), 37.

213 "Very dire for us and Lloyd": Albert Ballin to Max Warburg, May 25 (?), 1906, Warburg Archive, Hamburg, Germany.

213 "Just let the Russians sail": Max Warburg to Albert Ballin, May 25, 1906, Warburg Archive, Hamburg, Germany.

214 "That we have competed with each other": Georg Bessell, *Norddeutscher Lloyd, 1857–1957: Geschichte einer bremischen Reederei* (Bremen: Schünemann, 1957), 124.

214 "He was more an artist than an engineer": Max Warburg, "Eulogy for Albert Ballin," November 13, 1918, as quoted in Heinz and Ingrid Hueber, *Mein Urgroßvater Albert Ballin* (Privately printed, 2021), 408–11.

215 The first ran to 38 million marks: Lamar Cecil, *Albert Ballin: Business and Politics in Imperial Germany, 1888–1918* (Princeton, NJ: Princeton University Press, 1967), 219.

215 "demonic" side: Max Warburg to Bernhard Huldermann, December 28, 1922, Archives of M. M. Warburg & Co., as quoted in Chernow, *The Warburgs*, 104.

216 "A utopia . . . which I fear will only block": Cohen, *Jacob H. Schiff*, 163.

CHAPTER 16: IMMIGRATION RESTRICTION GOES MAINSTREAM

218 "We would have been spared the curse": Prescott Farnsworth Hall to Elihu Root, May 10, 1912, Papers of the Immigration Restriction League, Houghton Library, Harvard University, bMS AM 2245 (469).

219 "If we had the ways and means to distribute": Naomi W. Cohen, *Jacob H. Schiff: A Study in American Jewish Leadership* (Hanover, NH: Brandeis University Press, 1999), 119.

219 "the only constructive idea": Israel Zangwill, as quoted in Cohen, *Jacob H. Schiff*, 159.

219 "we must here give up our identity": Cohen, *Jacob H. Schiff*, 162–63.

219 "The port of Galveston invited entry": Proceedings of the Sixth National Conference of Jewish Charities, 1910, 124–25, as quoted in Cohen, *Jacob H. Schiff*, 162.

220 "Speaking as an American": Jacob Schiff, as quoted in Evyatar Friesel, "Jacob H. Schiff and the Leadership of the American Jewish Community," *Jewish Social Studies* 8, no. 2–3 (2002): 68, http://www.jstor.org/stable/4467629.

221 "Indeed, the Jews, the modern representatives": Jacob Schiff, May 13, 1891, Cyrus Adler,

ed., *Jacob H. Schiff: His Life and Letters*, vol. 2 (Garden City: Doubleday, Doran, and Company, 1928), 21.

222   "When this country conferred upon me the honor": Frieda Schiff Warburg, *Reminiscences of a Long Life* (New York: privately printed, 1956), 54.

223   "immigration increased over 14 percent in the same period": Prescott Hall to Henry Cabot Lodge, December 24, 1907, Papers of the Immigration Restriction League, Houghton Library, Harvard University, bMS AM 2245 (608), Box 7, Folder 2.

223   those with bond 142.2 percent: Prescott Hall to Henry Cabot Lodge, December 24, 1907.

224   "There are many immigrant ships on the Ocean today": William Williams to J. H. Patten, December 27, 1905, Papers of the Immigration Restriction League, Houghton Library, Harvard University, bMS AM 2245 (999), Box 11, Folder 1.

224   "The attempt to improve race stocks in recent times": Prescott F. Hall, "Eugenics, Ethics, and Immigration," *Publications of the Immigration Restriction League* 51 (1910), 1, Harvard Library, "Immigration to the United States, 1789–1930," https://curiosity.lib.harvard.edu/immigration-to-the-united-states-1789-1930/catalog/39-990100047200203941.

225   "I will talk to Mrs. Brooks": Madison Grant to Prescott Hall, February 13, 1907, Papers of the Immigration Restriction League, Houghton Library, Harvard University, bMS AM 2245, Box 5.

226   "no more use for the Constitution than a tomcat": Rich Rubino, "John Boehner Is Not the First GOP House Leader to Experience Dissention Within His Own Party," *Huffington Post*, February 24, 2014, https://www.huffpost.com/entry/john-boehner-is-not-the-first_b_4844228.

226   It would be composed of three senators: Robert F. Zeidel, "A 1911 Report Set America on a Path of Screening Out 'Undesirable' Immigrants," *Smithsonian*, July 16, 2018, https://www.smithsonianmag.com/history/1911-report-set-america-on-path-screening-out-undesirable-immigrants-180969636/.

227   Jacob Schiff had served as vice president: "Baron de Hirsch Fund," Encyclopedia.com, https://www.encyclopedia.com/religion/encyclopedias-almanacs-transcripts-and-maps/baron-de-hirsch-fund.

227   "Today the United States has probably more Jews": "Daily Digest of Public Opinion on Jewish Matters," Jewish Telegraphic Agency, January 24, 1926, https://www.jta.org/1926/01/24/archive/daily-digest-of-public-opinion-on-jewish-matters-42.

229   "I often ask myself what advantages our 'good society'": Friedrich Pöhl, "Assessing Franz Boas' Ethics in His Arctic and Later Anthropological Fieldwork," *Études/Inuit/Studies* 32, no. 2 (2008): 37, http://www.jstor.org/stable/42870269.

CHAPTER 17: HALTING THE MARCH TO ARMAGEDDON

231   "No Bismarck was needed": Bernhard Huldermann, *Albert Ballin*, trans. W. J. Eggers (London: Cassell & Co., 1922), http://www.gutenberg.org/files/44135/44135-h/44135-h.htm.

233   Thanks to Cassel, Ballin got to know Prime Minister Sir Herbert Asquith: Susanne Wiborg, *Albert Ballin*, trans. Peter Kuras (Hamburg: Ellert & Richter Verlag, 2000), 49.

233   "an unscrupulous press": Huldermann, *Albert Ballin*.

233   "You English are mad, mad, mad as March hares": "The Interview of the Emperor Wilhelm II on October 28, 1908," *Daily Telegraph (London)*, October 28, 1908, http://wwi.lib.byu.edu/index.php/The_Daily_Telegraph_Affair.

234   "A dark foreboding ran through many Germans": Bernhard Heinrich Karl Martin von Bülow, *Memoirs of Prince Von Bülow*, vol. 2 (New York: AMS Press, 1972), 96.

234   After the Kaiser, the position would make Ballin: Lamar Cecil, *Albert Ballin: Business and Politics in Imperial Germany, 1888–1918* (Princeton, NJ: Princeton University Press, 1967), 120.

234   Albert Ballin knew full well: Lamar Cecil, "The Creation of Nobles in Prussia, 1871–1918," *American Historical Review* 75, no. 3 (1970): 757–95, https://doi.org/10.2307/1854529.

235 And then there was the matter of principle: Phone conversation with Susanne Wiborg, May 22, 2020.

235 "You don't have more of this kind of people?": Cecil, "The Creation of Nobles in Prussia, 1871–1918," 757–95.

235 "a merchant could not rise any further in status": Dolores L. Augustine, "The Business Elites of Hamburg and Berlin," *Central European History* 24, no. 2 (1991): 135, http://www.jstor.org/stable/4546199.

236 "His error was perhaps a certain tendency": Wiborg, *Albert Ballin*, 30.

237 As the Ballins went from room to room: Ron Chernow, *The Warburgs* (New York: Vintage Books, 1993), 105.

238 Alice had so little confidence: Chernow, *The Warburgs*, 76.

238 On several occasions when he was in Hamburg: Cecil, *Albert Ballin*, 107.

239 "Kellner-Eleganz": Mark A. Russell, *Steamship Nationalism: Ocean Liners and National Identity in Imperial Germany and the Atlantic World* (Milton Park, UK: Routledge, 2020), 214.

239 "Consequently, it is necessary either to hang paintings": Russell, *Steamship Nationalism*, 214.

240 Albert Ballin was sick with the flu: Heinz and Ingrid Hueber, *Die Tochter des Reeders* (Privately printed, 2021), 159–63.

240 "My warmest thanks for your letter": Albert Ballin to Irmgard Bielfeld, undated, 1910, as quoted in Hueber, *Die Tochter des Reeders*, 167.

241 "While reading, she held his hand": Wiborg, *Albert Ballin*, 31.

245 "If the Jews of America, England, France, Germany, Italy, etc.": Zosa Szajkowski, "The European Aspect of the American-Russian Passport Question," *Publications of the American Jewish Historical Society* 46, no. 2 (December 1956): 86–100, http://www.jstor.org/stable/43058953.

CHAPTER 18: BETRAYING THE MORGAN TRUST

249 "[A]s far as it is possible to do so": Publicity leaflet for the RMS *Titanic*, September 1910, as quoted in Richard Howells, *The Myth of the* Titanic (London: Palgrave Macmillan, 1999), 139.

249 A third ship, to be named RMS *Gigantic*: After the *Titanic* disaster, White Star renamed the ship RMS *Britannic*. She was completed in 1915 as a hospital ship, and sank after striking a mine in the Aegean Sea, with a loss of thirty lives.

250 "The German lines have come to an agreement": Albert Ballin, as quoted in the *Hamburger Fremdenblatt*, March 18, 1907, HAPAG Archives.

251 "In accordance with the wish of the International Mercantile Marine Company": Legal Department, Norddeutscher Lloyd to HAPAG, March 9, 1912, HAPAG Archives, Hamburg State Archives.

252 The profit-sharing agreement was detrimental to HAPAG: Lamar Cecil, *Albert Ballin: Business and Politics in Imperial Germany, 1888–1918* (Princeton, NJ: Princeton University Press, 1967), 57.

252 "Tirpitz believed that the fleet's impact on the economy": Jonathan Steinberg, "The Tirpitz Plan," *Historical Journal* 16, no. 1 (1973): 198–99, www.jstor.org/stable/2637924.

253 "I do not need the protection of the German fleet for my ships": Albert Ballin to Maximilian Harden, as quoted in Susanne Wiborg, *Albert Ballin*, trans. Peter Kuras (Hamburg: Ellert & Richter Verlag, 2000), 50.

253 "It is said that as a man may be judged by the company he keeps": Cable to Mortimer Schiff from Otto H. Kahn, April 17, 1931, Otto H. Kahn papers, Box 238-15, Department of Rare Books and Special Collections, Princeton University, as quoted in Susie J. Pak, *Gentlemen Bankers: The World of J. P. Morgan* (Cambridge, MA: Harvard University Press, 2013), 81.

254 "When Communism does come": Stephen Birmingham, *Our Crowd: The Great German Jewish Families of New York* (Syracuse, NY: Syracuse University Press, 1967), 346.

255   131,910 Jews arrived on the island: "Jewish Immigration to America," Save Ellis Island, 2018, https://saveellisisland.org/about-us/blog/item/88-jewish-immigration-to-amer ica.html.

255   Between 1907 and 1914: Lloyd P. Gartner, "The Correspondence of Mayer Sulzberger and William Howard Taft," *Proceedings of the American Academy for Jewish Research* 46/47 (1979): 121–39, www.jstor.org/stable/3622461.

255   Of these, about one third went back: Drew Keeling, *The Business of Transatlantic Migration between Europe and the United States, 1900–1914* (Zurich: Chronos Verlag, 2012), 201.

256   "form the nucleus of a big export trade": "Backs Schiff's Charges," *New York Times*, November 19, 1911, https://timesmachine.nytimes.com/timesmachine/1911/11/19/1003414 62.pdf?pdf_redirect=true&ip=0.

257   "In 1861, public opinion insisted": Reel 681, W. Taft to Schiff, February 23, 1911, AJC Archives, "Minutes of the Executive Committee," February 23, 1911, as quoted in Naomi W. Cohen, *Jacob H. Schiff: A Study in American Jewish Leadership* (Hanover, NH: Brandeis University Press, 1999), 148.

257   "*Wir sind in Golus*": Cohen, *Jacob H. Schiff*, 148.

257   "and assimilated quickly. . . . On the other hand": James Pula, "American Immigration Policy and the Dillingham Commission," *Polish American Studies* 37, no. 1 (1980): 5–31.

257   "limitation of the number of each race arriving each year": Robert F. Zeidel, "A 1911 Report Set America on a Path of Screening Out 'Undesirable' Immigrants," *Smithsonian*, July 18, 2018, https://www.smithsonianmag.com/history/1911-report-set-america-on -path-screening-out-undesirable-immigrants-180969636/.

258   "There is a distinction, of course, between our people": Henry Cabot Lodge to Theodore Roosevelt, October 24, 1911, Theodore Roosevelt Center at Dickinson State University, Dickinson, North Dakota, https://www.theodorerooseveltcenter.org/Research/Digital -Library/Record/ImageViewer?libID=o71581.

CHAPTER 19: THE MARTYRS OF THE *TITANIC*

260   "Man, you are no match": Eli Moskowitz, *The Jews of the Titanic: A Reflection of the Jewish World on the Epic Disaster* (New York: Hybrid Global Publishing, 2018), 154.

260   Both lived in grand townhouses on the Upper West Side: PBS, *American Experience*, "Shirtwaist Kings," https://www.pbs.org/wgbh/americanexperience/features/shirt waist-kings/.

261   The entire women's garment industry employed: Tony Michels, "Uprising of the 20,000 (1909)," Shalvi/Hyman Encyclopedia of Jewish Women, Jewish Women's Archive, December 31, 1999, https://jwa.org/encyclopedia/article/uprising-of-20000-1909.

261   Two years earlier, the employees of the Triangle Shirtwaist Company: Michels, "Uprising of the 20,000 (1909)."

261   Clara quickly got a job in a garment factory: Annelise Orleck, "Clara Lemlich Shavelson," Shalvi/Hyman Encyclopedia of Jewish Women, Jewish Women's Archive, December 31, 1999, https://jwa.org/encyclopedia/article/shavelson-clara-lemlich.

262   "I have listened to all the speakers": Angie Boehm, "Triangle Shirtwaist Factory Women Strike, Win Better Wages and Hours, New York, 1909," Global Nonviolent Action Database, Swarthmore College, September 3, 2013, https://nvdatabase.swarthmore.edu /content/triangle-shirtwaist-factory-women-strike-win-better-wages-and-hours-new -york-1909.

263   A jury acquitted Max Blanck and Isaac Harris: *American Experience*, "Shirtwaist Kings."

263   "I would be a traitor to these poor burned bodies": Rose Schneiderman, "We Have Found You Wanting," Remembering the 1911 Triangle Factory Fire, Cornell University ILR School, https://trianglefire.ilr.cornell.edu/primary/testimonials/ootss_RoseSchneider man.html.

264   "the social, economic and political struggles": Rudolf Martin, *Yearbook of the Wealth and*

Income of the Millionaires of the Kingdom of Saxony (Berlin: Verlag Rudolf Martin, 1912), 111, Collection of Georg Gaugusch, Vienna, Austria.

265   and a salary of 400,000 marks: Martin, *Yearbook of the Wealth and Income of the Millionaires of the Kingdom of Saxony*, 8.

265   As one of about five hundred millionaires in Germany: Dolores L. Augustine, "The Business Elites of Hamburg and Berlin," *Central European History* 24, no. 2 (1991): 133, http://www.jstor.org/stable/4546199.

265   "The economic boom times of the last thirty years are unimaginable": Max Warburg, "Eulogy for Albert Ballin," November 13, 1918, as quoted in Heinz and Ingrid Hueber, *Mein Urgroßvater Albert Ballin* (Privately printed, 2021), 408–11.

265   He got his audience with Kaiser Wilhelm II: Cyrus Adler, unpublished manuscript of a biography of Jacob Schiff, Jacob H. Schiff Papers, Series B, Manuscript Collection No. 456, American Jewish Archive, 1877.

265   But according to Ballin's great-grandson Heinz Hueber: Interview with Heinz Hueber, October 5, 2021.

267   Nathan Straus and his wife stayed behind: Hanoch Teller, "Nathan Strauss, Netanya and the *Titanic*," NCSY Education, https://staff.ncsy.org/education/education/material/XkY7U2M0NI/nathan-strauss-netanya-and-the-titanic/.

267   Abraham's wife, Hattie: "Abraham Lincoln Salomon," Encyclopedia Titanica, Survivors, https://www.encyclopedia-titanica.org/titanic-survivor/abraham-salomon.html.

268   There were 44 passengers from Austria-Hungary: "Survivability Study of the 1912 RMS Titanic Disaster," Encyclopedia Titanica, https://www.encyclopedia-titanica.org/survivability-study-of-the-1912-rms-titanic-disaster.html.

268   "The influx of foreign emigrants": Dr. Sannemann to the Hamburg Emigration Station, April 13, 1913, HAPAG Archives, Hamburg State Archives, Hamburg, Germany.

269   When he was done for the day: Becca Martin-Brown, "Titanic Connections: Branson Museum Honors Jewish Passengers, Remembers the Holocaust," *Northwest Arkansas Democrat Gazette*, August 29, 2021.

270   Along with their personal belongings: Brigit Katz, "Sold: A Pocket Watch from the Titanic, Adorned with Hebrew Letters," *Smithsonian*, August 29, 2018, https://www.smithsonianmag.com/smart-news/sold-watch-titanic-adorned-hebrew-letters-180970169/.

270   After a few years, his parents hoped: Moskowitz, *The Jews of the Titanic*, 29.

271   Breakfast: Oatmeal Porridge and Milk: "Specimen Third Class Bill of Fare," Moskowitz, *The Jews of the Titanic*, 61.

272   As it was being lowered: Andrew Silow-Carroll, "A Famed Jewish Doctor Survived the Titanic—And Then Took His Own Life," Jewish Telegraphic Agency, April 14, 2017, https://www.jta.org/2017/04/14/culture/a-famed-jewish-doctor-survived-the-titanic-and-then-took-his-own-life.

272   He got into lifeboat number 1: "Abraham Lincoln Salomon," Encyclopedia Titanica.

272   "As we have lived, so will we die, together": "Isidor Straus (1845–1912)," Jewish Virtual Library, https://www.jewishvirtuallibrary.org/isidor-straus; "Isidor Straus and Wife, the Harlemites Who Died on the Titanic 1912," *Harlem World*, October 13, 2020, https://www.harlemworldmagazine.com/isidor-straus-and-wife-the-harlemites-who-died-on-the-titanic-1912/.

273   "Even among these people": Colonel Archibald Gracie IV, *Titanic: A Survivor's Story*; John B. Thayer, *The Sinking of the SS Titanic* (Chicago: Academy Chicago Publishers, 1998), 30–31.

273   Deep in her holds: "What Cargo Did the Titanic Carry?," Encyclopedia Titanica, https://www.encyclopedia-titanica.org/cargo-manifest.html.

273   More first-class men: "Titanic Disaster: Official Casualty Figures," Anesi.com, https://www.anesi.com/titanic.htm.

274   "The money has been placed in charge": "Sinai Kantor," Encyclopedia Titanica, https://www.encyclopedia-titanica.org/titanic-victim/sinai-kantor.html.

275 "No. 47.—MALE": "Eliezer Gilinski," Encyclopedia Titanica, https://www.encyclo pedia-titanica.org/titanic-victim/eliezer-gilinski.html.

276 "No. 96.—MALE": "Isidor Straus," Encyclopedia Titanica, https://www.encyclopedia -titanica.org/titanic-victim/isidor-straus.html.

276 "No. 283.—MALE": "Sinai Kantor," Encyclopedia Titanica.

276 The face of his silver watch was marked: Katz, "Sold: A Pocket Watch from the Titanic, Adorned with Hebrew Letters."

277 "Women and children first for the boats": "Thousands Mourn at Straus Memorial," *New York Times*, May 13, 1912.

277 "What made Isidor Straus so valued as an adviser": "Thousands Mourn at Straus Memorial."

278 "If we must die, we should die together": "Di korbones fun der shif Titanik—The Victims of the Ship Titanic. Disaster song by Morris Rund," Yiddish Penny Songs, http://www .yiddishpennysongs.com/2016/09/di-korbones-fun-der-shif-titanik.html.

278 "Children's fathers sank in the sea": "Di korbones fun der shif Titanik—The Victims of the Ship Titanic."

279 "At the time that the *Titanic* was lost": "Mr. Ismay and the White Star Line," *The Times (London)*, January 1, 1913, as quoted in Encyclopedia Titanica, https://www .encyclopedia-titanica.org/community/threads/news-from-1913-ismays-resignation -from-white-star.20582/.

280 "The king is dead. All New York is at half-mast": Vanderlip Papers, Columbia University, as quoted in Jean Strouse, *Morgan: American Financier* (New York: Random House, 2014), 680.

280 "The ocean was too big for the old man": *Wall Street Journal*, as quoted in Lamar Cecil, *Albert Ballin: Business and Politics in Imperial Germany, 1888–1918* (Princeton, NJ: Princeton University Press, 1967), 58.

CHAPTER 20: MY FIELD IS THE WORLD

281 "One is forced to think of the contrast between the front of a great house": Mark A. Russell, *Steamship Nationalism: Ocean Liners and National Identity in Imperial Germany and the Atlantic World* (Milton Park, UK: Routledge, 2020), 124.

282 The former housekeeper had the required twenty dollars in cash: Douglas C. Baynton, "Defectives in the Land: Disability and American Immigration Policy, 1882–1924," *Journal of American Ethnic History* 24, no. 3 (2005): 31, http://www.jstor.org/stable/275 01596.

283 The Fukos would be two of about forty-eight thousand returning immigrants: Hans-Hermann Groppe and Ursula Wost, *Über Hamburg in die Welt. Von den Auswandererhallen zur Ballinstadt* (Hamburg: Ellert & Richter Verlag, 2007), 65.

284 In 1913, 192,733 emigrants, the vast majority of whom: Groppe and Wost, *Über Hamburg in die Welt*, 21.

284 the first American issue of stock in the Hamburg-America Line: Lamar Cecil, *Albert Ballin: Business and Politics in Imperial Germany, 1888–1918* (Princeton, NJ: Princeton University Press, 1967), 57.

285 "There has been fairly good weather on the voyage": "Seas Test the Imperator," *New York Times*, September 13, 1913.

285 "[L]ife is conflict, and a strong man must always be armed for battle": HAPAG House Organ, as quoted in Frank O. Braynard, *Leviathan: The World's Greatest Ship*, vol. 1 (New York: South Street Seaport Museum, 1972), 31.

286 "First class got two-thirds of the ship": Peter Butt, *The Liners: Ships of Destiny* (1997, Australian Broadcasting Corporation).

287 Serbia rejected the ultimatum outright: James M. Lindsay, "TWE Remembers: Austria-Hungary Issues an Ultimatum to Serbia," Council on Foreign Relations, July 23, 2014, https://www.cfr.org/blog/twe-remembers-austria-hungary-issues-ultimatum-serbia.

288   "My dear friend": Drew Keeling, "A Century Ago, March Began to World War I," *Wharton Magazine*, July 24, 2014, https://magazine.wharton.upenn.edu/digital/a-century-ago-the-march-began-to-world-war-i/?fbclid=IwAR1uwmbLkPvFDMzjKMSHOTtcR3tKIISfBbpPp4aO0sHd8H4sqcH8qBoRyKQ.

288   "the unmarried Russians, male and female": Groppe and Wost, *Über Hamburg in die Welt*, 66.

289   "We will be compelled to make large refunds": File 1128, 621-1195, Korrespondenzen zur Erfüllung des Vertrages „Guido" zwischen HAPAG und Reichs-Marineamt zur Lieferung von Kohlen und Verpflegung für Kriegsschiffe, 1914, HAPAG Archives, Hamburg State Archives, Hamburg.

289   Paul Warburg was under scrutiny: File 4 4/18, 621-1195, Korrespondenzen zur Erfüllung, HAPAG Archives.

290   "Can you remit another $1 million?": September 14, 1914, File 4 4/18, 621-1195, Korrespondenzen zur Erfüllung, HAPAG Archives.

290   "[C]ould possibly offer property there in the form of land": File 4 4/18, 621-1195, Korrespondenzen zur Erfüllung, HAPAG Archives.

290   He admitted that HAPAG had gone to the investment banking firm: "Couldn't Get Loan on Ships," *New York Times*, February 19, 1915.

291   "I refer to Max Warburg, our director": "Couldn't Get Loan on Ships."

291   "Peace does not want to find the company without ships": "Couldn't Get Loan on Ships."

292   The promise, of course, came to nothing: Volume III A 1787, HAPAG Reederei 621-1195 2220, HAPAG Archives.

292   "this is only a line to tell you we are all right": Susie J. Pak, *Gentlemen Bankers: The World of J. P. Morgan* (Cambridge, MA: Harvard University Press, 2013), 135.

292   "The world will never be the same again": Naomi W. Cohen, *Jacob H. Schiff: A Study in American Jewish Leadership* (Hanover, NH: Brandeis University Press, 1999), 247.

293   Realizing that Wall Street was still a small world: Pak, *Gentlemen Bankers*, 115.

293   "I would just as little think of turning against [Germany] in this hour": Jacob Henry Schiff to Lucien Wolf, June 14, 1915, Jacob Henry Schiff Papers, MS 456, Box 4, American Jewish Archives, as quoted in Pak, *Gentlemen Bankers*, 115.

294   "I cannot stultify myself by aiding those who in bitter enmity": Jacob Schiff, as quoted in Stephen Birmingham, *Our Crowd: The Great German Jewish Families of New York* (Syracuse, NY: Syracuse University Press, 1967), 369.

294   "Kuhn, Loeb, German Bankers, Refuse Aid to Allies": Jacob Schiff, as quoted in Birmingham, *Our Crowd*, 370.

294   Otto Kahn and Mortimer Schiff decided to make loans: Pak, *Gentlemen Bankers*, 115.

294   "German Jewish Bankers are toiling in a solid phalanx": Cohen, *Jacob H. Schiff*, 196.

295   distributing $16.4 million a year to the four million Jews: Birmingham, *Our Crowd*, 382.

295   a unifying cause, regardless of ethnic origin: Paul Berger, "How World War I Shaped Jewish Identity and Politics," *Jewish Daily Forward*, June 25, 2014, https://forward.com/news/200509/how-world-war-i-shaped-jewish-politics-and-identit/.

295   "The Russian Government will rejoice": "Activities in the City," *American Jewish Chronicle*, vol. 1 (Chicago: Alpha Omega Publishing Company, 1916), 155.

295   Even the socialist *Forward* endorsed him: Cohen, *Jacob H. Schiff*, 222.

296   In November 1916, a group of wealthy German Americans threw a gala ball aboard the SS *Vaterland*: Christina A. Ziegler-McPherson, *The Great Disappearing Act: Germans in New York City, 1880–1930* (New Brunswick, NJ: Rutgers University Press, 2021), https://www.google.com/books/edition/The_Great_Disappearing_Act/yQpSEAAAQBAJ?hl=en&gbpv=1.

296   "Weakling! Ungerman pacifist!": Susanne Wiborg, *Albert Ballin*, trans. Peter Kuras (Hamburg: Ellert & Richter Verlag, 2000), 65.

296   the Kaiser would lose his throne: Albert Ballin to Arndt von Holtzendorff, June 1, 1916, HAPAG Reederei 1580, Volume 12, HAPAG Archives.

CHAPTER 21: A LIFE'S WORK RUINED

297   "The evolution of higher and of lower forms of life": Samuel S. Wyer, comp., *Authoritative Statements on Science, Evolution, Religion, and the Bible* (Columbus: The Ohio State University, 1926), 8.

297   an estimated 500,000 to 700,000 Jews fled: Stephen Birmingham, *Our Crowd: The Great German Jewish Families of New York* (Syracuse, NY: Syracuse University Press, 1967), 381.

298   "scientist, savant, traveler, and trained observer": Daniel Okrent, *The Guarded Gate: Bigotry, Eugenics, and the Law That Kept Two Generations of Jews, Italians, and Other European Immigrants Out of America* (New York: Scribner, 2019), 214.

298   "The Nordics are, all over the world, a race of soldiers": Madison Grant, *The Passing of the Great Race, or The Racial Basis of European History* (New York: Charles Scribner's Sons, 1916), 198.

298   "The mental characteristics of the Mediterranean race are well known": Grant, *The Passing of the Great Race*, 139.

298   "The process of conquering and assimilating these Alpines": Grant, *The Passing of the Great Race*, 117.

299   "The book is a capital book": Okrent, *The Guarded Gate*, 215.

299   "The worst deed that any man can do here": Address, October 11, 1897, Two Hundredth Anniversary of the Old Dutch Church of Sleepy Hollow (First Reformed Church, Tarrytown, NY, 1898), 104; "American People," Theodore Roosevelt Association, https://theodoreroosevelt.org/content.aspx?page_id=22&club_id=991271&module_id=339514&actr=4.

301   "a persistent foe of the tyrannical autocracy": Naomi W. Cohen, *Jacob H. Schiff: A Study in American Jewish Leadership* (Hanover, NH: Brandeis University Press, 1999), 202.

302   "The enemies of the workers are the capitalists of all countries": Vladimir Lenin, as quoted in Joshua Polster, *Stages of Engagement: U.S. Theatre and Performance, 1898–1949* (Abington-on-Thames, UK: Taylor and Francis, 2015), 165.

302   But Jacob Schiff feared that nothing good would come out of the new regime: Jacob Schiff, as quoted in Cohen, *Jacob H. Schiff*, 242.

302   "It has come to me, while thinking over the events of recent weeks": Jacob Schiff, as quoted in Cohen, *Jacob H. Schiff*, 248.

303   with twenty-five hundred wounded and dying soldiers: Hans-Hermann Groppe and Ursula Wost, *Über Hamburg in die Welt. Von den Auswandererhallen zur Ballinstadt* (Hamburg: Ellert & Richter Verlag, 2007), 66.

304   "I want nothing more for myself": Susanne Wiborg, *Albert Ballin*, trans. Peter Kuras (Hamburg: Ellert & Richter Verlag, 2000), 65.

304   "When Ballin saw me in my uniform": Wiborg, *Albert Ballin*, 70.

304   "must not be made too pessimistic": Theodor Wolff, *Through Two Decades*, trans. Ernest Walter Dickes (London: William Heinemann, 1936), 217.

305   Ballin confided to his diary: Tracey Hayes Norrell, *For the Honor of the Fatherland: German Jews on the Eastern Front During the Great War* (Minneapolis, MN: Lexington Books, 2017), 131.

305   "I too have more to do than wait around until it suits you": Wiborg, *Albert Ballin*, 66.

305   "But amid all the weariness and depression": Wolff, *Through Two Decades*, 218.

305   "I let him know that I would not back down": Wiborg, *Albert Ballin*, 70.

306   "Rough sailors with red nooses and cockades": Wiborg, *Albert Ballin*, 70.

306   Albert Ballin died: Wiborg, *Albert Ballin*, 71–72.

306   "bleeding of the stomach": Wiborg, *Albert Ballin*, 72.

307   "regular international all-worlds pogrom à la Russe": John C. G. Röhl, *The Kaiser and His Court: Wilhelm II and the Government of Germany* (Cambridge: Cambridge University Press, 1994), 210.

307   "the unfortunate war has come to an end!": Wiborg, *Albert Ballin*, 2.

307 "which we had acquired in a rush": Irmgard Bielfeld to Heinz Bielfeld, November 11, 1918, as quoted in Heinz and Ingrid Hueber, *Mein Urgroßvater Albert Ballin* (Privately printed, 2021), 406, trans. Peter Kuras.

307 "I see him lying there so still and peaceful": Irmgard Bielfeld to Heinz Bielfeld, November 13, 1918, as quoted in Hueber, *Mein Urgroßvater Albert Ballin*, 407, trans. Peter Kuras.

307 No members of the Hamburg Senate or City Council were there: Irmgard Bielfeld to Heinz Bielfeld, November 13, 1918, as quoted in Hueber, *Mein Urgroßvater Albert Ballin*, 407, trans. Peter Kuras.

309 "We live in a time of great death": Max Warburg, "Eulogy for Albert Ballin," November 13, 1918, as quoted in Hueber, *Mein Urgroßvater Albert Ballin*, 408–11.

309 In his will, he left 300,000 marks to his wife: Heinz Hueber to Steven Ujifusa, June 9, 2022.

310 The last year of his life, Albert Ballin had earned a total of 114,303.72 marks: Estate of Albert Ballin, as quoted in Hueber, *Mein Urgroßvater Albert Ballin*, 415.

310 The record is incomplete, but Albert Ballin died worth at least 1.2 million marks: Heinz Hueber to Steven Ujifusa, June 17, 2022.

CHAPTER 22: HE WHO SAVES ONE LIFE, SAVES THE WORLD ENTIRE

311 "He who carries out one good deed": "Wisdom: October 8," *Houston Chronicle*, October 7, 2017, https://www.houstonchronicle.com/lifestyle/houston-belief/article/Wisdom-Oct-8-12260852.php.

312 Despite his illness: Stephen Birmingham, *Our Crowd: The Great German Jewish Families of New York* (Syracuse, NY: Syracuse University Press, 1967), 397.

312 The cause of death was heart disease: "Jacob H. Schiff, Noted Financier, Dies in Fifth Av. Home After a Long Illness, Stricken by Heart Disease 6 Months Ago," *New York Times*, September 26, 1920.

312 Schiff had written checks worth over $500,000: "Jacob H. Schiff, Noted Financier, Dies in Fifth Av. Home After a Long Illness, Stricken by Heart Disease 6 Months Ago."

313 "Happy is the man who like Mr. Schiff can forbid": Naomi W. Cohen, *Jacob H. Schiff: A Study in American Jewish Leadership* (Hanover, NH: Brandeis University Press, 1999), 246.

313 The funeral fell on the Jewish festival of Sukkoth: Cohen, *Jacob H. Schiff*, 246.

313 1.2 million (1.4 percent of the American population) to 3.6 million (3.4 percent of the American population): Cohen, *Jacob H. Schiff*, 249.

314 "Today so-called aliens are deported": "Deportation Defied by Emma Goldman," *New York Times*, October 28, 1919.

314 "Great Britain and this country will have an enormous tonnage": Prescott F. Hall, "The Present and Future of Immigration," *North American Review* 213, no. 786 (1921): 599, http://www.jstor.org/stable/251511312.

315 "Mr. Schiff, who was as well informed as anyone": Hall, "The Present and Future of Immigration," 600.

315 "The best plan in sight for cutting down the total number of immigrants": Hall, "The Present and Future of Immigration," 607.

315 Among the supporters of the 1924 bill: "Gompers Dehands [*sic*] Total Immigration Restriction," Jewish Telegraphic Agency, January 1, 1924, https://www.jta.org/archive/gompers-dehands-total-immigration-restriction.

316 "these services were as simple as the ritual of the Episcopal Church would permit": "Final Rites Said for Senator Lodge," *New York Times*, November 13, 1924.

316 "Grandpa did the best he could": Lauren Bacall, *By Myself and Then Some* (New York: Harper, 1978), 4.

316 "I remember watching her sit in her chair": Bacall, *By Myself and Then Some*, 10.

317 "She was not demonstrative": Bacall, *By Myself and Then Some*, 3.

EPILOGUE: KADDISH FOR THOSE LEFT BEHIND

318   After Lenin's death in 1924, his successor, Joseph Stalin, resumed persecution of the Jews: "Joseph Stalin (1879–1953)," Jewish Virtual Library, https://www.jewishvirtuallibrary.org/joseph-stalin.

318   "The steamship line which a brave Jew": Letter to Henry Wollman, November 30, 1934, Felix Warburg Papers, B295 F4, as quoted in Ron Chernow, *The Warburgs* (New York: Vintage Books, 1993), 381.

318   SS *Hansa*: This was a different ship from the former SS *Victoria Luise* (ex-*Deutschland* of 1900).

319   "It seems strange that after a silence of about seven years": Daniel Okrent, *The Guarded Gate: Bigotry, Eugenics, and the Law That Kept Two Generations of Jews, Italians, and Other European Immigrants Out of America* (New York: Scribner, 2019), 361.

319   "better known for his countless benefactions": "Felix Warburg Dead at 66," Jewish Telegraphic Agency, October 21, 1937, https://www.jta.org/archive/felix-m-warburg-dead-at-66.

319   only a scant number of German Jews were able to find asylum: Chernow, *The Warburgs*, 475.

319   Most of the remaining two hundred thousand German Jews: Holocaust Encyclopedia, United States Holocaust Memorial Museum, https://encyclopedia.ushmm.org/content/en/article/german-jews-during-the-holocaust.

320   "Everything in that twilit evening was so remote": Ma XXVII, Tagebuch, Bertha Ehrenberg, July 15, 1939, Max Warburg Archive, as quoted in Chernow, *The Warburgs*, 470.

321   Tragically, 254 of *St. Louis*'s passengers: "Voyage of the St. Louis," Holocaust Encyclopedia, https://encyclopedia.ushmm.org/content/en/article/voyage-of-the-st-louis.

321   the deposed monarch also claimed that Jesus of Nazareth: As quoted in a review of John Röhl, *The Kaiser and His Court: Wilhelm II and the Government of Germany*, by Dr. Alan Sked, Reviews in History, January 1998, https://reviews.history.ac.uk/review/47.

321   "I am ashamed to be German": Michael Balfour, *The Kaiser and His Times* (New York: W. W. Norton and Company, 1964), 419.

321   In violation of his last wishes: Giles MacDonogh, *The Last Kaiser: William the Impetuous* (London: Weidenfeld & Nicolson, 2001), 459.

321   "They piled us into the train": Testimony of Lazar Rozin, Yad Vashem Archives, Record Group 0.33, File 7211, "The Iasi Pogrom," https://www.yadvashem.org/education/educational-materials/lesson-plans/iasi-pogrom.html#footnote4_n73ccxl.

322   "Monsters exist": Primo Levi, "The International Holocaust Remembrance Day," USC Marshall School of Business, January 27, 2015, https://www.marshall.usc.edu/blog/international-holocaust-remembrance-day.

323   she bequeathed her $9 million estate to her children: Julie Miller, "Frieda Schiff Warburg," Shalvi/Hyman Encyclopedia of Jewish Women, Jewish Women's Archive, December 31, 1999, https://jwa.org/encyclopedia/article/warburg-frieda-schiff.

323   "I'm sure he would be very pleased that his house is now being put to such use": "Interview: Ballin's Legacy—The Shipping Magnate Who Built UIL's Home," UNESCO Institute for Lifelong Learning, September 9, 2021, https://uil.unesco.org/interview-ballins-legacy-shipping-magnate-who-built-uils-home.

323   "Albert Ballin would never have gained the commanding position he held": Bernhard Huldermann, *Albert Ballin*, trans. W. J. Eggers (London: Cassell., 1922), http://www.gutenberg.org/files/44135/44135-h/44135-h.htm.

324   most of the estimated 1.2 million European migrants: Hans-Hermann Groppe and Ursula Wöst, *Via Hamburg to the World: From the Emigrants' Halls to Ballinstadt* (Hamburg: Ellert & Richter Verlag, 2007), 9.

Index

Holocaust, 319, 321–22
Holtzendorff, Arndt von, 296
Hornish, Ottlie, 71–72, 332n71
Hornish, Rudolph, 72, 332n71
Hornish, Selma, 71–72
Hornish, Willie, 71–72
Hotel Nord et Sud, 97
How the Other Half Lives (Riis),
103
Hueber, Heinz, 265, 323
Huldermann, Bernhard, 60, 95, 177,
203, 214, 323–24
Hunt, Richard Morris, 45
Hylan, John F., 313

Ignatiev, Count, 28
ILGWU. *See* International Ladies'
Garment Workers Union
Illinois Central Railroad, 40
IMM. *see* International Mercantile
Marine
Immigrant Jew in America, The, 165
immigration
costs, 154–55
European, 255
German, 35
German restrictions on, 13, 196
indirect migration, 16, 88, 191
Jewish, 46, 64–68, 77–78, 121,
141–43, 155, 169, 191, 193, 216,
255, 309, 313–14
non-Jewish, 191, 255
U.S. restrictions on, 79, 83–85,
110, 216–17, 300–301, 314–16
Immigration Act (1924), 315
Immigration Museum at Ballinstadt,
324
Immigration Restriction League
(IRL), 82–86, 169, 171, 218,
222–28, 258, 297, 316, 319
Imperator, SS, 216, 239, 251, 284–85,
286, 303, 306
influenza, 305–6, 307, 309
Inman Line, 19, 120
International Ladies' Garment

Workers Union (ILGWU),
106, 261, 263
International Mercantile Marine
(IMM), 2, 123, 134, 140,
142–49, 174–75, 209–10, 226,
241–42, 249–52, 279–80, 292
International Navigation Company,
118–19, 122
Inverclyde, Lord, 173–74, 195
Ireland
immigration to U.S., 21, 66, 83,
173, 257
Titanic passengers, 268
U.S. immigration quotas, 315
IRL. *See* Immigration Restriction
League
Ismay, Joseph Bruce, 124, 128, 147,
249–51, 266, 273, 279
Ismay, Thomas, 18, 19, 58, 123–24
Italy
immigration to U.S., 191
Triple Alliance, 231, 287
U.S. immigration quotas, 314,
315
Ivernia, RMS, 174, 191

Jadassohn, Salomon, 11
Jagow, Gottlieb von, 305
James, Henry, 260
Japan
Meiji Restoration, 178
Russo-Japanese War, 178–82,
184–89, 205–6
Treaty of Portsmouth, 205
Jefferson, Thomas, 44
Jenkins, William T., 73
Jewish Daily Forward (periodical),
258, 295
Jewish Encyclopedia, The, 154
Jewish Enlightenment (Haskala), 10
Jewish Museum, 323
Jewish people
Ashkenazi, 24
in Austro-Hungarian Empire,
62–63, 286–87

About the Author

STEVEN UJIFUSA is the author of *A Man and His Ship* and *Barons of the Sea*. He received an AB in history from Harvard University and a master's degree in historic preservation from the University of Pennsylvania and has given presentations across the country and on the high seas. He is the recipient of a MacDowell Colony Fellowship, the Washington Irving Medal for Literary Excellence from the Saint Nicholas Society of the City of New York, and the Athenaeum of Philadelphia's Literary Award. He lives with his wife, a pediatric emergency room physician, and his two sons in Philadelphia.